HEIDEGGER ON

Does adherence to the principles of logic commit us to a particular way of viewing the world? Or are there ways of being – ways of behaving in the world, including ways of thinking, feeling, and speaking – that ground the normative constraints that logic imposes? Does the fact that assertions, the traditional elements of logic, are typically made about beings present a problem for metaphysical (or post-metaphysical) prospects of making assertions meaningfully about being? Does thinking about being (as opposed to beings) accordingly require revising or restricting logic's reach – and, if so, how is this possible? Or is there something precious about the very idea of thinking the limits of thinking? Contemporary scholars have become increasingly sensitive to how Heidegger, much like Wittgenstein, instructively poses such questions. *Heidegger on Logic* is a collection of new essays by leading scholars who critically ponder the efficacy of his responses to them.

FILIPPO CASATI is Assistant Professor of Philosophy at Lehigh University. He is the author of *Heidegger and the Contradiction of Being* (2021) and of a number of articles in journals, including the *British Journal for the History of Philosophy*, *Synthese*, *Logic et Analyse*, *Philosophical Topics*, and *Philosophy Compass*.

DANIEL O. DAHLSTROM is the John R. Silber Professor of Philosophy at Boston University. He is the author of *Heidegger's Concept of Truth* (Cambridge, 2001), *The Heidegger Dictionary* (2013), *Identity, Authenticity, and Humility* (2017), and many essays, the editor of numerous volumes, and the translator of Mendelssohn, Schiller, Hegel, Husserl, Heidegger, and Landmann-Kalischer.

HEIDEGGER ON LOGIC

EDITED BY

FILIPPO CASATI
Lehigh University

DANIEL O. DAHLSTROM
Boston University

CAMBRIDGE
UNIVERSITY PRESS

Shaftesbury Road, Cambridge CB2 8EA, United Kingdom

One Liberty Plaza, 20th Floor, New York, NY 10006, USA

477 Williamstown Road, Port Melbourne, VIC 3207, Australia

314–321, 3rd Floor, Plot 3, Splendor Forum, Jasola District Centre, New Delhi – 110025, India

103 Penang Road, #05–06/07, Visioncrest Commercial, Singapore 238467

Cambridge University Press is part of Cambridge University Press & Assessment, a department of the University of Cambridge.

We share the University's mission to contribute to society through the pursuit of education, learning and research at the highest international levels of excellence.

www.cambridge.org
Information on this title: www.cambridge.org/9781108798792

DOI: 10.1017/9781108869188

First published 2022
First paperback edition 2024

A catalogue record for this publication is available from the British Library

Library of Congress Cataloging-in-Publication data
NAMES: Casati, Filippo, editor. | Dahlstrom, Daniel O., editor.
TITLE: Heidegger on logic / edited by Filippo Casati, Lehigh University, Pennsylvania, Daniel Dahlstrom, Boston University.
DESCRIPTION: Cambridge, United Kingdom ; New York, NY, USA : Cambridge University Press, 2022. | Includes bibliographical references and index.
IDENTIFIERS: LCCN 2022022791 | ISBN 9781108835794 (hardback) | ISBN 9781108869188 (ebook)
SUBJECTS: LCSH: Heidegger, Martin, 1889-1976. | Logic. | Metaphysics. |
BISAC: PHILOSOPHY / History & Surveys / Modern
CLASSIFICATION: LCC B3279.H49 H352265 2022 | DDC 193–dc23/eng/20220705
LC record available at https://lccn.loc.gov/2022022791

ISBN   978-1-108-83579-4   Hardback
ISBN   978-1-108-79879-2   Paperback

Contents

v

Contributors

FILIPPO CASATI is Assistant Professor in the Department of Philosophy at Lehigh University.

DAVID R. CERBONE is a professor in the Department of Philosophy at the University of West Virginia.

STEVEN CROWELL is the Joseph and Joanna Nazro Mullen Professor of Humanities and Professor of Philosophy in the Department of Philosophy at Rice University.

DANIEL O. DAHLSTROM is the John R. Silber Professor and Chair of the Department of Philosophy at Boston University.

FRANÇOISE DASTUR is Professor Emeritus at the University of Nice Sophia-Antipolis and an honorary president and founding member of l'Ecole Française de Daseinsanalyse, Paris.

SACHA GOLOB is Reader in Philosophy and Director of the Centre for Philosophy and Visual Art at King's College London.

STEPHAN KÄUFER is the John Williamson Nevin Memorial Professor in the Department of Philosophy at Franklin & Marshall College.

KRIS McDANIEL is a professor in the Department of Philosophy at the University of Notre Dame.

DENIS McMANUS is Head of Philosophy in the School of Humanities at the University of Southampton.

RICHARD POLT is a professor in the Department of Philosophy and Associate Dean at the College of Arts and Sciences of Xavier University, Cincinnati.

EDWARD WITHERSPOON is an associate professor in the Department of Philosophy at Colgate University.

KATHERINE WITHY is an associate professor in the Department of Philosophy at Georgetown University.

Acknowledgments

We are grateful to James Kinkaid for his help in editing and providing the index for this volume. We also would like to express our gratefulness to Hilary Gaskin and Nicola Maclean of Cambridge University Press for their cheerful and sage guidance and to Santhamurthy Ramamoorthy for his expert assistance in bringing this project to completion. Special thanks are also due to Professor Ricki Bliss, Max Dahlstrom, and Eugenie Dahlstrom for their support and encouragement.

Method of Citation

"SZ," followed by numbers in parentheses refers to the pages of the most widely used edition of *Sein und Zeit*. For example,

"(SZ 75)"

refers to

> Martin Heidegger, *Sein und Zeit* (Tübingen: Niemeyer, 1957), S. 75.

No corresponding English pagination is given since the page numbers of this German edition (issued in multiple years) are indicated in the margins of standard English translations of this work under the title *Being and Time*.

The German pagination of Heidegger's texts is cited as it appears in the respective volume of the Complete Edition (*Gesamtausgabe*) of his works, each published by Klostermann Verlag in Frankfurt. The letters "GA" followed by a number and comma refer to the volume and the numbers after the comma refer to the respective page numbers. For example,

"(GA5, 177)"

refers to

> Martin Heidegger, *Holzwege*, Complete Edition, Volume 5, edited by Friedrich-Wilhelm von Hermann (Frankfurt: Klostermann, 2003), S. 177.

Since most English translations include the respective page numbers of the volume in the Complete Edition, there is no need to cite the English translations. In the few instances where the pagination of the Complete Edition is not given, as in *Pathmarks*, the number of the corresponding pagination of the translation is given following the German volume pagination and a slash. For example,

"(GA9, 117/92)"

refers to

> Martin Heidegger, *Wegmarken*, Complete Edition, Volume 9, edited by Friedrich-Wilhelm von Herrmann (Frankfurt: Klostermann), S. 117/English translation: *Pathmarks*, edited by William McNeill (Cambridge: Cambridge University Press, 1998), p. 92.

The Bibliography contains full bibliographic information for all cited texts.

Introduction

In the Fall of 1946 Heidegger attributes the unfinished project of *Being and Time* to metaphysical pretensions that he had come to see as deeply and misguidedly humanistic. With its reliance on "the language of metaphysics," he admits, the project of thinking being without centering it in human being failed (GA9, 328). Questions of candor and revisionism aside, this repudiation of metaphysics, already commencing a decade earlier, contrasts sharply with Heidegger's commitment to metaphysics in the 1920s. That commitment can be traced to his 1919 letter to Engelbert Krebs, the priest who conducted his marriage ceremony. Heidegger writes Krebs that insights into historical knowledge have made "the *system* of Catholicism problematic and unacceptable to [him] – but not Christianity and metaphysics (the latter, to be sure, in a new sense)" (Denker et al. 2004, 67).

The metaphysics Heidegger had in mind was not theology but ontology – "in a new sense," to be sure, but nonetheless a recognizably modern version of this part of the subject matter of Aristotle's *Metaphysics*, what Baumgarten labeled *Metaphysica generalis*.[1] But this new ontology was not to be a formal ontology, the sort of ontology that would be the counterpart of formal logic and take its bearings from categories applicable to any science. Heidegger had designs instead on a fundamental ontology that would not make the mistake of overlooking the foundation of any ontology: distinctively human ways of being (existence) and the senses of being that are disclosed therein.

Yet, infamously, Heidegger found himself unable to convert the existential analysis in *Being and Time* into a fundamental ontology and, by the mid-1930s, he rejects "ontology" as well as "metaphysics" as rubrics for his ventures in thinking. Among the reasons given for this development,

---

[1] Scotus 1997, 14: "*Ideo de hoc quaeritur primo utrum proprium subiectum metaphysicae sit ens in quantum ens (sicut posuit Avicenna) vel Deus et Intelligentiae (sicut posuit Commentator Averroes).*"

perhaps the most prevalent is the notion that metaphysics, as a theoretical science, objectifies and thereby disastrously distorts the experience of
being, thus playing into an all-too-human delusion that being is equivalent to what is available, computable, reproducible, and – in the end –
ultimately exhaustible by technology, "the complete metaphysics" (GA7,
78–79).

But there is another possible, undoubtedly complementary reason for
this sea-change in Heidegger's thinking. Could it be that he gives up
on ontology because it is inherently illogical? That a logically coherent
ontology is an oxymoron? Or, if logic gets in the way of questioning
what "being" means, is he forced to set it aside as well? Particularly in
the first few years following the publication of *Being and Time*, reflections on logic and its import for ontology take center stage, raising new
questions about the extent to which, in Heidegger's eyes, logic should
regiment our thinking, especially when it comes to thinking about being
in contrast to beings.[2] Are these new questions part of the motivation for
abandoning a science of being in the early 1930s? And if so, is it because
he comes to see that any thinking about what it means to be founders
on logic, thereby requiring revising if not abandoning, not only ontology, but logic itself, as it is traditionally conceived? But in that case, is
not his own thinking deeply irrational since being – particularly, being
conceived as self-concealing – arguably cannot be described in noncontradictory terms?

Heidegger thinks that those who charge him with irrationalism
severely misunderstand him (GA66, 301). Indeed, he is often adamant in
his commitment to logical principle. One of his favorite tactics in critical
studies of interpretations of his predecessors and contemporaries is precisely to demonstrate that what seemed to be a contradiction is simply an

---

[2] The interest in logic is neither new nor passing for Heidegger. Inspired by Husserl's *Logical
Investigations* (1900–01), both Heidegger's dissertation and habilitation lie within the ambit of
debates over logic's autonomy; a 1912 essay canvasses "Recent Research on Logic" (with references
to Frege and Russell; GA1, 42f); and in 1915 he describes logic as "the discipline that interests
[him] the most" (GA16, 38). He finds in Scholastic thought (*ens logicum*) the equivalent to the
ideal character of propositions in themselves, a notion inherited by Husserl from Bolzano. Instead
of being reduced to the acts of entertaining or expressing propositions, logic is grounded in the
meanings of propositions (GA1, 276–278). Heidegger regularly develops his subsequent thinking
with a view to the status, conditions, and principles of logic. Thus, the question of the meaning
and scope of logic is not only a mainstay of his published and unpublished writings, but also the
explicit theme of lectures in the 1920s (GA21, GA26, GA62), 1930s (GA38, GA45), 1940s (GA55),
and 1950s (GA10, GA11, GA79).

instance of vagueness or ambiguity. In these contexts and elsewhere his allegiance to logical principle is patent. At the same time, however, given that logic, as he sometimes alludes, applies pre-eminently if not exclusively to beings that are on hand (*vorhanden*), it is hardly obvious what import it has for thinking about being. In the end, then, the question is inescapable: When it comes to Heidegger's own thinking, particularly his post-metaphysical thinking when he gives up on ontology and perhaps logic, is he compelled, if not to contradict himself, then to wallow in vagueness and ambiguity himself? Or does his thinking instead represent with exemplary and dogged clarity, as several contributors to this volume suggest, the limits of logic when it comes to thinking of being? Or is the morale of his thinking instead a reminder, as yet another contributor suggests, not to let ourselves be held captive by the very image of a boundary and, with it, the pretension of being able to think the limits of thinking?

Closely allied to these issues that have increasingly exercised philosophers of late are time-honored questions not simply regarding the normative reach of logic and its principles, but about the viability of raising such questions. Any attempt to question logic seems to force those who raise those questions to stumble as it were over their own logical feet. Can we plausibly ask for a reason for the principle of sufficient reason? If we take it upon ourselves to examine the validity of the principle of noncontradiction, are we not forced to beg the question or contradict ourselves? Or are there topics that can be meaningfully discussed but only by holding one or the other logical principle at bay? For Heidegger, at least at some junctures of his thinking, both being (in contrast to beings) and the nothing (in contrast to the naught) are those very sorts of topics. Yet when he discusses these topics himself, bending if not flaunting the logical and grammatical structure of our language, he exposes his thinking to the charge of producing non-sense. But what sort of non-sense? The phrase "the slowly not" is formally, that is, grammatically, nonsense, but in a way other than the phrase "round square" is. So, too, when Heidegger says that "being exists" is non-sensical since only beings exist (GA65, 30, 472–473), this sort of non-sense is less like the purely formal non-sense of "the slowly not" than the material non-sense of "round square," which rests on concepts that make obvious sense, as the analysis of the reasons for its non-sense make perfectly clear.

The chapters in this volume are ventures in thinking – indeed, radical, exploratory ventures (*avventure nel pensare*) – that attempt to address the questions raised above and many more that arise from Heidegger's reflections on logic in the context of his attempts to think and say what it means to be.[3]

Normativity, the Phenomenology of Assertions, and Productive Logic

The first cohort of studies of Heidegger on logic in our volume addresses the issue of logic's normativity as well as two crucial parts of the puzzle of his thinking on logic in *Being and Time*: his conception of assertions and his projection of his existential phenomenology as a "productive logic."

Beginning with the debate between descriptivists and normativists in the philosophy of logic, Steven Crowell (Chapter 1) argues that Heidegger's ontology offers a phenomenological version of the normativist thesis. Reviewing Gillian Russell's defense of the descriptivist thesis that logic is tied to normativity only in combination with "widespread background norms," Crowell argues that, for Heidegger, logic is intrinsically normative because it is constitutive of the practice of reason-giving, a practice demanded of us by our being as care. The argument begins by showing why Heidegger abandons Husserl's descriptivist claim that logic deals with "truths in themselves" and interprets assertion (A *is* b) instead as a communicative comportment that depends on experiencing A *as* b in a shared and normatively structured context grounded in what we care about. While this view leaves much of the descriptivist position intact as regards truth, it also entails that logic is intrinsically normative: In any such context, we are responsible for the normative force of the reasons we adopt and are answerable to others for those reasons. Logic is thus constitutively normative of a practice, reason-giving, that is not optional for us. Crowell concludes by considering what implications this has for the "original questioning" proper to phenomenological ontology itself.

The changeover from taking a *as* b to the assertion that a *is* b is central, as just noted, to Crowell's reading of Heidegger on logic, as it is to other interpretations represented in the volume. Stephan Käufer does us the

---

[3] In Heidegger's day as in our own, the term "logic" operates on various levels. As Edward Witherspoon notes in Chapter 8, it can stand for a formal system (e.g., predicate logic), for debates about the adequacy of such systems (e.g., debates about conditionals), and for inquiries into notions ultimately underpinning those debates (a realm of inquiries typically grouped today under "philosophy of logic" or "philosophical logic"). The chapters in this volume, like Heidegger's own investigations, fall under the third class of inquiries, as they examine the bearing of Heidegger's thinking on questions of sense, non-sense, paradox, and the limits of thinking, as well as questions of the authority, normativity, and revisability of logic and its basic principles.

service in Chapter 2 of providing a close analysis of the crucial passage in which Heidegger gives his account of this changeover (*Umschlag*). Käufer distinguishes a strong reading of Heidegger's account (where assertions can only intend present-at-hand entities) from the more plausible reading that the assertions in question (those that can intend only present-at-hand entities) constitute a limiting case of assertions. Käufer argues for the latter reading by pointing out that, for Heidegger, assertions commonly intend ready-to-hand entities. To better understand what Heidegger means by the changeover, he turns to Aron Gurwitsch's more thorough, Gestalt-theoretic phenomenology of themes. In this connection he likens Gurwitsch's account of "restructuration" (the acutest thematic modification) to the sudden and wholesale character of the changeover from taking *a* as *b* (where *a* remains ready-to-hand) to making the theoretical assertion "*a* is *b*" (where *a* becomes something present-at-hand). Käufer concludes by arguing that understanding the unthematic as a thematic field dissolves any appearance of a self-reference paradox in Heidegger's theoretical assertions about what is not present-at-hand.

Another passage in SZ, one that, by contrast, is often overlooked or passed over without comment, contains Heidegger's words of praise for the "productive logic" of Plato and Aristotle, coupled with the suggestion that his phenomenology is bent on something similar. But in what sense is his phenomenology a productive logic? Richard Polt answers this question in Chapter 3, first by contrasting productive logic with symbolic logic and its purely reproductive character, given its reliance upon the fixity (the onhandness) of its symbols and notation. Moving beyond the confines of SZ, Polt then suggests two recurring tropes exploited by Heidegger that serve as elements of a productive logic: the productive tautology of verbalization – making nouns into verbs, as in "the world worlds" or "the nothing nothings" – and the appeal to deficient modes – exceptions that prove the rule, such as the neglect that nonetheless exposes a concern or the loneliness that confirms our social nature. As is particularly evident from the first of these tropes, Heidegger's productive logic is aligned with an attunement to the creative possibilities of language, unregimented by formal languages.

Language, Logic, and Nonsense

We noted earlier Heidegger's adoption in his habilitation of the Bolzano–Husserl notion that propositions in themselves, as the elements of logic, are not to be confused with their verbalizations. Yet the relationship of

language to logic quickly becomes a more complicated matter in the ensuing years, from the analysis of discourse as a basic existential in *Being and
Time* to his mid-1940s gloss on language as "the house of being" (GA5,
310). Despite apparent retractions later, certain remarks in *Being and Time*
appear to entail that language is not on a par with attuned understanding in disclosing meanings. Hence, his understanding of language and
its logical import remains controversial. The next set of chapters weighs
Heidegger's distinctive attentiveness to language and non-sense from a
logical point of view, in the 1920s and beyond.

Sacha Golob begins his study in Chapter 4 by contrasting Dummett's
Frege-inspired view of philosophy, one that focuses single-mindedly on
linguistic analysis, and Dreyfus's view that this endeavor, however salutary
for the analysis of concepts, fails to broach the nonconceptual dimensions
unearthed by phenomenology. On Dreyfus's view, Heidegger is supposedly concerned with flagging the fact that the content of language (particularly assertions) fails to capture practical or perceptual content and
reduces everything asserted to something present-at-hand. Golob argues,
to the contrary, that the problem for Heidegger lies, not with assertions or
linguistic content as such, but with a way of thinking about them, a specific "meta-language" or "logic." In addition to removing grounds for any
self-referential paradox in Heidegger's use of assertions himself (to speak of
what is not present-at-hand), this interpretation has the virtue of identifying a strong point of continuity with Heidegger's later work on language.

After rehearsing the motivations for an "austere" conception of nonsense associated primarily with several prominent interpretations of
Wittgenstein's *Tractatus*, in Chapter 5 David R. Cerbone reviews
Heidegger's own invocation of nonsensical statements and how it both illu-
mines and challenges that austere conception. The import of Heidegger's
treatment of such statements shows, Cerbone contends, that a practical
ontological understanding – and not logic – is the primary source for identifying nonsense and that, by implication, logic is beholden to ontology
rather than vice versa.

Heidegger's "destruction" of logic is aimed, Françoise Dastur argues in
Chapter 6, neither at its elimination nor at some sort of irrationalism but
at de-constructing the reigning, derivative conception of logic as a technical discipline, exclusively preoccupied with beings and to which ontology
must be beholden. Heidegger undertakes the de-construction, Dastur contends, with a view to reinserting logic in ontology as a thinking of being
not beings. The deconstruction consists, Dastur shows, in exposing four
fraught presuppositions of that derivative conception of logic: the thesis

that truth resides exclusively in propositions, that the meaning of "being" is to be found in linguistic analysis of the copula, that logical negation is the source of all negativity, and that propositions and the implications of the predicative structure of assertions are logically and ontologically foundational for language.

Paradox, the Prospects for Ontology, and Beyond

Crowell and Cerbone argue, as noted, that Heidegger grounds logic ontologically, in who we are and what we do. But the very idea of this grounding raises issues of its own, questions about the reflexivity of logic and the very possibility of an ontology grounding it. In addition to familiar questions about question-begging and tripping over our own logical feet, Heidegger's own pronouncements about the ontological difference raise questions about the reach of logic and, indeed, the logical propriety of ontology itself. The next set of chapters addresses these concerns and Heidegger's approach to them, particularly after 1928.

In addition to stressing an "ontological distinction [*Unterschied*]" between ways of being, Heidegger speaks of the "ontological difference [*Differenz*]" between being and beings (GA24, 22, 109, 250, 454; GA26, 193, 200, 202; GA65, 250, 424, 465–469). Thus, he insists that being and beings (entities) are in each case different; being is never a being and whatever we can say about what a being is – formalized, for example, as Fx – does not amount to asserting that it exists, that is, ($x)(Fx). Prima facie the ontological difference presents a paradox that calls ontology into question. Since arguably only a being can be the subject of a proposition and since being itself is not a being, being cannot be such a subject. It is accordingly unsayable or sayable only by countenancing contradiction in its regard (the dialetheist recourse).

Denis McManus begins Chapter 7 by rehearsing reasons to think that, while appealing to a nonpropositional understanding does not appear to be a successful strategy in overcoming this paradox, a careful examination of its premises gives us good reasons to question its *exegetical* and *philosophical* force. Having said that, McManus also argues that, given Heidegger's philosophical framework, a different and more pressing paradox emerges. The reason is that, according to McManus, Heidegger is committed to the idea that Being in general is what determines *all* different ways in which entities are *thus-and-so*. However, since McManus argues that such a determining relation is irreflexive, he concludes that Being in general has no ways in which it is *thus-and-so*. And, if this is the case, Being cannot be what Being actually is, that is, Being cannot be the determiner of *all*

different ways in which entities are *thus-and-so*. Having said that, it should
be clear that, according to McManus, Heidegger's ontology does rest on
shaky ground. However, how to deal with such a paradoxical outcome is
less obvious and, for this reason, McManus simply sketches some possible
ways in which Heidegger might have tackled this problem and how philosophers might handle its implications.

While McManus offers reasons for thinking that ontology is ultimately
a logically forlorn enterprise (both in general and for Heidegger), Edward
Witherspoon argues in Chapter 8 that Heidegger countenances revisions
to logic in order to accommodate the possibility of thinking of being.
Witherspoon's chapter begins, much like McManus's, by setting up the
problem that the ontological difference presents for ontology and reviewing the interpretive options, including the dialetheist option, offered
by Casati and Priest, of countenancing contradiction. Witherspoon
also joins McManus in underscoring the differences between Priest's
and Heidegger's investigations. Witherspoon then argues that the ways
in which Heidegger's approach *differs* from Priest's are ways in which
it *resembles* Wittgenstein's. The central parallels between Heidegger and
Wittgenstein are their common resistance to privileging logic as a formal system and their common turn to the grammar that is embedded
in our language through our multiple attunements (to each other and to
the world). Drawing on Cavell's account of *Stimmungen*, Witherspoon
contends that the experience of nothingness in anxiety, so central
to Heidegger's conception of being, is an attunement (albeit a largely
repressed attunement) that engenders a mode of understanding that
accommodates a revision of logical principles.

Like Witherspoon, Kris McDaniel in Chapter 9 focuses on the question
of the authority of logic and contends that logic is rationally revisable. Yet
he argues that Heidegger rejects the authority of logic, not because of the
possibility of a transformative attunement, but for defensible metaphysical reasons. McDaniel describes a traditional theory according to which
logical principles present themselves as unrevisable. Such is the theory,
familiar to Heidegger, that logical entities – for example, propositions
and relations among them – have discernible essences mandating adherence to the laws of logic. McDaniel argues that, in Heidegger's view, the
representational properties of propositions are neither ungrounded nor
grounded in something internal to propositions, as the traditional theory
would have it. Instead they are grounded in the "deeper fact" of the primitive intentionality constituted by Dasein's pre-predicative openness to the
world. Given this derivativeness, logic loses its authority as a standalone

domain and, more importantly, one to which ontology must be beholden. Forfeited, too, is the idea of a formal ontology equivalent to formal logic, but not without opening the door to a nonformal ontology, a bottoms-up approach to ontology that takes its bearings from differing yet analogous modes of being.

As the glosses on the previous three chapters make clear, the implications of Heidegger's thinking for logic and ontology are much debated. Filippo Casati's contribution in Chapter 10 takes us in a sense beyond a version of this debate by questioning one of its premises. He begins by sketching Heidegger's rendering of the basic problem of squaring a logic for beings with philosophy's concern for being. After demonstrating irrationalist and rationalist interpretations of Heidegger's response to this problem, Casati identifies a common presupposition of these interpretations, namely, a pretension of thinking the limits of thinking. He concludes by making the case that Heidegger, particularly in his late work, calls this presupposition into question.

Logical Principles and the Question of Being

The last two chapters in the volume turn to Heidegger's construal of specific logical principles and their bearing on the possibility of think-ing of being. In Chapter 11 Katherine Withy shows how a version of the principle of sufficient reason resonates for Heidegger throughout the history of philosophy. Leibniz's modern formulation of the principle makes a claim on thinking only when it is understood as representing entities (as objects) to a subject. But the general principle (nothing is without reason) applies to all entities, insofar as they are grounded in being. However, the notion that being would itself have a reason in turn invites a regress and conflates it with entities. Yet while being is ontically indeterminate and ungrounded, it is historically determinate, relative to a respective epoch's response to the groundlessness of being's self-concealing. Whereas the Greeks preserve being's indeterminacy in this respect, medieval and moderns efface that groundlessness – they forget being by grounding it in an entity.

Heidegger's endorsement of the principle of noncontradiction as a law of thought is evident, Daniel O. Dahlstrom submits in Chapter 12, from his repeated strategy of exposing vagueness and ambiguity that create the illusion of contradiction. At the same time Heidegger acknowledges that the principle (together with the conception of the assertions constituting it) has been historically wedded to the idea that the principle applies solely to beings, not being, and, indeed, solely insofar as they are on hand (the metaphysics of presence) – an interpretation of the principle that rules out the very prospect of thinking about being and different modes of being. Dahlstrom reviews how Heidegger attempts to respond to this challenge, not by rejecting or flouting the principle, but by demonstrating how it is existentially grounded in and constituted by being-here with others. Dahlstrom concludes by suggesting how the principle of noncontradiction, so construed, remains in force in Heidegger's attempt to think beyng, not as presence, but as the hidden clearing, present and absent at once, albeit not in the same respect.

PART I

Normativity, the Phenomenology of Assertions, and Productive Logic

CHAPTER I

Heidegger's Phenomenology
and the Normativity of Logic

Steven Crowell

What is the normativity of logic? If logic is understood as "a specification of a relation of logical consequence on a set of truth-bearers," where consequence relations "preserve truth in virtue of logical form" (Steinberger 2017, 2), it is natural to think that logic has normative significance. For instance, noting that we often make errors in reasoning, one might assume that logic is not about how we do think but about how we *ought* to think. However, such a view runs into the problem that logical laws seem to say nothing about thinking; they are purely formal, while thinking is something we *do*, whether occasionally or all the time. How does a logical law gain normative traction on apparently psychological acts such as belief-formation or reasoning? One might think that it does so by means of a hypothetical imperative: If you want to preserve truth in such acts, then you ought to reason in accord with logical laws. Logic would be normative in the sense of providing evaluative norms that represent success-conditions for a practical project, that of preserving truth. But this leaves another normative question open: Why ought we to preserve truth in our thinking? And while the answer to this question may seem obvious, it can come into conflict with other desires we have, and so with other norms that pertain to them, such that, in some cases, thinking or reasoning or believing or asserting *ought* to ignore $((p \supset q) \ \& \ p) \supset q$.

To take one example, Gilbert Harman (1984) argued that logical principles are not directly normative for a theory of reasoning or belief-revision. To believe that *p* and that $p \supset q$ does not mean that one *should* believe *q*. Perhaps the preponderance of evidence speaks against *q*.[1] One response is to hold that logic supplies the *constitutive* norms for reasoning: Just as, in chess, if one consistently tries to move a knight diagonally,

---

[1] See Steinberger (2017, 17–24); for a more Husserlian response to Harman's challenge, see Kinkaid (2020). Kinkaid argues that the gap between psychology and logic can be bridged by a "genealogy of logic" that returns phenomenologically to "pre-predicative experience."

one does not count as playing chess, so too, if one continually embraces invalid inferences, one does not count as reasoning at all. Of course, I can make mistaken moves, but as long as "I acknowledge that my activity is answerable to the rules," then I still count as playing (Steinberger 2017, 14). Steinberger continues: "It is not easy to specify ... what the requisite acknowledgement or sensitivity consists in"; but it is just this, I hope to show, that is provided by Heidegger's phenomenological ontology of reasoning.

The interesting thing about constitutive norms is that they do not involve any "ought," so logical laws would simply specify what reasoning is. As Emanuela Carta (2021, 130) puts it, "contrary to deontic norms, *constitutive norms* do not engender obligations or place demands on agents to act or behave in certain ways." But with this we are back to the beginning: Reasoning just seems to be a game that we can either play or not play. The "normativity of logic," however, "does not seem to be optional in the same way" (Steinberger 2017, 8). And were one to argue that reasoning is somehow essential to us – that we cannot "be" without playing the game – then it needs to be explained how we can still be what we are even when we fail to reason logically. Beyond the game analogy, this is an *ontological* question that brings us to the threshold of Heidegger's approach to the normativity of logic.

I will argue that Heidegger, like Kant, provides an account of the constitutive normativity of logic; however, what logic is constitutive *of* is not something that is essential to us in the way it is for Kant.[2] Rather, it is constitutive of a practice that, for Heidegger (at least in the period covered in this chapter, up to 1930 or so), stands in a certain *opposition* to his ontological project, whose goal is not to explain entities and their properties but to clarify the "meaning of being" phenomenologically. Because phenomenology initially stands on an equal footing with logic in the project of ontology, it has normative parity, and so it is possible, as Heidegger famously claimed, that the "reign of logic ... disintegrates in the turbulence of a more original questioning" (GA9, 117/92). Of course, this introduces its own asymmetry between logic and phenomenology, a point to which we will return.

So, the "reign" or normativity of logic may not be absolute. Nevertheless, I will argue that, even for Heidegger, logic is not exactly optional either. Logical laws are constitutive norms of reasoning, and though we are not,

---

[2] On the Kantian origin of the idea of constitutive norms and its relation to the normativity of logic, see Tolley (2006).

"essentially," rational animals, reasoning is something we not only can do but are *obligated* to do thanks to what Heidegger calls the *care-structure* of our being. The ontology of care provides a normativity-first account of reason that shows why logic is more than a game: Logic formalizes "what we owe to each other" (Scanlon 1998) and belongs to the practice of coming to mutual understanding (Habermas 1990).

1.1 Contemporary Discussion of the Normativity of Logic

Before turning to Heidegger, it will be helpful to look briefly at how discussions of the normativity of logic that do not proceed phenomenologically understand the motivations for thinking that logic is normative, and how they frame the objections that have been raised to this idea. Gillian Russell examines three such motivations – the argument from "normative consequences" (**NC**), the argument from "error" (**E**), and the argument from "demarcation" (**D**) – on the way to arguing that logic is a purely "descriptive" enterprise that is only "weakly entangled" with normativity, that is, logic is normative only when combined with "widespread background norms about the relations between belief, reasoning, and truth" (Russell 2020, 387).

(**NC**) hold, roughly, that "is valid" or "is a logical consequence of," when used to describe an argument-structure, is epistemically normative: It tells us what we ought to *believe* (Russell 2020, 374). (**E**) appeals to the difference between descriptive laws, which are never violated, and norms, which are often violated, to argue that since we often fail to reason logically, logical laws cannot be descriptive. They must be normative. Finally, (**D**) addresses the worry that if logic is neither psychology nor semantics – neither the study of how we actually think or reason nor the study of truth-preservation in natural languages – then there is nothing for logic to be about. But if logic is about how we *ought* to think or reason, then it has a distinct domain (378).

(**D**) also addresses a worry that logic is merely conventional. If a classical logician accepts $\neg \neg p \supset p$ and an intuitionist logician rejects it, and if both systems can offer model-theoretic accounts that support their views, then either we can say that they "mean different things" by the entailment relation or we can ask which of them is the "real" entailment relation. But on a descriptivist approach, there might be no answer to this latter question. For instance, Steinberger (2017, 4) notes how this descriptivist result is reflected in Hartry Field's view that "validity" is primitive and that its normative meaning is determined by the "conceptual role" it plays *within* competing logical systems as a constraint on our "doxastic attitudes." On a normativist account, in contrast, we can ask, of either logic, whether it is how we *ought* to reason.

(D) involves what Russell calls the "strongest" degree of logic's "entanglement" with the normative. Normativity is (at least partly) constitutive of what *counts* as a logical theory. Disambiguations of "validity" (as in the dispute between classical and intuitionist logicians) do not count as logical theories unless they address what is demanded in **(D)**: Which one is normative for how we ought to reason? (Russell 2020, 379). Constitutive norms, as we saw, do not involve an "ought" in their formulation; nevertheless, their function cannot be understood without recognizing their normativity in regard to how something is supposed to be done. That is to say, constitutive norms yield *evaluative* norms for *success* in the "game" we are playing. While both "deontic" norms and "evaluative" norms include an "ought" in their formulation, only deontic norms constitute obligations on a specific *addressee*, while evaluative norms derive from the *eidos* of the type in question (Carta 2021). For this reason, evaluative norms are best expressed as "should be" (*Sein-sollen*) rather than as "ought to do" (*Tun-sollen*). Thus, the constitutive norms of a practice entail evaluative norms for assessing success in living up to the *eidos* of being a player; they do not demand that a player play a certain way.

A weaker view, represented by **(NC)**, is that logic is entangled with normativity because it has direct normative consequences for belief-formation and revision (for instance, if one takes "correctness" to be a normative notion). Weakest of all is the idea that logic has normative consequences not on its own but only "alongside other (perhaps quite prevalent) normative assumptions." If you make an error in arithmetic, for instance, then your sum is false. But this has normative significance only "in conjunction with the non-arithmetical normative fact that one ought not to believe false things" (Russell 2020, 380). Because the prior normative commitment does all the work, logic remains a descriptive theory. Like physics for mass and heat, logic simply tells us what "is" in regard to entailment or validity. The "widespread intuition that logic is normative" is explained by the fact that "when we make claims about entailment we are commonly also intentionally conveying normative information as well," and this conveyance "has a tendency to stick to logic" itself (382).

So, what does such a descriptivist position look like, and what answers does it provide to the three motivations for thinking that logic is normative? Russell's account will position us to see how a phenomenological approach – Heidegger's in particular – can put the debate on a new footing.

For Russell, "logic is the study of patterns of truth-preservation [e.g., entailment] on truth-bearers" (382). Thus, like physics, it has an object-domain ("sentences"), and just as physics studies certain properties of objects, logic studies how "the *property* of truth" is preserved in argument-forms (382). Taking logic to be about sentences can most easily be seen in artificial or formal languages, but Russell assumes that natural languages have such descriptive properties as well, though perhaps difficult to capture in formal notation. This is only an "epistemic difficulty," however, no more worrisome than are similar difficulties in applied physics (385n15).

On such a view, the arguments for the normativity of logic are easily dispensed with. (NC) is undermined because to say something is "valid" or "entailed by" is simply to say something about *truth*; any normative consequences come from a "conjunction with norms linking truth to belief and reasoning" (385). (E) is undermined by the observation that "there are no violations of logical laws" and cannot be any, since they are "descriptive laws of truth." Supposed violations of such laws are simply *mistakes*: I misapply or misunderstand the law, but I in no way "violate" it, since the law has nothing directly to do with application (386). Finally, (D) fails because, while it may be difficult to determine "whether or not an argument form is valid" for a given language, answering this question does not require us to consider whether it is "normative" for reasoning. We just need "better semantics," and ultimately the right model theory for it – that is, "more theory and evidence," not a normative conception of logic (386).

With this descriptivist account of logic in mind, we turn now to Heidegger, whose phenomenological approach to the connection between logic and truth gives us reason to accept the main claims of descriptivism but also to challenge the idea that appeal to "widespread background norms about the relations between belief, reasoning, and truth" (387) can adequately account for the kind of normativity that is intrinsic to logic.

1.2   Logic Is Not a Normative Discipline

From his earliest days as a student, Heidegger had an interest in logic. Though aware of the "logistics" of Russell and Whitehead (GA1, 41–42), Heidegger's attention lay elsewhere – namely, in the demarcation argument (D). In what domain do logical laws hold? If the laws of logic are supposed to pertain to thinking or reasoning, then they might appear to belong to psychology, suggesting that they are, at least in part, empirical and contingent. In his dissertation, Heidegger draws on Husserl to show that various current psychologistic theories of judgment misunderstand the character of logical laws, their a priori "validity" or "holding" (*Geltung*). Similarly, he argues that logical laws cannot be grounded in the "grammar" (vocabulary, sentence structure) in which judgments are expressed, since different languages express the same thing with different words and grammatical structures. Heidegger's initial attempt to address (D) thus settles on the idea that the domain of logic is the judgment's *ideal meaning*, the "proposition." Validity is a property of meaning (*Sinn*), and logic thematizes the entailment relations among propositions, given their categorial forms. The relation to truth is taken to lie in the fact that such judgment-meaning "holds" of the things about which the judgment judges. Logic is not a normative discipline but a *theoretical* one.

The details of this approach to the domain problem – which then as now are widely accepted – need not concern us, but a glance at Husserl's argument for it in the *Logical Investigations* (Husserl 1970, 74–89), which Heidegger adopts, will make the latter's eventual departure from it more perspicuous. Husserl's general argument is that all normative disciplines presuppose theoretical disciplines. For instance, to say that "a soldier ought to be brave" presupposes that we know what descriptive properties a soldier *has*, those properties that make up what it *means* to be a soldier (essence, ideal meaning). If bravery is among them, then we can always transform the descriptive statement "A soldier is brave" into a normative statement, "A soldier ought to be brave," where the "ought" here is an impersonal evaluative "should" expressive of the success-conditions for a certain *type* (here, soldiers). But this does not mean that our cognition of what a soldier *is* is intrinsically normative or presupposes a normative discipline. In the case of logic, the claim that in accepting p and $p \supset q$ one ought to accept q does not stand on its own; it is justified by the purely descriptive relations that hold (are valid) between the ideal meanings of p and q, that is, their status as *true*, and in that regard (as Harman reminded us), *evidence* can trump reasoning. Logic is not a normative discipline.

However, while appealing to Husserl's position throughout his dissertation, Heidegger concludes by turning the argument in a different direction: "What is the meaning of meaning?" "What *is* meaning?" (GA1, 170–171). By 1923, Heidegger had come to question Husserl's starting point on phenomenological grounds: By starting with "already known knowledge," that is, with ideal meanings (propositions) taken as elements of logically structured sciences, "truth" is taken to name a *property* of propositions, that is, their "holding" (*Geltung*) of their objects (GA17, 58–60; Dahlstrom 2001, 131–138). If ideal meaning is truth-functional in this sense, and if there are formal laws that preserve the property of truth through various transformations of meaning, then logic is the theoretical discipline that identifies such truth-preserving entailments. But Heidegger came to think that this schema is phenomenologically superficial: While it may appear, when one begins with developed sciences, that an ideal meaning's holding of an object is one of its properties, it is not. And if that is so, then the question of logic's normativity cannot be decided by appeal to Husserl's distinction between normative and theoretical disciplines, that is, by starting with already known knowledge. It demands a phenomenology of truth and so of "truth-bearers," one that illuminates what is "preserved" in logic.

1.3   The Phenomenological Ground of the Truth-Predicate

If the aim of Heidegger's early work can be described as an attempt to liberate logic from grammar – that is, to identify the logical elements of ideal meaning behind the surface grammar of sentences – *Being and Time* calls for "liberating grammar from logic" (SZ 165), an account of meaning that does not begin with the phenomenology of cognition. The supposed ideality of meaning – "validity" as the "object" of logic – is now declared to be "very questionable" due to its opaque because equivocal character (SZ 156): validity is understood *ontologically* as the "ideality" of judgment-meaning; *epistemologically* as the "objectivity" of that meaning, its "holding" of an object; and *pragmatically* as the "universal" validity, the "bindingness" of objective meaning "*for* everyone who judges rationally" (SZ 156).

Heidegger does not dismiss any of the phenomena that this equivocal term references, but he places "no advance restriction" on the "concept of 'meaning'" that would tie it to this whole "logical" problematic. At bottom, his target is the "unclarified separation of the real and the ideal," and he argues that "psychologism [is] correct in holding out against this separation" just *because* it is unclarified (SZ 217). However, Heidegger's point is not that logical psychologism is *correct*; rather, it is that there is a need for a phenomenological account of meaning, judging, and reasoning that does a better job of elucidating the ontological *ground* of cognition or "already known knowledge." And in pursuing this task, Heidegger suggests a different account of the normativity of logic: Logic is constitutive for a certain practice (hence it is descriptive, involving no "ought"), but the practice itself, reasoning, is normatively demanded of the kind of being we are.

The first step in Heidegger's phenomenological account is found in *The Basic Problems of Phenomenology*. In his criticism of Hermann Lotze, whose

Logik introduced "validity" as a *Zauberwort*, we can clearly see why, for Heidegger, truth is not, ontologically, a descriptive property of sentences.

To treat sentences as truth-bearers is to construe truth as a property of sentences. The sentence "Today, the sky is blue" has the property of being-true such that "The sentence 'Today, the sky is blue' is true" has the same logical form as the embedded sentence. As Heidegger shows, Lotze's account of the ideal meaning of such sentences rests on the centuries-old tradition, deriving from Aristotle, which holds that the "is" (or "copula") represents a kind of "combination" of subject-term and predicate-term. For this reason, Lotze maintained that "a negative copula is impossible," since nothing is combined in it, and this suggested to him that all judgments are really "double judgments." Thus, "S is p" should be understood as saying that "'S is p' is true," while "S is not p" says that "'S is p' is not true" – making explicit, in each case, that truth is or is not a property of the sentence.

This solution, which itself involves a sentence with a negative copula, threatens an infinite regress of such property-attribution, but if we respond by treating negation as a logical constant, moving it "outside" the sentence, $\neg$ (S is p), or by replacing the "combinatory" copula with the existential quantifier, $\neg$ ($\exists$x)(Px), we conceal what Heidegger sees as the primary *ontological* problem raised by logic: What mode of being (*Sein*) is represented by the copula?

Lotze answers that the copula represents the judgment-meaning's holding (being valid) of its object as a *known* object – its "objectivity" or "being-true" – and that this is co-intended in the copula by means of a "subsidiary thought" (GA24, 287–288). Heidegger, in turn, accepts the idea that the copula expresses the being-true of the assertion and that in "every uttered assertion [sentence] the being-true of the assertion is itself co-intended," but he denies that this co-intention is a "subsidiary thought" that attributes a *property* to something: "Truth is not a being that appears among other extant things" (GA24, 304). It is "never extant like a thing but exists" (GA24, 310).

So, in what way is truth co-intended in the assertion? Heidegger's answer goes back to Aristotle's claim that truth is not in things but *en dianoia*, in the "understanding." This does not mean that truth is a property of (some) thinking; it means that what truth *is* can be approached only "in the middle 'between' things and Dasein" (GA24, 305). For our purposes, the result is that truth-bearers cannot be understood as *any* kind of entity. Heidegger hints as much in *Being and Time*: "Assertion is not the primary 'locus' of truth" (SZ 226). Put positively, if we want to understand how logic can be the descriptive science of formal sentential truth-*preservation*, we must first understand how assertions, and so sentences, can be truth-*bearers* at all. For Heidegger, this is an ontological problem and so requires phenomenological reflection on the "being" of assertion. And central to his approach is the claim that assertion cannot be understood without taking its "reference to things" into account (GA24, 280).

This reference to things cannot be understood if we start with the "verbal sequence" (sentence) in which an assertion is expressed; rather, we must phenomenologically describe "the specific *contextual interconnection*" that belongs to the phenomenon: the "relational whole of word, signification, thinking, what is thought." And within this interconnection, the key point is that asserting is something we *do*; it is "one of Dasein's *intentional comportments*" (GA24, 294–295). A comportment is that for the sake of which (*Worumwillen*) we do what we are (currently) doing, so in asserting something, we act for the sake of being a truth-teller: "Prior to the assertion and *for the sake of making it*, the asserter already comports himself toward the relevant entity and understands it in its being" (GA24, 300, emphasis added). For this reason, Heidegger concludes that "being-true already lies in assertive comportment itself." It is co-intended, but not as a property of the assertion; rather, "truth exists. Truth possesses the mode of being of Dasein" (GA24, 313). But with this, we are still far from understanding the relation between *logic* and assertion, so we need to move a bit more slowly.

Heidegger's phenomenological analysis of assertion highlights three moments: "assertive comportment" is (1) *apophansis*, "exhibition": "letting something be seen as it is in itself." Apophantic exhibition is (2) *predication*: a "sundering" (*Auseinanderlegen*; *dihairesis*) of "the belonging-together of the manifold determinations of the being which is asserted about" so as to characterize it in a particular way (*synthesis*). Finally, assertion is (3) *communication*: an "understanding comportment toward the being about which the assertion is being made" in which that comportment (and not mere information) is or can be *shared* with others. In phenomenological terms, then, assertion is "communicatively determinant exhibition" (GA24, 297–300).

For Heidegger, each of these characteristics points to the fact that assertion is not our original access to things but is "related to something antecedently given as unveiled" (GA24, 296), that is, to something *available* as *understood*. Assertion exhibits something already there and, by sundering the manifold determinations that "belong together" in it so as to give it a *definite* determination, exhibits it in such a way that the comportment of truth-telling can be explicitly shared. Thus "assertion does not have a primary cognitive function but only a secondary one. Some being must already be unveiled" – available as understood – "if an assertion about it is to be possible" (GA24, 299).

If the "is" of assertion is understood or co-intended as "being-true," then truth is not a property of the sentence taken as a truth-bearer; rather, it "signifies a being *in its unveiledness*" (GA24, 303), its availability *for* assertive comportment. This being-available for communicatively determinant exhibition is what "bears" truth: Truth is *en dianoia*, in the understanding, not as a property of that understanding but as the availability of an entity in its organized manifold (meaning); and truth is also "in things," not as a property but as "a determination of the being of the extant, extantness" (GA24, 305). Truth, unveiledness – "'between' things and Dasein" (GA24, 305) – *befalls* things thanks to Dasein's "understanding of being." Here, we can begin to see why phenomenological reflection on intentional correlation, the "original" bearer of truth, has a certain priority over logic in an ontological investigation of what truth *is*.

The phenomenological picture, then, is this: The relation of assertion to truth does not involve positing a descriptive "third realm" of "valid meaning" (Husserl, Frege, Lotze) – truths in themselves – but is grounded in the ontology of Dasein as comportment. An assertion is true if its sundering-synthetic determination exhibits the entity as it is in itself. But such exhibition depends on the prior meaningful availability of the entity: Assertion "is a mode in which Dasein *appropriates* for itself the uncovered being *as* uncovered" (GA24, 312). Acting for the sake of being a truth-teller is appropriation, making one's own, but such comportment is possible only because Dasein itself is "unveiled to its own self for itself" (GA24, 308), that is, because Dasein "understands" both the being of things and *its own* being – in this case, what it means to be a truth-teller. As Heidegger puts it: "We take *being-true* in this wholly formal sense as unveiling" – that is, as *aletheuein*, "to take out of concealment" – with the result that Dasein "is true." But "being unveiled" is not a *property* of Dasein; it is its "way of being" (GA24, 307–308). In being unveiled to itself in its comportments, Dasein *uncovers* available entities such that they can be "encountered within the world," that is, "disclosed for the existent Dasein" in those comportments (GA24, 313).

In Section 1.4, we will examine how, exactly, Dasein is disclosed to itself in its comportments, and this should clarify the ontological ground of logic's normativity. But already we may note one consequence of Heidegger's approach. Heidegger argues that we may call an extant entity "true" *not* "intrinsically" but "as uncovered in the assertion" (GA24, 312).

Now, even though language is not an extant entity but "is as Dasein is," that is, "exists" (GA24, 296), a sentence *is* an extant entity – a structured string of written or spoken words – and so it is not *intrinsically* a truth-bearer but only "as uncovered in [an] assertion" *about* the sentence. Just this happens when logical theory asserts that truth is a *property* of sentences, but on Heidegger's view such an assertion is *false*. As Heidegger puts it, if assertions yield sentences, not all "sentences" can be "traced back to theoretical statements without essentially perverting their meaning" (SZ 158). Nevertheless, even if the sentence attributing the property of truth to sentences is false, logic might still be understood as describing truth-preserving entailments among sentences. In that case, though, what is "preserved" will not be a descriptive ("real") property of sentences. And if that is so, we have not yet decided the question of the normativity of logic when we have described such entailment relations. We would still need to reflect on the ontological ground of assertions and the sentences that express them, a ground that might yield a different understanding of the normativity of logic.

1.4   The Normativity of Meaning: "Is" and "As"

Being-true is co-intended in the assertion, not as a double judgment but as constitutive of assertive comportment. But the assertion itself can be "either true *or* false." What accounts for this possibility? In *Fundamental Concepts of Metaphysics*, Heidegger provides an extensive answer to this question, from which we will here draw only a few points relevant to the question of the normativity of logic.

In *Being and Time*, Heidegger argued that meaning does not originate in asserting but in what he calls the "hermeneutic 'as' of interpretation," the way we encounter something meaningfully *as* something: as a hammer, for instance, or as too heavy (SZ 158). Such interpretation "articulates" – that is, "takes apart" what it also "binds together" – that which is understood in my comportment. In saying something about what is so encountered, the hermeneutic "as" is reduced to the "apophantic as": The hammer *is* heavy. The "specialty of the assertion" (SZ 158) is thus to exhibit things in the "dimension" (GA29/30, 425) of the extant, the presence of a property "in" an object. This reduction is "formalized" as a "relation" and the assertion is thereby "dissolved logistically" and "becomes the object of a 'calculus.'" However, this conceals the way that logic is "rooted in the existential analytic of Dasein" (SZ 160). Only if this existential rootedness is excavated phenomenologically can we understand the sense in which logic is – and is not – normative.

The goal of Heidegger's phenomenology of logic is to show that the "is and the as have a *common origin*" – namely, Dasein's "fundamental comportment: being free in an originary sense" (GA29/30, 497). Unpacking this claim will show how the logical calculus is a descriptive theory of truth-preserving entailment relations, not a normative theory of how we ought to think. But it will also show that logic is not normatively optional for us either, since its laws are constitutive norms of a practice, reason-giving, that is *demanded* by our mode of being: "being free in an originary sense."

Heidegger's problem with formalization is that it eliminates the "dimension" in which a being is encountered "as" it is (GA29/30, 435–440). I encounter the hammer as too heavy when I find it unsuitable for the task at hand – that is, within the dimension of the available, the meaningful context (*Bedeutungsganzes*) in which the hammer shows up in its "equipmental" being.[3] The assertion abstracts the hammer from this dimension and constitutes it as an object possessing the property of heaviness. There is nothing *erroneous* about such abstraction, but it gives rise to the illusion that the subject-predicate form is *sui generis* and that the "meaning" or proposition expressed in the assertion can, by itself, be the bearer of truth. But, for Heidegger, such meaning is parasitical: "A *is* b" only *has* meaning thanks to the experience of A *as* b (GA29/30, 436).

Now, this sort of experience – the hammer as too heavy – is itself possible only if the hammer is encountered in a normatively structured context of *other* things in which it fails to serve as it ought to serve. Such contexts are possible only if I "hold *myself* in a *comportment*" in which I am "able to refer to [*meinen*, intend] these other beings as such" (GA29/30, 448). This same point holds of assertion as well: Since asserting is "an essential *manner of comportment*" belonging to Dasein (GA29/30, 486), it too is normatively suspended between success and failure. The "essence" of assertion, for Heidegger, is its *possibility* of being "true *or* false," such that *no* assertion can simply be "true" all by itself (GA29/30, 449). And if that is so, then the "falsity" of an assertion, like the "too heavy" of the hammer, depends on the context disclosed as meaningful in the kind of comportment that allows *assertive* reference to other beings – namely, the comportment of being a truth-teller. "Truth," then, is not a property of

---

[3] Kris McDaniel (2017) explicates Heidegger's ontological "pluralism" in terms of "quantifier variance"; for a discussion of problems with this approach, see McManus (2013a).

an assertion but a success-term, an *evaluative* norm that derives from the constitutive norms of the comportment of truth-telling. To see this, we need to take a closer look at Heidegger's phenomenology of comportment.

Comportment (*Verhalten*) is acting "for the sake of" (*hou heneka*) some *possibility* of being; that is, it is trying to *be* something: teacher, father, citizen, nurse, scientist, and so on.[4] To "try" in this sense is to care about succeeding or failing at one's practical identity – that is, to act in light of the norms that govern such success or failure. These norms are both evaluative (measuring the extent to which I succeed) and constitutive (measuring whether I count as trying-to-be at all). If I don't have the ability (*Seinkönnen*, "possibility" in Heidegger's sense) to do what is demanded of teachers or carpenters, then no matter what I do, I don't count as acting for the sake of being a teacher or carpenter. "Comportment," then, formally indicates the being of Dasein as care (*Sorge*): that being "for which, in its being, that very being is essentially an *issue*" (SZ 84). Put otherwise, Dasein *is* only in trying to be something.

The norms that govern practical identities are, in the first instance, public: One acts as one does around here. I "understand" what it means to be a teacher because teaching is an existing practice where I am from, a practice that, in complicated ways, reflects a common understanding of what teachers are supposed to do. But this normative "supposed to do" does not provide any recipe for being a teacher; it is not a technical or instrumental norm that can be expressed as an in-order-to. My success in building a birdhouse is measured by the result (the "work," *ergon*), and the work determines (in principle) the steps I should take to get there. In comportment (*hou heneka*), in contrast, success or failure is measured at every moment – which is another way of saying that the meaning of teaching, what a teacher should be, is *always* at issue.

Public norms institute criteria for counting as being certain things, of course: I cannot be a philosophy professor at Rice University unless I am hired to be one, hold classes at the appropriate time, and so on. But these – and other, tacit yet no less public – norms do not define what it means to be a philosophy professor, and in acting for the sake of the latter, I can bump up against these public norms. I can decide that giving grades does not belong to what I should do as a teacher, that it is not something that conduces to what I take teaching to mean, and while this may get me

---

[4] In Crowell (2013, chap. 11), I argue that this is Heidegger's phenomenological account of what Christine Korsgaard calls "practical identity." In what follows, I use this term as shorthand for *Worumwillen*.

fired, it does not mean that I have failed at being a teacher. Trying to be a teacher is nothing but acting in light of what I take to be best in the matter of teaching, and this "best" is nowhere anchored in "being"; it is always *at issue* in my comportment. So practical identities, no matter how ingrained in my "character" they may seem, are ultimately optional.

For Heidegger, then, one always finds oneself in a "factical" situation in which certain conditions obtain: institutional norms, social practices, and stereotypical roles, but also one's psychological makeup, drives, inclinations, history, and the like. Though I have no power over what is given in this way, I am not inert in the face of such things; I can choose how I take them up. I stand before them as "possibilities" for behaving in certain ways in light of what I think is best in going on for the sake of being what I am trying to be. As Heidegger puts this point, Dasein "never has power over its being from the ground up," but it *is* in such a way that it *must* "take over being a ground [*Grund*, reason]" (SZ 284).

On Heidegger's phenomenological account, then, Dasein is, "ontologically," a response to a *normative claim*: "you must take over being a ground."[5] To act for the sake of being a teacher, for example, is to *acknowledge* that one is responsible for what one takes to be best in how one goes on. But this means that to take over being a ground is just to take up one's factical grounds as *possible* – but *only* possible – *justifying* reasons. And because Dasein is essentially "being-with-others" (SZ 125), being responsible for reasons is also being answerable (*verantwortlich*) to others who might challenge one's reasons. Understood ontologically, then, reasoning is originally *reason-giving*: a practice that is not definitive of who we are (because it does not derive from a "faculty" we rational animals intrinsically possess) but is not optional for us either (because it arises from a demand to which we, as care, must respond, since what we "are" is precisely at issue).

Heidegger's phenomenology thus provides a *normativity-first* account of reason, and if logic is constitutive of the practice of reason-giving, then logic is not optional; logical laws are descriptively constitutive of reasoning, but their normative significance does not derive from "widespread background norms about the relations between belief, reasoning, and truth" (Russell 2020, 387). Rather, logic's normativity follows from the ontological *ground* of reasoning. It "follows," not as a logical entailment, a truth-functional consequence of statements about Dasein, but *phenomenologically*, as an

---

[5] This is phenomenologically grounded in Heidegger's account of the call of conscience. The full argument for the claims I make in this section can be found in Crowell (2013, pt. 3).

"intentional implication" of our ontological condition as beings who must take over *being* a ground (reason).[6] There "is" reason only because we are such that we cannot "be" without acting in the evaluatively normative light of what is best in regard to what we do and say. And this means that reason-*giving*, giving an "account" of oneself (justification, *Rechtgebung*), is normatively demanded of a being defined as care (GA9, 169–170/130–131).

1.5   The Normative Ground of Truth

Following this brief sketch of the phenomenology of comportment and its ontological significance, we may return, more specifically, to the question of how the assertion and its "truth *or* falsity" should be understood. If the truth of "A is b" is not a property of the sentence but is inseparable from the experience of A *as* b, what does propositional truth look like in the context of assertive comportment, being a truth-teller?

If we start with the traditional idea that truth is the "conformity [*adaequatio, homoiosis*] of thinking to the thing that is thought," our question is now: "what grounds the possibility of conforming to something?" (GA29/30, 497). "Conforming" is a success-term and so belongs within the normative realm, that is, it is intelligible only on the basis of a kind of freedom that can acknowledge norms and bind itself to them. In truth-telling, the thing itself is what provides the measure of what is said, so I must be able to bind myself *to* the thing *as* it is. Heidegger claims that "we are never able to say what it is about beings that binds us" because being an "object" (*Gegenstand*) is normatively indifferent: "not all 'standing-opposite' necessarily entails binding." Thus, "we cannot explain this binding character in terms of objectivity, but vice versa" (GA29/30, 525). Doing so requires a normativity-first approach to objectivity, and so also to propositional truth. The binding character of whatever it is that we encounter and conform our assertion to must become phenomenologically perspicuous in its *possibility*.

In *Fundamental Concepts of Metaphysics* Heidegger identifies comportment with *noein*, a "pre-logical openness" or manifestness of beings "as such" (i.e., as *being*) and "as a whole." This is no mere "givenness" but what Heidegger calls *world*, the normatively structured space of meaning in which beings are encountered *as* being *something* (GA29/30, 495–496).

---

[6] On the difference between logical entailment and intentional implication: My perception of a house intentionally implicates the existence of the house's unseen sides, but it does not logically entail such existence, since for logic there *are* no "unseen" sides.

Logos, in contrast, and so assertion, is a secondary "manifestness," one that stands within the possibility of being true *or* false, measured against the entity to which it refers. But how does the entity become a measure?

As we have seen, *every* comportment is already a "letting oneself be bound" by that for the sake of which one acts (GA29/30, 496), and in such "letting," beings as such and as a whole are at issue – disclosed, manifest – in some distinctively meaningful way. For instance, when I act for the sake of being a teacher, when I try to be one, I let myself be bound by norms that pertain to the meaning of teaching, I commit myself to – care about – a measure that is never simply given but remains at issue in my acting. This commitment allows me to apprehend (*noein*, *Ver-nehmen*) the *world* of teaching in which things show up as relevant or irrelevant *for* the comportment of teaching. In commitment, then, I give myself the measure, measure myself by what I take to be best in the matter of teaching, and this "giving of measure" is *eo ipso* "transferred to beings in advance in accordance with" my comportment, "so that conformity or non-conformity is regulated by beings" (GA29/30, 496–497). In short, *my* success or failure at being a teacher cannot be measured if I am indifferent to how *things are* in the world of teaching.

For instance, from an "objective" point of view a blackboard's placement in a classroom is normatively indifferent. But if I am trying to be a teacher, I might experience it *as* badly positioned (A as b), as other than it *should* be for teaching. Though what allows the blackboard to be experienced as badly positioned is my commitment to teaching, I have "transferred" this "binding character" *to* the blackboard, which thereby binds *me* because it belongs to the success-conditions of my comportment: I cannot be a teacher if I ignore the way blackboards are supposed to be in the context of teaching, just as I cannot be a chess player without responding to how a knight is supposed to be moved.[7]

If I find that I need help in moving the blackboard to a better position, I might say to someone, assert, "The board is badly positioned." I exhibit, determine, and communicate something the measure of whose success (truth *or* falsity) lies in beings as they are. This is because assertion, as we saw, is assertive *comportment*, acting for the sake of being a truth-teller, and, as with any comportment, I can only count as so acting if I am not indifferent to how things are. An assertion's being true or false, then, has the same ontological structure as the blackboard's being

---

[7] For the complexity of this "responding to," see Haugeland (1998, 331–333) on the "excluded zone."

well or badly positioned: The assertion "The board is badly positioned" is true (i.e., is as it should be within the comportment of truth-telling) if (*as a teacher*) I have encountered the blackboard as failing to be as *it* should be, and (*as a truth-teller*), I have succeeded in exhibiting, determining, and communicating this fact. Neither the blackboard nor the expressed assertion (sentence) has *any* determinate meaning when abstracted from this ontological ground: the comportmental "ap-prehending" (*noein*) of a normative space, or world, in which things (including sentences) can show up *as* succeeding or failing at what they are supposed to be. Further, since assertive comportment is a derivative mode of disclosing – that is, since the comportment of being a truth-teller attains *its* meaning only within some *other* comportment or practical identity – the "truth" of the sentence in which it is expressed is not only not a property of that sentence; it can get no purchase at all on the sentence in the absence of some other comportment. For instance, the assertion can predicate being badly positioned of the blackboard only if something like the board's optimal "positioning" is at issue within a context or "world" – here, the world of teaching.

But a major worry remains: It might seem that grounding the normativity of meaning (and so truth as an evaluative norm of assertions) in optional comportments or practical identities leads to a conception of logic as constitutive of a game that we can opt into or out of. But here we see how Heidegger's ontology allows for a striking reversal of roles. In cases where the comportments on which being a truth-teller depends are contingent practical identities, logic's normative grip on assertions is likewise contingent; but its normative grip is *not* contingent when it belongs constitutively to what Heidegger calls our "fundamental" comportment. Such comportment is not optional for us because it is the ontological basis for *all* comportments: "being free in an originary sense" (GA29/30, 497) is "responding to" the demand to take over being a ground.[8] No matter what I try to be, *taking over* being a ground means acknowledging responsibility for the normative *force* of what I take to be best in trying to be it. Only so can anything become "my" *reason*. And if Dasein is *Mitsein*, my responsibility *for* reasons is answerability *to* others. Thus reason, as reason-giving (*Rechtgebung*), is equally fundamental and so not optional for us. For Heidegger, this fundamental comportment, including the demand for reason-giving, is what originally "bears" truth.

[8] If one asks what I am trying to be in taking over being a ground, the answer, in *Being and Time*, is a "self," and in *Fundamental Concepts of Metaphysics*, "the Da-sein in ourselves" (GA29/30, 508).

Now, reason-giving is a *practice* in which assertions play a role and, like all practices, it rests on constitutive norms. Thus, no appeal to "widespread background norms about the relations between belief, reasoning, and truth" (Russell 2020, 387) is necessary to explain how logic gets a normative grip on reasoning. Logic codifies the norms constitutive of the ontologically demanded "game" of giving and asking for reasons. To talk of the "normativity" of logic is not to say that logic tells us how we "ought" to think, revise our beliefs, or reason. Logic's "intrinsic" normativity reflects the ontological fact that being answerable is *demanded* of us and that reason-giving is our response to that demand, a practice for which logic is constitutively normative. Further, because the comportment of truth-telling *depends* on the fundamental comportment of reason-giving – that is, on the way assertions are to be deployed within the practice of reason-giving – "truth" can, *within the limits of assertive reduction to the extant*, be "predicated" as a "property" of those assertions, and sentential logic can be formalized into a calculus of truth-preserving entailments.

So, we should agree with Russell that logical laws are descriptive of how truth is preserved in reasoning, but the "truth" in question is not what logic takes it to be. Logical laws *do* say something about truth, but in treating truth as a property of sentences, they do not say *enough* about it, since they capture only how truth *appears* in the dependent (and contingent) comportment of being a truth-teller. But logic's normative grip does not derive from this contingent comportment. It is intrinsic to the fundamental comportment of reason-giving. On Heidegger's phenomenological approach, then, logic formalizes the constitutive norms of a practice that answers to what we owe one another, and in which assertions are not first of all truth-bearers but reasons given to others that enable a *shared* comportment toward something at issue as I account for myself in a *dialogical* context aiming at mutual understanding.

1.6   Logic, Science, Philosophy

With this result in hand, I conclude with some brief remarks on the implications of Heidegger's account of the normativity of logic for the three "motivations" Russell provides for thinking that logic is normative.

Beginning with the argument from error (**E**), if Heidegger holds that logic is constitutively normative for reasoning, then errors in reasoning are either "local" mistakes arising from various kinds of inattention or "global" enough to indicate that the individual does not count as a reasoner at all. But, as we have seen, logic can also be taken to be purely *descriptive* if one accepts the ontological reduction to the extant that takes place in asserting a sentence. One is then free to *abstract* sentences from their phenomenological ground and treat them as elements of a system in which "reasoning" in the phenomenological sense does not take place at all. What could motivate such a view of logic?

The descriptivist position might be tempting if one focused on a practice whose constitutive norms seem to align entirely with those of being a truth-teller, that is, if truth-telling were, contrary to fact, not a dependent comportment. And there is indeed something *like* such a practice – namely, *science*. According to Heidegger, science is a comportment, "a freely chosen stance of human existence" whose constitutive norm is "to give the matter itself explicitly and solely the first and last word" (GA9, 104/83). This "submission to beings themselves" has a tendency to conceal science's status as a comportment, making it easy to embrace the abstraction in which truth appears as a property of the sentences science advances and organizes "theoretically" into a "truth preserving" whole. Such organizing, a *reconstruction* of knowledge according to logical entailment relations, anticipates the fully developed system of "already known knowledge." Pursuing scientific knowledge is, of course, a practice, but the proleptic reconstruction of such knowledge is not. It is an "ideal construct" that tells us something about truth – namely, that there can be no *violations* of logical laws because such laws just describe how truth is preserved in sentential form; they have nothing to do with application. The only price science pays for its self-effacement as a comportment, its "submission to beings," is to "stray into the legitimate task of grasping the extant in its essential unintelligibility" (SZ 153; see Crowell 2017).

In *Being and Time*, Heidegger's remarks on epistemology suggest that he leaves room for such a view. For instance, in discussing the ontological realism–idealism debate, Heidegger rejects the epistemological approach that begins with developed views on scientific knowledge, while admitting that this approach contains "a grain of genuine inquiry" and has "not gone so very far off epistemologically" (SZ 207). Nevertheless, even if the "epistemic" concern with truth as a property of sentences has a certain legitimacy and permits treating logic descriptively as the organizing form of science as "already known knowledge," it remains an ontological *abstraction* and cannot fully address the question of the normativity of logic.

This brings us to the argument from normative consequences **(NC)**, which holds that logical validity is intrinsically normative thanks to a *direct* consequence it has for what we ought to believe. Here Heidegger's phenomenological approach makes common cause with Gilbert Harman: Logic has no *direct* normative consequences for belief-formation and revision because belief is *independently* beholden to another norm, that of *evidence*. Husserl formulated this as the "principle of all principles: that each intuition affording [something] in an originary way is a legitimate source of knowledge," arguing, further, that "no conceivable theory can make us stray" from this principle because any theory can itself "draw its truth only from originary givenness" (Husserl 2014, 43). Despite having some objections to Husserl's formulation, Heidegger clearly embraces its basic sense: Belief, as cognition, must ultimately be based on "exhibiting [something] directly and demonstrating [*Ausweisung*] it directly," where "directly" refers to the kind of originary encounter or "intuition" of the matter in question (SZ 35).

So here too we find a *qualified* agreement with the descriptivist account of logic, but the qualification is important. Evidence and belief-formation presuppose comportments that ground practices, and all such comportments are *already* normatively constrained by the "fundamental comportment" of taking over being a ground. As we have seen, fundamental comportment phenomenologically entails answerability, such that logic is constitutively normative for the nonoptional practice of reason-giving. Any conflict between reasoning as logical *inference* and reasoning as appeal to *evidence* must be adjudicated "pragmatically" through *actual* argumentation (Habermas 1990, 94).

This, in turn, provides Heidegger's answer to the argument from demarcation (**D**). Motivation for conceiving logic as an account of how we "ought" to reason arose from the worry that the descriptivist position could not decide between mutually exclusive accounts of logical entailment, suggesting that logic might be altogether conventional. Russell defended descriptivism by arguing that deciding between competing accounts of entailment is an "epistemic" matter requiring better "semantics" – "more theory and more evidence" (2020, 386). While agreeing that logic is not about how we "ought" to reason, Heidegger shows that the descriptivist position is not the last word on logic's normativity. If truth is taken to be a property of sentences, and if sentences have meaning only within practices, then the decision about which notion of entailment best models a given practice may indeed be conventional. But if logic is constitutive of the "game" of giving and asking for reasons, then its "domain," reasoning, is *not* conventional but is ontologically grounded in something normatively *demanded* of us as beings who are answerable to others for what we do and say.

This point, finally, begs the question of how logic is related to Heidegger's *own* project, that is, to phenomenological *philosophy* as a practice with its own norms and stakes.

Unlike reasoning, philosophy is not something demanded of us by our very being; it is optional. And like all comportments, it stands under the "obligation" to give reasons, to answer for what, if anything, it asserts. However, phenomenological philosophy is not constituted, like *science* is, by the norm of giving *beings* the "first and last word." Rather, it aims at elucidating the *being* of beings – that is, the *meaning* thanks to which beings can show up *as* the beings they are. Philosophy *does* aim to speak truly, and so the comportment of being a truth-teller belongs to it as it belongs to science. But to tell the truth about being (meaning) is not necessarily to assert a sentence that can be seen as having a property, truth, that is preserved in relations of logical consequence. What *looks* like such a sentence may, in philosophy, be nothing of the sort. The "yield" of philosophical assertions must be understood from within the project of philosophy. Perhaps the "dependent" comportment of truth-telling *ought not always* observe logical entailment relations. Perhaps the form that reason-giving takes in philosophy cannot be formalized into a calculus. Indeed, on Heidegger's account of philosophy, the reduction to the extant (the "specialty of assertion") is phenomenologically offset by the use of "formal-*indicating* concepts" (GA29/30, 421–431) that lead the addressee of philosophical sentences back to the *evidence-situation* that alone provides access to what is exclusively of concern in philosophy: the *being* of beings (GA61, 157; Crowell 2001, 129–151).

For a time, Heidegger held that phenomenological ontology was "objectification of being" or "transcendental science" (GA24, 465), but he soon abandoned this idea as a holdover from the metaphysical tradition. In later writings Heidegger prefers the term "thinking" for inquiry into being. Thinking is neither cognition nor reasoning but phenomenological *Besinnung* – *sich auf den Sinn einlassen* (GA7, 63) – and in *that* context, what looks like a false assertion (for instance, a metaphor) might nevertheless communicate the shared comportment toward *being* required of thinking as the project of bringing meaning to light. If thinking is allowed the metaphorical "use" (Davidson 1984, 247) of sentences – and, as Hannah Arendt pointed out, thinking "cannot avoid them" (1978, 112) – this would signal a priority of phenomenology over logic in thinking, not an equal footing. If access to meaning comes not through cognition and reasoning but through thinking, phenomenology as *Besinnung*, then it may well be that the "reign of logic" in philosophy "disintegrates into the turbulence of a more original questioning" (GA9, 117/92).

CHAPTER 2

Heidegger on the Changeover in Assertions

Stephan Käufer

Heidegger criticizes logic at several points in *Being and Time*. The most central such criticism comes in §33, "Assertion as a Derivative Mode of Construal."[1] Here Heidegger argues that something about the structure of assertions, or judgments, precludes them from capturing basic features of entities in the world. He goes on to claim that philosophical logic, which takes the structure of judgments as basic, is "ontologically inadequate" and "not originary" (SZ 160). This is the most central criticism of logic in *Being and Time* because, for one, it prefigures the more rhetorically charged claims of Heidegger's "What Is Metaphysics?" lecture, that "logic dissolves in a whirl of more originary questioning" (GA9, 117/92). Those remarks drew Carnap's scorn and ridicule and hence contributed to driving a deep and misguided wedge between those who appreciate Heidegger's existential phenomenology and those who appreciate rigor and clarity in philosophy.[2] Furthermore, this criticism of logic is central because Heidegger presents it in terms of the distinction between readiness-to-hand and presence-at-hand, the principal ontological distinction that Heidegger introduces in Division One of his book. The ontological inadequacy of logic consists of the fact that it interprets and reveals entities only as present-at-hand and hence misses entire regions of being.[3]

---

[1] I generally follow the Macquarrie and Robinson translation of *Being and Time*, but will frequently modify it. Here, for example, "construal" is a more accurate and revealing translation for Heidegger's *Auslegung* than "interpretation," which suggests a more deliberate and cognitive process than what Heidegger has in mind.

[2] "What Is Metaphysics?" also bases its criticism of logic on structural limitations of assertion. Heidegger's focus here, however, is on the distinction between negation and "the nothing," while §33 of *Being and Time* focuses on the difference between practical construal of ready-to-hand equipment and theoretical assertions. For a detailed interpretation of "What Is Metaphysics?" see Käufer (2005a).

[3] In other places, *Being and Time* criticizes logic for the reliance of traditional theories of concepts on genus-species hierarchies, which cannot capture the relation between the one (*das Man*) and individuals (SZ 128–129); for the failure of traditional theories of inference to capture the structure of the hermeneutic circle (SZ 152, 315); and for its inability to grasp nothingness ontologically (SZ 285). For a discussion of Heidegger's criticisms of logic in the context of the traditional logic that still dominated German philosophy in the early twentieth century, see Käufer (2005b, 2001).

2.1 Assertions and the Ontological Inadequacy of Logic

The status of assertions is at the heart of the issue of logic's ontological inadequacy. The crux of the argument in this connection comes in a dense passage in the middle of §33. Schear (2007) and Golob (2013) give careful interpretations of this passage.[4] They both cite the text at length. Schear helpfully calls it "the influential passage." Because of the interpretive difficulties raised by Schear and Golob, I will call it the "controversial passage." Here it is:

> The entity which is held in our fore-having—for instance, the hammer—is proximally ready-to-hand as equipment. If this entity becomes the "object" of an assertion, then as soon as we begin this assertion, there is already a change-over in the fore-having. Something *ready-to-hand with which* we have to do or perform something, turns into something "about which" the assertion that points it out is made. Our fore-sight is aimed at something present-at-hand in what is ready-to-hand. Both by and for this way of looking at it, the ready-to-hand becomes veiled as ready-to-hand. ... The as-structure of interpretation has undergone a modification. In its function of appropriating what is understood, the "as" no longer reaches out into a totality of involvements. As regards its possibilities for articulating reference-relations, it has been cut off from that significance which, as such, constitutes environmentality. The "as" gets pushed back into the uniform plane of that which is merely present-at-hand. ... This leveling of the originary "as" of circumspective interpretation to the "as" with which the present-at-hand is given a definite character is the specialty of assertion. Only so does it obtain the possibility of exhibiting something in such a way that we just look at it. (SZ 157–158).

Heidegger here uses the term "assertion" or "utterance" (*Aussage*) rather than "judgment" (*Urteil*). He does this because he generally avoids terms that have an entrenched philosophical use and *Urteil* has a technical sense in the theories of judgment (*Urteilslehre*) of traditional logic. Further, he aims to explain the structure of judgments in terms of a derivation from utterances made in a practical context, something like speech acts. *Aussage* captures such continuity between contextual utterances and context-free judgments. Nevertheless, Heidegger's target in the passage above is precisely judgment as conceived in traditional logic. Note that just before this passage Heidegger criticizes the notion of

---

[4] Chaps. 1 and 2 of Golob (2014) contain a longer version of his interpretation leading to his broader argument that original intentionality in Heidegger is conceptual, but not propositional. Other helpful interpretations of this passage in the context of broader issues arising in §33 are Dahlstrom (2001), Carman (2003), and the groundbreaking Dreyfus (1991).

validity (*Geltung*) in Lotze's theory of judgments (SZ 155–156) and, as we already saw, §33 concludes with a comment on the inadequacy of logic due to its conception of judgment. Heidegger presents the paradigmatic case of assertion as a "categorical proposition" (*kategorischer Aussagesatz*) and his argument applies broadly to propositions as such, taken as the content of possible judgments, beliefs, or other propositional ways of intending entities (SZ 157).

On first look, Heidegger here argues that assertions, judgments, and propositions share a general structure and that this structure radically constrains how we can intend entities. Before we make an assertion, we comport ourselves toward equipment through skillful, circumspective use. But assertions are "cut off" from the practical significance of the ready-to-hand and our familiarity with the equipmental whole is "leveled down" into a uniform plane of present-at-hand properties.[5] Schear sums up the gist of this line of thought: "All and only present-at-hand entities are possible topics of judgment" (2007, 128). Golob similarly states that the passage supports the thesis that "if an entity E is intended by a propositional mode of intentionality then E is intended as [present-at-hand]" (2013, 884).[6]

So the controversial passage makes this controversial claim:

(A) *The strong assertion thesis*: Assertions can intend only present-at-hand entities.

This is not plausible. Both Schear and Golob argue convincingly that the strong assertion thesis is false. Most obviously, it is false on straightforward phenomenological grounds. We frequently make propositional assertions and judgments in the course of competently dealing with entities. We make them about entities in their contexts of use, pointing out opportunities for action or demands for adjustments in the course of skillfully dealing with them. "Their car to the airport is here." "You forgot to add

---

[5] So Heidegger's argument against logic in §33 is:

1. Readiness-to-hand is an important ontological region.
2. Assertions can intend only present-at-hand entities.
3. Logic ontologizes the structure of assertions.
4. Therefore, logic is blind to an important ontological region.

Below I show that Heidegger holds a limited and more plausible version of (2), namely: Assertions as understood in a certain strain of ancient ontology only intend present-at-hand entities. This is the ontology taken over by logic, so Heidegger's overall argument against logic still goes through.

[6] Golob aims to regiment Heidegger's loose use of "present-at-hand" by providing three distinct definitions of the term. The claim (assertions intend only present-at-hand entities) is false under all three definitions.

the salt." "Somebody knocked." These judgments, uttered or not, are integral to successful comportment in a familiar environment. They do not "level down" the entities (the taxi, the salt, the front door) to a "uniform plane of the merely present-at-hand." A second reason to reject (A) is that it seems to involve Heidegger in a somewhat embarrassing self-reference paradox. *Being and Time* consists of assertions and the vast majority of them are about entities that are not present-at-hand. Much of Division One consists of assertions about ready-to-hand equipment, and the entire book is about Dasein, whose mode of being is existence, not presence-at-hand. The possibility of such assertions is gainsaid by adherence to (A). This paradox is particularly poignant in the case of theoretical assertions that thematize their object. *Being and Time* consists precisely of theoretical assertions that thematize the equipmental whole and Dasein.[7]

Against the current of much Heidegger scholarship, both Schear and Golob therefore claim that we must reject any reading of *Being and Time* that commits Heidegger to (A). This raises the interpretive question of how to make sense of the controversial passage. The crux of the problem lies in the interpretation of the radical changeover (*Umschlag*) from comportment toward ready-to-hand equipment to intending present-at-hand things. In what follows I interpret the phenomenology of the changeover in a way that is textually and phenomenologically consistent with the following three claims:

1. Heidegger's view readily accommodates the possibility of making assertions about ready-to-hand entities.
2. Heidegger argues for a weaker version of (A).
3. *Being and Time* does not face a self-reference paradox regarding its theoretical assertions about equipment and Dasein.

I will do this by focusing on the textual nuances of the controversial passage and closely related sections of *Being and Time*, especially §16 and §69b. These sections use Heidegger's underdeveloped distinction between thematic and unthematic intentionality. These terms are discussed in more detail by phenomenologists close to Heidegger, especially Husserl and Gurwitsch. Gurwitsch's view serves as a model for how to interpret Heidegger's conception of the unthematic, the thematic, and the changeover, and hence sheds light on the argument of §33.

---

[7] The prospect of such a paradox is raised and discussed in detail by Dahlstrom (2001) and Blattner (2007). In this chapter I focus on assertions about ready-to-hand entities, as does Heidegger in §33. The case for assertions about Dasein is similar.

2.2 Assertions Commonly Intend Ready-to-Hand Entities

The first thing to notice is that Heidegger explicitly allows for assertions about ready-to-hand entities. In his phenomenological characterization of the structure of assertion as pointing-out, predicating, and communicating, he writes that "in the assertion 'The hammer is too heavy,' what is discovered is ... an entity in the way that it is ready-to-hand" (SZ 154). Further on Heidegger considers cases of assertions made in the course of concernful circumspection, in contrast to "theoretical judgments." Such circumspective assertions may be uttered and can "take some such forms as 'The hammer is too heavy,' or rather just 'Too heavy!', 'Hand me the other hammer!'" (SZ 157). They are of the same kind as an "action of circumspective concern—laying aside the unsuitable tool, or exchanging it, 'without wasting words'" (SZ 157). If you lay the hammer aside to take another one, the action construes the hammer as too heavy and expresses that construal, whether or not you utter words. Such construal, integral to competent use of familiar equipment, involves utterances that have the function of pointing-out.

Predicating also takes place within circumspective concern. Predication "is what it is only as a pointing-out" and it functions by "restricting our view [so that] that which is already manifest may be made explicitly manifest in its definite character" (SZ 155). This, too, need not be uttered in words. If you lay the hammer aside to heft a lighter one, you make manifest its weight or manipulability. If you lay it aside to pick up a chisel or screwdriver, you make manifest that it is too blunt or bulky for the current task. Even with the added explicitness of an utterance,[8] predicating utterances do not first discover the entity, but serve to determine an already discovered entity. So circumspective assertions point out and predicate ready-to-hand entities. Similarly, they communicate what they make manifest about ready-to-hand entities. Heidegger writes that communicating shares our being-toward an entity, even when the entity the assertion makes manifest is not present. "Their car is here" and "You forgot the salt" are obvious cases of utterances that point out, predicate, and share an aspect of an entity in the course of dealing with it.

---

[8] "Explicit" translates *ausdrücklich* in "durch die ausdrückliche Einschränkung ... ausdrücklich offenbar zu machen" (SZ 155). Perhaps a better rendering is "expressed" or "expressly." We can express determinate features of a situation or aspects of equipment in many ways, not only through words. The action of reaching for the other hammer expresses the unsuitability of the first one. Macquarrie and Robinson use "express" to translate *aussprechen* and *ausgesprochen*, which can be better rendered as "utter."

These examples of assertions appeal to the phenomenology of ready-to-hand equipment becoming conspicuous, that is, when the equipment fails to function smoothly and requires some adjustment. Strictly speaking, in such cases we are not dealing with purely ready-to-hand equipment. In §16 Heidegger calls this "a certain unreadiness-to-hand [*eine gewisse Unzuhandenheit*]" (SZ 73) and describes it as a dynamic between encountering ready-to-hand entities and those entities announcing their presence-at-hand. Throughout such encounters, the present-at-hand remains "bound up in the readiness-to-hand of equipment" (SZ 74). This is because we continue to make sense of this equipment within our broad background familiarity of the holistic network of involvement, the *Bewandtnisganzheit*: "Pure presence-at-hand announces itself in such equipment, but only to withdraw again into the readiness-to-hand of what we are dealing with, i.e. what we are putting into repair" (SZ 73). Depending on how skillful you are at using the equipment and how absorbed you are in the task, such adjustment can manifest the presence-at-hand of the entity to various degrees. A skilled carpenter can set aside an unsuitable tool and reach for the right one "without wasting words," as Heidegger writes, while an apprentice or unskilled hobbyist may need to step back further and stare at the other tools before hesitatingly choosing one and going on with the work. There seems to be a continuous scale of how far removed our comportment can be from fully absorbed coping, how thoroughly our circumspective sight is restricted, how many steps back we have to take in order to ascertain what is already manifest, how far we must dim down the entities. All along this scale we can make assertions: "Between the kind of construal that is still wholly wrapped up in concernful understanding and the extreme opposite case of a theoretical assertion about something present-at-hand, there are many intermediate gradations" (SZ 158).[9]

2.3   The Controversial Passage Is about Limiting Cases of Assertion

At some point there is a radical break in this continuity. Beyond this break lies the "theoretical statement" (*Aussagesatz*) that, Heidegger claims, functions as the paradigmatic case of assertion in logic. The theoretical

---

[9] Heidegger does not give an analysis of the propositional structure of these intermediate gradations because, he says, "they are intelligible once we have gotten clear on the limiting cases" (GA21, 158). See also his remark at GA21, 156n8. For an insightful discussion of the phenomenology of such intermediate cases of assertion, see Dahlstrom (2001), 202–205.

statement is the "limiting case" (*Grenzfall*) of assertion, whose phenomenological origin from construal Heidegger seeks to trace in the controversial passage. Theoretical statements are not merely further removed
from the ready-to-hand than any of the intermediate assertions. While
all the intermediate gradations of assertion still make manifest the entity
in the context of its involvement and therefore "cannot be traced back to
theoretical statements without essentially perverting their meaning," the
theoretical statement is "cut off" from the significance of equipment in the
environment and "no longer reaches out into the whole of involvements"
(SZ 158). It is a "limit" in the mathematical sense. Intermediate cases of
assertion point toward it, but never reach it. That requires a changeover.
It is this changeover that effects the restriction of assertions to the "merely
present-at-hand." Predication, or any other formal feature of assertions,
does not by itself bring about such a restriction. In fact, the very same
utterance, for example "The hammer is heavy," can intend a ready-to-hand
entity or be inherently restricted to the merely present-at-hand, according
to whether it is made under the condition of the changeover.

Heidegger endorses a version of (A) only for assertions made under the
conditions of the changeover, while he readily acknowledges all kinds of
assertions that point out ready-to-hand entities that are more or less conspicuous. Given this limitation on the scope of the controversial passage,
it argues for a weaker, more plausible claim:

> (A*) *The weak assertion thesis*: The limiting case of assertions, exemplified by
> theoretical statements, can intend only present-at-hand entities.

Unfortunately, the text of §33 leading up to the controversial passage is not
as clear as it should be on the point that the restriction to the "uniform
plane of the merely present-at-hand" applies only to the limiting case of
theoretical statements. Heidegger does make perfectly clear that he wants
to point out the modification from construal to assertion, and hence demonstrate that assertion is a "derivative mode" of construal, by "sticking to
certain limiting cases (*Grenzfälle*) of assertion" (SZ 157). But the controversial passage itself seems to address *all* assertions as such. It begins:

> The entity which is held in our fore-having—for instance, the hammer—is
> proximally ready-to-hand as equipment. If this entity becomes the "object"
> of an assertion, then as soon as we begin this assertion, there is already a
> change-over in the fore-having.

In the first sentence we are circumspectively dealing with the hammer. In
the second sentence we are making an assertion about it. It is tempting to

conclude that the changeover mentioned in the second sentence *simply is the modification* from construal to assertion that Heidegger is after. This, however, is wrong. There are different kinds of modifications that turn construal into assertions. The changeover is only one such modification. It is the most extreme one, the limiting case, and the one that, Heidegger thought, most convincingly demonstrates that assertions are derivative of construal.

It is worth pointing out a few subtleties of Heidegger's language here.

To begin with, "as soon as we begin this assertion" is a bad translation for *Aussageansatz. Ansatz* is not the beginning of the asserting act in time. It is the approach one takes toward the entity, the attitude or the slant that is implicit in and presumed by making assertions. Heidegger discusses this approach on the previous page ("*im bestimmenden Ansetzen liegt ferner schon eine ausgerichtete Hinblicknahme...*") and shows that for assertions, just like construal, it consists of a fore-having, fore-sight, and fore-conception (SZ 157). So this half of the sentence says something like: "In the approach we take toward entities with the assertion, a changeover already takes place in the fore-having."

Secondly, it is important to notice that the particular *Ansatz* (i.e., approach) mentioned here is specified in the conditional clause "If this entity becomes the 'object' [*Gegenstand*] of an assertion." Superficially this simply seems to say "if we make any assertion about the entity." But that is not the case, because not every assertion turns the entity it points something out about into a *Gegenstand. Gegenstand*, in *Being and Time*, is not a neutral term. Heidegger uses it in two connected contexts. First it means objects thematized by a science. So the environment can be the *Gegenstand* of biology (SZ 58), a corpse can be the *Gegenstand* of pathology and anatomy (SZ 238), antiquities can be the *Gegenstand* of history (SZ 392–394). In each case this requires the science to thematize the object, which, as Heidegger explains in §69b, requires establishing basic concepts, methods, regional delineations, and so on. Phenomenology, too, has its *Gegenstand* that it needs to thematize appropriately. The second context in which Heidegger uses the term is when he discusses philosophical theories that he is suspicious of. Cognition has its *Gegenstand*, though Heidegger points out that it is hard to see how it "has" it, how the cognitive subject "gets out" to its object (SZ 60–62). More relevantly, judgments in the theory of judgments of traditional logic have their *Gegenstand*. The account of truth that Heidegger finds unsatisfactory spells out truth as the agreement of the judgment or cognition with its *Gegenstand* (SZ 214). So by saying that an entity becomes the "*Gegenstand*" of an assertion or judgment, in the conditional clause Heidegger is specifically picking out theoretical judgments of a certain type. To underscore his suspicions of precisely this kind of assertion, Heidegger puts the term in scare quotes.

In summary, we can paraphrase the second sentence of the controversial passage as follows: If we make an assertion that thematizes the entity in a specific way so as to turn it into the *Gegenstand* of the assertion, then a changeover in the fore-having has taken place in the approach that such an assertion takes toward its entity. This sums up the limitation on the scope of the claim about assertions. It remains to explain what the changeover is and why it restricts assertions to present-at-hand entities.

2.4 "Theme" in Phenomenology

In addition to the distinction between presence-at-hand and readiness-to-hand, the argument of the controversial passage depends on a cluster of concepts that includes the changeover, *Gegenstand*, theoretical judgments, "categorical assertion," and the distinction between thematic and unthematic intending. These concepts pose difficulties for interpreters because Heidegger does not define them clearly. He does not define terms such as *Gegenstand*, theoretical judgment, or categorical statement because, along with the notion of presence-at-hand, he simply lumps them with a broadly Cartesian *style* of philosophy. Heidegger thinks this style, which he rejects as overly cognitive and committed to an ontology of substances, shows up in many different ways in work from Descartes to Kant, to the neo-Kantians and even Husserl. The distinction between thematic and unthematic and the notion of the changeover, however, do not belong to such an ontology of substances. They are phenomenological concepts used by Husserl and elaborated by Gurwitsch. A look at Gurwitsch's detailed treatment of "theme" helps make sense of what Heidegger means by the changeover.

Thema, thematisch, and its variants come up in three different contexts in *Being and Time.* The ordinary meaning is that something is the theme or topic of discussion, what it is about. For example, §9 explains what the theme (*Thema*) of the analytic of Dasein is. The being of entities is the "thematic object [*Gegenstand*] of the investigation" (SZ 27), thus reviving the question of being, which since Aristotle has "fallen silent—as the thematic question of genuine investigation" (SZ 2). Making this theme thematic again is the work of phenomenology: "What already shows itself in appearances, as preceding and accompanying them, albeit unthematically, can thematically be brought to show itself, and what thus shows itself in itself are the phenomena of phenomenology" (SZ 31). Throughout the book Heidegger reflects on how phenomenology can make relevant phenomena show themselves (such as in §28, "The Task of a Thematic Analysis of Being-in").

The second main context in which *Being and Time* considers the thematic is what Heidegger calls "thematization." As Heidegger explains in §69b, thematization projects a region of entities and makes them accessible for a positive science. A thematization constitutes a specific understanding of being; it provides basic concepts and readies the way for theoretical knowledge. The paradigmatic example of this, according to Heidegger, is how the development of modern mathematical physics is rooted in the work of Galileo and Descartes who articulated the mathematical projection of nature. Like theoretical assertions, such thematization involves a changeover (*Umschlag*) from circumspect dealing with entities to characterizing those same entities in a theoretical stance. Existential phenomenology has its own distinct thematization, that is, its way of ensuring a theoretical grasp of its entities.

The third context, which is directly relevant to the changeover in the controversial passage, comes in §§15–16 when Heidegger introduces his notion of the world, and again in §§31–33 on understanding, construal, and utterances. Heidegger here claims that sometimes we understand things correctly only when they are unthematic. For example, "in order for ready-to-hand equipment to be encounterable in its 'being-in-itself' [*An-sich-sein*] in everyday dealings with the 'environment,' the references and reference-wholes in which circumspection is 'absorbed,' must remain unthematic for it" (SZ 75). And later, "a thematic perception of things precisely does not encounter ready-to-hand equipment with respect to its 'in itself'" (SZ 354). The point of these passages is that ready-to-hand equipment functions as such only insofar as it remains in the background. Similarly, when Heidegger explains the structure of understanding as projection, he writes that "understanding has the characteristics of projection, and this also means that it does not thematically grasp the possibilities, i.e. the background against which [*woraufhin*] it projects" (SZ 145).[10] This background is our unthematic familiarity with the network of possible actions afforded by equipment. Sometimes particular nodes of that holistic

---

[10] *Woraufhin* is difficult to translate. In most passages "in light of which" or "on the basis of which" renders the idea. Here the *woraufhin* makes the projected possibility intelligible. So, for example, if you "project" the chalk onto its proper use of writing on the blackboard – that is, if you use the chalk in the course of lecturing – you do so against the background of your familiarity with classrooms, teaching, and so on.

network, such as conspicuous equipment, are articulated in a construal, but only briefly and partially: "The ready-to-hand is always already understood in terms of the wholeness of involvements. This need not be grasped explicitly in a thematic construal. Even if it has undergone such a construal, it again recedes into an understanding that does not stand out from the background" (SZ 150). Our ongoing, fundamental familiarity with the world of equipment is understood, but not thematic.

How an object is thematic in consciousness is a standard topic in Husserlian phenomenology. Husserl addresses the question in §122 of *Ideas I*. For Husserl, whether an intended object is thematic belongs to "an important group of general modifications of acts," modifications that move in a "completely different dimension from the difference between clarity and unclarity" (1913, 253f). The modifications Husserl has in mind here are *grasping* a content, *continuing to hold* it in our mental grasp as we synthetically add to the content to synthetically construct a cumulative theme (*Gesamtthema*) or move to a related content, or *turning to another theme*, in which case the original content "does not disappear from our consciousness, it is still conscious, but no longer in our thematic grasp" (1913, 254). He gives three concrete examples: First, I maintain what I have just now perceptually grasped, when I turn my grasping gaze to another object. Second, I run through the steps of a mathematical proof, going through each premise step by step. In so doing I do not abandon the previous steps of the proof, but maintain them in my grasp along with the new step in a "new thematic Ur-actuality." Finally, I may walk along a street engaged in thought when a whistle from the street momentarily distracts me from my thought. As I return to the thought, "the grasp of the sound is not extinguished, the whistle is still conscious in a modified way, but it is no longer in my mental grasp. It does not belong to the theme—nor to a parallel theme" (1913, 254).

Aron Gurwitsch analyzes the phenomenology of themes more thoroughly, particularly in his 1929 dissertation *Phänomenologie der Thematik und des reinen Ich*. In this dissertation Gurwitsch claims that some basic ideas of Gestalt psychology belong to phenomenology.[11] His fundamental observation is that "we never deal with a theme *simpliciter*; instead, we confront a theme standing in a field" (Gurwitsch 1929, 203). He gives the example of an inkwell that stands on his desk surrounded by pencils,

[11] A few years later Gurwitsch lectured on Gestalt psychology and its relevance to phenomenology in Paris. Merleau-Ponty attended these lectures and frequently discussed philosophy with Gurwitsch, whose ideas had an evident influence on the *Phenomenology of Perception*.

paper, books, and so on. If the inkwell is the theme of a perceptual act, the desk, pencils, papers, and so on make up its thematic field. Within the thematic field, there is a variety of relations that elements of the field bear to the theme, not as an "aggregate of single elements," but by virtue of a "Gestalt connection" (1929, 206). The desk supports the inkwell and, unlike the piano, is the proper place for it. The same perceptual act also sees the walls, and through the window the facade of the neighbor's house. These latter elements, Gurwitsch says, are "marginal co-givens." They do not belong to the thematic field, because they have no material relation to the thematic inkwell. "For this reason there is no continuous transition from the thematic field to that which does not belong to it. ... Its difference from that field is essential and radical" (1929, 206). The theme stands in "a special and privileged place" in its field. It is its organizing "center" and everything else in the field "is oriented with reference to this center" (1929, 203–204). Gurwitsch here points out that we can think of the structure of thematic field and theme as a ground that is organized around a figure. He refers to the investigations of Edgar Rubin's *Visuell wahrgenommene Figuren*, which "are relevant here so far as the figure–ground relationship studied by him is a special case of the general relation of theme to thematic field ... We can generalize the terms 'figure' and 'ground' beyond the visual realm in which they arose and identify them with the concepts of theme and thematic field" (Gurwitsch 1929, 204n).

The same Gestalt-theoretic concept also informs Gurwitsch's phenomenology of acts of "grasping" that make something thematic in the first place. His description differs substantially from Husserl, who suggested that attention functions like a ray that highlights and picks out one element in the field (Husserl 1913, 192). On Husserl's view, an object of consciousness can become the theme without affecting the remaining content of consciousness. Rather than such piecemeal spotlighting, Gurwitsch finds organization and reorganization of the whole. Considering Husserl's example of going through a mathematical proof, Gurwitsch writes:

> I am aware of a variety of propositions, of obscure, confused, and unarticulated thoughts in a more or less nascent state. Suddenly an orientation comes into unordered train of mathematical "phantasies" and musings; what was still simply floating by acquires relatedness to a thought of which I am aware clearly and articulately as my theme and which dominates my field of consciousness, centralizing and directing it. (1929, 204)

On the basis of this phenomenology of the relation between theme and thematic field, Gurwitsch distinguishes three "series of thematic modifications," or three different ways in which the theme of an act can change. The first series consists of a broadening of the thematic field, as memories or marginal objects gain relevance within the context of the theme. This modification leaves the content of the theme invariant, but "the theme is now differently oriented to the field and differently inserted in it" (1929, 227). The second series consists of changes in the status of the theme. It can disappear from consciousness, or it can move to marginal consciousness, as Husserl's whistle on the street does – still in conscious-ness but of no relevance to the current thought. Or the theme can move to the thematic field. This is how Gurwitsch characterizes the steps of a proof. As I go through them, the earlier steps of the proof cease to be theme and become part of the thematic field of the currently thematic step. This con-trasts with Husserl's analysis in which earlier steps are synthesized into a cumulative theme with the following steps.

The third series of modifications is "totally different" from the previ-ous two insofar as "through them the theme is affected in a deep-reaching way with regard to its very material content" (1929, 237). Gurwitsch calls such modifications "restructuration." If, for example, we see a rectangular piece of cardboard and are interested in its color, the rectangular shape is merely a support for the surface color; if we then focus our interest on the shape of the cardboard, the contour becomes active and compresses what lies within it. Rubin's figure–ground switches illustrate these phenom-ena: "We observe how the boundary between white and black changes its 'looks' and is totally transformed when we see it one time as the contour of the white vase and another time as that of the two black faces looking at each other" (1929, 238).[12] In such figure–ground switches, Gurwitsch claims, "objective identity becomes a problem":

> Nothing remains what it was. A stroke in one configuration of lines (e.g. the contours of Rubin's goblet) and the "same" stroke—the "same" objectively speaking, i.e., as far as the physical stimulus is concerned—in *another* con-figuration (the contour of the two faces) appears phenomenally as totally different; is by no means the same stroke. (1929, 239)

Because of restructurations, Gurwitsch rejects Husserl's claim that "atten-tional modifications are without import for the noematic material what" (1929, 265). Shifting our attention from the color to the shape of an

---

[12] Gurwitsch has in mind the figure that can be seen either as a white vase against a black background or as two dark faces in profile against a white background. This figure is now commonly called "Rubin's goblet," though it was in part inspired by an earlier paper by Lillien J. Martin (1914–1915). See Rubin (1921, 32n).

object effects a restructuring akin to a figure–ground switch, in which the intended object is no longer the same. It is the same physical object, but it is not the same intended object in phenomenal consciousness.

2.5 The Changeover and the Specialty of Assertion

There are some obvious similarities between Gurwitsch's phenomenology of thematic fields and Heidegger's view of the unthematic and the changeover.[13] Like Gurwitsch, Heidegger thinks of the unthematic in terms of a field that is centered on a theme and organized according to a general structure that gives each entity within the field its particular significance. This organizing structure is the holistic structure of references and affordances, the *Verweisungsganzheit* and *Bewandtnisganzheit*. The centering theme is what shows itself in everyday dealing, for example the work, the task, or the activity (*Werk*), like building bookcases or teaching a class. The thematic task is made possible by our familiarity with the unthematic background. The task also "sustains the holism of references in which we encounter equipment" (SZ 70), because it organizes what has a bearing on what. The task, in Heidegger's language, construes (*auslegen*) the ready-to-hand equipment. Because it depends on and sustains the network of ready-to-hand equipment, the work – be it a bookcase or a lecture – itself has the being of the ready-to-hand. We do not have separate understandings of being for the work and for the background.

Second, like Gurwitsch, Heidegger considers distinct modifications of the field. For instance, Heidegger discusses conspicuousness, obtrusiveness, and obstinacy as three distinct modes in which equipment can become unready-to-hand. When equipment breaks, goes missing, or otherwise fails to function smoothly, it activates a new task and we have a "modified encounter of the ready-to-hand" (SZ 74). The equipment emerges from its inconspicuousness in the thematic field and becomes salient as

---

[13] Heidegger did not take these ideas *from* Gurwitsch. Gurwitsch's dissertation was published in the journal *Psychologische Forschung* in 1929. It is not clear if Heidegger was familiar with it, and he obviously could not have read it before writing SZ. On Carl Stumpf's recommendation, Gurwitsch spent a year in Freiburg in 1922 to study with Husserl. But he did his work on the dissertation and Gestalt psychology later, during the mid-1920s while he was working with Adhemar Gelb in Frankfurt, so it is not likely that Gurwitsch and Heidegger discussed this Gestalt-inspired phenomenology of themes in Freiburg. Edith Stein is another phenomenologist in Husserl's ambit who had familiarity with Gestalt concepts. While studying with Husserl in Göttingen she participated in Rubin's figure–ground experiments. The German translation of Rubin's *Visuell wahrgenommene Figuren* was published in 1921. On Heidegger's generally positive opinion of Gestalt psychology, see Radloff (2007, 22f).

we construe it in various tasks of "preparing, assembling, maintaining, improving, augmenting" (SZ 148). The conspicuous equipment is now the theme and the entire field undergoes a modification. Before the hammer broke, the nails and wood had an immediate bearing on it in the activity of building a bookcase. Now that we need to fix the hammer, the glue or the other hammer has a bearing it did not have before. During this modified encounter of equipment we continue to understand the equipment as ready-to-hand.

> The modes of conspicuousness, obtrusiveness, and obstinacy have the function of bringing to light the characteristic of presence-at-hand in what is ready-to-hand. But the ready-to-hand is thereby not yet merely *observed* and gawked at; the presence-at-hand that announces itself is still bound up in the readiness-to-hand of equipment. Such equipment does not yet veil itself into mere things [*verhüllt sich noch nicht zu bloßen Dingen*]. (SZ 74)

Finally, like Gurwitsch's restructuration, Heidegger singles out a type of modification that is sudden and wholesale, the changeover (*umschlagen* as opposed to *modifizieren*). Our construal of conspicuous equipment points *toward* this changeover as its limiting case that does *not yet* constitute the encounter of entities. As Heidegger puts it, with the changeover entities are "merely observed"; their presence-at-hand no longer is bound up with the readiness-to-hand of equipment; and equipment "becomes veiled as ready-to-hand" (SZ 158) and thus "veils itself into mere things" (SZ 74). In Gurwitsch's words, with this restructuring, "nothing remains what it was" or the same entity "appears phenomenally as totally different" (1929, 239).[14] The unthematic hammer that functions smoothly while you build a bookcase is the same entity as the conspicuous hammer when it breaks or is too heavy for the job. It is the same entity because its meaning is understood in terms of the holistic network of involvements. It *is* still *for* hammering, even though it does not work well right now. If, however, you merely observe it and it is veiled in its readiness-to-hand, then it is no

---

[14] Gurwitsch himself interprets the changeover in Heidegger as a kind of Gestalt switch illustrated by Rubin's images. He suggests that changeovers are fundamental phenomena for exploring what is constitutive of certain objects. See Gurwitsch (1931, 118). Here he again illustrates the changeover as a figure–ground switch. This illustration requires some care. In Rubin's goblet, the way of looking, the perceptual approach we take to the image, does not change with the switch from vase to faces. What changes is the organization that determines what is ground and what is figure *within* the overall perceptual approach. To use Heidegger's terminology, the entities switch, but the being of the entities remains the same. In a changeover, on the other hand, the *being* of entities switches. This does not merely affect the relation of entities to each other within a field, but produces an entirely different field of entities and ways they have of relating to one another.

longer the same entity. The place of the entity in the network of involvements is eliminated in the changeover from equipment to "mere things."

A changeover, for Heidegger, implies a change in the being of entities, not a modification of entities within the same domain of being. For instance, if an inauthentic person becomes authentic, that is a modification within existence, that is, within the being of Dasein (SZ 130). If a person dies, however, that is an *Umschlag* from existing to merely-being-present-at-hand (*Nur-noch-vorhandensein*), a "remarkable phenomenon of being" (SZ 238). If a hammer becomes the *Gegenstand* of a "theoretical statement," there is an *Umschlag* from the fore-having that understands the *Bewandtnisganzheit* to one that is cut off from it (SZ 158). This is a changeover in the understanding of being (SZ 361), not merely a modification of the entity. In the controversial passage, Heidegger writes that the changeover takes place in the fore-having. In Heidegger's vocabulary, the fore-having, fore-conception, and fore-sight make up the background of a projection (*das Woraufhin des Entwurfs*) in terms of which an entity can be understood. To understand the being of an entity is to project that entity onto this background. Heidegger also calls this the *sense* (*Sinn*) of an entity (SZ 151). The hammer makes sense in terms of our familiarity with the affordances that connect equipment and certain tasks. The fore-having here consists of the way in which we have already adapted to, and are oriented toward, this background of uses, affordances, typical arrangements, and so forth.[15]

When the understanding of being changes over at the limit of dealing with broken hammers and the like, the familiar background loses all relevance. We experience them in a different understanding of being by "looking at the ready-to-hand things we encounter *in a new way*" (SZ 361). They now make sense in a different way, projected against a different background. We get an example of such a new way of looking in §69b. Here Heidegger outlines the "mathematical projection of nature" (SZ 362), the specific thematization of nature achieved by natural science with the work of Galileo. The place of the hammer in the network of affordances that structures its being as a tool is replaced by "a spatio-temporal position, a world-point, which is in no way distinguished from any other" (SZ 362). Looked at in this way, the hammer and the nail each makes sense as a material thing with extension, weight, acceleration, and so forth, but they have no bearing on one another.

---

[15] In German, *ein Vorhaben* is a project, a purpose, or an undertaking. This colloquial sense further clarifies the fore-having; what we are up to shapes how we encounter entities.

It did not take the work of Galileo to understand the being of entities as merely present-at-hand. The modern scientific understanding of being is a development of a more basic one that has been available to Dasein all along. Like the scientific projection, this original understanding of entities as present-at-hand projects them onto a "uniform plane." Cut off from the *Bewandtnisganzheit,* this understanding of being does not make sense of entities against the differentiated topography of a background that withdraws and gives salience to a specific organization of the field. It does not distinguish between theme and field and it does not require familiarity with cultural background practices. There is no specific task that organizes the field of entities. The entity loses its place in the holism of involvements. But entities do not thereby stop making sense. The "specialty" or "merit" (*Vorzug*) of assertions is precisely that we can make sense of entities in terms of mere properties from a standpoint that is completely uninvolved (SZ 158). This understanding of being has been "the methodological basis on which ancient ontology arose" (SZ 160).

2.6   There Is No Self-Reference Paradox

Finally, understanding the unthematic as a thematic field, or the ground of a figure, shows how the apparent self-reference paradox dissolves. *Being and Time* can make theoretical statements about the phenomena of readiness-to-hand and Dasein without thereby misrepresenting those phenomena as something present-at-hand. Consider, for comparison, Rubin's goblet. This image illustrates the drastic difference between perceiving a colored field as a figure and perceiving it as ground. If we experience the vase as the figure, we do not notice or recollect anything about faces in profile. And yet, the background is not absent in our visual experience. We experience it correctly, *as* ground, insofar as we experience it as not drawing attention to itself, as withdrawing. There are quite a few things we can meaningfully assert about the ground without giving up on the claim that as ground it necessarily withdraws as long as it functions as the ground for the figure. Much of Rubin's *Visuell wahrgenommene Figuren* consists of such assertions. He states, for example, that the ground does not have a shape, that we see it as continuing under the figure and into the surrounding space beyond the edge of the picture, that we see it without definite edges, that we see it as being located further away than the figure, and so on (Rubin 1921, 35ff.). All of these statements thematize the ground explicitly, without thereby turning it into a figure. Rather, they articulate explicitly what it is like for us to see the ground "unthematically."

Articulating theoretical statements about the ground or the unthematic, then, is no more paradoxical than making precise statements about vagueness, or determinate statements about indeterminacy. While there is no self-undermining paradox, the difficulty lies in the challenges of discovering just what to say about structures that by their nature are hard to grasp. Rubin's experimental subjects faced this difficulty when they were asked to describe their experience of the ground while attending to the figure. Heidegger worries about precisely this difficulty in his methodological reflections on phenomenology. The interpretation of Dasein, he writes, has its "peculiar difficulties grounded in the way of being of the thematic object [*Gegenstand*] and the thematizing comportment" (SZ 16). The peculiarity is that the essence of this thematic object (Dasein) is that it covers itself up, while the thematizing comportment is one that uncovers. The same difficulty arises for equipment; "in itself" this thematic object withdraws, while phenomenology draws attention to it.

Heidegger's conception of phenomenology is designed to handle this peculiar difficulty. "What is it that phenomenology is to 'let us see'? ... It is something that proximally and for the most part does *not* show itself at all. It is something that *lies hidden*, but at the same time essentially belongs to what does show itself, in such a way that it constitutes its meaning and its ground" (SZ 35). Phenomenology finds ways to make explicit and analyze structures that lie hidden. Heidegger's description of his phenomenological method emphasizes a kind of passivity with respect to its theme. The passivity comes from the fact that "we achieve phenomenological access to the entities by thrusting aside the tendencies of interpretation that suggest themselves all along" (SZ 67). If done correctly, the entities show themselves, "announce themselves," "light up," or "shine forth," and so on (SZ 72, 75). With respect to ready-to-hand equipment, "the pre-thematic entities become phenomenologically accessible when we put ourselves in the position of concerning ourselves with them" (SZ 67).[16] They remain accessible as the entities that they are so long as we continue to put ourselves in the position of concern. If we cease doing so, the phenomenological concepts and statements can become "denatured," "empty," "uprooted," and "free-floating" (SZ 36). Such methodological reflections indicate the thematization of existential phenomenology, that is, the specific way in which phenomenology seeks to grasp, conceptualize, and make thematic

[16] *Das phänomenologisch vorthematische Seiende* means the entities before they are thematized in phenomenology, not the "preliminary theme" as Macquarrie and Robinson have it. These entities, that is, equipment, become thematic when we gain phenomenological access.

assertions about equipment, readiness-to-hand, world, Dasein, and other ontological structures whose way of being is to withdraw or cover themselves up.

2.7   Conclusion

Following Schear and Golob, I have argued that Heidegger does not hold the strong assertion thesis. There is ample textual evidence that in the controversial passage Heidegger proposes a weak version of this thesis, which restricts it to limiting cases of assertions. Such limiting cases have the same structure as other assertions. They point out, determine, and communicate. But they intend entities from within a different understanding of being. This understanding of being, which consists of the projection of the being of entities, is nonpractical, not absorbed, and not circumspective. It veils the ready-to-hand and isolates entities from the holistic network of references. In so doing, this understanding of being reveals properties as the only determinations of entities. The criticisms of logic that Heidegger voices in §33 still go through. They depend only on the weak assertion thesis because logic itself adopts the understanding of being that Heidegger outlines in the controversial passage.

This reading of the controversial passage is supported by an interpretation of Heidegger's conception of the unthematic and the changeover that draws on Gurwitsch's detailed Gestalt-influenced phenomenology of theme and thematic field. This phenomenology shows that the changeover radically restructures the entire field of entities.

CHAPTER 3

Heidegger's Productive Logic

Richard Polt

Heidegger never pursues formal logic, which he sees as a debasement of genuine logic. Logic ought to ask "the question of truth" (GA21) and investigate *logos* as the process of meaning – the way we appreciate and articulate the significance of what *is* (Shirley 2010). Such a process is not simply our doing; as he increasingly emphasizes, it springs from an "appropriating event" that establishes a meaningful space and grips us, calling for an appropriate response. *Logos* has human beings, not the other way around (GA40, 184). Heideggerian logic, then, would attend to how this event of sense literally *takes place*.

Formal logic takes the event of sense for granted. It works within a world that has already been established, whose significations have already been highlighted and distinguished in a "discourse" more fundamental than explicit language (SZ 160–166). As we dwell in a world, we can (but need not) express discourse in words. We can (but need not) use our words to form statements, offering propositions that assert correct or incorrect claims about entities. These propositions can (but need not) be arranged into coherent arguments and theories. Formal logic may then describe patterns of coherence among propositions.

This pursuit is perfectly legitimate within its proper boundaries; Heidegger never claims that, if one is trying to establish a coherent set of assertions, one is free to contradict oneself or to let loose a series of non sequiturs. Perhaps even "essential thinking" must respect formal logic, to the extent that such thinking "posits propositions" (GA55, 156). But he is interested in the phenomena that formal logic presupposes: discourse, dwelling, and the event of sense.

Such phenomena cannot simply be summed up in a set of claims. They call for a discourse that is underway and that provokes us to transform ourselves. Otherwise, we are operating within an established way of being in the world, rather than attending to the unfolding of the world itself. To notice the world itself, in its "worldhood" or "worlding," would be to think in a special way. In his earlier work, Heidegger refers to the logic of such thinking as "formal indication" (Kisiel 2006; Nelson 2006). It invites "understanding to twist free of the vulgar conceptions of beings and properly transform itself into the Da-sein within it" (GA29/30, 428). Such thinking is "shot through with the finitude of existence" and points to "the already implicit sense of factical experience" (Hatab 2016, 2).

From the point of view of formal logic, this thinking may often look sloppy, arbitrary, or nonsensical. But Heidegger claims that, when it comes to the event of sense, his thinking is more rigorous than formal logic, because it is more suited to the issue at stake. What counts as rigor in thinking depends on the topic of thought (SZ 153).

There are no formal rules or techniques for Heideggerian thinking. However, like every thinker, he has certain favorite moves or turns of thought that we can call *tropes*. Their purpose is often to provoke us to attend to the deeper *logos*, the event of sense – and this demands a development in our way of thinking. Heidegger's tropes are meant to be transformative, to generate new concepts. They are a *productive logic*.

Heidegger himself uses this expression in *Being and Time*, but he does not explicitly identify the elements of his own productive logic or explain how they help us think. Based on what he does say, I will consider two of his typical practices that embody such a logic: verbalization (turning nouns into verbs) and the phenomenology of deficient modes (exceptions that prove the rule). These two tropes are found in every phase of Heidegger's career. Can they transform our concepts? Can they focus us on the event of sense? And can they also mislead us and lend themselves to abuse?

3.1 The Concept of Productive Logic

Organized, theoretical research into a particular field of beings presupposes the pre-theoretical disclosure of that field. Accordingly, in the introduction to *Being and Time*, Heidegger distinguishes the kind of logic that merely investigates the method of an established discipline from a *productive* logic that discloses the very being of the entities in a field through new concepts:

> Fundamental concepts are the determinations in which the substantive domain [*Sachgebiet*] underlying all the objects a science takes as its theme arrives at an advance understanding that leads all positive investigation. Only after the area itself has been thoroughly researched in advance in a corresponding manner do these concepts become genuinely demarcated and "grounded." But since every such area is itself obtained from the

domain of entities themselves, this advance research that creates the fundamental concepts signifies nothing else than an interpretation of those entities with regard to the fundamental constitution of their being. Such research must run ahead of the positive sciences, and it *can.* The work of Plato and Aristotle proves this. Laying the foundations for the sciences in this way is different in principle from the kind of "logic" that limps along after, investigating the condition of some science as it chances to find it, in order to find its "method." Instead, it is a productive logic—in the sense that it leaps ahead, as it were, into some determinate area of being, discloses it for the first time in the constitution of its being, and, after thus arriving at the structures within it, makes these available to the positive sciences as transparent assignments for their inquiry. (SZ 10)

For example, investigating the historicity of historical entities is more fundamental than analyzing the methods of historians (SZ 10, 392–397); and Kant's first *Critique* is of greatest value as an investigation of the being of natural entities, not as a theory of natural science (SZ 10–11). Productive logic generates concepts that indicate what it means to *be* in, say, a historical or natural way.

Productive logic is crucial to hermeneutic phenomenology, which interprets the being of entities, and particularly the being of Dasein – the entity to whom being makes a difference (SZ 38). In contrast, merely *apophantic* discourse makes assertions using established concepts (SZ 34, 219).

The germ of these ideas is already found in some of Heidegger's earliest lectures, where he proposes a "concrete logic" focused on the characteristics of various domains of entities: "The manner and structure of concept formation is indicated in advance by the sense of the substantive domain" (GA58, 74). His teacher Rickert had investigated concept formation in the "individualizing" sciences, such as history, in contrast to the "generalizing" natural sciences (Rickert 1913; GA56/57, 169–176). For Heidegger, this Neo-Kantian, epistemological approach is too superficial (GA58, 211, 226); phenomenology must go deeper and investigate the being of the domains in question. If "the problem of philosophical concept formation" is taken in this deep sense, "it is the philosophical problem at its origin ... the problem of obtaining philosophical experience" (GA59, 169).

The term *productive logic* makes an appearance in Heidegger's lectures of Summer Semester 1922. He praises the Greeks' "unprecedented ruthlessness of seeing": they developed "a wealth of ontological, categorial explications that has never again been achieved, but was only modified within the tradition and accepted as a guide in the most disparate philosophical contexts" (GA62, 230). In contrast, contemporary logic is a mere theory of knowledge, instead of research into entities themselves:

> A hermeneutic situation ... can never be attained through a programmatic, formal reflection.... Phenomenological hermeneutics is the methodology of philosophical research, i.e. [this methodology] can be developed only in connection with such research and for it. Logic of philosophy—productive logic—[vs.] logic *post festum* [after the feast, i.e., derivative]; in Lask's logic, the calamity: no "feast" there; the idea of logic—just a formal repetition of the disguise of logic as epistemology, in the sense of Neo-Kantianism— without any substantive result. (GA62, 232–233)

The challenge is to "feast" eagerly, ravenously, upon our experience of what *is*, so as to form concepts that are suited to its way of being.

Heidegger makes much the same point in 1925:

> *Logic* will then no longer be a supplementary formulation after the fact of scientific procedures, but rather a basic guide that runs ahead of the sciences and discloses their fundamental concepts. To this end, we need the history of philosophy, so that we may understand the ancients anew. We must press forward so that we may once again be equal to the questioning of the ancient Greeks. (Heidegger 2010, 272)

Productive logic is

> the advance disclosure and conceptual penetration of possible fields of objects for sciences. It does not, like traditional theory of science, run after the particular fact of a ... given science and investigate its structure. Instead, it is a logic that leaps ahead into the primary substantive field of a possible science, and first prepares the basic structure of the possible object of this science by disclosing the constitution of the being of this field. This is the procedure of *original logic* as it was exhibited by Plato and Aristotle—albeit only within very narrow limits. Since then, the concept of logic has been buried, and it is no longer understood. (GA20, 2–3)

Unless we understand "the genesis of the concept from raw signification [*rohen Bedeutung*] ... every logic is merely a construction or a matter for dilettantes" (GA20, 60).

Note that productive logic is not just a theory of how to think, but substantive research. It cannot be completely formalized and pursued independently of a phenomenological investigation.

In contrast, formal logic aims to abstract from the content of thinking. It can also be called *reproductive*: It applies only to apophantic discourse, it essentially relies on the stability and reproducibility of concepts, and it presupposes the disclosure of a field of beings. For example, "all men are mortal" and "Socrates is a man" imply that Socrates is mortal, *if* "man" and "mortal" are repeatedly used in the same senses – which they can be as long as we keep within a certain unchallenged understanding of what it means to be human. Symbolic logic can analyze far more complex deductive reasoning than syllogistic can, but again, such reasoning relies on fixed concepts.

Even probabilistic, inductive logic typically does not address concept formation and transformation, but assumes that the hypothesis under investigation has a fixed sense. It asks how one can verify or falsify an empirical proposition such as "All ravens are black." But it does not usually consider how the concepts at stake may, and often do, shift during an empirical investigation. Findings may make us reconsider what we mean by our words, or realize that our concepts were not as precise as we had assumed. (When major conceptual shifts take place, a science undergoes a creative crisis (SZ 9).) To disprove the proposition about ravens, "it is not enough to find that there is a raven correctly described by the *word* 'white,' we also have to know what kind of whiteness we want—and that is not a simple matter (assume a bunch of ravens lost colour because of some sickness—how shall we deal with this event?)" (Feyerabend 1991, 32). Productive logic would form richer, more revealing interpretations of what counts as white, as a raven, as a bird, or as a living thing.

Heidegger cites Plato and Aristotle as practitioners of productive logic. To expand a little on his suggestion: Plato's dialogues offer many examples of deductive arguments and Socratic elenchus, both of which follow reproductive logic. The former draw conclusions from a consistent set of premises; the latter derive contradictions, showing that the premises are inconsistent and thus that Socrates' interlocutor is at odds with himself. But between these arguments, there are often fluid and imaginative passages in which new concepts are being formed. In the *Republic* (331e), Polemarchus asserts that justice means giving everyone what is owed. By employing reproductive logic but also introducing a variety of new questions and creative proposals, Socrates brings Polemarchus to the point where he confesses, "I don't know what I meant" (334b). He has to rethink the very concept of owing. This is productive logic at work disclosing the domain of human relationships.

Aristotle develops a syllogistic logic and holds up an ideal of scientific knowledge as a demonstrative system that applies universal truths to more specific truths (*Nic. Eth.* VI.3). But his own texts hardly ever exemplify such a science; they are productive, not reproductive. In the *Physics*, for example, he draws on a variety of observations, puzzles, traditional opinions, and philosophical theories to refine his concepts of fundamental phenomena in the domain of nature, such as time, place, and motion. This is why, for example, in early Freiburg lectures (GA61, GA62) and later in

Marburg (GA18, GA19), Heidegger repeatedly takes Aristotle as a model of hermeneutic phenomenology.

We should also mention Hegel's logic, which attempts to show how fundamental concepts develop dialectically. Heidegger's confrontations with Hegel are many and complex (GA28, GA32, GA68, GA86). But in general, we can say that from a Heideggerian standpoint, Hegel refuses from the start to engage in genuine productive logic because he does not begin with a world that is disclosed in a finite experience. He presupposes the supremacy of creative, self-conscious subjectivity over receptivity. In contrast, for Heidegger, we find ourselves immersed in *logos* as the event of sense, or even seized by it. *Logos* is not produced by concepts; to the contrary, concepts are obliged to respond to *logos* as a phenomenon that they cannot capture, but only indicate.

We turn now to two tropes that Heidegger often employs in his attempts at productive logic: verbalization and deficient modes.

3.2   Verbalization: Productive Tautology

Verbalization verbalizes. It turns a noun into a verb.

Heidegger experimented early on with this trope, notably in his break-through lecture course of 1919, "The Idea of Philosophy and the Problem of World Views": "Living in an environment, it signifies to me overall and always, it is all worldly, '*it worlds*'" (GA56/57, 73). When worlding is in full swing, I experience what happens as an event of my own (*Ereignis*) rather than an objectified process that passes before my gaze (*Vor-gang*) (GA56/57, 73). When events are degraded to processes, "the 'it worlds' is extinguished" (GA56/57, 89).

The invented verb *welten* was to become a durable part of Heidegger's vocabulary, reappearing in important texts such as the 1936 "The Origin of the Work of Art" (GA5, 30). He invokes the word, again in conjunction with *Ereignis*, in a 1949 lecture that makes a point strikingly similar to the one he had made thirty years earlier: When nearness is lacking, "World does not world. Thing/world does not take place [*ereignet sich nicht*]" (GA79, 23).

Heidegger also experiments with variations on *welten* and combinations of it with other distinctive words and concepts. A few examples: "The world ... *in its worlding pervades* [*durchweltet*] every *encounter* with beings and their *presencing*" (GA87, 100); "Worlding—as *owning*-over [*Welten— als über-eignen*]" (GA73 1.258); "World worlds so that beyng may essence [*Welt weltet, damit das Seyn west*]" (GA94, 211).

This last word is not Heidegger's invention. The archaic and poetic verb *wesen* means, more or less, to live and be. The noun *das Wesen* derives from the verb (Grimm 2021, s.v. *wesen*). In the *Contributions to Philosophy*, Heidegger favors *wesen*, or its gerund *Wesung* (essencing), as a word that applies to "beyng" (*Seyn*). The usual concept of essence asks "what 'makes' an entity into what it *is*, thus *what* constitutes its *what*-being, the being-ness of the entity" (GA65, 288). It is conceived as a generality that applies in common to a set of entities (GA65, 287–288). But if beyng is not an entity, it would be a gross confusion to say that it "is," or to apply the usual concept of essence to it. Instead, "essencing" designates "the happening of the truth of beyng" (GA65, 288) – "not something over and *above* beyng, but what gives word to its innermost" (GA65, 286).

Being and Time, too, adopts some existing verbs in order to describe what certain key phenomena "do." Thus: "Temporality has different possibilities and different ways of *temporalizing* itself [*Zeitlichkeit kann sich … zeitigen*]" (SZ 304). Or: "The historizing of history [*Geschehen der Geschichte*] is the historizing of Being-in-the-world" (SZ 388). In everyday German, *sich zeitigen* means to ripen, and *geschehen* means to happen. Heidegger is not disregarding these meanings, but trying to find resources within them that allow for a transformation into deeper concepts.

Heidegger's verbalizations can often be difficult to translate. A notorious example is *das Nichts selbst nichtet*: the nothing "nihilates" or "noths" (GA9, 116).

Sometimes the connection between noun and verb may wholly escape the English reader, as when he says that "language speaks." In German, there is an obvious connection: *die Sprache spricht* (GA9, 72; GA10, 143; GA12, 10; GA100, 32).

For a last example of verbalization, we might cite the pronouncement from the most famous of Heidegger's late lectures, "Time and Being," that "appropriation appropriates" (*das Ereignis ereignet*) (GA14, 29).

What does verbalization achieve?

Nothing, perhaps. It is easy enough to cast doubt on this way of talking. To say that *x* is *xing* is just to say the same thing twice – in other words, to say nothing, according to the usual logic (GA14, 29). What can "appropriation appropriates" mean other than "appropriation is appropriation"? This says as little as "it is what it is." It is simply a tautology, a failure to predicate anything new about a subject, a failed attempt at meaning.

Carnap was particularly scandalized by the Heideggerism *das Nichts selbst nichtet*. Not only is it illegitimate to turn a mere negation into a noun, but then to verbalize the noun is the sheerest nonsense (Carnap

1959, 70–71). This is to say nothing at all, while imagining that one is invoking a deep Nothing.

Heidegger is not without a response to Carnap. In 1935, in some material for *Introduction to Metaphysics* that he chose not to read in the lecture hall, he lashes out against logical positivism:

> What is going on here is the uttermost reduction and deracination of the traditional theory of judgment under the illusion of mathematical scientificity. Here one draws the ultimate conclusions of a thinking that began with Descartes, for whom already truth was no longer the openness of beings— and accordingly, the integration and grounding of Dasein within the beings that are opened up—but truth was diverted into *certainty*. ... (GA40, 228)

In 1964, he more generously suggests that he and Carnap share questions about the nature of objectification, thinking, and speaking (Heidegger 1976, 24). But of course, they do not share answers. For Heidegger, our immersion in openness – the event of *logos* – is prior to propositional thought and irreducible to cognitive certainty. This phenomenon requires creative language – although he does not specifically explain how coining the verb *nichten* is supposed to help.

As for tautology, he asserts in a late remark that "tautological thinking ... is the primordial sense of phenomenology" (GA15, 399). The point, perhaps, is that by pairing a noun with its corresponding verb, we notice the distinctive behavior of what we are considering. The technique focuses "on the phenomenon ... rather than trying to explain it in terms borrowed from a different kind of entity" (Braver 2014, 101). For example, Heidegger writes that "the very aim of this exposition is to lead us face to face with the ontological enigma of the movement of historizing in general" (SZ 389). The historizing of history is how this phenomenon takes place or "moves," and the goal of the phenomenologist is not to explain the "enigma" but to experience it.

One might argue that there is another risk here: that we will neglect to research the deeper causes of a movement. Sometimes the quest for explanation is reductive, and it is right to resist it in the name of understanding – but at other times, resisting explanation can amount to obscurantism. Consider the line from Angelus Silesius that Heidegger likes to quote: "The rose is without a why. It blooms because it blooms." Silesius points to the blossom's blossoming, encouraging us to appreciate its unfolding without demanding a cause. But we know that such blossoming *is* caused: it is the product of intricate but identifiable genetic structures, and it functions to attract pollinators and reproduce the plant. This function may be viewed as a final cause, to use Aristotelian terms, or simply as a moving cause that tends to spread the rose's genes. In any case, the rose is *not* without a why. Are Silesius and Heidegger promoting a mysticism of the worst sort, an antirational, antiscientific myopia?

Heidegger himself admits that "botany will easily point out to us a chain of causes and conditions for the growth of plants. ... Everyday experience speaks for the necessity of the grounds of growth and blooming" (GA10, 55). But according to his interpretation, Silesius does not mean to deny that there are grounds for blooming; he is saying that the rose itself has no need to ask "why." Human beings, in contrast, do (GA10, 56–57).

Heidegger's intent, though, is to curb our thirst for grounds, to limit it, in a thought that has some affinity to Kantian critique: Seeking reasons for entities within the world is legitimate, but the fundamental fact that we are exposed to entities and their being should simply be appreciated as the ontological enigma of "worlding."

Even if one rejects this view as mysticism, one may grant that understanding should precede explanation. To use Aristotelian terms again, one should grasp the formal cause – the essence of a thing – before one tries to identify final, moving, or material causes. Verbalization focuses us on essence.

But the impact of verbalization may go deeper than that: It may challenge the traditional distinction between essence and existence, as well as the way existence claims are handled in symbolic logic. Here, perhaps, is a more powerful Heideggerian answer to Carnap than the retort he himself offers.

It was once routine among analytic philosophers to dismiss Heidegger by claiming that his vague talk of "being" conflates some elementary logical distinctions. The peculiar verb "to be" and its counterparts in various Indo-European languages do triple duty: "be" is used not only for predication, but for claims of existence and identity. But symbolic logic healthfully eliminates this ambiguous verb and makes metaphysical nonsense impossible. The obsolete "problem of being" is thus resolved into distinct logical operations.

To my knowledge, Heidegger never thoroughly addresses this criticism, but he is certainly well aware that, as Aristotle puts it, "being" is said in many ways. He does not see this as a mere equivocation. Instead, he treats "what-being" (*Was-sein*), "that-being" (*Daß-sein*), and "how-being" (*So-sein*) as various modes that are somehow connected. He is interested in finding the root meaning of all the traditional senses of "being," and then challenging the predominance of that root meaning, which can be called presence or presencing. His technique of verbalization is, as we will see, part of this ambitious program.

The distinction between what-being and that-being is present in ancient philosophy, but it is not always clearly articulated (for one clear statement of the distinction see Aristotle, *Post. An.* II.1). The medievals sharpen the concepts of existence, essence, and accident. These distinctions are radicalized in modern symbolic logic, which follows Kant and Frege in holding that claims about the existence or nonexistence of an object must be kept strictly separate from claims about its attributes. To claim that a thing *is* (exists) is logically distinct from claiming that it is this or that kind of thing, or has such and such properties. Kant insists on this distinction in order to defuse the illusory ontological argument for the existence of God: no description of God (say, as a perfect being) can imply anything about whether there actually *is* such a being. Likewise, in symbolic logic, existence is not predicated of an object, as if it were just another characteristic; an existence claim is a "quantifier" that asserts that at least one object with certain characteristics is in fact given. For instance, one can define the concept "even prime number" or "hippogriff"; one can make universal statements based on such definitions, such as "all hippogriffs are animals"; but whether such objects *exist* is a completely separate question that cannot be settled by definition.

No doubt, this way of treating questions of existence brings some clarity and helps us avoid some confusions. Most factual questions cannot be settled simply by appealing to concepts. However, the approach also creates opacity when it comes to the meaning of "exists." It seems that the concept of existence cannot be specified at all, or can only be described with rough synonyms such as those we used above: "actually is," "is in fact given." For symbolic logic, if we try to attribute certain properties to existence itself, we must be confused: We are really talking about attributes of objects, not the question of whether there *is* an object. Thus any attempt to find content in the concept of existence beyond the existential quantifier is "a forlorn cause" (Quine 1969, 97).

But in fact, we mean different things when we say that different kinds of beings "exist." For a number to exist is, one might say, for it to be constructible or identifiable given the rules of arithmetic. For a dog to exist is for it to live and breathe. For justice to exist is for it to be applied equitably. And so on: "Existence" has a different nature and implications depending on the kind of entity that exists. It would make no sense – it would be ontologically inappropriate – to say that a dog is applied equitably, or that the number two lives and breathes (see GA14, 48–49;

GA40, 95–98, 223).[1] So although Heidegger certainly understands that it can be useful to distinguish essence from existence (or actuality), he insists that actuality comes in a variety of different essences:

> Actuality itself essentially varies, along with essence in the narrow sense, which expresses only what-being. But the full essence of an entity—we must learn to understand this—concerns both the *what* of an entity and the *how* of its possible or actual actuality. Of course, what a thing is must be determined without regard to whether it is actual or not; the essential definition of a table also applies to a possible table or one that is no longer present-at-hand. However, if we disregard whether the what-being is actual or not, this must in no way mean that now it makes no difference to ask how this actuality is, according to its essence—the actuality that is indicated for the what-being that is determined in this or that way. (GA33, 223)

When we leave the meaning of "existence" utterly abstract and unspecified, the risk is that we will insensibly let it revert to a default meaning, a predominant sense that arises from a particular field or mode of life, thus distorting or blocking our understanding of other domains. According to *Being and Time*, the default meaning of being, at least in the Western philosophical tradition, is presence-at-hand. This concept is never precisely defined in that text, but its general sense emerges through contrast. To be present-at-hand is to exist as an object with identifiable properties, as revealed through theoretical inspection. In contrast, to be ready-at-hand is to function within the web of purposes and interpretations that constitutes Dasein's world; and to exist as Dasein is to be faced with one's own being as a temporal issue. Unless we appreciate these distinctions, we are liable to take ourselves, along with the familiar things in our world, as mere objects. This is not just a philosophical confusion; it leads to inappropriate treatment of human beings and things. Quite a lot may depend, then, on avoiding the emptiness of the existential quantifier.

Heidegger's later work develops a more elaborate and dramatic story about the default meaning of being. In the "first inception" among the early Greek thinkers, being meant presencing: the manifestation of an enduring fullness (GA65, 31). Later developments in philosophy, the sciences, and technology narrowed presencing into presence-at-hand, objectivity, and

---

[1] Quine observes that "there is no simple, general answer" to "what counts as evidence for existential quantifications": Evidence for the existence of a rabbit is of a different kind from evidence for the existence of a number (Quine 1969, 97). Heidegger would argue that it is the rabbit's and the number's *ways of existing* that determine what is appropriate evidence. McDaniel (2009, 2017) and Edwards (2018) argue for a similar ontological pluralism in an analytic idiom; McDaniel incorporates Heidegger in his arguments. For a defense of the Quinean view against McDaniel, see van Inwangen (2009, 2014).

"standing reserve," or the availability of resources to provide energy and obey human will (GA7, 17). Again, these shifts in interpretation have practical implications. In the technological age, entities of all kinds are actually reduced to standing reserve – processed, exploited, and annihilated.

Verbalization resists reduction by drawing our attention to *how* something exists, happens, or takes place. If we say that a tree is "treeing," we imply that a tree, as tree, *does* something other than possessing objective attributes or serving as a lumber resource. It has a special way of existing determined by "the essencing of the respective uniqueness and rank of the entity" (GA65, 66).

In sum: Verbalization can contribute to productive logic by stimulating us to form concepts that indicate the way of existing, or being actual, that distinguishes entities in a certain domain within our world – or indicate "worlding" itself.

3.3   Deficient Modes: Exceptions That Prove the Rule

Heidegger's concept of certain phenomena as "deficient modes" is another form of productive logic. This concept, too, has a complex history and raises important ontological questions. We will touch on these before considering some concrete uses of the concept as well as some critiques of it.

In 1925, Heidegger claims that "in the pure perception of a thing, the world shows itself in *deficient significance*." He explains that he uses "the expression 'deficient,' *deficiens*, in reliance on the old term" (GA20, 300). The medieval concept of *deficientia* derives from Aristotle's *sterēsis* (*Met.* Δ 22, *Phys* I.9; cf. GA9, 294–297). Both Aristotle and the medievals take their bearings from being as presence and actuality; the most actual or "perfect" entity is supremely present. As Augustine puts it in *City of God* XII.7, to be deficient is "to defect from that which supremely is, to that which has a less perfect degree of being" (Augustine 1998, 507). He applies the concept of a "deficient cause" to the evil that characterizes human beings as finite, imperfect creatures.

Needless to say, Heidegger does not share this metaphysical and theological agenda, but he too understands deficiency as a deprivation, a falling away from a certain fullness. For instance, if mere perception is a deficient form of the significance of the world, "it lacks something that it properly has, and should have, as a world" (GA20, 300).

There is a phenomenological difficulty here. Understanding deficiency is a paradoxical achievement, like seeing darkness or hearing silence (Augustine 1998, 508). What is at stake here is the evidence of nonevidence:

One might take *sterēsis* (absencing) as the mere opposite of presencing. But *sterēsis* is not simply absence ... Today we say, for instance, "the bicycle is gone," and we do not just mean it has left; we mean that it is lacking. If something is lacking, then the *lacking thing* is gone, but the *gone* itself, the lacking, is just what bothers and troubles us—and "lacking" can do this only if it itself is "there," or *is*, i.e. constitutes a [way of] being. *Sterēsis* as absencing is not simply absence, but *presencing*, the kind of presencing in which *absencing*—not the absent—is present. (GA9, 296–297)

As Heidegger puts it in *Being and Time*, missing something "is by no means a non-presenting [*Nichtgegenwärtigen*], but a deficient mode of the present [*Gegenwart*] in the sense of an un-presenting [*Ungegenwärtigen*] of something expected" (SZ 355). The German prefix *un-* helps him make his point here. It does not express mere absence, but suggests a distorted or perverted presence.

Since the passage just above from GA9 is a discussion of Aristotle, and the second (SZ 355) refers to ready-to-hand beings, whose being is a form of presencing, Heidegger makes his point in terms of presence. But we can state it more broadly: In a deficient mode, a phenomenon shows itself as not fully showing itself. The idea remains enigmatic, but assuming that such a phenomenon is possible, deficient phenomena can clue us in to fundamental ways of being and may help us form new ontological concepts.

In *Being and Time*, deficient modes first appear when Heidegger writes, "If historiology [*Historie*] is lacking, this is not evidence *against* Dasein's historicality; on the contrary, as a deficient mode of this state of being, it is evidence for it. Only because it is 'historical' ['*geschichtlich*'] can an era be unhistoriological" (SZ 20). The idea is that only an entity who exists historically can neglect historical research; it would make no sense to claim that a whale, a lichen, or a cloud is guilty of such neglect.

This line of thought is mirrored when Heidegger writes that being unconcerned with ready-to-hand beings – "leaving undone, neglecting, renouncing, taking a rest" – is a deficient mode of concern (SZ 57).

He makes a different point about situations where ready-to-hand things inconveniently become unusable. Here we are not neglecting them, but haplessly staring at them. This is a deficient mode of concern that reveals the mere presence-at-hand of a ready-to-hand being (SZ 73; GA20, 300).

But deficient modes of concern can also disclose phenomena that are irreducible to presence-at-hand. In fact, they may do more than engaged concern does to explicitly reveal "the region," the meaningful context for equipment (SZ 104). For example, I may come home and find that my pocket is empty – my house key is not in its place. This is a deficient mode, in that I am unable to use the key – but its lack urgently highlights a whole set of purposive spatial relationships.

As for relationships with other people, "being-alone is a deficient mode of being-with; its very possibility is the proof of this." That is, others can be missing and missed only for an entity who is essentially with others (SZ 120). Inconsiderateness and disregard are deficient modes of caring for others, and they are the most common, everyday modes (SZ 121, 123–124).

Heidegger also applies the concept of deficient modes to our relationships with ourselves. One's fundamental self-knowledge – understanding the possible way of being that one is projecting for oneself – can never completely disappear as long as one is Dasein, but it tends to lapse into the deficient mode of self-ignorance or self-misunderstanding (SZ 336). We thus need to get to know ourselves (SZ 124). Similarly, we are always already in a mood, so the "lack of mood" is actually a mood of satiety (SZ 134).

Heidegger makes comparable points using the term *privation* – which he admits is not very clear (SZ 286). Mere life must be understood privatively, as a diminished version of full Dasein (SZ 58). Mere staring is a privation of interpretive understanding (SZ 149). To fall into inauthenticity is "merely the *privation* of a disclosedness which manifests itself phenomenally in the fact that Dasein's fleeing is a fleeing *in the face of* itself" (SZ 184). Avoidance points to what it avoids.

Although Heidegger drops the term *deficient mode* after *Being and Time*, he does not abandon the pattern of thought. In 1955, for instance, he writes: "whoever spends time in some foreign place is denied the dwelling-relationship to a home…. But this lack of relationship is itself an essential facet of the relationship called 'homesickness.' Hence a relationship can consist precisely in its lack" (GA10, 62).

These thoughts are akin to the claim in the *Black Notebooks* that the "un-essence" (*Unwesen*) is crucial to the essence (GA95, 1) or the related idea in "The Question Concerning Technology" that salvation is to be found within the danger itself (GA7, 29–35). Here, the seemingly inoffensive concept of a deficient mode takes on major implications for how we are to dwell on the earth and live together (Polt 2019, 134–137).

We could sum up several of Heidegger's main points in terms of various kinds of "care" – caring for oneself, for other individuals, for one's community and its history, and for things. In English we have three "antonyms" to care: One may be careless (German *unsorgfältig*), carefree (*sorgenfrei*), or uncaring (not normally expressed in German with a form of *Sorge*). For Heidegger, even careless, carefree, and uncaring behavior are forms of care, albeit in deficient modes.

Carnap would have a field day with such statements. The logical objection is expressed well by Klaus Hartmann:

a deficient mode appears to be the negation in concreteness of what the existential pre-ordains in abstraction. The deficient mode, overtly the flat denial of the existential, is subject to the existential of which it is the denial, for it is still a mode of what it denies.

For example, concern is an abstract existential, but Heidegger claims that the concrete phenomenon of *not* being concerned is itself a form of concern:

> The curious thing is how to accept that an existential, which stands for a principle, could provide for its negation on the ontic level. Clearly, such a "logic" is paradoxical and could not hold between the two levels, just as a species cannot be the denial of its genus. ... Indeed, the relation of mode and existential becomes trivial: anything could be claimed as a mode of anything. (Hartmann 1974, 123)

This line of criticism is crystal clear, from the point of view of reproductive logic. But if Heidegger is aiming at a *productive* logic, which generates new concepts, the criticism is not on target.[2] Let us look more closely, then, at the conceptual transformation that can happen when we encounter the claim that carelessness is a deficient mode of caring.

1. At first sight, the claim is a contradiction: not having care is an example of having care.
2. We can then think of the claim not as a contradiction, but as a paradox – a challenge to *doxa*, conventional opinion and sense. We look for the deeper meaning of the claim and begin to play with different interpretations of its words.
3. The claim emerges as a case of "the exception that proves the rule" – a kind of paradox that is itself described paradoxically.[3] What seems to be a counterexample to a rule may be seen as a case of it, if we are willing to take a word in two different senses. For instance, if even "sleepers are workers" (Heraclitus, Diels-Kranz frag. B75), those who are obviously not working in the conventional sense must be working in a different, unconventional sense.

---

2 Daniel Lachenman's response to Hartmann has several merits, but when he asserts that *Being and Time* "neither has a logic nor requires one" (Lachenman 1981, 56), he overlooks the concept of productive logic. For Hartmann's rejoinder, see Hartmann (1981). Parapuf (2005, 46) points out that the existential–existentiell relation, contra Hartmann, is not a genus–species relation.

3 The meaning of this saying is itself ambiguous and controversial. Although I am treating it as a paradox, its origin in Roman law is not paradoxical: Specifying an exception (on snow days, you do not have to go to school) implies a rule in other cases (normally, you do have to go to school). On the logic and jurisprudence involved, see Holton (2010); on some political implications, see Kistner (2011).

4. The unconventional sense must be broad enough to embrace both the conventional sense and its negation. It must be fundamental and essential enough that it can remain in place even when more superficial characteristics waver between one opposite and another. For example, there must be a sense of "work" that applies to both rest and exertion. At this point, we may feel "that something crucial has been forgotten without our being able to recall what" (Lachenman 1981, 67).

5. We now have to generate a new concept, because everyday concepts tend to fall into oppositions that describe accidental, not essential traits of things. These concepts are ontic, so we must work to transform them into ontological ones. We usually lack the words and grammar to speak of being instead of beings (SZ 39). But we cannot just "invent a new language for beyng"; we must "say the language of beings as the language of beyng" (GA65, 78). This is where productive logic must happen, if we are to make any philosophical progress – and at this point, we have to delve into the phenomenon at stake, letting a deep experience of it guide our thought.

6. What emerges from this process, if it is successful, is a new ontological concept. For instance, "care" is no longer one of a pair of ontic opposites, but covers both opposites and describes fundamental features of a certain domain (*Dasein*). For Heidegger, "care" comes to describe the entire temporal structure of our existence: being ahead of oneself, already being in a world, and being amidst (*bei*) the entities in the world (SZ 192).

But if the objection from reproductive logic misses the mark, it is not yet clear that the trope of deficient modes is above board. Is it any more legitimate to say "sleepers are workers" than to say "workers are sleepers"? Why take rest as a deficient mode of concern, instead of concern as a deficient mode of rest? On the face of it, in the abstract, neither claim is more or less paradoxical than the other. We may suspect, then, that by choosing one over the other, Heidegger is privileging certain ontic states over their opposites – and this may reflect his own ideological prejudices.

We should also note that claims about deficient modes seem unfalsifiable. If apparent counterexamples to a principle can be counted as evidence *for* it, as the exceptions that prove the rule, then the principle can never be disproved: "clearly Heidegger's set of existentials can cover everything if non-instantiation is confirmation" (Hartmann 1974, 134). We could compare his thinking to Freud's, where any mental phenomenon that does not seem to reflect a fundamental drive can be interpreted as a repression, a disguise, or resistance to the analyst. No one can refute a

Freudian or a Heideggerian, which is why such thought is ideology rather than a rational investigation:

> the principle is a foregone conclusion. ... in ideology, facts contrary to the basis, to what is essential, or conformal to the principle, are rationalized as a function of that very basis in a reductionist manner. ... ideologies are always right ... [they] are confirmed by their denial. (Hartmann 1974, 124)

The case of homesickness might seem especially telling. As we have seen, Heidegger takes it as a deficient mode of having-a-home (GA10, 62). But is this an instance of his prejudice in favor of belonging and rootedness, against "Semitic nomads" (Heidegger 2013, 56)? Could we reverse the thought, and develop a "nomadology" (with a tip of the hat to Deleuze and Guattari 1986) that sees dwelling as a special case of homelessness?

This is a strange thought, but it is one that Heidegger himself pursues at an important juncture in *Being and Time*: "The kind of being-in-the-world that is tranquilized and familiar is a mode of Dasein's uncanniness, not the reverse. *From an existential-ontological point of view, the 'not-at-home' must be conceived as the more primordial phenomenon*" (SZ 189).

This claim complicates any simplistic critique of Heideggerian dwelling. Without exposure to a certain nondwelling, dwelling cannot be authentic. Without the threat of anxiety – an encounter with "nihilation" – care could not be care. Likewise, being alone (not *with* others in the ordinary sense) is a deficient mode of being-*with* (in another, more fundamental sense), but this fundamental being-with in turn presupposes the possibility of a radically individualizing experience in which one discovers that one is not *with* others in some third, still more fundamental sense.

Clearly, the productive logic of deficient modes allows for further twists that generate still more new concepts.[4] Such twists may well come across as dialectical tricks. Heidegger would insist that in order to avoid mere wordplay, we have to keep the phenomena in our sights.[5] The "things themselves" will decide which formulations work. In this text, for instance, he argues for a claim about deficient modes on the basis of experience:

> A critique of "experience"[6] asserts—appealing to the principle that we overlook what is closest [cf. SZ 15]—that "being-amidst" is not the ground of knowing, but rather a deficient mode of knowing. (The "already-being-amidst"

---

[4] Each new twist "renders a conceptual distance or oblique angle with respect to the terms of the previous account, enabling them to be fundamentally rethought" (Bahoh 2020, 43).

[5] Hartmann sees Aristotle's use of *sterēsis* as empirical, while Heidegger deals in "idealities removed from concreteness" (Hartmann 1974, 128). Of course, Heidegger would disagree.

[6] Heidegger probably has Georg Misch in mind; just below, he refers to Misch's "misunderstanding" of already-being-amidst in his *Lebensphilosophie und Phänomenologie* (1930).

over-looked.) This is "logical": first I must know *something*, in order then to be *amidst* it! First to know—*ego cogito*—"I"—as if nothing were first present, whereas actually, familiarity [*Kennen*], not just knowing [*erkennen*], is grounded on the revelation of what is present. (GA76, 247)

The phenomena should guide us in selecting what should be treated as a deficient mode.

Of course, Heidegger could also have chosen to transform the sense of "knowing," so that it would come to mean exposure to the event of sense. The choice of which words and concepts to adopt and transform must consider which traditional philosophical prejudices are most pernicious and most in need of resistance.

3.4   Conclusion: Beyond Reproductive Logic

One such prejudice affirms the supremacy of reproductive over productive logic.

How many philosophical breakthroughs have been enabled by Aristotelian syllogistic? Certainly not Aristotle's own.

How many have been enabled by the symbolic logic that so many doctoral programs still impose on their students, in obeisance to a long-discredited logical positivism? Symbolic logic has borne fruit in mathematics, but to take it as a constraint on thinking in general is to thwart the creative illumination that makes great philosophers worth studying.

Along with the fresh content of what they disclose, philosophers develop characteristic tropes that are appropriate to that content. The logic of Heraclitus' thinking on *logos* is not the logic of Lao Tzu, Nāgārjuna, Fichte, or Peirce. Great thinkers engage in *productive* logic – but there are no abstract rules for such logic, or a set of privileged tropes that could be imposed in advance, before an exploration of the issues at stake.

We learn how to think by thinking with a thinker about that thinker's questions – and then thinking with other thinkers. Every philosophy is a venture. None of these ventures can certify itself absolutely, either by its results or by a formal logical method that it adopts a priori. We will never be sure that a philosophy is "right"; we will always be faced with the possibility of a new productive logic, a fresh revelation.

For all of Heidegger's limitations, it is to his credit that he not only admits the finitude of his thinking, but insists on it.

PART II

Language, Logic, and Nonsense

CHAPTER 4

Logic, Language, and the Question of Method in Heidegger

Sacha Golob

This chapter examines the relationship between "logic," language, and methodology in Heidegger. I begin by contrasting two ways in which one might understand that relationship: Dummett's position as articulated in *The Logical Basis of Metaphysics* and Dreyfus's influential reconstruction of *Sein und Zeit*. Focusing on *Sein und Zeit* §33, I distinguish Heidegger's own view from each of these. First, drawing on his discussions of "grammar," I show where and why he diverges not just from someone like Dummett, but also from Kant. Second, I argue for the difference between my approach and the Dreyfusian one: For Dreyfus, Heidegger's attack on logic is ultimately a question of content; for me, it is ultimately a question of method. I close by indicating how this analysis might be extended to texts from the 1924 *Platon: Sophistes* lectures to *Die Sprache* in the 1950s, paying particular attention to the concept of a "meta-language."

4.1 Dreyfus, Dummett, and the Philosophical Role of Language

"Analytic philosophy" is a highly contested category. But historically one of its central markers has been a certain view of language. As Dummett put it:

> The fundamental axiom of analytical philosophy [is] that the only route to the analysis of thought goes through the analysis of language. (Dummett 1994, 128)

This is not much use as a gloss on how the label is actually applied: As Dummett admits, Evans is not an analytic philosopher on his construal, but *The Varieties of Reference* is surely not what people have in mind when they praise or damn "continental" thinkers. Nor am I concerned in any strict sense with the causal history of "analytic philosophy" and Dummett's place in it. Rather, I want to use Dummett as exemplifying one particular, and highly influential, strand of the analytic approach. It is a strand defined not by the details of Dummett's own commitments, but by its basic methodology. For example, it yields the "Good Old-Fashioned Oxford Philosophy (GOOP)," as Noë recently dubbed it, of Stanley and Williamson's intellectualism:

> I have referred to Stanley and Williamson as practicing GOOP. But really, what they practice is something like good old-fashioned Oxford philosophy all souped-up with contemporary linguistics. But new-fangled GOOP has many of the same old problems as old-school GOOP. The biggest problem with GOOP is that it directs our attention to considerations about language (how people talk), when theorists of mind (in philosophy or cognitive science) are interested in human nature and the nature of mind. (Noë 2005, 288)

The approach exemplified by Dummett, and rejected by Noë, is thus characterized by privileging linguistic analysis as a philosophical guide. Of course, this does not mean that surface grammar can simply be taken as a reliable indicator. Rather, the method, and here one can see its history back through Russell and others, mandates an absolute focus on the relationship between such surface grammar and language's underlying logical form.

It is in this context, despite his many differences from Dummett, that we need to see events such as Carnap's famous attack on Heidegger. As Carnap put it:

> It may happen that such a sequence of words looks like a statement at first glance; in that case we call it a *pseudo-statement*. Our thesis, now, is that logical analysis reveals the alleged statements of metaphysics to be pseudo-statements. (Carnap 1959, 61, original emphasis)[1]

Dummettian analytic philosophy thus simultaneously privileges language and sees a certain lack of attention to it as a founding philosophical sin: As Frege himself put it, "a great part of the work of the philosopher consists in … a struggle with language" (Frege 1979, 270). The use of the formal tools and techniques of modern logic therefore becomes essential to balancing these tensions. By extension, authors such as Heidegger are natural targets precisely because they fail to employ such methods. This makes them vulnerable to accusations such as Carnap's, that it is a flawed relationship to language that fatally undermines their thought.

---

[1] My interest here is in Carnap's remark as exemplifying the "analytic" approach I am charting; I cannot address the details of his attack on Heidegger, which hangs in large part on the differences between what they understand by "metaphysics."

I now want to introduce a very different approach, set out by Dreyfus in dialogue with Heidegger, and elaborated with enormous sophistication by those influenced by him. At its core is the belief that certain levels of experience have been neglected by traditional philosophy. Dreyfus's 2005 Presidential Address to the American Philosophical Association gives a good flavor of the key idea:

> But, although almost everyone now agrees that knowledge doesn't require an unshakeable foundation, many questions remain. Can we accept McDowell's Sellarsian claim that perception is conceptual "all the way out," thereby denying the more basic perceptual capacities we seem to share with prelinguistic infants and higher animals? More generally, can philosophers successfully describe the conceptual upper floors of the edifice of knowledge while ignoring the embodied coping going on the ground floor; in effect, declaring that human experience is upper stories all the way down? This evening, I'd like to convince you that we shouldn't leave the conceptual component of our lives hanging in mid-air and suggest how philosophers who want to understand knowledge and action can profit from a phenomenological analysis of the nonconceptual embodied coping skills we share with animals and infant. (Dreyfus 2005b, 49)

Similarly, in his enormously influential commentary on SZ, Dreyfus talks of the need to get back to "a more basic form of intentionality" than that studied by the canon (Dreyfus 1991, 3).

Dreyfus's own stance on language is at times unclear, since it seems to fall on both sides of the "coping" framework he often uses.[2] But there is a striking tendency in his work and that of others influenced by him to contrast the primitive level of "nonconceptual embodied coping skills" with linguistic content. This, for example, is how he casts his relationship with Brandom and Sellars:

> Phenomenologists therefore disagree with conceptualists in that phenomenologists claim that a study of expertise shows that nameable features are irrelevant to the current state of mind of the [chess grand] master when he acts ... If, as Robert Brandom claims, "Sellars' principle [is] that grasping a concept is mastering the use of a word" then, according to Sellarsians,

---

[2] For example, Dreyfus draws a distinction between "the practical function of language" where it "functions as equipment" and the "thematizing use of assertions" in "theoretical reflection" (Dreyfus 1991, 208, 212). But where does, say, fully absorbed discussion of pure mathematics fit in? More broadly, Dreyfus's account relies on a theory of breakdown or disturbance in which the "available" or *zuhanden* is equated with the pre-breakdown level and the "occurrent" or *vorhanden* with explicit, "post-breakdown" awareness (Dreyfus 1991, 208). Blattner offers acute criticisms of this larger framework with which I am in agreement (Blattner 1995, 325–326). For a more detailed analysis of the problems with Dreyfus's various formulations, see Golob (2014, 25–47).

> master chess play is nonconceptual. Yet clearly, what is given to the chess
> master in his experience of the board isn't a bare Given ... A "bare Given"
> and the "thinkable" are not our only alternatives. (Dreyfus 2005a, 56)

Sellars and Brandom are obviously very different thinkers from Dummett.
But what is striking is how close the Dummettian picture of analytic philosophy is to Dreyfus's own view of that movement: In both cases, the
defining assumption is that concepts are to be analyzed in linguistic terms.
Dreyfus is happy to accept that this is a legitimate enterprise; his com-
plaint is that this focus on the "nameable" misses something more fundamental: While "analytic philosophers ... continue their work on the upper
stories of the edifice of knowledge, perfecting their rigorous, fascinating,
and detailed accounts of the linguistic, conceptual, and inferential capacities," they have ignored the "non-linguistic, nonconceptual discrimina-
tions" unearthed by phenomenology (Dreyfus 2005a, 62).

For Dreyfus, the problems exemplified by "analytic" philosophy are
not, however, unique to that movement. Indeed, pre-Heideggerian phenomenology falls into much the same trap. Carman gives perhaps the most
elegant formulation of this aspect of the view:

> Husserl's theory of intentionality thus stands as perhaps the supreme expres-
> sion of the *semantic paradigm* in the philosophy of mind. Unlike empiricist
> versions of the theory of ideas, which construe mental representations on
> analogy with pictures or images, the semantic model conceives of mental
> content in general ... on analogy with linguistic meaning. (Carman 2008,
> 18, original emphasis)

Heidegger, in contrast, recognized the vital need to avoid "any surrepti-
tious reading of the structures of propositionally articulated thought back
into" the explanatorily basic levels of experience (Carman 2003, 217).
Avoiding this danger is vital if we are, in line with Dreyfus's ambition, to
do justice to the primary forms of intentionality:

> [I]ntentional attitudes and experiences do not ... —pace Sellars—typically
> contain propositional claims. (Carman 2003, 217)

What we have seen so far is the way in which the Dreyfusian approach
defines itself by its stance on language: Both "analytic philosophy," understood in an essentially Dummettian way, and Husserlian phenomenology
fail because they bought into the "semantic paradigm." As Dreyfus always
stresses, the claim is not that these schools are simply wrong: they *do*
help delineate the "upper stories" of experience. But they simultaneously
risk radically misconstruing the "ground floor" of being-in-the-world on

which thought and language depend. This fundamental move has extensive implications for everything from the philosophy of action to epistemology. Consider this from Cussins:

> Many years ago, I used to ride a motorcycle around London. And I would often exceed the speed limit. One time a policeman stopped me and asked, "Do you know how fast you were travelling?" ... On the one hand, I did know, and know very well, how fast I was travelling. I was knowingly making micro-adjustments of my speed all the time in response to changing road conditions. These micro-adjustments weren't simply behaviours, the outputs of some unknown causal process. They were, instead, epistemically sensitive adjustments made by me, and for which I was as epistemically responsible as I was for my judgements. On the other hand, I did not know how fast I was travelling in the sense of the question intended by the policeman ... the speed of my motorcycle was not made available to me as that which would render true certain propositions, and false certain others. The speed was given to me not as a truth-maker—for example, a truthmaker of the proposition that I was exceeding the speed limit—but as an element in a skilled interaction with the world. (Cussins 2003, 150)

For Cussins, what is needed is a philosophy of action that operates at the level of "micro-adjustments," not propositions; it is precisely this that the Dreyfusian program aims to provide.

4.2   *Sein und Zeit* on Language and Assertion: The Content Model

With this sketch of the Dreyfusian approach in place, I want now to look more closely at how it treats language within early Heidegger. I will then explain both where I think that approach goes wrong, and what a better alternative might look like.

In the preceding section, I stressed the explanatorily derivative status ascribed to language within the Dreyfusian model: It is dependent on the "lower floors" of nonlinguistic capacities. And this clearly has some support in Heidegger's text: most famously, *Sein und Zeit* §33, "Assertion as a derivative mode of interpretation." We can press the point further: The Dreyfusian approach cashes the derivative status of language in terms of a particular story about *different forms of meaning* or *content*. Consider, for example, this from Carman's commentary on SZ: Heidegger associates the idea of "dimming down" with assertion at SZ 156:

> Predicative assertions, that is, let things be seen in a specific light as this or that. Dimming down and so letting things be seen ... is a kind of abstraction or decontextualisation against a background of prior practical familiarity.

Propositional content therefore derives from a kind of privation, or perhaps a refinement or distillation, of practical interpretative meanings. Indeed "levelling down" the interpreted intelligibility of entities of all kinds to mere determinations of [present-at-hand] objects is "the speciality of assertion" (SZ 158). (Carman 2003, 219)[3]

Likewise, this from Wrathall:

In natural perception, then, we ordinarily perceive a whole context that lacks the logical structure of linguistic categories. When we apprehend things in such a way as to be able to express them in assertion, however, the act of perception is now brought under the categories of the understanding ... Thus assertion manifests things differently than they are given in natural perception ... This allows us to see an object with a thematic clarity that is not present in our natural perception of it. (Wrathall 2011, 20)

When Heidegger talks about the derivative status of *Aussage*, he leaves it unclear what exactly his target is and why. Is the problem, for example, with assertion as opposed to questions or suggestions? Or is it with something much more general like propositionality? What we see in these remarks from Carman and Wrathall, and in Dreyfus's Presidential Address, is the decision to gloss this derivative status in a particular way: There is a kind of basic meaning, the practical or perceptual, which language cannot capture.

This move is vital to the structure of the Dreyfusian interpretation for two reasons. First, it allows an immediately satisfying explanation of Heidegger's insistence that "assertion" is *both* derivative *and* that it is linked to an ontology of the present-at-hand, an ontology of "things" [*Dinge*].[4] This dual claim is evident both in the key section of SZ, for example SZ 157–159, and in many other texts, such as GA41, 62–64, or GA29/30, 419. Within the framework defended by Carman or Wrathall, the link is straightforward: Assertions reduce entities to "presence-at-hand" precisely because assertions distort or at best "distil" the irreducibly rich perceptual and practical content of being-in-the-world. This is why propositional intentionality always implies a "narrowing of content" (SZ 155). This is a significant exegetical achievement of the Dreyfusian school. After all, there is no other obvious reason why just making assertions should confine you to any particular ontology: Surely, I can talk about everything from emotions to numbers to tools to Dasein?

---

[3] Carman uses "occurrence" for *Vorhandenheit* and its cognates; I have altered the citation to allow terminological continuity.

[4] I use *Ding* as it is used in texts like SZ or GA41 (see, for example, SZ 80 or GA41, 60–62). Heidegger later changes his valuation of the term radically based on its supposed Germanic heritage (GA7, 176).

Second, the move positions Heidegger in a specific way within the canon, namely as a phenomenologist engaged in a project very much like Merleau-Ponty's. Indeed, as Carman acutely notes:

> Although Heidegger is the figure to whom Dreyfus most frequently appeals, his argument frequently draws more directly from the *Phenomenology of Perception* than from *Being and Time*. (Carman 2008, 224)

Bringing these points together with those of the preceding section, we can see the power and sophistication of the Dreyfusian position on language. Philosophically, it positions Heidegger as having grasped capacities that are explanatorily prior to those studied by either Husserl or analytic authors; exegetically, it seems to make excellent sense of SZ §33, including its otherwise puzzling insistence that language links to the present-at-hand. The problem, I will now argue, is that things are not quite as neat as they seem.

4.3   *Sein und Zeit* on Language and Assertion: The Methodological Model

I want to begin with the link postulated by texts such as SZ 157–158 between assertion and the present-at-hand: Assertion somehow pushes the world back into the "uniform plane of that which is merely present-at-hand" (SZ 157–158).[5] Elsewhere Heidegger frames the point in terms of *Dinge*:

> We cannot emphasize this fact too often: those determinations which constitute the being of the thing [i.e. *katagoria*] have received their name from assertion [i.e. *kataphasis*] ... The fact that since then in Western thought the determinations of being are called "categories" is the clearest expression of the point I have already emphasized: that the structure of the thing [*Ding*] is connected with the structure of the assertion. (GA41, 62–64; similarly, GA29/30, 419)

Earlier Heidegger defined a thing as "the present-at-hand bearer of many present-at-hand yet changeable properties" (GA41, 33), and the corresponding passage at GA25, 295–296, uses "present-at-hand" directly, so for current purposes I will take the two formulations as equivalent. The idea of a connection between certain forms of representation and certain ontologies is, of course, also central to Heidegger's later work and its attack on *Vorstellen* (for example, GA5, 305). So, the claim that language might mandate a particular ontology has a comforting Heideggerian familiarity to it.

---

[5] In what follows, I extend some arguments sketched in Golob (2014).

But, this should not blind us to the fact that we face immediate problems when we try to get clear on what exactly SZ is saying.

First, even within a single period the key terms typically lack a stable meaning. For example, "present-at-hand" and "thing" are associated variously with substances in the Aristotelian, Cartesian, or Kantian senses (SZ 318; GA20, 232–233; GA41, 62–64, 107–108; GA25, 295); with entities individuated by their spatio-temporal or causal properties (GA20, 49–50; SZ 361), and with entities cut off from the network of relations that define the Heideggerian world (SZ 83–86, 157–158). But none of these is remotely equivalent. For example, substantiality is neither necessary nor sufficient for individuation by spatio-temporal or causal properties, as both empiricists and Leibnizian monadologists can attest. Likewise, being cut off from the world is neither necessary nor sufficient for being individuated by spatio-temporal or causal properties: Consider some aleph number divorced entirely from our social practice or any world that makes sense of objects precisely in terms of their primary qualities (a building yard, for example).

Second, the basic idea remains puzzling: Why should merely making assertions about something commit me to a particular ontology for it? Consider some of the disambiguations of "presence-at-hand" that I just flagged. Why should assertions about loneliness or number theory or that damn noise from my neighbor force me to see emotions as substances or numbers as spatio-temporally individuated or that racket as cut off from the world?

The Dreyfusian approach, as we saw, explains this lacuna in terms of the rich perceptual content of lived experience; such assertions necessarily arise from a kind of "privation, or perhaps a refinement or distillation" of some richer form of meaning (Carman 2003, 19). But here is another option: Perhaps Heidegger's point is not about propositions or assertions or linguistic content at all, but rather about a particular philosophical *theory* of those things. As I read him, many of the issues that Heidegger raises with language are not problems with assertions or propositions per se, but rather with a *particular way* of thinking about them, a particular methodology. There is a genuine danger in forcing Heidegger into the idiom of analytic philosophy, but it also has some benefits of accessibility: If one were to do so here, my claim would be that his problem is not with language at all, but rather with a specific "meta-language."[6] Heidegger's

---

[6] I am indebted to audiences in Paris and Oxford for discussion of the idea of a meta-language in this context.

blanket term for the suspect philosophical approach, or the suspect "meta-language" if one is willing to talk in those terms, is "logic." Hence his aim is to "liberate grammar from logic" by exposing the link between logic and the present-at-hand (SZ 165).

I now want to show how this might help make sense of central texts such as SZ §33.

I will begin with the key passage at SZ 154–155. Note first that assertion's "primary signification," "pointing out," does not just comprise my indicating an entity, but also includes my saying something about it: "the hammer is too heavy" (SZ 154). Since the "primary signification" of assertion says something about something, it constitutes a declarative sentence and so propositional content as that idea is standardly understood: In other words, we already have propositions in place several pages *before* Heidegger turns to the problems of SZ 157–158. The second signification, which Heidegger labels "'predication,'" (note the scare quote punctuation), then introduces "a narrowing of content as compared to the … first signification" (SZ 154–155). It is this second signification that "dims down" or "restricts" our view. In other words, contra Carman as cited above, "dimming down" is something that is done *to*, not *by*, propositional content. This occurs insofar as "logic" assumes a particular way of understanding how the assertion works:

> Prior to all analysis, logic has already understood "logically" that which it takes as its theme, for example, "the hammer is heavy," under the heading of the "categorical statement." The unexplained presupposition is that the "meaning" of this sentence is to be taken as: "This thing—a hammer—has the property of heaviness." (SZ 157)

What is at issue here is a particular method for analyzing assertions, a method that generates what Heidegger calls "theoretical assertions" (SZ 157). This refers not to theory in the sense of the natural sciences – the predicate is still "heavy" as opposed to "having mass" – but rather to philosophical notions such as "'categorical statement'" (SZ 154). Note how Heidegger here again uses scare quotes: We can now see that their function is to flag the suspect theoretical terms, the suspect parts of what in analytic jargon would be the "meta-language."

Having introduced "logic," Heidegger starts to flesh out its ontological implications. This finally gives us the full context for his remarks concerning "the uniform plane of that which is merely present-at-hand":

> The entity which is held in our fore-having—for instance, the hammer—is initially ready-to-hand [*zunächst zuhanden*] as an item of equipment. If this entity becomes the "object" of an assertion ["*Gegenstand*" *einer Aussage*],

then as soon as we begin with this assertion, there is already a changeover in the fore-having. The ready-to-hand entity with which we have to do or perform something, turns into something *"about which"* [*"Worüber"*] the assertion that points it out is made … Only now are we given any access to *properties* or the like. When an assertion has given a determinate character to something present-at-hand, it claims something about it *as* a "what" and this "what" is drawn *from that* which is present-at-hand as such. The as-structure of interpretation has undergone a modification. In its function of appropriating what is understood, the "as" no longer reaches out into a totality of involvements. As regards its possibilities for articulating reference-relations [*Verweisungsbezügen*], it has been cut off [*abgeschnitten*] from that significance which, as such, constitutes environmentality. The "as" gets pushed back [*zurückgedrängt*] into the uniform plane of that which is merely present-at-hand. It sinks to the structure of just letting one see what is present-at-hand in a determinate way. (SZ 157–158, original emphasis)

We can immediately note the scare quotes again picking out the key terms of the problematic approach; he also uses italics here for the same purpose, for example with *"properties."* Heidegger's claim here is that giving philosophical weight to this type of theoretical framework not only alters the way in which assertions are understood but equally modifies the way in which one views the entities intended by those assertions: They are thematized as "'objects'" of "categorical statements" and bearers of *"properties."*

How exactly does this work? A full discussion would require close treatment of both the ambiguities in Heidegger's talk of the "present-at-hand" and his views on modern symbolic logic, which he knew partly through Cassirer. But I can indicate the basic point by using two examples.

First, consider the conception of the present-at-hand as a substance in an Aristotelian, Cartesian, or Kantian sense. Heidegger is pointing out the close links between the ontologies of these thinkers and a philosophy of language based around a combinatorial analysis of propositional form that privileges the subject–predicate structure. The classic example is Kant's claim in the Metaphysical Deduction to have derived the categories from the logical forms of judgments.[7] Heidegger sees exactly the same problem in Leibniz:

> Leibniz sees that this interpretation of substance takes its bearings from predication and therefore a radical determination of the nature of predication, of judgment, must provide a primordial conception of substance … Here the ontic subject, the substance, is understood from the viewpoint of the logical subject, the subject of a statement. (GA26, 41–42)

---

[7] Kant (1902, KrV A70–80/B95–106).

He views others, such as Aristotle, as making the same move albeit in a less systematic fashion (GA41, 62–64; GA25, 295). These authors happily endorse the link between assertion, "logic," and the present-at-hand because they regard the resultant substance ontology as a positive; what Heidegger is doing is using that very same ontology as the basis for a *modus tollens* against the underlying philosophy of language. In making this move, Heidegger is in good company: Thinkers from Nietzsche to Russell have made similar observations. As Russell puts it, in perhaps the sole line in his corpus that could equally have been written by Heidegger:

> The ground for assuming substances—and this is a very important point—is purely and solely logical. (Russell 1937, 49)

By extension, for Nietzsche and for Russell, classical subject–predicate logic is both misleading and ontologically dangerous.[8] This is exactly the point Heidegger is making.

This brings me to the second case: How should we understand Heidegger's attacks on "logic" once we move outside the pre-Fregean subject–predicate framework? Heidegger is consistently scathing of modern logic, so it is clear at least that he does not think, as Russell did, that modern logicians have fixed the problem (SZ 88). Matters here are complex and a full treatment would require a detailed discussion of Heidegger's broader philosophical methodology.[9] But the basics are clear enough: Heidegger is worried that a focus on the logical structure of the assertion will necessarily lead to a concomitant neglect of the existential, that is, the pragmatic social and environmental context in which language actually functions. It is in this sense that entities within a logic-dominated philosophy are "cut off" from their "significance" and "pushed back into the uniform plane of that which is merely present-at-hand" (SZ 158). An analysis such as Russell's would no longer talk of a "categorical statement"; as Russell stressed, such outdated logic is utterly unable to deal with the inferential status of relational properties. Heidegger's worry, however, is that the modern ingenuity expended on analyzing such properties, on grasping the "empty formal idea of relation," ironically leads to the "suppression of the dimension within which the relevant relation can be what it is," namely, its worldly context (GA29/30, 424). By extension, his own preferred alternative is to

---

[8] On Nietzsche, see Nietzsche (2002, §16) and *Twilight of the Idols* in Nietzsche (2005, III/5).
[9] I have tried to supply the necessary context in Golob (2014, 50–62).

approach assertion from within and only from within an analysis of Dasein – to start not with syntactic or semantic form, but with the various roles of assertion within the rich social and instrumental context in which Dasein deploys it. Thus, we are far better off with Aristotle's *Rhetoric* than we would be if he had written a philosophy of language since the former treats speech "as a basic mode of the being of the being-with-one-another" (GA18, 171). As Heidegger puts it himself, his aim is to move "from the question of what language is to the question of what man is" (GA38, 38).

If we now turn back to the Dreyfusian account, we can see why my position is strikingly different. In Dreyfus the link between assertions, propositions, and the present-at-hand was explained in terms of differing forms of *content or meaning*, specifically the inability of propositional intentionality, and by extension assertion, to capture perceptual or practical awareness. On my approach, in contrast, things are very different. Propositions and assertions are not the problem, and there is no story about inexpressible meaning. The problem is rather with a particular way of thinking about language. It is an issue of *method*.

The distinction between the two approaches is real. First, my view avoids trapping Heidegger in a self-reference paradox: He refers to his own claims as both "propositions" and "assertions," a fact that would, on the Dreyfusian approach, imply that merely in writing about Dasein he had already leveled it off (GA24, 461).

Second, I avoid the pressure created by the Dreyfusian approach to conflate Heidegger and Merleau-Ponty: After all, the perfect candidate for a primal form of intentionality uncapturable by language is the fine-grained meaning characteristic of perceptual motor intentionality. Such a conflation is characteristic of the Dreyfusian reading and it is a mistake. As I put it elsewhere:

> The problem is that SZ would, effectively, state Heidegger's views without giving any argument for them: there is little discussion there of the type of detailed motor intentional case study needed to motivate the view that such content even exists. This absence is even more striking in Heidegger's other works. For example, GA3 and GA25 detail his disagreements with Kant, yet the body and embodiment receives no treatment at all. Could one conceivably have said the same of a similarly extensive confrontation with Kant written by Merleau-Ponty or Todes? ... Ultimately, an appeal to motor intentionality risks turning ... Heidegger's key arguments into ... a promissory note to be cashed by the *Phenomenology of Perception*. (Golob 2014, 46)

On my account, in contrast, Gadamer is a much more natural interlocutor: The task in texts such as SZ §33 is primarily "to liberate the verbal nature of understanding from the presupposition of philosophy of language" (Gadamer 2006, 404).[10] As Dreyfus presents it in his Presidential Address, analytic philosophy has done a fine job of elaborating the "upper floors" of experience, advancing "rigorous, fascinating, and detailed accounts of the linguistic, conceptual, and inferential capacities that are uniquely human"; the problem is that they have missed the "lower stories." But this is very far from Heidegger's view. The problem as he sees it is *not* that we have a decent philosophy of language but have missed something else. It is rather that the existing philosophies of language amount to "a monstrous violation of what language accomplishes" (GA36/37, 104).

The distinction between my reading and the dominant Dreyfusian one is thus a genuine one. But it can also be easily obscured. This is because there is a natural tendency to talk as if the suspect methodology were automatically built into terms such as "proposition." Using this idiom, one might say that my account, like the Dreyfusian one, also regards propositions as necessarily derivative and necessarily tied to presence-at-hand. Heidegger himself is deeply conflicted on this and on the general question of existing philosophical terminology. This is exemplified in his treatment of terms such as *logos*, which he alternately tries to retrieve for his own purposes and to replace with coinages such as *Rede* (compare GA40, 128 and 194).

However, I think it much better to separate out propositions per se, that is, the content of declarative statements, from the pernicious theory that has accompanied them. Most obviously, failing to do so obscures the points just made about the differences between my approach and the Dreyfusian one. Such a failure also makes dialogue with analytic philosophy extremely hard. This is because, whatever one's view on the standard Fregean/Russellian/Evansian/possible worlds options, almost all analytic authors will regard "the noise downstairs is very loud" as a proposition – and this kind of claim was never the target of SZ §33. While the Searle–Dreyfus dialogue was complicated by many issues, one of the most persistent was a simple misunderstanding as to what each author meant by basic terms like "proposition": We should avoid framing things in a way that will systematically generate such misunderstandings (see, for example, Searle 2000).

---

[10] I deliberately say only "interlocutor"; I certainly do not think that Heidegger shares all of Gadamer's positive views on language.

4.4   Extending the Methodological Approach
to Heidegger's Later Work

In line with the scope of this chapter, I have focused on SZ. I will now indicate how my reading might be expanded to Heidegger's later work.

Heidegger's "later work" is, of course, a blanket way of describing a vast range of stylistic, terminological, and conceptual shifts to which I cannot do justice here. But, one can see how the argument I picked out reoccurs throughout Heidegger's corpus; indeed, it is, in my view, one of the few absolute points of continuity. For example, three years before SZ, he rails against the way *Satzlogik* has distorted language:

> As orientated in this way, i.e. as taking the theoretical proposition for its exemplary foundation, propositional logic [*Satzlogik*] at the same time guided all reflections directed at the explication of logos in the broader sense, as language [*Sprache*], and insofar as it did so the whole of the science of language, as well as, more generally, the entire philosophy of language, took their orientation from this propositional logic. All our grammatical categories and even all of contemporary scientific grammar—linguistic research into the Indo-Germanic languages etc.—are essentially determined by this theoretical logic. Yet there does indeed exist the task of conceiving logic, once and for all, much more radically than the Greeks succeeded in doing and of working out thereby, in the same way, a more radical understanding of language itself and consequently also of the science of language. (GA19, 253)

This is exactly my claim: The key contrast is between language and pernicious theories of it.

The same point is also clearly visible in texts from the mid-1930s. I mentioned above the 1933/34 lectures *Sein und Wahrheit* (GA36/37). The problem, Heidegger states, is that "grammar" was dominated by "logic"; the result is a very specific "representation of language," one that amounts "to a monstrous violation of what language accomplishes" (GA36/37, 104). In place of this theory, Heidegger enjoins us to "consider a poem or a living conversation between human beings" (GA36/37, 104; similarly, GA54, 102). This is the strategy I suggested Heidegger had in mind in SZ §33, a philosophy of language grounded on our social practices of assertion and speech. The task, in short, is "destabilizing the grammatical representation of language" (GA36/37, 104).

Another particularly interesting case is the lecture course GA38, *Logik als die Frage nach dem Wesen der Sprache*, delivered in the Summer of 1934. This illustrates the complex development of Heidegger's thought during the mid-1930s: Recognizable themes from SZ, such as the *Augenblick* or *Selbstverlorenheit* are interwoven with new vocabulary, in particular that of the *Volk* (GA38, 50, 57). It is, rightly, hard to read Heidegger's casual examples of *SA-Dienst*, but for current purposes what is important is the absolute consistency of Heidegger's position on the status of language. The task, as he sees it, is to revive "logic," as the study of *logos*, and to "ask about the essence of language." One sees again his ambivalent stance on existing terminology: In this text, even "logic," rightly construed, can be saved. The difficulty, precisely as above, is that language has been radically misconstrued:

> Hence, we ask first of all about the essence of language [*Wesen der Sprache*], but not via a philosophy of language, which degrades language to a specific, separate area. (GA38, 30)

Only by doing this can we understand the nature of the human being; indeed, a grasp of that and a genuine grasp of language are inseparable (GA38, 31). Exactly as in SZ, the problem is thus *not language as opposed to perception, but language rightly understood as opposed to language as conceived by the tradition*. And, exactly as in SZ, only by understanding Dasein and language together can progress be made.

We see exactly the same points again in *Die Sprache* from 1950. The orthodoxy that Heidegger rejects is one on which:

> [A]ll statements are referred in advance to the traditionally standard way in which language appears. The already fixed view of the whole nature of language is thus consolidated. (GA12, 13)

How far can we push these claims of continuity once we get to Heidegger's postwar period? One feature of my account is that it becomes possible to understand many of his various writings as more closely continuous than is often believed. After all, if SZ's warnings really are directed against language per se, as on Dreyfus's model, it is harder to explain its later role as the "house of being" without positing a radical break. In contrast, on my approach one could read even SZ as accepting the same foundational role for language visible in the later works – it would oppose only the misguided methodology sketched above. I do not however, want to make that further claim here, in part because I agree with Wrathall that the meaning of terms such as *Sprache* in the later work is complex; in part, because that would require a vastly more detailed treatment of SZ.

But what we can say is this: A central concern in Heidegger's thought from the 1920s through the postwar period was to identify a series of problems not with language but with the ways in which language had been conceived, systematized, and misconstrued. In SZ, these worries are framed in terms of the present-at-hand; in the latter work, they are often

put in terms of the threat of technology. In both cases, they are often sum-
marized by talk of "logic."

One can also see how deep the worries run. For example, as noted, one
natural way to articulate Heidegger's point in an analytic context is by
talk of a "meta-language." The problem from a Heideggerian perspective
is that such philosophical idioms are never simply neutral or transparent;
indeed, he sees that very phrase as itself bound up with the underlying
problems he traces, with an attitude that misconstrues language and –
by extension – the entities that it names. As he characteristically puts it,
"meta-language and Sputnik are ... one and the same" (GA12, 160). Later
Heidegger thus seeks both a new understanding of language and a new
way of articulating that understanding within a transformed philosophy.
It is in this sense that:

> The liberation of language from grammar into a more original essential
> framework is reserved for thought and poetic creation. (GA9, 314)

We see here both the difficulty Heidegger faces in articulating his views
and the ease with which he slides between different formulations. SZ
sought to "liberate grammar from logic" (SZ 165); the very same task is
now presented as liberating "language from grammar," that is, from a conception of grammar corrupted by traditional philosophy.[11]

4.5   The Apophantic and the Hermeneutic "As"

I want to close with one final issue: the status of the "as" – what Derrida
rightly called the "great phenomenological-ontological question" (Derrida
1992, 289). How does my position bear on this? As we will see, this is
intricately related to another question: What would happen if Dreyfusians
were to simply adopt my gloss on SZ §33?

Consider, for example, the distinction SZ 158–159 draws between the
hermeneutic and the apophantic "as." One simple option would be to use
my approach and then to align the "hermeneutic" with assertions properly understood, and the "apophantic" with those treated in terms of the
problematic philosophy. But I think things are more complex – Heidegger
uses "apophantic" and its cognates in SZ 154–155 to introduce both the
basic features of assertion and its gradual appropriation by the problematic
theory. Instead, as I see it, the reference to the "hermeneutic as" alludes to

---

[11] I am indebted to Daniel Dahlstrom for highlighting this point.

a further claim, namely, that assertion, even when correctly understood, still remains derivative on some prior form of intentionality. It is this further claim that is in play in passages such as the following:

> The proposition "a is b" would not be possible with respect to what it means, and the way in which it means what it does, if it could not emerge from an underlying experience of "a as b." (GA29/30, 436)[12]

Now one might wonder whether in accepting this I have suddenly acquiesced in the Dreyfusian interpretation. After all, that interpretation also viewed language as derivative. The answer is no. On my account, there are *three* things in play and it is vital to keep them distinct: (1) the "as" structure, identified by Heidegger as the primary level of intentionality, (2) assertion, and (3) assertion as construed by the philosophically problematic methodology. Heidegger holds that (2) is explanatorily dependent on (1). He further holds that (3), a distortion of (2), introduces a deeply pernicious ontology: This is the claim that links assertion and presence-at-hand. The Dreyfusian model, in contrast to my account, conflates the problems of derivation *and* the pernicious ontology: Assertion is seen as the source of a present-at-hand framework *because* it is seen as derivative, unable to capture the underlying form of intentionality.

Why does this fine difference in argument structure matter so much? Well, I have argued above that we should not go back to anything like the standard Dreyfusian story; we cannot, for example, impose Merleau-Ponty's concepts onto SZ. So, whatever my story regarding (1) and (2) is, it will need to differ from that. To put the point another way, if not all assertions are linked to the present-at-hand, then the priority of (1) over (2) cannot be a function of the supposed fact that the latter is a privative representation of the former; it cannot simply be that "assertion manifests things differently than they are given in natural perception" (Wrathall 2011, 20). So, the task becomes offering an analysis of the "as"/"is" distinction in early Heidegger that recognizes *both* that language is not the primary form of intentionality *and* that language, properly understood, can nevertheless do justice to that experience. To put the point another way, we need to show how Heidegger can avoid collapsing into a McDowellian-style view on which the "as" is tacitly propositional. Doing that, I have argued elsewhere, requires us to fundamentally rethink the relationship between the nonconceptual, the conceptual, and the propositional.[13]

---

[12] Compare GA26, 158.
[13] Golob (2014). My thanks to the Editors and to audiences in Paris, Oxford, and Kennebunkport for their extremely helpful comments on earlier versions of this material.

CHAPTER 5

Nonsense at Work
Heidegger, the Logical, and the Ontological
David R. Cerbone

> Don't *for heaven's sake* be afraid of talking nonsense! But you must
> pay attention to your nonsense.
> — Wittgenstein, *Culture and Value*

A central feature of a cluster of readings of the early analytic tradition –
culminating in what has come to be known as a *resolute* reading of
Wittgenstein's *Tractatus* – is an insistence on an "austere" conception of *non-sense*.[1] What makes the conception austere is its rejection of the idea that non-sense – or at least some nonsense – can arise as a result of what the constituent
parts of the nonsensical sentence or utterance *mean*. Viewing nonsense in the
latter way is characteristic of what has been dubbed a *substantial* or *natural*
conception of nonsense. As James Conant, an advocate of austerity, puts it:
"Substantial nonsense is composed of intelligible ingredients combined in an
illegitimate way" (Conant 2000, 176). This idea of "intelligible ingredients"
is a principal target of the austere conception. As Cora Diamond notes, "if
a sentence makes no sense, *no* part of it can be said to mean what it does in
some other sentence which does make sense" (Diamond 1991, 100).[2]

5.1 The Caesarian Section

Diamond's example here, "Caesar is a prime number," would appear to be
fodder for precisely the view the austere conception rejects. According to

---

[1] All citations of the *Tractatus* are from Wittgenstein (1961).
[2] Notice that what Diamond says here goes beyond what Wittgenstein says at *Tractatus* 5.4733, namely,
that nonsense arises "because we have failed to give a *meaning* to some" of a would-be proposition's
"constituents." Wittgenstein here leaves open the possibility that some "ingredients" in a nonsense-sentence might be intelligible. In Wittgenstein's central example, "Socrates is identical," the predicative
expression is identified as the culprit, since no meaning has been "assigned" to "is identical" understood
as ascriptive rather than relational. But Wittgenstein's discussion seems to leave in place the idea that
"Socrates" refers to Socrates, which is not exactly as austere as contemporary advocates of austerity seem
to want. More on these passages below. See Glock (2015) for criticism of the austere conception.

that view, all the "ingredients" of this sentence look to be perfectly in order: Everyone knows what "Caesar" means and everyone – or pretty much everyone – knows what "is a prime number" means. Diamond's example does not contain any obvious "nonsense words" or phrases (like Diamond's *piggly wiggle tiggle*). Moreover, the "ingredients" are put together in grammatically correct form. On the natural view, the problem lies with the way these "intelligible ingredients" are "combined" in this sentence: given the *kind of thing* Caesar is and the *kind of things* prime numbers are, Caesar is not the kind of thing that *could* be found among the prime numbers. We have in this case a kind of "clash" of categories: Roman emperors and prime numbers belong to distinct categories that could not possibly overlap and so the attempt to "combine" them yields nonsense.

For both austere and substantial conceptions, nonsense is to be contrasted with sentences that are merely *false*. It is of course possible to have thoughts that are false – I can think, falsely, that Julius Caesar was a Persian king, for example – but to say those thoughts have a *sense* means that *understanding* them involves (essentially) knowing *what it would be* for the thought to be true. At *Tractatus* 4.01, Wittgenstein writes:

> A proposition is a picture of reality.
> A proposition is a model of reality as we imagine it.

And shortly thereafter, at 4.021:

> A proposition is a picture of reality: for if I understand a proposition, I know the situation it represents. And I understand the proposition without having had its sense explained to me.

Merely false propositions accord with these remarks, as they manage to represent situations, albeit ones that do not obtain. When it comes to "Caesar is a prime number," however, these ideas of picturing or modeling break down. Were someone to say "Caesar was a great Persian king," I both know it to be false *and* understand what is being said; I know, in other words, what it would mean for that sentence to be true. In the case of "Caesar is a prime number," while it is tempting to say that it is not just merely but laughably false, the problem is that there is nothing there would be for that sentence to be true, no situation represented, however erroneously. At 4.022, Wittgenstein says:

> A proposition *shows* its sense.
> A proposition *shows* how things stand *if* it is true. And it *says that* they do so stand.

The problem with "Caesar is a prime number" is that it shows no such thing.

Notice what Wittgenstein says in 4.021 about understanding without explanation. That does not always happen: Sometimes we come across something that has been written or hear someone say something whose sense needs to be explained. On those occasions, my interlocutor and I will work together to figure out what situation or model the initially opaque sentence expresses. We might look to the subsentential components, point to their uses in other, more readily understood sentences, and then figure out how they hang together in *this* sentence so as to express a thought, so as to be a "model of reality." In the Persian king example, I can point to maps of the Persian empire, find statues of Caesar, references to him in works from antiquity and by contemporary historians, and so on. *Who* the sentence is about and *what* is being (falsely) said of him can be cashed out in a variety of ways, even when all parties to this process know the sentence to be false. Such procedures come to naught in the case of "Caesar is a prime number."

These considerations appear to support the natural view in the following way: While the whole sentence is opaque, the subsentential components of "Caesar is a prime number" are *clear enough* to send us looking in particular directions in trying to make sense of the sentence, that is, in the direction of Roman emperors, on the one hand, and prime numbers, on the other. That those procedures lead only down blind alleys, as it were, ultimately reinforces the initial impression that the sentence is nonsensical.[3] Doesn't this show that we do indeed have "intelligible ingredients combined in an illegitimate way"? However, from the standpoint of the austere reading, these ideas only serve to show what is seductive about nonsense-sentences like "Caesar is a prime number": Such sentences are composed of *signs* that appear to be the same signs as those that appear in meaningful propositions such as "Caesar crossed the Rubicon in 49 BCE" and "Fifty-three is a prime number." But appearances can be misleading, as sameness of sign does not guarantee sameness of meaning (in the parlance of the *Tractatus*, the same sign can *symbolize* in different ways). Suppose, for example, that I hear my friend say, "Caesar is a great Persian." I interject rather pedantically that Caesar was not Persian, but Roman, thereby correcting my friend's rather embarrassing mistake. As it turns out in the sequel to my interjection, *I* am the one in need of correction, as my friend was talking about his *cat* named Caesar.

---

[3] As Bronzo (2015, 308) notes, "there are determinate routes into illusions of meanings."

So the mistake of the substantial conception of nonsense can be traced to the following problematic line of reasoning: Because other sentences involving "Caesar" and "is a prime number" make sense, and because the words making them up are there functioning meaningfully, what they mean *there* in some way "clings" to them in the sentence "Caesar is a prime number." Because the meanings that "cling" to those words do not play together nicely, as it were, we end up in the case of "Caesar is a prime number" with something nonsensical.[4] According to the austere reading, the mistake here is to think of sentences as "made up of ingredients, words-assigned-to-certain-categories"; instead, on the austere view, sentences are

> constructed on patterns, where the category of a word in a sentence depends upon the pattern (or patterns) in accordance with which the whole sentence may be taken to be constructed; and [would-be examples of substantial nonsense] have only superficial resemblance to the patterns we at first discern in them, and in accordance with which we try to construe them. (Diamond 1991, 105)

Diamond's appeal to *whole sentences* signals the austere reading's guiding idea, namely, Frege's Context Principle, from the beginning of *Foundations of Arithmetic*. There, Frege says that we are "never to ask for the meaning of a word in isolation, but only in the context of a proposition" (Frege 1980, x). If we begin with sentences that make sense, we can discern the signs such propositions comprise, as well as the contributions those signs make to the sense of the whole. But where the whole does not make sense – where we have nonsense – we should not see whatever it is that we might discern at a subsentential level as somehow *trying* to make a contribution and yet failing. If the whole does not make sense – if it has no meaning – then there is nothing at the subsentential level that contributes to the meaning of the whole sentence (since, as nonsense, it lacks meaning). To think otherwise is to fall afoul of one of the other two principles that frame Frege's *Grundlagen*: separating the logical from the psychological. Thinking of words as antecedently meaningful "ingredients" mistakes what words in isolation conjure up in us psychologically (images, associations, and so on) for the *logical* contribution signs that symbolize make to meaningful propositions.

---

[4] On the idea of "clinging," compare §117 of Wittgenstein (2009), which critically examines the idea of meaning as "an aura the word brings along with it and retains in every kind of use." The suspicion Wittgenstein here directs toward the idea of meaning as an "aura" has roots that run all the way back to the *Tractatus*.

The primacy of whole sentences points to a deeper motivation for the austere conception of nonsense, having to do with the relation between the logical and the *ontological*. Conceiving words as antecedently intelligible ingredients of sentences transposes into formal mode what in the material mode is the idea that we grasp reality via an understanding of *entities* prior to, or independent of, our ability to form thoughts expressible in propositions. On this conception, we know what entities are without necessarily knowing how they can be modeled or pictured. We know the kind of thing Caesar is and the kind of thing a prime number is, and so we both understand the sentence "Caesar is a prime number" *and* understand it to be nonsense.

Wanting it both ways courts the idea of *illogical thought*, a recurring target of Wittgenstein in the *Tractatus*. One important stretch, starting at 5.473, ties together Frege's Context Principle, the "*impossibility* of illogical thought" (5.4731), and the austere conception of nonsense (5.4733):

> Frege says that any legitimately constructed proposition must have a sense. And I say that any possible proposition is legitimately constructed, and, if it has no sense, that can only be because we have failed to give a *meaning* to some of its constituents.
> (Even if we think we have done so.)
> Thus the reason why "Socrates is identical" says nothing is that we have not given *any adjectival* meaning to the word "identical." For when it appears as a sign for identity, it symbolizes in an entirely different way—the signifying relation is a different one—therefore the symbols also are entirely different in the two cases: the two symbols have only the sign in common, and that is an accident.[5]

What might initially appear to be a relatively minor quibble about whether or not "Caesar" means Caesar in the sentence "Caesar is a prime number" is something more like the light-hearted tip of a more serious philosophical iceberg, encompassing issues of the relation between logic and psychology, logic and ontology, and the nature of meaning itself. Endorsement of the austere reading of nonsense is in this way not an isolated or frivolous position, but indicative of much deeper commitments to the primacy of the proposition and ontology's subordination to logic. Rejecting austerity appears to run afoul of those commitments, reviving the specter of psychologism, for example, or subscribing to a problematic "realism" that depends upon viewing our thought from "sideways-on," in McDowell's oft-cited phrase.[6]

[5] The parenthetical between the two main paragraphs underscores the close connection between Frege's Context Principle and the desire to keep the logical and the psychological clearly distinguished.
[6] See Introduction II of Diamond (1991), as well as Goldfarb (2011).

While comprehensive exploration of how these commitments hang together is well beyond this chapter's scope, I want to explore them from a seemingly oblique but (I hope) fruitfully critical perspective: Heidegger's 1926 *Logic* lectures. In Part One of those lectures, Heidegger explores interconnections among the proposition, truth, and falsity in ways that resonate with Tractarian ideas. Intriguingly, at more than one juncture, he adduces examples of *nonsense* that merit close scrutiny. Despite apparent lines of convergence with the austere conception of nonsense, Heidegger's *diagnosis* of nonsensical sentences moves away from the kind of austerity some readers find in the *Tractatus*. For Heidegger, Wittgenstein's remark that "whatever is possible in logic is also permitted" (5.473) is indicative of the limitations of logic's ability to police the bounds of sense. On Heidegger's analysis, the kind of sense that is the concern of logic – the sense associated with propositions – facilitates rather than hinders the formation of nonsense. If, for Wittgenstein, "logic must look after itself," Heidegger's concern is what happens when logic is left to its own devices. Heidegger's handling of nonsense is ultimately irresolute, but not in ways that threaten a revival of psychologism. Instead, what "clings" to words in nonsensical sentences is the residue of the *practical* meanings that form the backdrop for logico-linguistic sense. One of Heidegger's ambitions in the lectures is to illuminate this practical orientation and its primacy in relation to the (merely) propositional. Nonsense, irresolutely understood, serves to further that ambition.

5.2 Heidegger's Chalk Talk

Heidegger's inquiry into the nature of the proposition revolves around the basic idea that "the proposition has a peculiar relation to truth" (GA21, 135). The peculiarity lies in the fact that a proposition "is the kind of speech that is neither true as such nor false as such, but can be *either* true *or* false" (GA21, 135). Heidegger explicates the notions of *being true* and *being false* as *uncovering* and *covering-over*, respectively: To say something that is true is to uncover something – an entity – as it is, whereas to say something false is to represent the entity in a way that it is not. Structurally, these are not two separate features or aspects of the proposition, but are coeval: What *can* be true must at the same time be something that *can* be false. The possibility of representation is inseparable from the possibility of *mis*-representation: "The possibility of being true or false – which is the essential feature of any statement – is as such necessarily grounded in one and the same *logos*" (GA21, 135).

Heidegger's running example of a true statement throughout this discussion is the simple – and, for his audience, eminently evident – statement "The chalkboard is black." The statement's truth consists in representing the chalkboard as it is, as black. He contrasts it with "The chalkboard is gray," which is no less a statement even if false. Both statements say something about something, that is, the chalkboard, representing it as being a certain way, black in one case and gray in the other. The difference is that one of them is a misrepresentation. Heidegger's point here is that a *mis*representation is equally and fully a *representation*. We *understand* what "The chalkboard is gray" is saying, even while looking at the black chalkboard and seeing that the statement is false, because we understand what it *would be* for the chalkboard to *be* gray. Since being either true or false is the essential feature of the proposition as such, we can say that any true proposition is also possibly false while any false proposition is possibly true; in both cases, our understanding what it would mean for them to be otherwise is internal to our understanding them at all.

Although false, "The chalkboard is gray" still manages to say something about the chalkboard even while covering over the chalkboard by misrepresenting how it is. Heidegger emphasizes the assertoric-representational character of this false statement by contrasting it with a third case. He writes:

> At any rate, the second statement ["The chalkboard is gray"] doesn't simply assert *nothing* about the thing it names—as would be the case if we claimed that "The chalkboard is not ambitious." The statement, "The chalkboard is not gray," in fact does assert something, because the chalkboard could very well be gray. Our uncertainty about statements like these comes from the fact that the statements are artificially stripped of any real context in which they might be made. They are put forward in a form in which we hardly recognize them. (This is a problem that as a matter of principle should be explained in logic.) (GA21, 139)

What are we to make of this third case, "The chalkboard is not ambitious"? While we might be inclined to say that the statement is false – it certainly does not uncover anything about the chalkboard as it is – it is important to note the way Heidegger contrasts it with the straightforwardly false "The chalkboard is gray." As Heidegger emphasizes, in the case of the false statement, it still contains within itself the structure common to both true and false statements. Moreover, if we were to say, truly, "The chalkboard is not gray," we would have thereby uncovered the chalkboard, albeit more indirectly than when we say "The chalkboard is black." But if we consider "The chalkboard is not ambitious," do we still have that structure of *either* true *or* false? While "The chalkboard is not gray" is true-but-possibly-false, is that the case with "The chalkboard is not ambitious"? What would it *mean* for the chalkboard to be ambitious? If nothing is forthcoming with respect to this last question, then "The chalkboard is not ambitious" is not true-but-possibly-false, which further means that it does not partake of the *either* true *or* false structure constitutive of propositions. Whether we say "The chalkboard is not ambitious" or "The chalkboard is ambitious," we have not really managed to say anything about the chalkboard: neither uncovers or covers over the chalkboard; neither is any more or less (mis) representational than the other. It would thus appear that "The chalkboard is not ambitious" is not a proposition at all, which accords with how Heidegger begins this passage: "The chalkboard is not ambitious," unlike the straightforwardly false "The chalkboard is gray," asserts *nothing* of the thing it names.

Whereas "The chalkboard is gray" makes sense but is false, "The chalkboard is (not) ambitious" misfires in a different – and more radical – way. The distinctive "misfiring" can be discerned in my inclusion of the parenthetical "not." Neither the addition nor the deletion of the negation sign yields a statement that uncovers anything about the chalkboard, which indicates the way this sentence is not structured as being *either* true *or* false. Neither "The chalkboard is ambitious" nor "The chalkboard is not ambitious" makes sense, since what is being said about the chalkboard is in either case, as Heidegger notes, uncertain. Heidegger elaborates on this uncertainty "about statements like these" by noting that they "are artificially stripped of any real context in which they might be made." While words can – in some sense of "can" – be put together this way, it is not at all clear why anyone *would* say such a thing in a "real context" involving chalkboards (or ambition, for that matter). As Heidegger notes, "They are put forward in a form in which we hardly recognize them," which I take to mean that such statements – or "statements" – leave us puzzled in a way that ordinary false statements do not.

Notice that Heidegger ends the passage we have been considering with a parenthetical: "This is a problem that as a matter of principle should be explained in logic." What exactly is the problem here and in what way might logic be called upon to explain it? For Heidegger, the answer to this question begins with the way sentences such as "The chalkboard is not ambitious" are formed in a kind of vacuum, divorced from "any real context." In this case, the closest we have to a "context" is a lecture, one of whose topics is sentences that do not make sense. That is not exactly a *real* context in that the work the sentence is being enlisted to do does not depend upon the specifics of the sentence itself; the sentence is to a large extent *arbitrary*. "The chalkboard is not cantankerous" would have served just as well. Words have here become dislodged from their context of use and in ways where the prospects for giving them a context look dim. In the sequel to this passage, Heidegger turns his attention to these contexts of use, and so to the kinds of practical significance that founds and sustains the significance of language. In doing so, Heidegger provides insight into the origins of nonsense.

5.3   Of Hammers and Word Salads

Consider the hammer. In our comportment, the hammer is manifest *as* something with which to hammer nails. Heidegger considers this "as" *pre-predicative*: In picking up and using the hammer, I manifest my understanding of it *as* a hammer but without explicitly predicating something of something. I simply pick it up and use it. "My being in the world *is* nothing but this already-operating-with-understanding in those various ways of existing" (GA21, 146). As an "operating-with-understanding," comportment is thus oriented toward *meaning*: "The result of an act of sense-making is precisely *sense* or *meaning* – not what we usually call the 'meaning of a word' but the primary meaning to which words can then accrue" (GA21, 150). As pre-predicative, the meaning manifest in comportment is manifest as *belonging* to whatever it is I am taking up and using: My experience is not separable into different components – the hammer-thing and the meaning in terms of which I experience it – but has a more primordial unity.

In §15 of *Being and Time*, after noting that equipment such as a hammer "is not *grasped* thematically," Heidegger notes how "the hammering does not simply have knowledge about the hammer's character as equipment, but it has appropriated this equipment in a way which could not possibly be more suitable" (SZ 69). In understanding the hammer *as* a hammer, I understand it as "suitable" for hammering; I understand what the hammer is *for* and how it is *supposed* to be used. That does not mean the hammer *cannot* be used in other ways. I can use the hammer to prop up a window, smash tin cans, ward off an intruder, and so on. Yet, as noted above, the hammer has a "primary meaning to which words can then accrue." That primary meaning accords with the primary way of making sense of the hammer – as suitable for hammering – and accordingly marks other uses of the hammer as deviations from that primary meaning. That is, a hammer *retains* that primary meaning even when it is being used in other ways: When I use a hammer to prop up the window, it does not cease to be (understood as) a hammer. It is still manifest *as* a hammer, but as being out of place or put to an unaccustomed use, albeit in a handy way. The suitability of the hammer for hammering makes it unsuitable for other purposes, such as serving soup or repairing cloth. The hammer's primary sense in this way *allows for* some further ways of making sense of the hammer, but not others. We might call the hammer's primary sense a *material* sense involving a primary material application, coupled with a range of material compatibilities and incompatibilities. We can think of the latter as dividing between *sense* and *nonsense*: Nut-cracking with a hammer makes sense, serving soup with a hammer does not. Of course, one can *try* to serve soup with a hammer, in which case it would be experienced as retaining its primary sense, even while being enlisted in a task for which it is eminently unsuitable.

On Heidegger's account, these primary practical meanings to which we are attuned in comportment are not to be understood as *verbal* meanings, but they are the meanings to which words "accrue." Understanding-as-comportment, as a primary mode of sense-making oriented toward primary practical meanings, is the basis for linguistic meaning:

> Only insofar as this capacity to understand—to make sense of—already belongs to existence, can existence express itself in sounds, such that these vocal sounds are words that now have meaning. Because existence, in its very being, is sense-making, it lives in meanings and can express itself in and as meanings. Only because there are such vocal sounds (i.e., words) that accrue to meanings, can there be individual words, i.e., the linguistic forms that are stamped by meaning and can be detached from that meaning. (GA21, 151)

This last sentence – with its talk of *detachment* – hints at a significant difference between the material senses canvassed above and verbal senses. By "detached from *that* meaning" (emphasis added), I take Heidegger to be referring to the kinds of practical, material meanings manifest in our comportment toward various kinds of entities. The meaning of the hammer – as *for hammering* – manifest in the competent use of it is bound up with the hammer itself. As Heidegger says in §15 of *Being and Time*: "The less we just stare at the hammer-thing, and the more we seize hold of and use it, the more primordial does our relationship to it become and the more unveiledly is it encountered as that which it is—as equipment" (SZ 69). Heidegger continues by noting the way "the hammering itself uncovers the specific 'manipulability' of the hammer" (SZ 69). While that meaning "accrues" to the word "hammer," the *word* – unlike the item of equipment – is utterable quite apart from actually *hammering*. I can talk about hammers without being anywhere near an actual hammer.

Perhaps it belabors the obvious but I think it is worth putting it this way: The word "hammer" is *not* a hammer, indeed, *nothing like* a hammer. This is one way to understand what Heidegger is after in talk of detachment here, which he subsequently connects to talk of *flattening*. In the verbal statement, "the '*as*' of the primary understanding is simultaneously flattened out into the pure and simple determination of a thing" (GA21, 153). Although this talk of flattening is typically understood as emphasizing the way predicative judgments – what gets expressed in assertions – foster the tendency to view the item of equipment as an isolated (*vorhanden*) *object*, I want here to emphasize that in the accrual of the primary meaning to a *word*, that meaning is transposed into a medium of *uniform* consistency.[7] There is nothing materially specific about words, no specific material medium that words *need* for their efficacy (one and the same word can be written in chalk, ink, or graphite, represented by pixels on a screen, scratched into the ground, and so on) and so there are no material features that they must have. As a result, the material compatibilities and incompatibilities are no longer preserved in the way they are in the case of the primary meaning. As Heidegger puts it, "when *logos* gets cut loose, so to speak, from the specific relation of the subject matter (the about-which) and the predicate (the as-what), it gets passed off as the relation of anything to anything, equivalent to formal synthesizing as such" (GA21, 160).

Consider again the hammer and the word "hammer." The hammer is materially incompatible with tasks like serving soup or mending fine fabric. But it is no more difficult to write the sentence "Henry served the soup with his trusty hammer" than to write "Henry hammered in the nails with his trusty hammer." While *hammers* do not "allow" themselves to be of use for serving soup, the English language is perfectly compliant when it comes to writing sentences about serving soup with hammers. Recall that this discussion began with Heidegger's example "The chalkboard is not ambitious," which he took as pointing to a problem "that as a matter of principle should be explained in logic." My suggestion here is that his account of the "flattening" of the "as" in the accrual of primary (material) meanings to words contributes to that explanation. The uniformity of words and the "frictionless" character of predication (in contrast to the kind of material compatibilities and incompatibilities of primary meanings) allow for combinations of words that have all the trappings of

---

[7] The difficulties engendered by the uniform *appearance* of language, which can obscure the multiplicity of *uses*, are a theme of the opening passages of Wittgenstein (2009). See especially §§11–12.

predicative statements while not exactly making sense. "Henry served the soup with his trusty hammer" is a kind of nonsense, just as "The chalkboard is not ambitious" is a kind of nonsense. The frictionless character of predication allows for even more attenuated combinations: "Henry smashed the square root of two with his trusty hammer" begins to chart Lewis Carroll territory.[8] But we also in a way understand such sentences because we recognize the primary meanings that accrued to the words in the first place. As Heidegger notes, "the statement's modification of the as-structure always presupposes the original as-structure, the underlying understanding of the thing that gets flattened out in and through the statement" (GA21, 159).

5.4   The Deer Hunter

Heidegger's first use of nonsense in the *Logic* lectures – "The chalkboard is not ambitious" – initially suggested an affinity with the austere conception of nonsense: Given that such a sentence (or string of words) does not embody the either-true-or-false structure essential to propositions, it cannot be understood as *saying* something about the chalkboard. However, for Heidegger, the sentence's failure to say something does not impugn the idea that the constituent parts have sense. Indeed, quite the contrary: The practical senses to which words "accrue" can still be discerned in those parts; our appreciation of those senses is what enables us to see that the whole is indeed nonsensical. We thus seem to have, to use Conant's words, "intelligible ingredients combined in an illegitimate way" (Conant 2000, 176). Importantly for Heidegger, the illegitimacy is a kind of *practical-ontological* illegitimacy, reflecting our understanding of the kinds of things chalkboards are and ambition is.

Toward the end of Part One of the lectures, Heidegger offers a second example of nonsense via his analysis of *perceptual* falsehood, thereby enlarging the scope of the practical understanding already emphasized in the course. Attention to this second example underscores the primacy of practical-perceptual understanding. At the same time, the example highlights a *productive* role for nonsense to play for Heidegger: Although a kind

---

[8] Lewis Carroll's "The Mad Gardener's Song" provides a clear example of the English language's tolerance for nonsense. McManus (2014) also appeals to Lewis Carroll to make a similar point, although McManus is primarily interested in the way some of Carroll's sentences trade on our capacity to hear a word in more than one way. The nonsense of "The Mad Gardener's Song" does not exploit such oscillations. I should also note here my debt more generally to McManus's criticisms of the austere reading in his paper.

of degenerative byproduct of the flattening of the "as," our recognition of some sentences *as* nonsense serves to delineate precisely the practical-perceptual understanding at work in that recognition. That nonsense has this productive role casts further doubt on the austere conception of non-sense, since it is precisely the *intelligibility* of the "ingredients" that gives such sentences a productive role.

Heidegger's example of perceptual falsehood or deception in the *Logic* lectures involves nothing outlandish or contentious.[9] The example is one of walking in the forest and taking something to be a deer, only to discover that it was a bush:

> Say I am walking in a dark woods and see something coming toward me through the fir trees. "It's a deer," I say. The statement need not be explicit. As I get nearer, I see it's just a bush that I'm approaching. In understanding, addressing, and being concerned with this thing, I have acted as one who covers-over: the unexpressed statement shows the being as something other than it is. (GA21, 187)

My taking the bush to be a deer is a *mis*taking, and so I am mistaken, taken in by whatever it was about the way the bush looked (its size and shape, for example), or the poor light (the glimmer of moonlight on the leaves resembled the characteristic fluttering of a deer's tail), or my eagerness to see deer (I've spent the day hunting for deer, not squirrels). Heidegger embeds the example in an analysis of perceptual falsehood as involving three conditions:

1. The orientation to the uncovering of things – the prior intending and having of the subject matter.
2. Within this basic comportment of uncovering – in fact, dominated and guided by it – there is the showing of the subject matter in terms of something else. Only on the basis of this structure is there any possibility of passing something off as something *else*.
3. At the same time, such showing-something-as-something-*else* is based on the possibility of synthesizing something with something (GA21, 187).

Heidegger's appeal in the first "structural condition" to "the orientation to the uncovering of things" refers to the way perception is situated and already structured by my orientation toward that broader situation. Walking in the woods, I am in, as it were, "forest mode," perceptually attuned to

---

[9] As Wrathall (2011) has emphasized in his discussion of the example, it is not the philosopher's custom-built hallucination.

those surroundings and so *ready* to perceive a variety of things (trees, animals, birdcalls, and so on). Consider the difference between hearing birds chirping while on a hike and hearing a wayward bird's sudden chirping inside the house. The latter is startling and disorienting. It might take me a moment even to hear the series of noises *as* a bird's, since, puttering in the kitchen or typing at my desk, I was not at all ready or *poised* to hear a bird's chirp.[10] Walking through the woods, I am, to varying degrees, poised to perceive some things and not others. I say "to varying degrees" because my specific perceptual orientation will be structured in many ways by what I'm doing in the woods. If I'm just going on a walk, my readiness will be rather loose and shambling: "Oh look, a tall tree." "Hey, a mushroom." And so on. If, on the other hand, I'm out with my gun during hunting season, I am *on the lookout* for a deer and *what I see* while hunting shows up in terms of *not a deer, possibly a deer,* and *deer* (or, really, "Holy shit, a deer at last!"). In some ways, being poised to see a deer makes me more primed to be deceived. This is what Heidegger is getting at with the second condition, where he refers to the "possibility of passing something off as something *else.*" That latter "something *else*" is shaped by my prior perceptual orientation. I am more likely to mistake something *as a deer* insofar as I am particularly on the lookout for a deer (hence the dangers faced by rambling hikers and their dogs when out in the woods during hunting season).

I want to focus especially on the third condition, which concerns the *range* of my prior perceptual orientation, of what I am poised to see. What does it mean to talk about *possibilities* here and how is such a *range* demarcated or determined? While perceptually encountering anything involves "the general possibility of synthesis," that is, perceiving something *as* something, Heidegger contends that this possibility in any "concrete deception," which after all takes place in a concrete situation, "includes within itself a range of indications." Heidegger elaborates:

> To take the above example, I would not, in fact, think that what was approaching me was the Shah of Iran, even though something like that is intrinsically possible. The Shah is a being that *could* appear among the trees in a German forest at night, whereas there is not a chance that I could see anything like the cube root of sixty-nine coming toward me. (GA21, 188)

Heidegger's examples here illustrate the idea of "a range of indications." Given my perceptual orientation, I am poised to see the bush *as a deer,* but I am not at all poised to see the bush *as the Shah of Iran* even though,

---

[10] I take the term "poised" from Wrathall (2011).

as Heidegger notes, he *could* appear in a forest among the trees (at least
in 1926). While I am not in any way poised to see the Shah of Iran (in
Heidegger's example), there might be situations – however unusual or
outlandish – where my poise *is* so structured. Consider: I work for the
United Nations and am taking part in a retreat for select world leaders.
During breaks from the intense talks, the leaders go for walks in the surrounding woods. A sudden fog descends and some of the leaders go missing, including, to update the example, the Supreme Leader of Iran. While
out with the search party, I am exquisitely poised for Supreme Leader
sightings. In that situation, I may be more likely to mistake Heidegger's
bush for the Supreme Leader than for a deer, even while my more general
out-in-the-woods orientation toward things is still in play.

But what about Heidegger's second alternative? Even though the example of the Shah is an *outlandish* possibility, the example still possesses (in
1926) what Heidegger calls *intrinsic* possibility. The latter is illustrated by
the UN example. So while there *could be* a situation where I am perceptually poised to see the Supreme Leader of Iran and so in that way liable to
mistake something (a bush, a deer) for him, there is no possible situation
in which I am perceptually poised to see the cube root of sixty-nine. That
possibility is, we might say, off the table, as indicated by Heidegger's "not
a chance." We thus appear to have a range of cases:

(D) I mistake a bush for a deer.
(S) I mistake a bush for the Shah of Iran.
(C) I mistake a bush for the cube root of sixty-nine.

As we move from (D) to (S) to (C), it appears that we are in each case
taking a step further out in terms of a possible way of being deceived. In
Heidegger's example, (D) is eminently possible; (S) is not really possible,
but still stands as intrinsically possible; while (C) is not at all possible.

The transitions from (D) to (S) and then to (C) exemplify what might
be called an *attenuation* or *diminishment* of *sense*. Case (D) is straightforward and unremarkable – a case of perceptual deception that is familiar
enough and readily understandable – whereas (S) is far less so. Describing
a situation wherein I see a bush in the distance but think "That's the Shah
of Iran" or, alternatively, I discover that what I see is in fact a bush but
think "I could have sworn that was the Shah of Iran" takes a great deal
more in the way of stage-setting (e.g., the example of wayward leaders on a
UN retreat). But while the transition from (S) to (C) is in a sense just a further step in the process of diminishment, it seems misleading to describe
it as being a matter of *degree*. That is, (C)'s relation to (S) (and to (D) for

that matter) is not simply a matter of being a *more* attenuated possibility, a case where the question "What are the odds?" still admits of an answer. Rather, (C) does not appear to name or constitute a *possibility* at all. There is *no situation* I can, however implausibly, describe as involving *that* kind of perceptual deception, which suggests that there is no longer a kind of perceptual deception at issue at all. In other words, the transition from (S) to (C) marks not a *diminishment* of sense so much as a *lapse* in sense, a passage from sense, however attenuated, to *nonsense*.

Consider now the following questions:

1.   What makes (C) nonsensical?
2.   What *work* does (C) do in the context of Heidegger's discussion?

I want to suggest that different answers to (1) have a bearing on the answer to (2). More specifically, I want to suggest three things: first, that Heidegger's answer to (1) diverges from the answer dictated by a resolute understanding of nonsense of the kind illustrated by Diamond's handling of "Caesar is a prime number"; second, that Heidegger's answer to (1) provides a way of answering (2) such that (C) does a kind of work, work that I'll refer to as ontological; and third, that the kind of answer to (1) that the resolute understanding of nonsense provides makes an answer to (2) more opaque.

Here is what I take to be Heidegger's answer to the first question. What makes (C) nonsensical has to do with the *kinds of things* under consideration: Unlike a bush or a deer, the cube root of sixty-nine is *not the kind of thing* that one can perceptually encounter in a forest. This is why the transition from (S) to (C) is different from the one from (D) to (S): However remote the chance of spotting the Shah of Iran is, the Shah (at least in 1926) is still the kind of thing that one can see in the forest. If we consider the sentence schema "I mistake a bush for X," we can see that the words "the cube root of sixty-nine" refer to something that belongs to the *wrong category* to yield a properly meaningful sentence. (C) is nonsense, but it has a kind of nonsensical sense in that all the words mean what they usually mean, which is precisely *why* the sentence as a whole misfires. In this respect, Heidegger's answer is in accord with what Diamond labels the natural conception of nonsense. But Heidegger does not simply embrace that natural conception; instead, he goes further by offering an account of the *sources* of the intelligibility that the natural conception simply takes for granted.

To spell out this last claim, consider what might be said from Heidegger's perspective about the second question in light of what I take to be his answer to the first question. Let's start by first considering the immediate context where (C) comes into play. Heidegger is here sketching an account of perceptual deception that involves a prior orientation, a matter of being perceptually poised to perceive some things and not others. I think it is fair to say that this perceptual poise involves a kind of *understanding*. Further, I think it is fair to say that this understanding is *ontological* in that it is oriented toward what things *are* and the way they fall into different categories, however inchoate that understanding might be. In this context, thinking about the transition from (D) to (S) serves to "light up" that orientation in that I can appreciate the remoteness of (D) from (S) and in that way learn something about how perceptual poise works. But the transition from (S) to (C) does a kind of work as well. While the first transition involves a kind of strain, the second transition is more a matter of the gears grinding to a halt. That "grinding" further "lights up" our understanding of categorical distinctions, thereby delimiting what Heidegger refers to as "the possibility of synthesizing something with something."

So (C) does *work* by being nonsensical, but emphatically not because the meaning of one or more constituent parts of the sentence is undetermined. If that were the problem with (C), then it would not be at all clear what it contributes to Heidegger's example. If the topic in the series of sentences went from *deer* to *Shah of Iran* to *squiggle-squoggle*, the final sentence would indeed be (at least partly) a nonsensical string of words but it would no longer illuminate as (C) does: With "squiggle-squoggle," there is only the absence of understanding rather than the delineation of one category (perceivable things) from another (abstract objects, e.g., the cube root of sixty-nine).

A sentence of the form "I mistook the bush for the cube root of sixty-nine" appears attenuated in much the same way as "Julius Caesar is a prime number." If the latter is nonsensical, then so too is the former. Given the austere conception of nonsense central to resolute readings of the *Tractatus*, the diagnosis of the nonsensicality of each sentence should be the same. Again, the sentences are nonsense not because of what their constituent parts mean but because of a failure to give one or more constituents of the sentences a meaning. Consider the following series of sentences:

The cube root of sixty-nine is irrational.

The cube root of sixty-nine is between four and five.

I mistook a bush for **the cube root of sixty-nine.**

The first two sentences make sense and the meaning of the boldfaced phrase is the same in both, making the same contribution to the respective sentence. We thus can say that each of the two sentences is *about* the cube root of sixty-nine. In keeping with Wittgenstein's *Tractatus* remarks about Occam's Razor,[11] we can say that the phrases are doing the same kind of *work* in the two cases.

But what are we to say about the third sentence and its relation to the first two? Recall that at *Tractatus* 5.4733 Wittgenstein says that "any possible proposition is legitimately constructed." So if the third sentence symbolizes a proposition, then it is legitimately constructed. But does it? What proposition would it symbolize if it did? It seems that the only thing we can do here is simply *repeat* the sentence. We saw that Wittgenstein also says in this passage that there can be situations where we have failed to give a meaning to some of the constituents of a sentence (we have used signs that don't symbolize) while *thinking* that we have. This means that we can *think* that the third sentence symbolizes a proposition – and so is legitimately constructed – and yet be *wrong* about that. We are led in this direction because the boldfaced phrase in the third sentence looks and sounds just like the phrases that appear in the first two sentences, tempting us to see the phrase in the last sentence as symbolizing in the same way. This is again the idea of the meaning as "clinging" to the parts of the sentence, and thereby transferable to others. We can *feel* this kind of clinging by comparing:

I mistook a bush for the cube root of sixty-nine.

I mistook a bush for gibbety gobblety goo.

In the latter case, that a constituent of the sentence has not been assigned a meaning is patently obvious. Indeed, we might even say in this case that we are not presented with *signs* at all, let alone signs that symbolize. Psychologically, there is nothing to associate with "gibbety gobblety goo," and so there is no real possibility of *thinking* one means something while failing really to do so. There is, in other words, no temptation to think one has meant something with the last phrase. On the austere conception of nonsense, what differences there are between the last two sentences are *psychological* differences, but when it comes to *logic* their status is the same: Neither symbolizes any proposition.[12]

---

[11] See *Tractatus* 3.328 and especially 5.47321.

[12] Although we might question the invocation of this distinction here by arguing that there is a logical difference as well: "I mistook a bush for the cube root of sixty-nine" is logically – and not just psychologically – related to "I mistook a bush for a number between four and five." Camp (2004) makes a strong case for that idea that we do understand (in however attenuated a sense) what she calls "cross-categorial predications." Her argument in part involves the idea that such nonsensical-looking sentences nonetheless "possess substantive inferential roles" (212).

Notice here that the category of the *psychological* is being enlisted to do a great deal of the explanatory work.[13] While the austere conception of nonsense typically appeals to a rather anemic notion of the psychological – mental images, feelings, and the like – more careful reflection on the *passage* from sense to nonsense reveals a far richer psychological landscape that involves such notions as *understanding, realizing, recognizing, discovering*, and so on. Rather than a mere play of images, these processes engage – or operate – with *senses*. Diamond's own discussion betrays a reliance on a more robust conception of the psychological – as involving understanding, realizing, recognizing, discovering, and so on – than her official position allows. Consider again Diamond's rejection of the idea that sentences are "made up of ingredients" in favor of the claim that they "are constructed on patterns." On her view, nonsense sentences such as "Julius Caesar is a prime number" or "I stumbled over the cube root of sixty-nine on my hike" have "only superficial resemblance to patterns we at first discern in them, and in accordance with which we try to construe them" (Diamond 1991, 105). What does it mean here to *at first discern* a pattern and what exactly does it mean to *try to construe* something as being in accord with a pattern? Furthermore, how is it that the *attempt* to construe breaks down: What is it that we *come to realize* in this case? Discerning a pattern could be understood purely syntactically: We recognize a sequence of *signs* as being the same *signs* as occur in other sentences we understand. That sameness at the level of signs is what encourages us to construe them as "being in accord" with those other patterns. But what happens when we do that? To construe here would appear to mean that we try to understand the signs as symbolizing as they do in other sentences, as in the series of sentences above. We construe "the cube root of sixty-nine" as *meaning* or *being about* the cube root of sixty-nine and we construe "stumbled" and "hike" as *meaning* or *being about* stumbling and hiking, but then find ourselves at a loss as to how to fit those back together. But why are we at a loss? We are at a loss because we do not understand how the cube root of a number is something I *could* stumble over while on a hike. This is nothing like a mere play of images or loose associations. In accord with what we saw in the previous section, our coming to see that the sentence is nonsense is underwritten by a *practical* familiarity with hiking and stumbling, as well as cube roots, a prior grasp of practical-material senses. Notice that what happens here is in many ways different from the kind of discernment involved when it comes to "Caesar is a great Persian." While we might initially see

<hr>

[13] Suspicions about the appeal to the "psychological" in austere readings are a focus of McManus (2014).

this sentence as in accordance with a pattern that includes sentences such as "Caesar is a great general," "Caesar crossed the Rubicon in 49 BCE," and so on, when I construe "Caesar" as the name of a friend's cat, I *then* see it in accordance with a whole other pattern: "Caesar prefers canned food to kibble," "Caesar likes to nap upstairs in the afternoon," and so on. In the case of nonsense such as "Caesar is a prime number," there is no *other* pattern with which we see this sentence as being in accordance.

We could of course *stipulate* that "Caesar" in this case just means the number fifty-three or that "is a prime number" just means "is a great general." Such stipulations – or "construals" – would indeed rescue "Caesar is a prime number" from being nonsensical. As Diamond notes:

> "Caesar is a prime number" can be made sense of in two ways: it can be taken as saying of Caesar something *it makes sense to say about a person*—in which case it contains the proper name of a person but not a numerical predicate; or it can be taken as saying of a number something *it makes sense to say about a number*—in which case it contains a numerical predicate but not the proper name of a person. (Diamond 1991, 102, emphasis added)

Diamond's proposal points in two directions: construe "Caesar" as referring to a number or construe "is a prime number" as not being a numerical predicate. That *these* two ways suggest themselves suggests that we already – initially – understand the constituents of the sentence as being about a person *and* a numerical predicate. It is only when we find that we cannot do anything with the sentence as a whole – only when we find the sentence to be nonsense – that we then cast about in those two directions. That it is just those two directions shows a reliance on the usual meanings of "Caesar" and "is a prime number." Notice, though, that if we follow Diamond's proposal, then the sentence is no longer available to do the kind of work *Heidegger* wants it to do. If we construe one or more constituents of the sentence so as to have it make sense, then it will no longer be the kind of nonsense that indicates categorical distinctions. In other words, *making sense* of "Caesar is a prime number" is exactly what Heidegger *does not* want to do. What matters for him is the way "Caesar is a prime number" fails to make sense on the most natural way of construing "Caesar" and "is a prime number." That failure shows us something about the structure of our understanding.

This last point in turn points to something further and deeper about Heidegger's discussion. Concerning Diamond's proposal for making sense of "Caesar is a prime number," consider the following question: How do we decide – or how do we know – what it makes sense to say about a person or what it makes sense to say about a number? What fixes or determines the range of what it makes sense to say? Heidegger's contention in the *Logic* lectures is that *logic* is not what determines that range; indeed, logic is all too permissive when it comes to forming nonsense sentences. Instead, it is our practical familiarity with chalkboards and numbers, deer and bushes that serves to demarcate that range. That prior familiarity is what motivates us to construe the parts of the sentence in the way Diamond describes so as to have the sentence make sense after all. We are motivated precisely because we recognize that construing the sentence in the most straightforward way – where "Caesar" means *Caesar* and "is a prime number" means *is a prime number* – yields nonsense. We recognize – or understand – that it makes no sense to say the one thing of the other because we (already) understand *things* like Roman generals, prime numbers, chalkboards, deer, forests, and world leaders.

Heidegger's strategic use of nonsense illuminates, rather than confounds, that understanding, or, we might say, it illuminates that understanding precisely *by* confounding it. At the same time, that use confounds the austere conception of nonsense in a way that promises to reconfigure the relationship between logic and ontology.[14]

[14] Earlier versions of this chapter were not presented at any conferences or workshops, but I would like to thank Kate Withy for reading and commenting on an early draft, Filippo Casati for numerous Zoom conversations on the matters at issue, and Daniel Dahlstrom for his care and attention in preparing the final version of the chapter.

CHAPTER 6

Heidegger's "Destruction" of Traditional Logic

Françoise Dastur

The title of Heidegger's habilitation, *Duns Scotus' Doctrine of Categories and Meaning*, may suggest that it is a largely historical investigation. Yet it is essentially because the young Heidegger dealt with the problems of contemporary logic and, indeed, principally those outlined in Husserl's *Logical Investigations* that he was led to take an interest in Scholastic logic.[1] Far from being simply a resumption of Aristotelian syllogistic theory, Scholastic logic contained in his eyes genuinely phenomenological elements, notably what Husserl deems a "formal apophantic," a logic of meaning that is concerned, not with objective validity, but with the a priori laws that establish the conditions of the unity of meaning. The privileged object of this logic, that is, the locus of that meaning, is the assertion, the propositional statement. Heidegger discovered the matrix of such a logic of meaning in the semiotics attributed to Duns Scotus, and it was from this "logic of meaning" that he awaited an essential clarification of the question of the leading meaning of Being. The latter question, as he emphasizes in his self-interpretation a half-century later, constituted "the question that set [him] on the way," beginning in 1907 with his first philosophical reading: Brentano's dissertation (GA14, 93).

In fact the same project, that of the development of a logic of meaning oriented toward judgment – in contrast to a logic of validity, oriented toward the object – still guides Heidegger in his enterprise of "destruction" (*Destruktion*) or "critical deconstruction of traditional logic" (*kritischer Abbau der überlieferten Logik*), an expression he uses in the lecture course of the summer semester 1928 devoted to *The Metaphysical Foundations of Logic*. What Heidegger seeks to clarify in this course is precisely the metaphysical status of the initial metaphysical principles of logic, that is to say,

---

[1] Parts of this chapter present, in a substantially revised and developed form, some material first aired in Dastur (1987) and in Dastur (2007, 121–151). For a review of Heidegger's early preoccupation with logic and the motivation behind it, see Dastur (1987), 55f.

III

its properly philosophical character that, by means of the *Destruction* of
the Leibnizian theory of judgment, that is, its reorientation to its metaphysical foundations, can be defined as a "metaphysics of truth" (GA26,
126, 132). For it was still essential for Heidegger, during the entire Marburg
period, to "make more originally conceivable" what we call logic and to
make visible "the idea of a philosophical logic" (GA26, 7). But this philosophical logic can be established, not by an external connection of logic
and philosophy, but only by a more originary appropriation of traditional
logic, through the attempt to "make it less compact, so that central problems appear in it" in order "to let us be led by the content of these problems themselves to its presuppositions" (GA26, 7). We can see here that
the task of *Destruktion* that is determined as an *Auflockern*, a loosening of
what is too knotted, too intertwined, too compact, consists in *de-struere*, in
dismantling an assemblage, in identifying the various layers of a construction, rather than throwing down or destroying.

It is therefore only by such a de-construction that one can truly found
a philosophical logic. This is what Heidegger explicitly says in this same
course: "We do not have a ready-made metaphysics in which we could
house logic, but the *Destruktion* of logic is itself a part of the foundation
of metaphysics" (GA26, 70). As Heidegger repeatedly points out in this
course and as he will recall in 1929 in the introduction to *Kant and the
Problem of Metaphysics*, founding metaphysics does not consist in replacing one already established foundation by another, as if metaphysics were
already a completed building and a ready-made discipline, but the foundation is on the contrary the projection of a new architectural plan and at the
same time the concrete determination of metaphysics (GA26, 13; GA3, 1f).

What then is "logic," a term that Heidegger most often puts in quotation marks, precisely to indicate that it poses a problem (GA26, 1, 23)? The
Greek term *logikè* is the abbreviation of *logikè epistèmè*, which means the
science of a determined district of being, that of *logos*, alongside that of
ethos and *phusis*, in accordance with the division of philosophy into three
branches in the Platonic and Aristotelian schools (GA21, 1ff). This division
essentially isolates each of these regions of being and separates philosophy
into three different sciences, each of which, having its own defined object,
becomes a positive science. Heidegger considers these schools' enrollment
of thought as nothing less than a decline, merging as it does with what
he will later call in the *Letter on Humanism* "the technical interpretation
of thought" that transforms philosophy into a technique of explanation
by ultimate causes, thus subjecting it to the unconditioned domination
of logic (GA9, 314f). Instead of being a dimension of *phusis*, as is the case

in the pre-Socratic way of thinking, *logos* acquires in *epistèmè logikè* an independent existence, a positivity recognizable in propositions insofar as they are enunciated. From this point of view, it also acquires the mode of being of something subsisting, something given and *vorhanden*. Such a conception of *logos* will find its apogee in Bolzano's theory of "propositions in themselves"(*Sätze an sich*). However, this new status of *logos* does not in itself explain why the propositional *logos* can become "*the* normative region," "the place of origin of the determinations of being" (GA40, 196) – that is to say, what it is in the doctrine of categories that defines as such the project of an ontology, a science of and a discourse on being. For this, the propositional *logos* must appear as the place of truth, the place where truth occurs and where it can be preserved.

The explanation to which Heidegger appealed in the 1930s and 1940s was the transformation of the essence of truth that occurred with the Platonic determination of being as an *idea* and its implication that the truth of *phusis* is now a matter of vision. This transformation of the meaning of *logos* brings with it a different meaning of being itself, and in both cases it means substituting for original being something that is only its effect, the essential consequence (*Wesensfolge*) of it (GA40, 192). Heidegger indeed emphasizes that the Platonic interpretation of being as *idea* is the necessary consequence of the fundamental interpretation of being as *phusis*. This interpretation is therefore not in itself a decline, and of Plato, Heidegger says that he is "the completion [*die Vollendung*] of the beginning." But the decline begins when the effect or result of being takes the place of being itself, that is to say, when the *idea* becomes the only normative interpretation of being. At this point being as un-concealment (*alètheia*) no longer determines the presence of things. Instead being-seen determines being as such; that is to say, the *idea* by itself determines the presence of things, with the result that *logos* as the gathering of their presence only happens for the benefit of seeing itself. The *logos* then devolves into merely a means of retaining the presence of the visible, of the *idea*, in the form of a propositional statement that can be repeated even in the absence of any actual seeing. And in this way the proposition becomes the place of truth.

We then understand why ontological determinations are called categories, that is to say statements, according to the primary meaning of the verb *katègorein* (GA9, 252).[2] Presence, in traditional ontology, is only seen in the perspective of a determinate form of language, the predicative

---

[2] Heidegger recalls here that *katègoria* comes from *kata-agoreuein* and originally means to accuse somebody on the *agora*, that is, in a public manner.

statement insofar as it says something of something (*legein ti kata tinos*). It is not, however, self-evident, as Heidegger points out, that all ontology must take the form of a doctrine of categories. As the young Heidegger learned from Aristotle via Brentano's Dissertation, "being can be said in multiple ways"; in addition to signifying categories, "being" can also stand for a property (accident), for possibility and actuality, and, above all, for truth.

Brentano's way of solving the question of the unifying determination of being, one that governs this quadruple significance, is to give the categorial meaning of being the lead over the other meanings, including the sense of being as truth, since for him the being of the copula merges with the *einai hos alèthès* (Brentano 1960, 37). While he knew that Aristotle conceives truth in the *Metaphysics* both as a logical function of judgment and as a characteristic of things themselves, Brentano tends to give the nod to the former conception (Brentano 1960, 31f). By contrast, Heidegger privileges passages discussing the ontological conception of truth, in particular *Metaphysics*, Theta 10, deeming the latter "the apogee" of Aristotle's thinking of being since unconcealment (*Unverborgenheit*) appears there as being's fundamental feature (GA9, 232). Later, in "The Word of Anaximander" (1946), Heidegger goes so far as to affirm that Aristotle, when he thinks of being on the basis of *kategoria*, does not interpret being "logically" any more than Parmenides, that is, on the basis of the propositional statement and its copula. Instead Aristotle simply takes up entities as already there *for* the assertion, as what is present each time in the unconcealment (*das unverborgen jeweilig Anwesende*) (GA5, 351).

The least we can say is that Heidegger refuses to see in Aristotle what tradition deems him, namely, the "father" of logic and the "inventor" of the copula. For Heidegger, traditional logic is a product of schools, and it is therefore to the editors of Aristotle's works rather than to Aristotle himself that we owe the purely instrumental status of logic as an *organon*, and this will remain unchanged until Kant. To be sure, it was Kant who "first gave logic a central philosophical function" (GA24, 252) with his transcendental logic (a logic of the object with ontological implications) and it was Hegel who, continuing in the same ontological direction, identifies logic and philosophy rather than seeing the former as merely the instrument of the latter. Yet despite these innovations on the part of Kant and Hegel, it is nonetheless necessary to repeat once more Kant's words, true for Kant himself and later for Hegel, that since Aristotle "logic has not taken a single step forward" (GA40, 197). The apparent extension of its domain to the a priori knowledge of objects with Kant and to all possible ontological knowledge with Hegel leaves its foundation unchanged. Hegel, in identifying logic and metaphysics, brought to its completion only the "initial end" of Western thought and not its true beginning; Hegel closes the chapter only on the determination of being as *idea* and that of *logos* as *katègoria*.

What matters to Heidegger is neither extending the reign of logic nor dissolving the ontological into it. The task is instead that of bringing logic back in ontology. The very future of philosophy depends on accomplishing this task and moving beyond Hegel, as Heidegger put it in 1927 (GA24, 254). It is against this backdrop, I suggest, that we should read Heidegger's often-quoted line: "The idea of 'logic' itself disintegrates into the turbulence of a more original questioning" (GA9, 117/92).

This statement has mistakenly been read as a sign of the total rejection of reason and logic and the admission of irrationalism. But this misunderstanding comes from the fact that the positivity of phenomenological destruction remains ignored. Logic has its own limited validity, derived from a larger "idea" of *logos*. In the 1943 Afterword to *What Is Metaphysics?* Heidegger indeed notes that "'logic' is only *one* interpretation of the essence of thought, an interpretation that precisely rests, as the word already indicates, on the experience of being reached in Greek thought" – which means that logic cannot govern a thought "which finds its source in the experience of the *truth* of being" and thereby exposes the limitation of the Greek thought of being (GA9, 308/235, my emphasis). What is questioned here is precisely the unquestioned supremacy of logic throughout the history of Western philosophy. However, as an element of the phenomenological method, destruction cannot be separated from the two other elements, reduction and construction. For this very reason, the destruction of traditional logic entails both tracing logic back to its foundation (i.e., *logos* in its original sense) and constructing a true philosophical logic.[3] The more original questioning into whose "turbulence" the idea of logic dissolves is that of the meaning of being, albeit no longer merely its *categorial* meaning, which determines it according to the *logos* qua proposition, but above all its *temporal* meaning, which alone makes it possible to think of being as unconcealment and bring out a meaning of *logos* different from the restricted meaning of the *apophantikos logos*. Such a questioning involves what can be called the *Destruktion* of traditional logic, that is to say, the "critical deconstruction" (*kritischer Abbau*) of the fundamental

---

[3] In his 1925–26 lecture course (§3) Heidegger opposes traditional school-logic and philosophizing logic (*traditionelle Schullogik und philosophierende Logik*), a rejection signifying nothing other than the movement toward the philosophical appropriation of its genuine philosophical content.

theses on which the domination of logic over Western thought as a whole is founded (GA24, 31), namely:

1. A thesis concerning truth: The place of truth is judgment.
2. A thesis concerning being: Being has no other meaning than that of the copula.
3. A thesis concerning negation and nothingness.
4. A thesis concerning language: The propositional statement constitutes the essence of language.

Heidegger devoted a large part of his Marburg courses and conferences and the beginning of the second Freiburg period to this work of deconstruction and foundation of a philosophical logic. The period in question stretches from the course *Logic: The Question of Truth* in the winter semester 1925–26 to the famous course *Logic as the Question Concerning the Essence of Language* in the summer semester of 1934 (GA38). Heidegger himself notes that the latter course constituted for him a decisive moment, that of the transformation of logic into the question of the *Wesen der Sprache*, the unfolding of the being of language (GA8, 158; GA12, 89). This clarification makes it possible to understand that the *Destruktion* of logic is a task that remains essentially centered on a certain conception of discourse and language, the same one that one finds in *Being and Time*, namely, a conception that sees in language (*Sprache*) a set of words (*Wortganzheit*) and the oral exteriorization of speech (*Hinausgesprochenheit der Rede*) (SZ 161).[4]

From the moment when language is no longer identified with the totality of words and sounds but understood from its *Wesen*, that is to say not from its *essentia* but according to the meaning of the old verb *wesen*, as the advent of the clearing of being,[5] there can no longer be any question of bringing logic back to fundamental ontology, that is to say, of "making clear that the 'logic' of *logos is* rooted in the existential analytics of *Dasein*" (SZ 160, emphasis added). The task is to move beyond thinking merely about this derived mode of the *logos* that is the *apophantikos logos* and to exhibit its hermeneutic-existential "foundation" by asking the question of

---

[4] Heidegger distinguishes here in a clear manner discourse (*Rede*) and speaking (*Sprechen*). But he is still following the distinction made by Husserl between signification and expression, as shown by the commentary he added later to the passage in which he had said that significations "found the possible being of words and language": "Untrue. Language is not superimposed [*aufgestockt*], but *is* the primordial essence of truth as there [*Da*]" (GA2, 88 note c).
[5] GA9, 326: "Language is the clearing-concealing advent of Being itself."

the being of *logos*, the "initial" being of the derived *logos*. It will therefore no longer be a question of a deconstruction of logic understood as a return to its initial foundations in order to reveal the metaphysical origin of logic, but rather of seeing in it only the invention not of philosophers, but of school teachers (GA40, 129) and the result of the technical interpretation of thought that signifies its decline, now reduced to having only an instrumental value, which is somehow confirmed by the traditional definitions of logic as *organon* or *canon* (GA9, 314–315/240–241). One can however consider that the "destruction" of logic to which Heidegger proceeds in his courses and conferences between 1925 and 1930 is a task that prepares for the "turning point" of the mid-1930s, since it clearly highlights, with regard to truth, being, nothingness, and language, the derived character of their traditional determination. We could thus show that the domination of logic over Western thought and the primacy over philosophy itself that has been traditionally accorded to it as an *organon* are founded on the fundamental theses on which the Heideggerian critical deconstruction systematically starts working in the Marburg and Freiburg courses.

6.1   Criticism of Logic's Thesis Concerning Truth

The criticism of the traditional thesis of truth is deployed in particular in the course of 1925–26 entitled *Logic, The Question of Truth*, in the form of a critical discussion of the Husserlian theory of truth to which a whole long "Preliminary consideration" (almost 100 pages) is devoted. It is in Heidegger's last seminar, the 1973 Zähringen seminar, that we find summed up in a concise formula what Heidegger considers as the fundamental contribution of Husserl's *Logical Investigations*: "With his analyses of categorial intuition, Husserl freed being from its attachment to judgment" (GA15, 377). In the 1925 summer semester course *Prolegomena to the History of the Concept of Time* (the "preparatory part" of which, with the title "Meaning and task of phenomenological research," covers more than 170 pages), we already find a similar remark: "Phenomenology breaks with the limitation of the concept of truth to acts of connection, to judgments ... It returns, without having an express awareness of it, to the breadth of the concept of truth which enabled the Greeks – Aristotle – to also call 'true' both perception as such and the simple fact of perceiving something" (GA20, 73). It is this broader concept of truth that can be found in the *Sixth Logical Investigation* at the level of categorial intuition, which attests that being is not a simple concept, a pure abstraction – it is not a real predicate, as Kant already said – but that it is *given* in an intuition of a special nature, analogous to the sensitive intuition that is the basis of the perception of the phenomenal world.

Yet in the *Prolegomena of Pure Logic*, Husserl refers to another concept of truth, that of truth in the sense of validity (*Geltung*). In his 1925–26 course, Heidegger shows that the origin of this concept of truth in the sense of validity, which will even take the sense of value (*Wert*) in Rickert and in the Baden school, is to be sought in Hermann Lotze's *Logic*, which identifies the propositional statement, as far as it is valid, with truth itself (GA21, 82f). Lotze's conception of validity therefore represents the culmination of the traditional thesis that judgment is the place of truth. Husserl adopts this definition of truth, truth as propositional truth (*Satzwahrheit*) or as the truth of *logos* (*Logoswahrheit*), in order to fight against psychologism, which does not distinguish between the act and the content of judgment, that is to say, between reality and ideality, and thus ruins the very foundation of the idea of truth. For Lotze himself, the proposition is not the result of a psychic act, but a form of actuality (*Wirklichkeit*) that cannot be produced by consciousness, but only recognized, affirmed (*bejaht*) by it. This is the reason why he identifies the proposition with the Platonic *idea* and attributes a timeless character to it. Husserl therefore adopted the Lotzean theory of validity in order to preserve the timelessness of truth from psychologism's relativism.

However, in order to understand the real objective pursued by Husserl, we must not stop at the *Prolegomena* but go as far as the *Sixth Logical Investigation*. Because there it becomes clear that Husserl's main problem is not so much that of the distinction between reality and ideality as that of their correlation. How can the actual act of judging have as correlate the ideal content of the judgment? It is the notion of intentionality that constitutes the answer to this question: It means that each psychic act is in itself linked to something actual (*wirklich*) in the sense that Lotze gives this term; in Husserlian terms, this means that the real psychic act is in itself linked to the ideal content of the act. Furthermore, it is always possible to experience the identity of the intention and its object; Husserl called this act of identification "obvious." It is here, in the *Sixth Logical Investigation*, that we find the true phenomenological concept of truth: not truth in the sense of validity, but truth in the sense of the identity of intention and intuition, which Heidegger designates in the 1925–26 course as the truth of intuition (*Anschauungswahrheit*) or also as the truth of *nous* (*Nouswahrheit*), because the Greek term *nous* is able to account for the broad sense of the Husserlian intuition that includes categorial intuition alongside sensible intuition.

The question obviously remains why we find two concepts of truth in the *Logical Investigations* and how they are articulated with respect to each other. How then is it possible to "locate" truth either in the proposition or in intuition? The proposition explains or articulates intuition. Being thus an expression of intuition, it can be repeated without the "lively" presence of the object in question. It therefore constitutes an "empty" representation (*ein Leervorstellen*) and, as such, it is identical to one of the members of the identity relation that constitutes intuitive truth. The proposition can therefore only be said to be true because it is part of a more original truth. The terms of the problem are thus radically transformed. For Lotze, the proposition is true because it is "valid" and therefore grants real things their validity and their truth. For Husserl, the proposition is "valid" because it can be legitimized by things themselves as possible objects of intuition. Heidegger has thus shown that in Husserl, it is intuitive truth that serves as the foundation for propositional truth, unlike what happens in Lotze, who bases intuitive truth on propositional validity. For Husserl the proposition can be said to be "valid" as the expression of intuition only as an empty representation of the intended object that can be legitimized at any time by the effective presence of the object.

Husserl's merit in the *Logical Investigations* consists in having renewed the truth of the *logos* for *us* and in having thus, through his expanded concept of intuition, contributed to shaking the foundation of traditional logic, that is, the localization of the truth in the propositional statement alone. This is why he somehow is in accordance with Aristotle, who in *Metaphysics* Theta (1051b24) defines the truth concerning noncomposed beings (*asuntheta*) as the simple act of touching and expressing (*thigein kai phanai*). Aristotle here takes into account what Heidegger calls the prepredicative level of truth and falsehood, which implies that being is no longer considered as the object of a logical determination and therefore that the *logos*, as judgment, no longer constitutes the guide for the ontological inquiry. In this passage, however, Heidegger sees Aristotle going even further than Husserl himself with categorial intuition, because in opposition to the entire Western tradition, he determines truth no longer as a character of *logos*, but as a character of being itself.

Heidegger thus broke decisively with the usual interpretation of Aristotle's thought, which saw in him the author of two well-known theses: first, the proposition is the place of truth, and secondly, truth is the adequacy of thought and being. To refute the first of these theses, Heidegger emphasizes the true meaning of *apophansis*, which means letting beings show themselves, which implies that the proposition as *apophantikos logos* must be understood on the basis of the originating dimension of a discovery of being that alone can give it its truth. If the proposition is thus only the expression of what has already been discovered at the more original level of the openness to the world of *Dasein*, it can no longer be understood as the condition of possibility of truth, but on the contrary must be understood as itself made possible on the basis of a more original truth. We thus arrive at a veritable reversal of the traditional priority, a reversal that Heidegger expresses by this lapidary formula: "The proposition is not the place of truth, but truth is the place of the proposition" (GA21, 135).

6.2   Critique of Logic's Thesis Concerning Being

Such a critique of propositional truth already includes in itself the criticism of logic's thesis on being, which defines being solely in terms of the copula. Heidegger engages in the discussion of this thesis in the 1927 course *Basic Problems of Phenomenology*. The entire first part of this course is devoted to the examination of four traditional theses on being that have been formulated during the history of Western philosophy. The most general thesis – the only one, among the four that are analyzed, that cannot be referred to a determined period of history – is the "logic thesis": the definition of being as copula. Here we are confronted with the extreme form of the oblivion of being by which it has been possible to relegate to the domain of logic a fundamental problem of philosophy. The fact that logic took on the appearance of a separate science has had the effect of interrupting the *gigantomakhia peri tès ousia*, this fight of giants over being that is discussed in *Sophist* 244a, and thereby of setting aside the project of a science of being (SZ 1). Insofar as it is identified with the copula, that is to say with a simple sign of connection, being is exposed to the danger of being considered only as a simple *flatus vocis*, a simple meaningless sound. But if the project of a science of being is not absurd, it means that the little word "is" must find again its enigmatic character and the plurality of its meanings. It is from this perspective that Heidegger examines a certain number of conceptions concerning the meaning attributed to the copula. Given the importance that Heidegger will subsequently accord to the *Logical Investigations* in the genesis of his own question, namely, the question of the meaning of being, we are a little surprised to find no reference in this course to Husserl himself, who expressly confronted the problem of the meaning of the copula in the *Sixth Logical Investigation* (see Dastur 2003).

The goal that Heidegger pursues is indeed to show that any investigation concerning the meaning to be given to the copula cannot lead to seeing in it only a pure sign or a pure sound, but on the contrary implicitly gives an ontological meaning to the little word "is." It must however first be explained that Aristotle is in no way responsible for the determination of the copula as a simple sign. Rather, it has for him the meaning of a co-signifier (*prossemainei*), which implies that the copula has no meaning in itself, no independent signification, but only in relation to something else, that is, in a synthesis, which is not the case for the other elements of the *logos apophantikos*, the nouns and verbs (*onomata* and *rhèmata*) (GA24, 256f). In addition, because the "is" cannot have the meaning of a given being, of something on hand (*Vorhandenes*), it is only in thought (*en dianoia*) and the synthesis that it expresses is a synthesis in thought only (*sunthesis noèmaton*). The interpretation of "is" as *ens rationis* gives it precisely an enigmatic character that is not present in pure nominalism. The ensuing discussion of Hobbes's nominalism aims to show that extreme nominalism cannot be sustained. Even Hobbes, who sees in the proposition a simple gathering of words, cannot be satisfied with the determination of the copula as a simple sign. The copula is certainly a *signum*, but not in the sense that only a phonetic function would be recognized in it: It gives an indication of the reason (*causa*) that causes two names to be joined in a proposition. But this reason cannot be discovered at the level of simple language, which implies that there is a relationship between names and things, a meaning of names in relation to the quiddity of what they name. The meaning of the copula in Hobbes's extreme nominalism is therefore nevertheless an ontological meaning: Being here also means *essentia* (GA24, 260–273).

But this is not the only meaning that can be given to the copula. The discussion of two other conceptions, those of John Stuart Mill and Lotze, which cannot be explained in detail here, show in a similar way that the copula can have the two other ontological meanings of *existentia* in the case of Mill and of truth in the case of Lotze. What the examination of the thesis of logic on being as copula discovers is therefore its *enigmatic* character, because the plurality of its possible ontological meanings cannot appear on the level of language alone. What Heidegger calls the "indifference" – in the sense of plurivocity (*Vieldeutigkeit*) – of the meaning of the copula comes in fact from the subordinate nature of the statement (GA24, 300). It is therefore fundamentally wrong to seek its meaning at the level of the signitive and vocal complex, since as Heidegger already says in *Being and Time*, there are not word-things to which we add meanings, but on the contrary words themselves arise from meanings (SZ 161).

Here again we find the same traditional thought process that consists in taking a derivative element as the starting point for reflection, here a sequence of words. But it is impossible, starting from the given presence of the *logos* in the complex of words that constitutes the utterance, to find a path that leads to meanings. Rather, we have to go in the opposite direction and see words emerge from the meanings, which can never be taken as independent beings. This is the reason why a language can never be identified with the whole of a lexicon. It does not have the character of a given presence, what Heidegger calls *Vorhandenheit*, but the historical character of existence (GA24, 296). Language, or more precisely speech (*Sprache*), must be understood from discourse (*Rede*) because discourse is a behavior of *Dasein* in which it expresses its own being-in-the-world.[6] The emission of words is only the expression of an understanding of the being that originally takes place at the level of factual existence. This explains why the proposition cannot by itself have discovering power and that its enunciation presupposes the previously discovered being of the things of which it speaks. We can therefore understand why the meaning of the copula remains indeterminate: It is simply because its meaning has already been previously determined in the factual understanding *before* the enunciation of the judgment. The "indifference" of the copula is not a lack of meaning that should encourage us to see in the little word "is" only a pure *flatus vocis*, but an effect of the subordinate nature of the judgment compared to the factual understanding that articulates beings in accordance with their ontological modalities (GA24, 301).

Furthermore, the copula is not only related to modal differences of being, such as *essentia, existentia*, given presence, and so on, but, because the statement does not relate only to beings in general but to beings in their unveiling, the copula has also the meaning of unveiling, that is, being itself. The critical discussion of the status of "is" thus brings us back to the ontological question, that is to say, to the complexity of the idea of being that cannot find its expression at the level of language alone, and this is why it cannot be reduced to the merely phonetic or even logical function of the copula. Reviving the *gigantomachia peri tès ousias* therefore means nothing other than breaking with the status traditionally attributed to being, that of the copula of judgment.

---

[6] See GA21, 134: "The fundamental movement: not from speech to discourse, but from discourse to speech."

6.3   Critique of Logic's Thesis Concerning Nothingness

If, as we are right to think, at least as regards the problematic before the "turn" of the 1930s, the ontological difference is indeed the fundamental notion of Heidegger's thought, we must then recognize the vital importance of the phenomenon of negation for the definition of Being (*Sein*) insofar it is precisely not a being (*ein Seiendes*). Besides, in the foreword to the 1949 edition of *On the Essence of Ground* (the essay dedicated to Husserl in 1929), Heidegger himself explicitly declares that "nothingness [*das Nichts*] is the not [*das Nicht*] of being and thus Being [*Sein*] experienced from being [*Seiendes*]" and that "the ontological difference is the not [*das Nicht*] between Being and being" (GA9, 123/97). We know that it was during this same year, 1929, that in the inaugural course that marked his accession to the chair from which Husserl was retiring, Heidegger pronounced, in relation to negation, nothingness, and logic, a certain number of statements that would be considered by logicians, in particular by those of the Vienna Circle, as a violent attack on logic. Everyone knows that three years later Rudolf Carnap published a response consisting in showing the absurdity of Heidegger's remarks on nothingness in his article entitled "Overcoming of Metaphysics through Logical Analysis of Language" (Carnap 1959). The main thesis that Heidegger sets out in this inaugural course consists in asserting that it is nothingness that is the origin of negation and not the reverse, which implies that logical negation is precisely not the source of all negativity and that negativity must be sought in a phenomenon more original than logic itself, which can therefore no longer be considered as the supreme instance of philosophical thought.

What logical positivism in general and Carnap in particular find objectionable in Heidegger's analysis of anguish and nothingness is precisely that it consists in the formulation of syntactically absurd statements. Heidegger, however, had himself foreseen the objection by underlining from the outset the danger that awaits any statement, positive or negative, about nothingness: Can we, he asked, refuse to speak of it without conceding it, but can we ever concede it if we do concede nothing? "Perhaps our confused talk already degenerates into an empty squabble over words," he suggested (GA9, 106/84). A little further on, he does not hesitate to assert that questioning about nothingness "turns what is interrogated into its opposite" and that such a question about the being of nothingness deprives itself of its own object, so that "with regard to nothingness question and answer alike are inherently absurd" (GA9, 107/85). Likewise, in his 1935 course, with regard to the question "Why is there Being in general

and not rather nothing?" he underscores that "whoever speaks of nothingness does not know what he is doing," since he thereby makes something
of it, thereby contradicting himself and derogating from the fundamental rule of *logos*, from logic (GA40, 27f). Heidegger therefore recognizes
in advance that speaking of nothingness goes against the very nature of
thought, which is always thought of something, at least as long as we take
the fundamental rules of logic as criteria. In a sense he anticipates Carnap's
criticism and would no doubt readily admit that any metaphysical utterance is syntactically wrong – and in particular any utterance containing
the term "nothingness," since this word, as a substantive, is only the abbreviation of negation, that is to say, of a simple factor of judgment.

The question, however, is whether the syntactic or propositional point
of view is the only possible point of view and whether we must submit all
words to the logic held up as a "tribunal instituted from all eternity and
forever" (GA40, 28). It remains to be asked whether logic in this sense
is perhaps only the imposition of a measure inappropriate to thought, a
measure, as Heidegger puts it in the *Letter on Humanism*, that sanctions
the technical interpretation of thought whose origins go back to Plato and
Aristotle (GA9, 315) and puts thought in the service of doing and producing. What is therefore contradictory from the syntactic-logical point of
view is not necessarily devoid of all meaning, and the meaning of the "true
discourse on nothingness," which remains always unusual and rebellious
to any popularization (GA40, 29), is certainly not directly accessible and
presupposes precisely the experience of strangeness, the *epokhè* of anguish,
and the abandonment of the familiarity which is that of our usual relationship with the world.

Heidegger, by asserting in the inaugural lecture of 1929 that the sciences
want to know nothing about nothingness, insists on the fact that "the
nothing is at first and for the most part distorted [*verstellt*] with respect
to its originality," and this comes from the fact that "we usually lose ourselves altogether among beings" and "the more we turn towards beings
in our preoccupations, the less we let beings as a whole slip away as such
and the more we turn away from the nothing" (GA9, 116/91–92). What is
thus described is the condition that Heidegger in *Sein und Zeit* calls "falling prey" (*Verfallenheit*), which, it should be emphasized, is always falling
prey to the "world" (*Verfallenheit an die "Welt"*). Heidegger writes "world"
with quotation marks to indicate that here the world is understood as the
totality of beings and not as the world as such, in which he sees precisely
in 1928 a "nothingness," not in the sense of a *nihil negativum*, the simple
and absolutely empty negation of something, but a *nihil originarium*, in

the sense that it is not a being, but a nothingness that is temporalized originally and arises purely and simply in and with the temporalization (GA26, 272). Such a "falling prey," not to be construed as a "fall from a purer and higher primordial condition," characterizes the being near the world of *Dasein*, preoccupied insofar as it is *absorbed* by intramundane tasks so that the movement of transcendence that carries it beyond being is, so to speak, suspended (SZ 176).

For, as Heidegger underlines, "the question of the nothing pervades the whole of metaphysics since at the same time it forces us to face the problem of the origin of negation, that is, ultimately, to face up to the decision concerning the legitimacy of the rule of 'logic' in metaphysics" (GA9, 120). For if philosophy is dominated by the principle of noncontradiction that prohibits any question relating to nothingness, a metaphysical question can longer be asked, and Carnap's project of "going beyond metaphysics" becomes legitimate. If, on the contrary, the negation of logical propositions is linked to a more original dimension that is the true source of all negativity, then traditional "logic" is not the only sort of thinking required and metaphysics is possible. Such is the metaphysics of *Dasein* and finitude, the *re-founding* of which Heidegger, in the same period, projects in his book on Kant. And in this case, as he underlines it in 1935, the question "Why then is there being and not rather nothing?" is the first of all questions (GA40, 3), the one that opens us up to the experience of nothingness, which is therefore not that of a *nihil absolutum*, of an absolute of nothing, but that of Being itself insofar it is *not* a being. Nothingness is not external to being; it "does not remain the indeterminate opposite of Being, but reveals itself as belonging to the Being of beings" (GA9, 120).

It then becomes clear that traditional logic is itself possible only because the human being is originally open to being. What is therefore called into question here is the original character of logic: its claim to regulate all modes of thought and its status as a fundamental science with regard to metaphysics.

6.4   Critique of Logic's Thesis Concerning Language

For the last thesis of logic concerning the status devolved to language, we can take as our reference the 1929–30 course *The Fundamental Concepts of Metaphysics*, which takes up the analysis of the propositional statement that can already be found in the 1925–26 lecture course and in *Being and Time*. This course contains a final, and the most detailed, analysis of the *apophantikos logos* in Aristotle. It is only possible here to characterize very schematically the general line that Heidegger follows in this course, as indeed already in the previous texts: that of a retrocession from the propositional statement to the dimension where the as-structure (*Als-Struktur*) that characterizes it finds its origin (GA29/30, 416). Heidegger insists on the fact that the problem of the proposition is not a special problem, reserved either for logicians or for philologists, but that on the contrary it refers to the experience of daily discourse, from which the "normal" form of the statement comes, namely, the predicative form. This is therefore to be compared with the level of daily existence, a level where beings are considered to be purely subsisting (*vorhanden*).

It is because everyday speech is the preponderant form of discourse that it is determining not only for the philosophical theory of discourse, that is, logic, but also for the general theory of language in the form of grammar. To free grammar from logic – a task that Heidegger explicitly proposes in *Being and Time* (SZ 165) – it is necessary to have access to the dimension on which the as-structure is based – the ground (*Grund*) of *logos* – and this implies the still transcendental style of Heidegger's questioning in this course. It is indeed always a question of seeing in discourse as a statement "the fundamental primordiality and scope of an existential" and thus to give to the science of language "an ontologically more primordial foundation" (SZ 165). It is therefore at the level of the structures of human existence, in *Dasein* itself, that we must seek the foundation of the *logos*.

But, in the 1929–30 course, a theme emerges – that of the human being as *weltbildend*, as configuring the world – which must be connected with the essential role that Heidegger attributes in his interpretation of the *Critique of Pure Reason* to imagination as a power of ontological configuration. What is thus refused to the animal, "poor in world," is this power of schematization that is rooted in imagination understood as *exhibitio originaria*, the originary presentation of the object (GA25, 417), which is itself made possible only by the project of that finite being that is *Dasein*. In this regard, it should be remembered that this analysis takes place in a course devoted to the three fundamental questions of metaphysics: world, finitude, and solitude. It is precisely to the question of finitude that Heidegger attributes the median role of the original and unifying root of the other two, because it expresses the brokenness (*Gebrochenheit*) of *Dasein*, which is both oppressed by the distant world and isolated by what constitutes his solitude, namely, the exceptional and unique character of his *Da-sein* (GA29/30, 253). Heidegger says in *Kant and the Problem of Metaphysics* that this finitude of *Dasein* in the human being is more original than the human being, because it is thanks to it that

Being can become manifest as such (GA3, 229). It is by this inclusion in nature that places it *in the midst* of beings and *devotes it* fundamentally to them that *Dasein* can "understand" (*verstehen*) them, that is to say, make them stand up and bring them to standing (*ver-stehen*),[7] take them for true (*wahr-nehmen*), perceive them *as such*[8] and so *let* them be what they are, which implies that the horizon of their possible encounter has always been already projected. During this period when Heidegger is still trying to bring to its completion the problematic developed in *Being and Time*, the human being is therefore essentially understood on the basis of the notion of *Bildung*, which means indissolubly in German at the same time the capacity to give form and configure, and the formation of the human being in the sense of education and culture. It is therefore in this capacity to give form that the difference between the human being and the animal resides.

Heidegger then has to think of the phenomenon of language from this essence of the human being, starting from what Aristotle teaches us about the *apophantikos logos,* namely, that it is this particular species of *logos* that can be true or false. Heidegger emphasizes the fact that it is essential to take into account not only the "normal" propositional form, the true affirmative proposition, but also the other possible forms of propositions, the true negative proposition and the false affirmative and negative propositions, because it then becomes clear that the essence of logos lies in the possibility of either truth or falsehood. The mode of being of the *logos* is therefore not of the order of a given presence (*Vorhandenheit*) and the *logos* does not consist of a purely subsisting set of word-things, but it lies only in the possibility that the human being has to refer to beings as such, as opposed to the animal's way of being "taken up" in numbness (*Benommenheit*) by its environment. Truth and falsity as characters belonging to the proposition in fact find their foundation in a behavior of *Dasein* by which it is possible for it to discover or to conceal beings. What constitutes the essence and the foundation of language is therefore not the predicative structure of the proposition, but something more original: the pre-logical opening to being. What is new in the 1929–30 course in relation to *Being and Time* and anticipates what is found in *On the Essence of Truth* (whose first

---

[7] *Verstehen* derives from *stehen* and therefore belongs to a semantic area different from that of the Latin *intelligere.* Heidegger himself links this term with the Greek word *epistemè*, whose primary meaning is that of standing and remaining *(istèmi)* close to *(epi)* being.

[8] See GA 29/30, 376, where Heidegger states that, although the animal can see, it can never perceive *(vernehmen)* something as such.

version also dates from 1930) is the indication of a connection between truth and freedom. This is because being able to discover or conceal beings means for *Dasein* a being-free (*Freisein*) for beings. The foundation that makes the statement possible is then nothing other than freedom itself: "In short," Heidegger declares, "the *apophantikos logos* as a statement is only possible where there is freedom" (GA29/30, 492).

As noted earlier, Heidegger teaches us in *The Fundamental Problems of Phenomenology* that, as an element of the phenomenological method, destruction is inseparable from the method's other two elements: reduction and construction. The destruction of traditional logic therefore implies the reduction of the *apophantikos logos,* that is to say, the process of leading it back to the foundation that makes it possible – a task that Heidegger, it seems, ventures to accomplish in the 1929–30 course. But what about the project of constructing a logic other than Scholastic logic – a *philosophier-ende Logic,* as the 1925–26 course puts it – which would consist in bringing the logical back to the philosophical? The *logos* of this new logic could no longer take the predicative structure as normative in the way that Hegel, for example, continues to regard it in his dialectical logic, the last and most powerful attempt to subject being to reason's imperatives. To be sure, by making room for contradiction in the form of the speculative proposition in which subject and predicate exchange their positions, Hegel's dialecti-cal thinking seems to operate beyond traditional logic's constraints. Yet far from being destroyed, the general predicative structure remains intact dur-ing the whole dialectical process. Precisely in this sense, then, logic reaches its supreme significance in Hegel's thought, a conclusion underscored by Heidegger in the late 1930s as follows: "'Logic'; metaphysics thus receives this name there where it reaches *full* (the greatest possible) *awareness of itself*: in *Hegel*" (GA9, 253).

In order to construct this new logic, however, is it enough to question the foundation of the predicative proposition and to see in *logos* an existen-tial? Is it not necessary, on the contrary, to detect in language something other than *Dasein's* comportment – that is, to see in it an inherent dimen-sion of being itself? Considerations such as these, it seems, lead Heidegger from 1934 to question the being – in the verbal sense of *Wesen* – of lan-guage. Far from enjoying a normative status in relation to being, the *logos* of the Heideggerian "logic" must proceed from being itself. We can gather that Heidegger is suggesting as much when, in the final lines of the *Letter on Humanism,* he projects what thinking in the future (thinking that is no longer philosophy) should be:

Thinking descends into poverty of its provisional essence. Thinking gathers language into simple saying. In this way language is the language of being, as clouds are the clouds of the sky. With its saying, thinking lays inconspicuous furrows in language. They are still more inconspicuous than the furrows that the farmer, slow of step, draws through the field. (GA9, 364)

Such a *logos* does not do violence to being and so it is not party to the conceptual dimension that would determine what is and what is said. It stands instead on the side of the Parmenidean tautology and what Goethe called a "pure remark" (*reine Bemerkung*). It does so because tautology, like a pure remark, has the capacity to reveal what is most unapparent in being, what Heidegger, translating Parmenides in his last seminar (1973), calls "the presencing presence" (*das Anwesend-Anwesen*). Herein lies what Heidegger was trying to say toward the end of that final seminar: "Tautology is the only possibility of thinking what dialectic can only cover over" (GA15, 400).

PART III

Paradox, the Prospects for Ontology, and Beyond

CHAPTER 7

Heidegger, Being, and All That Is and Is So
On Paradoxes, and Questions, of Being

Denis McManus

In recent years, a number of readings of Heidegger's reflections on the "question of being" have emerged that place at its heart what has come to be called a "paradox of being." We find these readings in work by Filippo Casati, Adrian Moore, Graham Priest, and Ed Witherspoon, though earlier work by Daniel Dahlstrom traces related themes. I discuss all of these commentators below, but my principal focus is the interpretations that Casati and Priest offer. They compare the paradox that they identify with others in the history of philosophy, paradoxes that, they argue, call for a radical change in our understanding of logic: in particular, the embracing of dialetheism, the view "that some contradictions are true" (Priest 2014a, xviii). In light of these readings, Priest argues not only that Heidegger should have embraced this too, but also that dialetheism makes available an *answer* to the "question of being," one invisible to Heidegger in his lingering "*horror contradictionis*" (Priest 2014a, 15).

In what follows, I present the "paradox of being" that these and the other readings mentioned identify. I consider how one might respond to that paradox, and argue that we have reason to doubt whether it rests on an interpretively and philosophically sound basis. I go on to defend the notion that another paradox of being can, nonetheless, be found in Heidegger's work, one with rather different and perhaps sounder foundations, and one that becomes visible when we consider more closely *which* "question of being" is at stake in Heidegger's work.

Before beginning, a note on *Sein* and *Seiendes*. In translations of his work and in the work of his commentators, one finds "Being" and "being" as renderings of *Sein*. For uniformity's sake, I employ "being" and impose this regimen on the above sources when quoted. (Similarly for "the nothing," where the same issue arises.) Heidegger contrasts *Sein* with *Seiendes*, which commentators render variously as "beings," "entities," and "objects."[1] There are philosophical reasons for favoring particular renderings but I have left this variation in place, as imposing uniformity – I can report, having tried it – only causes more confusion and, in our present context, I believe that we can treat the above terms as synonymous.

7.1 A Paradox of Being

In the opening pages of *Being and Time*, Heidegger tells us:

> In the question which we are to work out, *what is asked about* is being—that which determines entities as entities, that on the basis of which entities are already understood. (SZ 6)[2]

In the dialetheist case for believing that this "working out" leads to paradox, two passages are key:

(I)   Everything we talk about, mean, and are related to is in being in one way or another, as is what and how we ourselves are. Being lies in the fact that something is, and in its being as it is [*im Dass- und Sosein*]; in reality, presence-at-hand [*Vorhandenheit*], subsistence, validity, *Dasein*, and in the "there is" [*es gibt*]. (SZ 6–7)

(II)   The being of beings "is" not itself a being. The first philosophical step in understanding the problem of being consists in avoiding telling the *mython tina diegeisthai*, in not "telling a story," that is, not determining beings as beings by tracing them back in their origins to another being – as if being had the character of a possible being. (SZ 6)

(I) is taken to imply an exclusionary claim of something like this form:

(E) Only a being can be the subject of a proposition

which, when combined with

(BNB) Being is not a being,

derived from (II), entails that there are no propositions about being. As Priest puts it,

[1] On these issues of translation, see Witherspoon (2002, n. 3).
[2] While I follow the present volume's format of referencing, I diverge on occasion from the standard English translations of Heidegger's works.

[I]f being is not a being, it follows that one cannot say anything about it. For to say anything of the form "Being is [so and so]" would be to attribute being to it, and so make it a being, which it is not. (Priest 2001, 240, square brackets in the original)

What is paradoxical about this conclusion is that it – and Heidegger's own work – is full of propositions about being. With (E) and (BNB),

[Heidegger] … has shown that being is such that one cannot say anything about it. Yet it is clear that one can say things about it. [His works] are littered with assertions about being, as even a casual perusal suffices to verify. (Priest 2001, 245)

For the dialetheists, faced with this "paradox of being," Heidegger should "simply accept the fact that is staring him in the face—that he *can* speak of *being* … albeit inconsistently" (Priest 2001, 247). He should "simply accept such a contradiction as true" (Casati 2019, 1011). Priest has argued that this kind of outcome is one to which philosophers have been led repeatedly[3] and – crucially and distinctively – that it is an outcome that we should embrace: "some contradictions are true." To many, this denial of what Aristotle called "the most indisputable of all beliefs" (*Metaphysics* 1011b12–13) is a kind of philosophical madness.[4] But for the dialetheist, "there are criteria for rationality other than consistency, … such as simplicity, problem-solving ability, nonadhocness, [and] fruitfulness," "the combined force" of which, they maintain, "may trump inconsistency" (Priest 1998, 420; cf. Priest 2006a, 123–125). For example, responses to paradoxes such as the Liar that sacrifice all other "rational virtues" for the sake of consistency "are complex," "often have strong ad hoc elements," and "pose just as many problems as they solve," Priest argues; moreover, "it is not clear that, in the last instance, they really solve the problem they are supposed to"; and hence, "rationality speaks very strongly in favour of the simple inconsistent theory," the dialetheist acceptance that some contradictions are simply true (Priest 1998, 421).[5]

However, presented with the prospect of "crossing the bridge of inconsistency," many still think it looks pretty rickety, and seek to take "evasive action" (Priest 2014a, 15; Casati and Priest 2018, 280). The next

---

[3] See, in particular, Priest (2001, 2014a).
[4] References to the work of Aristotle are to the translations published in Barnes's *The Complete Works* (Aristotle 1984).
[5] Another key element in dialetheists' response to the belief that their view entails that anything goes is their insistence on paraconsistent logics that specifically deny that "contradictions entail everything" – "*ex contradictione quodlibet*" (Priest 1998, 411).

two sections look at two such attempted detours around the above "paradox of being."

7.2 Reactions to the Paradox – I: Appealing to Nonpropositional Understanding

One response is to propose that what the paradox shows is that we must appreciate the nature of being through a species of nonpropositional understanding. For example, Moore has argued on the basis of versions of (BNB) – citing passage (II) – and of (E) – "only beings can be the subject of propositions" – that "[t]he sense-making required to make sense of being is in Heidegger's view non-propositional" (Moore 2012, 483, 480).

In one sense, there is obviously a place for nonpropositional forms of understanding in Heidegger. For example, he depicts our grasp of *zuhanden* entities – paradigmatically, tools (SZ 68) – as a form of "know-how" that is irreducible to propositional knowledge.[6] But Moore's proposal is that nonpropositional understanding might play something *like* the reflective role that philosophy is traditionally seen as playing: The proposal is not that our "pre-ontological understanding" (SZ 13) is nonpropositional – though it might well be – but that ontological understanding might somehow take such a form, or, in some sense, have its place taken by something that does.

Casati and Priest are critical of attempts to deal with the paradox by "making an appeal to some non-literal notion of expression (such as metaphor or analogy)" (Priest 2001, 246), criticizing two maneuvers that might be seen as instantiating the appeal we are discussing,[7] ones that the later Heidegger and Moore himself explore.[8] One is the "technique of writing under erasure," that is, "crossing out the very word 'being' while allowing it to remain visible" (Moore 2012, 483; GA9, 412). Echoing his assessment of "evasions" of the Liar, Priest insists that this practice "does nothing to solve the problem": "Whether one likes it or not, [it] appears to refer to being" – which, by (E), renders it an entity – "or how are we to understand what Heidegger is on about?" (Priest 2001, 245; 2016, 251). A second maneuver is to deploy "poetic language [as] a way of referring to being that

---

[6] For discussion, see McManus (2012), and for criticism, Priest (2015, 289).

[7] What might seem to be a third instance is the proposal that silence plays a part in acknowledging the nature of being. But dialetheist readers seem to have a more ambivalent view of this proposal; for example, contrast Casati and Priest (2018, §3.4) with Casati (2019, 1008; and 2018, 299).

[8] For Priest's assessment of Moore's invocation of nonpropositional sense-making in the broader project that Moore (2012) undertakes, see Priest (2015), and for Moore's reply, Moore (2015b, 369–373).

[does] not imply any reification or objectification of being itself" (Casati and Priest 2018, 293; Moore 2012, 484). Against this, Casati and Priest argue that "for one who appreciates the poetry … being is still an object of intention, and so an object" (2018, n. 50). Just as "Heidegger's own explanation of writing under erasure … refers to the notion of being in the more usual way" (Priest 2001, 245), grasping the *point* of using this "poetic solution" (Casati and Priest 2018, 293) might seem to do the same.

One might place Witherspoon's understanding of Heidegger's predicament here too, not least because it invites similar criticisms. Witherspoon believes that "Heidegger seeks to convey" an "inexpressible insight," an "unstatable doctrine" (2002, 104, 109). This means that he sees him in this effort employing "sentences that appear to have cognitive content" but that, in fact, "fail[] to express anything"; Heidegger cannot "give a positive formulation of the insight" in question but "the discerning reader" will come to grasp it when they come to "see[] the precise way in which the[se] sentence[s] misfire."[9] The sentences Heidegger uses, Witherspoon continues, "do not *say* anything," but they do "*show* something through their breakdown" (2002, 103, 104).

Witherspoon here alludes to a distinction that we find in Wittgenstein's *Tractatus*, and reflection on that book lies in the background of all of the discussions of the paradox of being that we are considering. As Moore puts it, when considering the paradox, "[i]t is impossible not to be reminded of the early Wittgenstein" (2012, 481).[10] Similarly, Casati and Priest's criticisms of "writing under erasure" and the "poetic solution" echo long-standing worries that there is a problematic double-think – an "irresolution," as the *Tractatus* literature now puts it[11] – in the notion of unsayable but showable insights. These worries date back to Frank Ramsey's famous remark that "what we can't say, we can't say, and we can't whistle it either."[12]

Moore and Witherspoon are well aware of these issues. Witherspoon invokes ideas from the "resolute" literature as a basis for *criticism* of the approach that he believes Heidegger adopts.[13] Moore's notion of "non-propositional understanding" emerges partly through efforts aimed

---

[9] See Moore (2012, 492) for a similar-sounding thought.

[10] Cf. Dahlstrom (1994a); Priest (2001, 246–247, ch. 12); and Casati and Priest (2018, 26).

[11] Goldfarb (1997) is normally credited with introducing this terminology.

[12] Quoted in Hacker (2000, 355); Dahlstrom (2001, 456 n. 85). My own discussion of these issues (see McManus 2006) argues that, in Wittgenstein, the notion of "showing" plays a part in a maneuver more akin to the "nonissue" response that I examine briefly below.

[13] See Witherspoon (2002, 111–113), and, for one of his own contributions to that literature, Witherspoon (2000).

precisely at avoiding "irresolution,"[14] but whether he succeeds is a matter too difficult to settle here. More generally, hoping to illuminate the issues with which we are presently concerned by turning to "writing under erasure," the "poetic solution," or the *Tractatus* may well seem an instance of *obscurum per obscurius*. In the last of these cases, for example, it is attempting to explain what we have come to suspect is puzzling in Heidegger by turning to what we have always known is deeply puzzling in Wittgenstein. Hence, echoing again Priest on evading the Liar, these responses to the "paradox of being" may well seem to "pose just as many problems as they solve." Perhaps these are resolvable; but perhaps they are not, so I will move on now to other responses.[15]

7.3   Reactions to the Paradox – II: Questioning Its Premises

Dialetheists distinguish their belief "that *some* contradictions are true" from a "trivialist" belief that *all* are (Priest et al. 2018). Priest himself insists that "if we have views that are inconsistent then we are probably incorrect" and "should go back and examine why we hold such a view" (Priest 1998, 424). Perhaps then, too, the most obvious response to the "paradox of being" is to re-examine its premises, and the present section does so. Questions of exegesis do, of course, differ from questions of justification – the question of what Heidegger said differs from the question of whether he ought to have said it. But if the paradox of being matters – if it is to be more than an instance of some German chap a hundred years ago getting confused – we need grounds for thinking that the premises that lead to it have something going for them; and another response to the paradox then would be to question whether they do, whether (E) and (BNB) are good thoughts to have.

One version of this response proposes, in the spirit of the later Wittgenstein,[16] that the paradox is a pseudo-problem the supposed

---

[14] See, e.g., Moore (2003). For discussion of Moore's reading of the *Tractatus*, see McManus (2015b).

[15] McManus (2013b) identifies another interpretation of the proposal that the kind of understanding that Heidegger seeks to convey might be nonpropositional. But this interpretation rests on a specific understanding of what philosophical confusion and its alleviation are, in light of which Heidegger's writing practices are specifically not envisaged – "irresolutely" – as another way of doing what propositions about being would do if they could but can't. Nor do I envisage this interpretation as resolving the worry over the unity of being that is central to §4. As I argue (McManus 2013a) concerning invocations of a quasi-Wittgensteinian "showing" in this particular connection, showing rather than saying only helps if there *is* something to show, and the worry is that there is not.

[16] "Resolute" readers of the early Wittgenstein would have it that it is his spirit too. For discussion, see McManus (2006).

premises of which include one or more pseudo-propositions. Indeed one could argue that (E), which entails that there are no propositions about being, entails that (BNB) must be a pseudo-proposition. If so, the paradox collapses: One of what appear to be its two premises requires abandonment of the other. A similar concern would be that (E) entails that "the question of being" too cannot be formulated. As Priest himself puts it,

> Never mind answering the question of being; if one cannot refer to being with a noun phrase, one cannot even ask it. ("What is being?") (2016, 251; cf. Casati and Priest 2018, 294)

The above Wittgensteinianism might prompt one to say here that there is then no question; that it had sense was just an illusion and the fact that its supposed answer might turn out to be paradoxical should then come as no great surprise. Not that this is the dialetheist response, of course. That response is: But there is a question! You just asked it! "What is being?" And their response to the paradox is similar: "There is a paradox! You just posed it."

Again there are complex issues at stake here.[17] But here I set aside this way of questioning the paradox's premises – questioning whether they have meaning – to consider instead other, less radical ways. As Priest puts it, "[a] paradox is an argument with premises" and a "solution" to such a paradox "would tell us which premise is false" (Priest 1979, 220). With many of the paradoxes that he has discussed – such as the Liar and Russell's Paradox – the premises seem compelling: they include the truth-schema – "'p' is true iff p" – and the "naïve notion of set" – the "connection between satisfying a condition and being in a set" being "about as simple and natural a conceptual connection as there can be" (Priest 2001, 144, 279). But the situation seems significantly different with the paradox of being: specifically, whether (E) and (BNB) are true – and indeed what they mean – is far less clear.

7.3.1   Questioning (E)

I mentioned in the introduction that the notion that there might be such a thing as a "paradox of being" has a pre-history of sorts in earlier discussions, central to which is Daniel Dahlstrom's proposal that we find in

---

[17] For example, McManus (2014) argues that "the standard tests of meaningfulness" (Priest 2015, 289) to which Priest is apt to turn in arguing that such premises are not meaningless distinguish instead sentences that we might mistakenly be tempted to take as meaningful when they are not from those that would not so tempt us.

Heidegger a "paradox of thematization." Dahlstrom argues (citing, e.g., SZ 158) that Heidegger's remarks on assertions commit him to the view that since assertions presuppose that what is asserted is objectified and on hand (*vorhanden*) in some sense, their use is at least a hindrance to any attempt "to indicate, specify, and communicate" the other forms of being (Dasein, *Zuhandensein*, etc.) that he insists we must acknowledge (Dahlstrom 1994a, 778), and this is a paradoxical outcome in that that is precisely what a work like *Being and Time* appears to aim to do.[18] But this also gives us reason to doubt that Heidegger's account of assertions does indeed have the implications that Dahlstrom claims it does.[19] I have argued elsewhere that it may not,[20] and for reasons that also make clear that what Heidegger precisely means by "the *Vorhanden*" isn't obvious either. I will not rehearse that argument here. Instead I will indicate why (E) raises similar concerns.

With the thought that "to say anything about" something is to "make it a being," Heidegger may seem to be either giving a misleading presentation of what is, in fact, a tautology or making a claim about the expressive powers of our language that is simply false. If "a being" just *means* "that which is the subject of a proposition," then there is nothing troubling in the claim that "say[ing] anything of the form '[x] is [so and so]' would ... make [x] a being." The claim would then just be that saying anything of the form "x is so and so" makes x the subject of a proposition.[21] In that spirit, one might hear passage (I), which inspired (E) above, as principally meant to be *inclusive* rather than exclusive – that "beings" includes not just "medium-sized dry goods" or the entities revealed by the natural sciences, but everything we might find ourselves "talk[ing] about, mean[ing], and [being] related to": events, states of affairs, persons, actions, ways of acting, artifacts, institutions, locations, dates, periods, properties, ways of possessing properties, and so on. Indeed the sentence that precedes (I) stresses this plurality, the need to be inclusive rather than exclusive: "there are many things which we designate as 'being ['*seiend*], and we do so in various senses" (SZ 6).[22] (This reaction also echoes a theme in dialetheist

---

[18] Cf. Cristina Lafont's identification of "Heidegger's self-posed problem of how assertions, the objectifying tools *par excellence*, can be used to thematize the unobjectifiable" (2002, 233).

[19] See, e.g., Heidegger's comments on "assertions in and for a practical function" (GA21, 156 n. 8) that are "wrapped up in concernful understanding," including "accounts of the ready-to-hand" (SZ 158).

[20] See McManus (2012) and, for further discussion, Schear (2007) and Golob (2014).

[21] Cf. Priest (2014a, 15): "[W]e can refer to it, quantify over it, talk about *it*. If this does not make something an object, I am at a loss to know what could."

[22] GA21, 23: "There are automobiles, negroes, Abelian functions, Bach's fugues. 'Are there' truths too? Or how could it be otherwise?"

readings of Heidegger: In reply to the above Wittgensteinian attempt to "dissolve" the paradox – which cited (E) as reason to believe there are no such propositions referring to being, (BNB) included – the dialetheist reader says: "But you can refer to it; you just did!")

So to retain their paradox, it would seem that dialetheist readings need an independent notion of "a being" in play here and to retain a construal of (E) as possessing substantive exclusionary power. Establishing that these needs can be met will not be easily done, certainly if one hopes to do so in what might seem the most natural way, that is, consistently and by uttering propositions of the form "You cannot refer to *x* using a proposition," which will, of course, meet the rejoinder "But you just did." Dialetheist readings do, of course, have good *textual* grounds available to them for claiming that Heidegger believed the above needs can be met in, for example, passages such as that which inspired (BNB). (II) *says* that "[t]he being of beings 'is' not itself a being," a proposition that, with its use of inverted commas, seems to flag its own questionable character, but to do so in expressing what also seems a clearly exclusionary thought: Being is not a being. But then is *that* a good thought to have?

7.3.2   Questioning (BNB)

In his 2016 essay "The Answer to the Question of Being," Priest proposes that Heidegger "takes [(BNB)] to be so obvious that he does not give an argument for it," and that "it is actually hard to find arguments for the claim in the Heideggerian corpus," though "one might essay" some on his behalf. There Priest offers two – "one metaphysical, one grammatical" (2016, 250) – though elsewhere he has offered another, one which turns on Heidegger's puzzling remarks on "the nothing."

The "grammatical" argument is a nod, and not Priest's first in discussing Heidegger, to Frege. Consider the sentence "Heidegger is":

> "Heidegger" refers to an object, a being. If "is" referred to a being then the italicized phrase would simply be a list of two objects: Heidegger and being. But it is clearly not a simple list. In an obvious sense, it has a unity that a pair of objects lacks. (Priest 2016, 250)

The proposition would seem to fall apart unless one or other of the entities referred to is un-object-like: One must be, as Frege puts it, "unsaturated" (Frege 1997 [1892]).

This argument might seem to show too much. "Heidegger walks" and "Heidegger sleeps," for example, aren't mere lists either and therefore, by the above argument, "… walks" and "… sleeps" aren't beings either. Frege might, of course, be happy with this. But walking and sleeping at least might seem to count as beings according to passage (I). "… walks" and "walking" are, of course, different parts of speech. But it does seem to be possible to use both without, one could say, changing the subject. Intuitively, and passing over Frege's debate with Benno Kerry *very* rapidly, it seems to be a resource of languages like English that one can make the subject of a proposition out of what figures in others as predicates.[23]

As Priest notes elsewhere, one might insist instead that really there is "only one item with a predicative function: 'instantiates'" (2014a, 7). But English seems to have the resources to make this, too, the subject of a proposition. In an earlier discussion by Priest of the Fregean connection, we read that "'is' is the generic form of predication" and that "[o]ne cannot, therefore, refer to being, since … to say anything about being one would have to say something of the form 'Being is …'" and so "treat it as an object" (2001, 240). But this invites the response "But you can refer to being! It's the generic form of predication." So, by (E), and *pace* (BNB), being would be an entity after all. This is, of course, a *very* Priestian response, and where we have ended up might seem to be precisely where the dialetheist reader wants us to: Being is a being *and* it is not a being. But let us not forget the stage of the argument that we are at: We are still trying to find a reason to think being is not a being. We are examining the credentials of (BNB).

The remarks of Heidegger's on "the nothing" that have prompted Priest to essay another argument for (BNB)[24] have attracted the attention of many readers, including – infamously – Carnap, but also Moore and Witherspoon in substantiating their cases for a paradox of being.[25] These remarks point to a parallel paradox concerning "the nothing":

> What is the nothing? … In our asking we posit the nothing … as a being. But that is exactly what it is distinguished from. … [So] the question deprives itself of its own object. … With regard to the nothing question and answer are alike inherently absurd. (GA9, 107)

---

[23] Cf. Priest (2001, 245; quoted above) and dialetheist criticism of responses to the paradoxes that deny "plain facts concerning natural language and our thought processes" by, for example, insisting on the use of metalanguages "expressively weaker than English" (Priest et al. 2018, §3.2).

[24] It is unclear whether Priest remains wedded to this argument – which is prominent in Priest (2001), absent from Priest (2016), and then presented again, though rather cautiously, in Casati and Priest (2018, 300) – or to its key claim that "being and nothing are identical," which remarks in *One* (Priest 2014a, 54 n. 17) seem to question.

[25] See Moore (2012, 482–484) and Witherspoon (2002, 100), quoted below.

In Priest's treatment of such remarks, he identifies an argument in support of (BNB) that rests on the premises that "being and nothing are identical" (Priest 2001, 242) and nothing is not an entity. Again, Priest is admirably cautious: "Heidegger's reason for supposing that being and nothing are the same is difficult to discern" (Priest 2001, 243).[26] But our concern here is why we ought to think that nothing is not an entity.

Carnap, of course, thinks it is not because "'nothing' is a quantifier phrase, not a noun phrase" (Priest 2001, 241). But here Priest sides with Heidegger, in that he agrees that "'nothing' can be used as a substantive"; in this sense, "*[n]othing*, then, may indeed be a thing" (Priest 2001, 241). But, in a dialetheic spirit, Priest also believes that Heidegger also believes that it is *not*:

> One cannot ... say anything of *nothing*. To say anything, whether that it is something or other, or just that it is, or even to refer to it at all, is to treat it as an object, which it is not. (Priest 2001, 241)

Priest has plenty of textual evidence upon which to draw for Heidegger holding this latter view. But *our* question is why he – and perhaps we too – *should* hold it, other than by virtue of the nothing being identical with being, as assessing the claim that being is not a being is the concern that brought us here in the first place.

Priest follows up the last of his remarks that we have just quoted with "*[n]othing* is the absence of all objects" (2001, 241; 2014a, 55; and Casati and Priest 2018, 301). As we will see shortly, I think this stress on "*all* objects" points us in the right direction. But given our present concerns, the obvious question that this claim invites is why that absence is not all the same an object. Metaphors of space and its filling, and of backgrounds and foregrounds, are at work here. A spatial object needs a space if it is to appear, a space *in which* to appear; it needs an absence in order to be present. But why not think of such a space as an object? It is not the same *kind* of object as the objects that it lets be present. But why not an object full stop? Similarly, Priest says:

> [A] being is, and can only be, because it is not a nothing. It stands out, as it were, against nothingness. If there were no nothing, there could be no beings either. (Priest 2001, 242; 2014a, 180)

The nothing is then something that necessarily does not "come forward" in order that entities might instead (GA9, 115, quoted at Priest 2001, 243).

---

[26] For textual evidence of this supposition, see Priest (2001, 242 n. 7).

But again, why not think of this backgrounding nothing as a being? It may not be the same *kind* of being as that which shows up against it. But it is not clear why that should mean it is not a being at all.[27] So again, it seems to me, we are some way short of seeing why (BNB) must be the case.

The "metaphysical" argument that Priest essays on Heidegger's behalf is as follows:

> Being is the ground of beings. As such, it is not the kind of thing that can be a being. It can function as the ground only if it, itself, is beyond being, and so not a being. (2016, 250)

As Section 7.5 will explain, there is something important here, but we need to do some work to identify what that is, as it is not – I will argue – crucially to do with grounding.

Casati and Priest have focussed much attention recently on this latter notion and for two good reasons. One is that Heidegger does indeed make remarks to the effect that being grounds beings.[28] The other, taking us back to SZ 6's specification of "being," is that what "determin[ing] entities as entities" means is less than obvious. Other glosses Casati and Priest have used include "[b]eing is what it is that makes beings be" (Casati and Priest 2018, 300) and "[t]he being of something is that in virtue of which it is" (Priest 2016, 255; cf. Casati and Priest 2018, 290 and Casati 2018, 292, quoted in n. 30). But these too are neither transparent nor unproblematic, inviting causal construals, for example, which cannot be correct in light of Heidegger's repeated criticism of previous philosophers for understanding being as something like a first cause, as passage (II) above illustrates. Casati and Priest have thus also turned to the gloss that "[b]eing grounds entities" (Casati 2018, 294). But while

---

[27] Similar concerns apply to Witherspoon's treatment of Heidegger's remarks on the nothing. We find there too a version of (E) – "the topic of questions, assertions, or judgments ... must be an entity" – and an analogue of (BNB) – "Heidegger declares that the nothing is distinct from entities"; when combined with the fact that "he wants to think and talk about the nothing," Heidegger commits himself paradoxically "both to the claim that the nothing is not an object of thought and to the claim that the nothing is an object of thought" (Witherspoon 2002, 100). But – and I suspect this simply reflects the exegetical focus of his discussion – Witherspoon does not give us why we should accept (E) or the above analogue of (BNB). He tells us that the passage in which he presents his version of (E) is informed by "an argument ... based on Heidegger's discussion of assertion in *Being and Time*" (2002, 100 n. 13), but not what the argument is, or why we too should embrace it; and, as we have already noted, the upshot of that discussion is the subject of much debate. Similarly, Witherspoon tells us that "Heidegger *declares* that the nothing is distinct from entities" (2002, 100, my emphasis), but not whether – or why – he (or we) should. As argued above, the paradox will be more interesting – and less of a quirk of the psychology of some chap from Messkirch – the more philosophically well-founded it proves to be.

[28] See, for example, GA9, 172: "being ... *grounds* things in an originary manner."

Heidegger's allusions to the concept of ground are indeed fascinating and certainly call for exploration, I have doubts about whether turning to them helps with our present concerns.

For some who have driven the recent explosion of interest in this concept in analytic philosophy – such as Jonathan Schaffer – grounding is "a natural and intuitive notion" (Schaffer 2009, 375). But others, such as Jessica Wilson, have argued that grounding claims that invoke an abstract, "coarse-grained," "(big-G) 'Grounding'" relation "admit of such underdetermination" that "even basic assessment" of them is impossible; for that, we "cannot avoid appealing to … specific 'small-g' grounding relations" (Wilson 2014, 535, 540; cf. Koslicki 2015). Crucially, moreover, none of those treatments typically discussed in the recent literature – such as "token identity, realization, the classical extensional part-whole relation, the set membership relation, [and] the proper subset relation" (Bliss and Trogdon 2016, §8) – seems to be what Heidegger has in mind.[29]

But, as I have said, the passage in which Priest presents his "metaphysical" argument points us in the right direction. As Section 7.5 will explain, the crux of the matter is that what "determines *all* entities as entities" cannot be an entity. One can translate this claim into the grounding idiom if one likes, and one might read Priest's passage as doing that. But that translation is misleading if it suggests that it is essential to understanding why there is a "paradox of being" that we recognize being's relation to entities as one of grounding. The crux of Priest's passage then will be not that the ground of a being cannot be another being, but rather that the ground

---

[29] There are other candidates, though these too are problematic. For example, turning to the genus–species relation as a relevant "grounding" relation (Koslicki 2015, 316) must contend with Heidegger's insistence that "the 'universality' of 'being' is not that of a *class* or *genus*" (SZ 3) – an insistence that is, in itself, a can of worms (see McManus 2013a) – and the suggestion that being is a determinable realized in different determinates must contend with reasons to think that it is determinates that ground determinables (Rosen 2010, 128). Casati and Priest allude to a grounding relation of particulars in universals: "as the redness of the rose makes the rose red, the being of all entities makes all entities be" (Casati and Priest 2018, 289). But Priest ascribes to Heidegger an Aristotelian conception of being's character as a universal (Priest 2016, 2 n. 5), and elsewhere characterizes such a conception as one according to which universals "have their being in virtue of being said of individual substances" (see Bliss and Priest 2017, 75), which – again – would then suggest instead that beings ground being. Casati (2018)'s lengthy discussion of the being–beings relation as a grounding relation focuses on working out the formal characteristics of that relation in light of the taxonomy of possibilities that Bliss and Priest present, a taxonomy that "abstract[s] away from the *nature* of such dependence relations and focus[es] on *structural features*" (Bliss and Priest 2017, 64); and other discussions of the relation that Casati and Priest present circle back to the already-problematic glosses presented above; for example, "being ontologically grounds all entities – being makes all entities entities" (Casati 2018, 294).

of *all* beings – "*the* ground of beings" – cannot be another being. But *that* then is the notion on which we need to concentrate, as we will below.[30]

Before moving on from this assessment of the foundations on which (BNB) or (E) might be thought to rest, we should note that even if "there is general agreement [among commentators] on the fact that, on Heidegger's view, being is not an entity" (Casati and Wheeler 2016, 487), there are points at which Heidegger himself makes remarks that must serve to question either (BNB) or (E). For example, in the important *Basic Problems of Phenomenology* lectures given immediately following the publication of *Being and Time*, Heidegger claims that the "[t]emporal projection" that the *Being and Time* project seeks "makes possible an objectification of being and ... thereby constitutes ontology in general as a science [*als Wissenschaft*]." It is clear that, in this context, Heidegger understands "objectification" in a Fregean manner: as no more – and no less – than "thematization," being made the subject matter of a body of propositions, a *Wissenschaft*. For example, he talks of "condition[s] of possibility that being should be objectified, that is, thematized [*vergegenständlicht, d. h. thematisiert*]" (GA24, 398).[31]

I do not claim that my discussion here of (E) and (BNB) is decisive. But as Priest consistently notes in connection with the paradox that he identifies, "Heidegger's reasoning is unclear" (Priest 2001, 240), and the considerations that this section presents do seem to give us reason to wonder whether that paradox really does force itself upon Heidegger, or upon us. Nevertheless, I think that there is present in Heidegger's early work something that merits the label a "paradox of being." To see what it is, we must consider just what it is that Heidegger thinks makes being a question.

7.4   What Is Questionable about Being?

Given the failure of his early work to reach the fruition that Heidegger proposed it would in *Being and Time* – a work Herbert Spiegelberg famously described as "a torso" (Spiegelberg 1965, 271) – identifying Heidegger's

---

[30] We do see a concern with "being in general" in Casati's proposals that "every thing is grounded in being" and that "Heidegger's being is the ground of literally everything because being is what makes any entity an entity" (Casati 2018, 306, 292). But this totalizing theme is typically absent from – or at best implicit in – his presentations of his "paradox of being." The same might also be said of Moore's discussions, despite the centrality in his work of the notion that "[m]etaphysics is the most general attempt to make sense of things" (2012, 1), itself included.

[31] Cf. GA29/30, 521: "Not every assertion and opinion is ontological, but only those that speak of [*ausspricht*] entities as such, and with respect to that which makes entities into entities, the 'is'—and that is just what we call the being of entities."

"question of being" is difficult. But I will present here two questions concerning being that are clearly central to the work of his early period.

The first is "[t]he question of the possible *multiplicity of being*" (GA24, 170). Heidegger challenges "the domination of the ontology of the 'substantial,'" under which "entities are ... conceived of as ... Things (*res*) ... [and] substantiality becomes the basic characteristic of being," proposing instead what has become known as an "ontological pluralism."[32] A key inspiration here is Aristotle and his famous proposal that "being is said in many ways" (*Metaphysics* 3.2 1003a33):

> [F]or instance, some things are characterized by the mode of composition of their matter, e.g. the things formed by ... being bound together, e.g. a bundle ... and others by being glued together, e.g. a book; ... and others by position, e.g. a threshold and a lintel (for these differ by being placed in a certain way); and others by time, e.g. dinner and breakfast; and others by place, e.g. the winds; and others by the affections proper to sensible things, e.g. hardness and softness, density and rarity, dryness and wetness. ... Clearly, then, the word 'is' has just as many meanings; a thing is a threshold because it lies in such and such a position, and its being means its lying in that position, while being ice means having been solidified in such and such a way. (Metaphysics 8.2 1042b15–28)

In a similar spirit, Heidegger argues that we must distinguish *Vorhandenheit*, *Zuhandenheit*, and both of these from the mode of being of the world within which entities of those sorts are found, and from that of the entity that encounters them in that world, *Dasein*.

A benefit to note in passing of having these particular ways of being in mind is that Heidegger's being–beings relation, and *some* of the glosses of that specification previously mentioned, take on natural senses. There does seem to be a natural sense, for example, in which it is locatedness that determines a threshold as a threshold – that a threshold is a threshold by virtue of locatedness – and that usability for certain purposes makes a hammer a hammer. (Does usability *ground* hammers? This seems a little less natural, and principally for the reason discussed above: "ground" meaning what?)

But let us turn now to our second question concerning being, one that Heidegger claims that he found "concealed" in Aristotle's "being is said in many ways" (GA11, 145; Heidegger 1963; GA14, 93). Our first question – that "of the possible *multiplicity of being*" – raises "at the same time" an "urgent" question "of the *unity of the concept of being in general*" (GA24, 170), "urgent" because the very possibility of ontology seems to depend on

---

[32] See, for example, Turner (2010).

there being such a unity. By embracing ontological pluralism, one might seem to dispense with any such worry over unity; but one does not: It remains "concealed" there in that, if there is no "single unifying concept of being in general that would justify calling these different ways of being ways of *being*" (GA24, 250), then whatever distinctions such a pluralism may mark, one will not be entitled to label them "*ontological* distinctions." For example, in distinguishing the *Zuhanden*, the *Vorhanden*, and Dasein, one distinguishes – roughly speaking – something's being usable for some purpose, something's occupying a certain space, and something's understanding a world around it. But are these variations on a single "achievement" – "existence," "being"? To use Aristotle's examples, are "lying in such and such a position" and "having been solidified"? If not, ontology – the "science … [that] stud[ies] all things that are, *qua* being" (*Metaphysics* 3.2 1003b15–16) – would seem to lack a topic, a subject matter.[33] The worry is that the science we believe we have in mind when we talk of "ontology" is an illusion, conjured up by our use of a single term, "being," for a deeply heterogeneous collection of phenomena – usability, occupying a certain space, understanding, and so on. Such a science would belong with the science of locks – a lock-ology that would seek the unifying principles governing small quantities of hair, some door fastenings, and systems of gates and sluices used to change a canal's water level – and a bank-ology that would explore the deep underlying unity of financial institutions and riversides.

Heidegger sees at stake then, in his search for a "horizon" for "being in general," "the possibility … of ontology as such" (GA24, 324) – pluralistic or otherwise. One does hear it said that "Heidegger *assumes*" that, although "[b]eing takes various forms … all the varieties of being cohere," "so that we can ask what it means to be in general" (Polt 2005, 2, my emphasis). But Heidegger would respond that all ontologists – all who consider being, and believe ontology possible – make this assumption; and what is distinctive about his project is not that he makes this assumption, but that he recognizes the need to justify it and tries to do so.[34] As Steve Crowell observes, an appreciation of the need for pluralism about the basic ontological categories was not unique to Heidegger but was "shared by many

---

[33] Heidegger is not alone in seeing this dialectic in Aristotle, nor in his assessment of its metaphilosophical importance. See G. E. L. Owen's reading of Aristotle (McManus 2013a, §3).

[34] A solution to these difficulties sometimes ascribed to Aristotle is that "[t]he primary sense" of "being" "is that in which substances … exist," that other "ways of being" are derivative, in that the notion of substance "reappear[s] as a common element in our analyses of the existence of non-substances such as colours or times or sizes" (Owen 1986, 217; *Metaphysics* 3.2 1003b5–18). But for Heidegger, this is precisely "the domination of the ontology of the 'substantial'" at work.

philosophers at the turn of the century" (2001, 80). But what Heidegger believed such philosophers did not share was an appreciation of the need – "concealed" within such pluralism – for an account of the topic on which such pluralism is a view, of what makes these categories *ontological*, unified in indicating different ways of *being*.

The key reason I raise here Heidegger's pursuit of a "horizon" for "being in general" is, however, that that pursuit leads to paradox, or so I will argue. The paradox in question, which I have sketched in earlier work (McManus 2013a), rests on premises that are less contentious both interpretively and philosophically than those presupposed by the paradox that Casati, Moore, Priest, and Witherspoon offer. Indeed, as we will see, it also gives us an account of why a rather particular version of (BNB), a premise for which these commentators have struggled to account, does indeed force itself upon us. In addition, this second paradox is – to my mind – deeper than the first in concerning not the expressibility of being, but whether there is anything there to be expressed.

7.5 A Second "Paradox of Being"

The "horizon" for "being in general" that Heidegger seeks and that he believes every ontologist must assume can be found is one against which all that is will show up, all modes of existence and all entities that realize them. But that leaves an awkward outstanding issue: the being of that horizon itself. The worry is not "How ought we to characterize the horizon?" nor "*Can* we characterize – describe or express – it propositionally?" Rather it is "Can we make sense of it being thus-and-so at all?"

If we want to claim that we can, then it would seem to be necessary for this horizon to possess a mode of being, too. But in that case, it does not seem to fit its "job description": It was to have been the horizon against which all modes of being were – as Heidegger puts it – to be "projected." But now it appears that they, along with its mode of being, must be projected against a yet-further horizon, which might make a stronger claim to be the horizon that Heidegger seeks – until, that is, it is recognized that its being (or lack thereof) raises the very same issue.

One might worry that this paradox relies heavily on Heidegger's use of the metaphor of "horizons" and that, paralleling worries that Section 7.3 raised, we face it only if we adhere to a metaphor we really need not (McManus 2013a, n. 82). But we can reformulate our paradox – or one that is at

least very closely related – without such reliance. The first premise we need is
the minimal specification of "being" with which Section 7.1 began:

(1) Being is that which determines entities as entities.

The second is:

(2) The relation, "determining entities as entities," is irreflexive.

Can we help ourselves to this second premise, when – as I argued earlier –
what it is for something to "determine an entity as an entity" is less than
transparent? Certainly, the notion that an entity might perform such a
feat for itself is unintuitive – to imagine that a tree, for example, might
"determine" itself as a tree; and while a rock might *illustrate* what it is to
be a rock, it is difficult to envisage what it would be for a rock to determine
what it is for it to be a rock. So much for ordinary entities like trees and
rocks, one might object, but mightn't an extraordinary entity – though
an entity all the same – achieve this feat? God, for example?[35] It is hard to
argue against such a proposal, but surely in part because the invocation
of God here plays a role not dissimilar to that which Wittgenstein saw
"the mental" as playing in accounts of "meaning or thinking as a peculiar
mental activity": "the word 'mental' indicat[es] that we mustn't expect to
understand how these things work" (Wittgenstein 1969, 39).

If one is tempted to suggest that reading being's "determining entities as
entities" as being's "grounding entities" might help settle the truth of (2), then
unfortunately the doubts I expressed above about the value of such a gloss resur-
face here. Grounding is standardly taken to be an irreflexive relation (Schaffer
2009, 376). So, to that extent, the gloss might perhaps provide a degree of
support for (2). But Wilson, for example, argues that some grounding claims
can be reflexive (2014, 570–575). The examples she considers – identity claims
and logical analyses – do not seem to be what Heidegger has in mind. But
what that shows is that insisting that (1) does indeed capture a grounding relation will only get us closer to settling whether (2) is true if we can also identify
which more specific – "small-g" – grounding relation Heidegger *does* have in
mind. If all we can ascribe to him is a "course-grained" notion of grounding,
then (2) will be another grounding claim that, to echo Wilson again, "admits
of such underdetermination" that assessment of it will be impossible.

With these uncertainties acknowledged, I will rely hereafter on (1) – as
every reader of Heidegger must – and (2) – not least on the basis of the

---

[35] In a discussion of ontological dependence, Bliss and Priest observe that "God, for Leibniz, depended
on Himself" (Bliss and Priest 2017, 77; Priest 2001, 39).

ad hominem consideration that (BNB), which is a commitment of the versions of the paradox that I wish to challenge, seems itself to entail such irreflexivity.[36]

What we certainly do not have yet, however, is reason to think that what "determines an entity as an entity" cannot itself be an entity. To revert to two of our earlier examples of ways of being, usability for some purpose may determine the *Zuhanden* as *Zuhanden* and locatedness may determine thresholds as thresholds. But why should we think that usability and locatedness aren't entities? They obviously aren't *physical* entities; perhaps they are abstract objects; but they certainly do seem to be matters we can thematize and so – by GA24, 398 – objectivize. However, we do have reason to think that things will differ in one particular and special case: that of being *in general*, what "determines *all* entities as entities." Being in general – by (2) – cannot fall within the set of entities that it determines as entities, and that is all the entities that there are. So being – at least when that means being *in general* – is not an entity. We have then a case for thinking (BNB) plausible after all on at least one interpretation or in at least one case, though it is one upon which – according to the argument that Section 7.4 presented – we draw also in contemplating particular ways of being *as* particular ways of being and entities as partaking in them.

But still, where is the promised "paradox of being"? It lies concealed, as Heidegger might say, within the case just presented. To see this, let us return to another important feature of Heidegger's understanding of "being," which we can articulate in a third premise of our paradox:

> (3) Being determines what it is for something to be and what it is for it to be thus-and-so.

– its *Dass- und Sosein*, as (1) puts it. When we were considering that which determines particular kinds of entities as the entities that they are, no

---

[36] Both Casati and Priest have considered the notion of being grounding itself (or analogues thereof), but that notion forms for them part of explicitly inconsistent, dialetheic theories. For example, in one of his discussions of "the third man" argument – with a version of which the "paradox of being" that I have identified might perhaps be identified, or so Kate Withy has suggested to me in conversation – Priest discusses a theory of forms that would allow "self-predication," whereby "the regress" in question would be "broken"; but it is a commitment of that theory that "the form is both identical to and different from itself" (2014a, 111). This suggests, I think, that, if one can escape the paradox that irreflexivity helps generate, one can do so only by embracing paradox elsewhere: One flattens the carpet in one corner but only by it rucking up in another. A similar thought might apply to the proposal that, although something's determining what it is for it itself to be is not something trees and rocks can pull off, God might. In an unpublished paper, Withy discusses the possibility that Heidegger's opposition to "ontotheology" (GA9, 450) might be seen as affirming that a version of our irreflexivity premise applies here. too.

particular reason emerged there to think that what does this determining work cannot be an entity too. By (2), such determinants are not among the entities that *they* determine as entities, but that does not mean they are not entities all the same, with their own *Dass- und Sosein*. Indeed one might well think that they had better be, if we are to make sense of this determining relation, in that that would seem to require that there be determinate facts about these determiners – their possessing features that fit them to play the determining role, features that might give us a sense of *how* they perform that role, and of what that determining *is*. To do that, we seem to need to be able to make sense of these determiners as being thus-and-so. For them too then, there must be something that determines their *Dass- und Sosein*.

But what of being *in general*? That which determines all modes of *Dass- und Sosein*, it seems, must lack *Dass- und Sosein*. We can articulate why in two ways. Any candidate for the role of "being in general" that did possess *Dass- und Sosein* couldn't do the job. On the assumption of (2) – that the determining relation is irreflexive – it would not be fit to determine all modes of *Dass- und Sosein*, since it could not determine its own. Any candidate for the role cannot – by (2) – have a form of *Dass- und Sosein* among the forms of *Dass- und Sosein* that it determines; but if so, it cannot be the determiner of all forms of *Dass- und Sosein* after all; whatever it is, it cannot perform that role.

We can arrive at the same point by noting that the supposition that there are facts of the matter about "being in general" – what is to determine *all* the ways in which things can be and be thus-and-so as ways in which things can be and be thus-and-so – leads to paradox: *If* it itself were to have a way of being and being thus-and-so, then – by (2) – that way both *cannot* fall within that totality, and yet *must*, if that totality is indeed *all* the ways in which things can be and be thus-and-so. Hence, formulated in either way, we arrive at the conclusion that there can be no determinate facts of the matter about being in general.

7.6   Dialetheist Readings Revisited

Where then does our discussion leave dialetheist readings of Heidegger? I have argued that the paradox I have identified rests upon foundations that are sounder interpretively and philosophically than the foundations upon which the paradox that those readings identify rests. Here I will indicate a further negative moral, though also a more positive second moral.

In light of Section 7.4's discussion, Priest's claim to have answered Heidegger's "question of being" does not hold up. What he offers as an answer is an account of what it is for an entity to be *an* entity, to be unified rather than just a congeries of parts. According to Priest, because "being and unity come to the same thing" (2016, 253), and his account answers the question of what it is to be one, it also answers the question "what is it to be?" and "[t]hat is the question of being" (Priest 2001, 238; also 2014a, 51; 2016, 255). His account is complex and dialetheic – postulating what he calls "gluons," "inconsistent object[s]" that unify entities by acting as "binding agents" (2016, 252) – but we need not go into its details to recognize that, while Priest may answer *a* question of being here, there must be doubt about whether he answers *Heidegger's*. What he sought was a horizon by reference to which different modes of being could be understood *as* different modes of *being*. But if so, Priest's account of what it is for an entity to be one – and, in that sense and for the sake of argument, to be – does not seem to be the kind of account Heidegger needs to answer *his* question of being.

Priest might seem to come closer when his book, *One*, extends the gluon theory to account for "what one might call being *an sich*," "being as universal" (2014a, 53). There Priest subsumes "being" under a "gluon theory of universals" (2014a, 44), a general account of the unity that is multiple entities instantiating a single property. Priest applies this general account to the particular case, "being," to provide an account of what unifies the many entities that fall under that universal, "being" – the many entities that are and hence, in one sense perhaps, "the *unity of the concept of being in general*" (GA24, 170, quoted above). But again – and again the details of his account need not concern us – the relationship between the "question of being" that Priest's account answers and Heidegger's question is distinctly loose, the latter being motivated by particular concerns about being's possible fragmentation. Priest's general account of what unifies instances of a universal does not address Heidegger's concern that "being" may, in fact, not be such a universal – that the "being" that subsumes *Vorhandenheit, Zuhandenheit,* Daseinhood, and so on may be no more a universal than the "bank" that subsumes financial institutions and riversides.[37]

---

[37] In light of its being a "torso," and the widely held view that the project that Heidegger builds around the "question of being" must therefore fail, commentators have often seen their task as that of stripping the body for what might still be of use, which is typically taken to be the analysis of Dasein. (How that analysis and that project relate is a complex question and for some discussion, see McManus 2015a.) This points to another respect in which the dialetheist approach may seem to focus on a notional version of *Being and Time* rather than the book we actually have, because – in terms that Section 7.2 used – dialetheist readers have focussed to date almost exclusively on what

But let us turn now to a second and more positive moral. The formulations of Section 7.5's paradox with which that section ended may already have rung some bells, bringing to mind other paradoxes that Priest's work explores, ones that arise when we pursue structurally similar ventures, such as numbering the numbers with Burali-Forti, making a set of all sets with Russell, and so on (Priest 2001, ch. 8–9). A further interesting twist to the paradox I have presented is that it fits Priest's over-arching understanding of the paradoxes that he traces through the history of philosophy, and perhaps better than the Heideggerian paradox that Priest has himself presented.

The paradox I have offered is what Priest calls an "inclosure-paradox," one that fits his "inclosure-schema":

> [Such a paradox] arises when there is an operator, δ, and a totality, Ω, such that whenever δ is applied to any subset, x, of Ω, of a certain kind—that is, one which satisfies some condition ψ—it appears to deliver an object that is still in Ω, though it is not in x. A contradiction will then arise if Ω itself satisfies ψ. For applying δ to Ω will produce an object that is both within and without Ω. (Priest 2014a, xx)

By way of further explanation, Priest offers a figure (Figure 7.1) "where X marks the contradictory spot—something that is both within and without Ω" (2014a, xx–xi).[38] Dialetheist readers have presented their paradox of being as an inclosure-paradox too, but only in the broad sense that it presents us with "a certain object" – here, being – that "must be within a certain totality" – in their case, the expressible – "but also must be without it" (Priest 2001, 245; also Casati and Wheeler 2016, 489, 497 n. 5). The paradox I have offered tracks more closely than that the finer contours of Priest's inclosure-schema above.

---

a reflective grasp of being is, rather than on Dasein and its pre-ontological grasp of being, where that is a – indeed arguably *the* – central theme of the book we know as *Being and Time*. (Priest 2001 dedicates a paragraph to these matters (see p. 240); and while §3 of Casati and Wheeler 2016 discusses how Heidegger's thought challenges representational theories of mind, they devote only one sentence (on p. 493) to addressing how that challenge might relate to the concerns of dialetheist readings.) Efforts to extend the dialetheist approach to these matters might generate interesting lines of thought. There are reasons, for example, to think that "world" – as Heidegger understands that notion – might harbor paradoxes not dissimilar to those that "being in general" does, as others, indeed, have suggested (Witherspoon 2002, §1 and §4; Casati and Wheeler 2016, 493, the sentence mentioned above). If so, might not Dasein's "being-in-the-world" itself turn out to have a dialetheic structure? Elaborating such possibilities is, however, work that remains to be done. A further lacuna is, as Casati and Wheeler concede, that, "even if we assume that being is a true contradiction," "we still don't know how being makes entities entities" (2016, 490). That remark leads into a discussion of Priest's gluon theory but, as argued above, the bearing of that theory on Heidegger's core concerns is questionable.

[38] Priest informs me that the figure was originally drawn for him by Greg Restall.

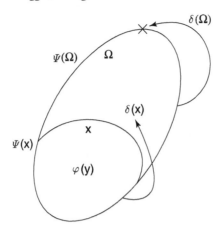

Figure 7.1   Priest's inclosure-schema

In our case, Ω is "all that which is thus-and-so" and δ "determines that which is thus-and-so as that which is thus-and-so." When we apply the latter to some subset of that which is thus-and-so, x – the subset of Ω picked out as that which satisfies ψ – it can deliver something that is still in Ω – something that is thus-and-so – though not itself a member of x, because δ is irreflexive. But a contradiction arises if Ω itself satisfies ψ: that is, if ψ "is that which is thus-and-so," the misnamed "subset", x, is the whole of Ω, and the particular instance of δ under examination is "determines all that which is thus-and-so as that which is thus-and-so." Then, what that operator delivers must fall on "the contradictory spot." It must fall *outside* the x to which it is applied – which here is Ω, all that is thus-and-so – because δ is irreflexive. But it must also fall *within* Ω if it is to have a mode of being – if there are to be any facts of the matter about it.

When discussing (1) above, I proposed that we can ascribe a natural enough sense to notions such as that locatedness determines a threshold as a threshold. A threshold is a threshold by virtue of locatedness, and locatedness makes a threshold a threshold, whereas a hammer is a hammer by virtue of usability, usability making a hammer a hammer. The range of ways thresholds can be and the range of facts that can hold of thresholds are determined then, we might say, by how locatedness is, by the facts about locatedness. But when we consider what "determines *all* that which is thus-and-so as that which is thus-and-so," there are no such further facts to which we might turn. Unlike locatedness – where how it is falls outside of the relevant x, as the irreflexivity of δ requires, but still within Ω – how the all-encompassing determinant is must fall outside of Ω – as here the relevant x is Ω – yet Ω takes in *all* the ways that matters are. So before we get as far as wondering what that determinant might be – for instance, that it might have something to do with time in some sense or other – we face the problem that there is no room, as one might put it, for this determinant to be any way at all, or for there to be facts about how it is. Yet there must be such room, one feels, if there is to be anything about this determinant in virtue of which it fulfills the determining role we envisage it as fulfilling. To turn to another earlier formulation, there must be such room if it is to possess features that fit it to play that determining role, features that might give us a sense of how it performs that role and of what that determining role here is.[39]

Not that this predicament would necessarily be the dialetheist's conclusion, of course. She sees no *reductio* in such an object both having and not having properties, in there both being and not being facts of the matter about it, being in general being an "inconsistent object," a "strange beast" (Priest 2016, 252, 256). But if one still does not like the look of the "bridge of inconsistency," then one's conclusion will instead be that Heidegger is in deep trouble, and perhaps so are we. (Or, as the critic of dialetheism will, of course, want to have it, *another* kind of deep trouble.) We have seen that a "paradox of being" arises when one tries to find an *all-encompassing* "determiner of entities as entities." It is in helping us think about what the philosophical options might then be – in light of similar totalizing projects that have failed before – that I think the greatest importance of our paradox fitting Priest's inclosure-schema may yet lie. Exploring those possibilities properly lies beyond the scope of this chapter, though I will flag some in closing.

7.7 Some Concluding Thoughts

Naturally, fairness requires that we scrutinize our second paradox as, in Section 7.3, we did the first, that is, by going back to examine once again its premises. Some scrutiny has already fallen on the relation upon which so much of our discussion of that paradox depends, that of "determining entities as entities" and, in particular, its irreflexivity. As indicated, we seem to

---

[39] Another conciliatory note is that Priest has recognized elsewhere the kind of paradox I identify; the Heideggerian paradox Priest identifies stands to it in something like the way that his Gluon Paradox #1 stands to his Gluon Paradox #2 (2014a, 200–201), and a "contradiction concerning the limits of expressibility" stands to an "ontological contradiction," both of which he finds in Nāgārjuna: The upshot of the latter is that "[r]eality ... is not in any way at all" (Priest 2001, 265, 267).

have a reasonable sense of what that relation amounts to when considering particular ways of being – locatedness making thresholds, for example – and it seems there clearly irreflexive. It is less clear that the quite general relation of determining entities as entities must be too, but surely in part because it is less clear what we have in mind when we contemplate that relation. This should perhaps come as no surprise if this application of the relation does indeed descend into paradox, as I have argued; but either way, we encounter an issue here with which all readers of Heidegger would seem to need to wrestle.

One might also wonder whether there is a lingering influence in our second paradox of something akin to (E). That there can be no facts of the matter about being in general will strike many – in particular, non-diale-theists – as entailing that being in general must be a fiction, a will-o'-the-wisp. But might a certain conception of what it is to grasp something – for something to be intelligible – be casting here an ontological shadow, as one might put it, making us think that only things about which there are facts of the matter – facts being things that one grasps *propositionally* – could be *non*-wills-o'-the-wisp, there to be thought about or otherwise engaged with in intelligible ways? This takes us into murky, though not unfamiliar, waters, I think, in pointing us back perhaps to the other principal way in which, as Section 7.2 discussed, one might respond to the first paradox – that is, by appealing to the notion that being might be the object of a kind of nonpropositional understanding.

If there is a significant worry here, then what we should conclude on the basis of the second paradox is perhaps instead that ontology as a body of facts makes no sense. (Again, I set aside here the dialetheic interpreta-tion of the paradox.) To some, that would mean that there is no such thing as ontology – what else might it be? Others might conclude perhaps that ontology must take another form – whatever that might be – or that whatever urge has found expression through the pursuit of a body of onto-logical facts actually calls for some other mode of expression altogether – whatever that might be.[40]

Which of these or other options Heidegger himself may have seen as available is a difficult question to answer.[41] It seems to me that we see an awareness of our second paradox already in *Being and Time* but deepening in the years that follow. In *Being and Time*, Heidegger seems optimistic

---

[40] Cf. n. 15.
[41] Certainly a mere retreat – as it were – to regional ontology was not an option for him, if the argu-ment that Section 7.4 set out is sound. Heidegger here seems to share Priest's intuition that, in philosophy, "completeness or totalisation is … conceptually unavoidable": "[t]otalising is part of our conceptual machinery—like it or not" (Priest 2001, 86, 162).

that whatever issue lies here can be contained – by containing the "is" of propositions about being in inverted commas and assigning to "temporality" – the horizon for "being in general" that Heidegger there postulates – a predicate all its own: "[t]emporality ... is not, but it *temporalizes* [zeitigt] itself" (SZ 328). We see this optimism in the *Basic Problems* lectures too: "the propositions of ontology are *temporal propositions* [*temporale Sätze*]," as a "temporal projection" "constitutes ontology in general as a science" (GA24, 459–460). Ontology is certainly a special science – "at bottom temporal science" (GA24, 461) – but a science all the same.

Things have clearly changed, however, by the time Heidegger gave his 1929 inaugural lecture, "What Is Metaphysics?" where "the nothing" supplants "being" from center stage. The very familiarity of this supplanting – as we look back on it some ninety years later – must not blind us to how clear a signal this will have sent that Heidegger felt he had underestimated – and his contemporaries continued to underestimate – just how very different philosophy's "subject matter" is, just how different its kind of reflection is and its questions are, to the point where they even pose "the question of [their] questionability" (GA9, 108). There certainly are continuities: The nothing too is assigned its own predicate – "*[d]as Nichts nichtet*" (GA9, 116). But the cautious "is" of passage (II) is supplanted by the flat-out insistence that the question "What is the nothing?" "deprives itself of its own object" and Heidegger now insists that "[p]hilosophy can never be measured by the standard of the idea of science" (GA9, 107, 122).

Perhaps most strikingly of all, the inaugural lecture not only does not mention temporality or a temporally constituted science of ontology; it also sets the very term "ontology" aside. In the introduction to *Being and Time*, Heidegger insists that a concept of "being in general" must be available to us because "[o]therwise there could have been no ontological knowledge heretofore" (SZ 8). But in the semester that followed his inaugural lecture, Heidegger urges his audience to "ponder the following: it is nowhere written that there must be such a thing as ontology" (GA29/30, 522). If we are, he continues, to "ultimately unfold" "the problem of the distinction between being and beings" – the "enigmatic nature" of the "ontological difference" – we must face "the danger of arriving at a position where we must *reject all ontology in its very idea*": "yet what," he asks, "are we then to put in [its] place?"[42]

[42] For helpful comments on material on which this chapter is based, I would like to thank Lee Braver, Adrian Moore, Stephen Mulhall, Graham Priest, Joshua Tepley, Ed Witherspoon, Kate Withy, and the editors of this volume.

CHAPTER 8

Logic and Attunement
Reading Heidegger through Priest and Wittgenstein

Edward Witherspoon

What is the relation between logic and metaphysics? A robust tradition in Western philosophy supposes that logic should guide metaphysics, along at least two dimensions: (1) logic sets out the rules for correct thinking, which metaphysical investigation must of course observe, and (2) the structure of logic defines the possibilities for the structure of reality, so metaphysics should look to logic for its most basic categories. Heidegger challenges this tradition, along both dimensions. He asserts that metaphysics is a more fundamental discipline than logic, and so it cannot rely on logic for its structure. He even goes so far as to question whether the rules of logic apply to metaphysical investigation. As he puts it in one of his most notorious remarks, "the idea of 'logic' itself disintegrates in the turbulence of a more fundamental questioning" (GA9, 117/ 92).[1]

Why does Heidegger seek to dethrone logic? And if he does contemplate a revision or rejection of the principles of logic, on what basis could such a thing be done? This chapter explores these questions. To understand how Heidegger's thought puts pressure on logic, I compare it to that of Graham Priest, who overtly calls for rejecting the law of noncontradiction. Priest advocates *dialetheism*, the view that some contradictions are true, and he argues that Heidegger's project would benefit from the explicit embrace of that position. I argue, however, that Heidegger's challenge to logic is fundamentally different from Priest's. The difference springs from differences in the kinds of investigations they are pursuing and in the kinds of reasons they give for their revisions of logic. Priest embraces dialetheism on the basis of a rational weighing of theoretical costs and benefits. Heidegger finds himself in conflict with the principle of noncontradiction as a consequence of a fundamental experience of

---

[1] In the original edition of "What Is Metaphysics?" the word "logic" in scare quotes is qualified as "the *traditional* interpretation of thinking." The significance of this qualification emerges in Sections 8.3 and 8.7 below.

anxiety – his name for the mood in which one encounters *the Nothing* and, with it, entities as a whole.

How could an *experience* lead someone to revise logic? Doesn't logic articulate the limits of what it is possible to experience? To explore these questions I draw on Wittgenstein's later philosophy and Stanley Cavell's reflections on it. I argue that systems of logic are distillations of the grammar of our language and that our language has the grammar it does thanks to our sensibilities, or what Cavell calls our "attunements." An alteration of our attunements can open new possibilities for grammar, can create new ways of making sense. Like Wittgenstein and Cavell, Heidegger thinks that what we can talk about depends on our attunements. He adds that some experiences can alter those attunements. In particular, the experience of anxiety brings about an attunement that provides a new mode of understanding. If this understanding involves a revision of our logical principles – revision even of the principle of noncontradiction – so be it.

8.1.   A Problem with the Question of Being

While Heidegger discusses the nature of logic throughout his career, in this chapter I focus on three works that form a unit: *Being and Time* (1927), in which he formulates the question of Being without exploring in detail the logical puzzle that springs from it; "What Is Metaphysics?" (1929), his 1929 inaugural address at Freiburg, in which he explicitly faces up to this logical conundrum; and, mediating between these works, *The Metaphysical Foundations of Logic* (1928), his last lecture course at Marburg. I do not explicitly address the question of whether Heidegger later modifies any commitments made in these texts, but "What Is Metaphysics?" remains a touchstone for Heidegger for decades: He adds a postscript to it in 1943 and an introduction in 1949 (GA9).

Heidegger's challenge to logic springs from the project at the heart of *Being and Time*. This project is to pose the question of the meaning of Being. Heidegger thinks that this should be the central question of philosophy, but that it tends to be covered up and forgotten. He therefore attempts to recover this question and to lay out a route for answering it. As we will see, however, that route leads to paradoxes.

What is Being? An initial characterization emerges from the observation that every thing *is* some way or other; every entity has a determinate, intelligible character. This is to say, entities *have Being*. Hence Heidegger begins with the thought that Being is "that which determines entities as entities, that on the basis of which entities are already understood, however we may discuss them in detail" (SZ 6). This of course does not *answer* the question of the meaning of Being, but it is a preliminary indication of what we are seeking, namely, the source (in a yet-to-be-determined sense) of entities and of our understanding of them.

Heidegger thinks that the only viable approach to the question of the meaning of Being is to exploit the understanding of Being that we – as instances of Dasein – already possess (SZ 5). This is a "vague average understanding," exhibited in our various ways of interacting with entities, for example in our use of tools, our relationships with other people, and our theoretical reflections. In any interactions with an entity, we understand it *as something*, which is to say, we understand it as having Being, and, moreover, as having Being of a particular kind. But this understanding is typically implicit. So it looks as though answering the question of Being is a matter of making these implicit understandings explicit and explaining how they are related, that is, explaining what makes them all understandings *of Being*.

This project, while immense, appears to be feasible. But when Heidegger tries to make *Being* itself the topic of his inquiry he runs into profound difficulties. The goal of the inquiry would seem to be making true assertions about Being. But when Heidegger comes to analyze the concept of an assertion, he concludes that any assertion must be about some *thing*. This is a problem because, as Heidegger argues, Being is not a *thing*; it is (to a first, inadequate, approximation) that which makes every thing the thing it is. And so it appears that we cannot make assertions about Being.

We can express the obstacle in the way of philosophizing about Being as the conjunction of the following three theses:

1. Being is distinct from any entity.
2. What an assertion is *about* is always an entity or a set of entities.
3. It is possible to make assertions about Being.

This is an inconsistent triad: The truth of any two of these theses entails the falsity of the third.

When we are confronted with an inconsistency, the rational response is to give up one or more of the inconsistent propositions. Many commentators on Heidegger have sought to do just that – to argue that Heidegger need not be committed to all three of these theses. To exhibit the depth of the paradox Heidegger faces, I adumbrate the philosophical and textual bases for attributing each of these positions to Heidegger. I do not pretend to give an exhaustive defense of the theses or of the correctness of attributing them to Heidegger; for my purposes it is enough to show that they are at least plausible, and are plausibly attributable to Heidegger.

Thesis (1) is a recurrent theme in Heidegger's writings. A representative passage is: "Being [*das Sein*] is different from entities [*das Seiende*], and only this difference, the possibility of this difference, allows for an understanding of Being.... We term this distinction ... the *ontological difference*" (GA26, 193, translation modified).[2] The ontological difference is the difference between, for example, (a) a *hammer* and (b) *what makes a hammer the thing that it is*. Even if we do not yet know how to characterize (b) – it expresses, after all, part of what the question of Being is to answer – it is clear that (b) is different from (a).

Thesis (2) follows from Heidegger's analysis of the concept of assertion. According to this analysis, assertion is a "derivative" form of interpretation that *points something out*. Our understanding of Being (however vague and everyday) is what allows us to point something out. What can be pointed out is an entity; Being, as that which makes entities available for pointing out, cannot itself be pointed out (SZ 154–156).

Thesis (3) allows for the possibility of philosophical inquiry into Being. That Heidegger believes that philosophical inquiry into Being is *possible* needs no argument: Such inquiry is his life's work. Moreover, it seems obvious that philosophy traffics in questions and assertions, which we evaluate as true or false. So in attempting to answer the question of Being, it seems we will be making assertions about Being. Indeed, Heidegger's own writings – as well as commentaries like this one – are full of sentences in assertoric form employing "Being" as a referring expression. These bear every earmark of being assertions about Being.

It thus appears that Heidegger has plausible reasons for maintaining each of theses (1)–(3). As readers of Heidegger we thus face a conundrum: How shall we understand Heidegger's philosophizing about Being in the face of these inconsistent commitments?

8.2   Interpretive Options

This conundrum and its close variants have elicited abundant commentary. As a way of placing the main concerns of this chapter within this interpretive space, I start with a brief overview of the options available to Heidegger's readers.

---

[2] The brackets display the German expressions that Heidegger uses to mark the difference. *Das Sein* is the nominalized form of the verb "to be," so "Being" is a suitable translation. *Das Seiende* could be literally translated as "what is"; I adopt the terms "entity" or "entities." (Unlike many translators I do not use "beings" because I want to avoid any risk of confusing *das Sein* and *das Seiende*.)

These options may be arrayed under two main headings. The first family of options is to abandon one of the three theses listed above. Doing so would remove the inconsistency and might thereby open an avenue for philosophizing about Being. For each of the above theses, commentators can be found who believe that Heidegger should or does abandon it. One could deny that there is an ontological difference. But as exegesis this runs up against the stubborn fact that Heidegger frequently and consistently asserts that respecting the distinction between Being and entities is essential to philosophizing about Being (SZ 6; GA9, 305–306/233). One could maintain that assertions do not have to be restricted to *entities*, so that *Being* could be the topic of assertions. However plausible this suggestion might seem, it faces the exegetical problem that Heidegger frequently insists that assertions can *only* be about entities (e.g., GA29/30, 466). Finally, one could maintain that it is not possible to make assertions about Being. Reading Heidegger in this fashion would then require a way of philosophizing about Being without making assertions about it.[3] There are various versions of this position, but they all face the challenge of explaining away the fact that Heidegger's text appears to be rife with assertions about Being.

In light of Heidegger's commitment to theses (1)–(3), a reader of Heidegger should be willing to explore a second main interpretive option. This is to read Heidegger as retaining all three theses, while continuing to philosophize *in the face of their inconsistency*. This approach reads Heidegger as rejecting the principle of noncontradiction, thereby allowing that there are some true contradictions. While this will strike many philosophers as a counsel of desperation, there is significant textual evidence that Heidegger considers – and perhaps embraces – just this option. When his account of the Nothing in "What Is Metaphysics?" runs afoul of the "commonly cited ground rule of all thinking, the proposition that contradiction is to be avoided," Heidegger responds by continuing to discuss the Nothing. Indeed, he explicitly presses the question as to whether "logic" is sovereign over his inquiry (GA9, 107/85). As I noted above, Heidegger seems to conclude that it is not: "the idea of 'logic' itself disintegrates in the turbulence of a more fundamental questioning" (GA9, 117/92).

Entertaining the possibility of revising logic raises a host of questions. On what basis could it be legitimate to cast off a fundamental principle of logic? Could a revision of logic ever be rational? How must we understand

---

[3] One such interpretation is suggested in Witherspoon (2002). An overview of several other such interpretive approaches can be found in Casati (2019, 6).

logic if it turns out that logic can or should be revised? In this chapter I explore these questions as part of an investigation into whether Heidegger should be read as promoting a revision of logic.

8.3   Varieties of Logic

In order to describe the kinds of debates that can arise around the acceptance or rejection of a logical rule or principle, I now introduce some distinctions between things that can all, with some justification, be called "logic." These distinctions can be found in *The Metaphysical Foundations of Logic*, although I express them in nomenclature quite different from Heidegger's own.[4]

The word "logic" can refer to a set of techniques and algorithms for symbolizing arguments and testing them for deductive validity. Any such body of techniques and rules is a *logic-as-formal-system*. The most familiar one is first-order predicate logic, but there are many others, such as relevance logic, intuitionistic logic, and three-valued logic.

The goal of these systems of rules is to issue correct verdicts on the goodness or badness (typically the validity or invalidity) of any argument to which it can be applied. (How exactly we determine when such a verdict is correct will be a crucial question as we proceed.) One can investigate how well a proposed logic-as-formal-system meets this goal. For example, different introductory logic textbooks present different formal systems: Some use truth-trees, others truth-tables; some use one formulation of the rules for inferences involving quantified statements, others use a different formulation; and logicians debate their respective merits. In addition, logicians can identify kinds of reasoning that are not susceptible to existing formal systems (e.g., drawing inferences from a database containing inconsistent data) and can try to devise new formal systems to capture them. The arena for debates about the adequacy of formal systems is what I will call *logic-as-discipline-of-formalization*. It is within this discipline that logicians compare systems of natural deduction, debate theories of conditionals, and advocate relevance logics or intuitionistic logics or three-valued logics as against classical logic.

Within logic-as-discipline-of-formalization, as philosophers debate the adequacy of contending formal systems, they rely on notions like *object*, *proposition*, *truth*, and *necessity*. The same goes for any particular

---

[4] For an attempt to work through Heidegger's terminology in detail and to apply that terminology to the notorious remarks in "What Is Metaphysics?" see Witherspoon (2003).

logic-as-formal-system: Such a system may define a "valid inference" as *a deductive inference that necessarily preserves truth*, but it does not investigate theories of truth or of necessity. That is perfectly appropriate, given the aims of these projects, but Heidegger pursues a more fundamental inquiry into the nature of propositions, truth, and – of course – Being. This inquiry is what he calls "metaphysics," in particular "the metaphysics of truth" (GA26, 131), and he says that metaphysics too can be regarded as a kind of "logical" investigation (GA26, 138). Hence we have another philosophical discipline: *logic-as-metaphysical-inquiry*. And it will issue in an account of these fundamental notions, or what I call a *logic-as-metaphysical-system*.

These distinctions between different notions of logic are not meant to suggest that philosophers should engage in just one form of investigation at a time. For example, a dispute about which formal system is most appropriate for a particular kind of inference (logic-as-discipline-of-formalization) may involve questions about the subject matter of those inferences themselves (logic-as-metaphysical-inquiry). The point of making these distinctions is to allow us to give a coherent description of how within logic (in one sense) a philosopher could challenge logic (in another sense); this possibility in turn opens an interpretive space for understanding Heidegger's own challenges to logic.

8.4   Priest on Revising Logic

Whatever else Heidegger's challenge to logic might be, it certainly appears to involve challenging and even rejecting the principle of noncontradiction. We may formulate this as the principle that the conjunction of a statement and its negation (p & $\sim p$) is necessarily false. For anyone curious about the status of the principle of noncontradiction, Graham Priest is an essential philosopher. As I noted above, he defends dialetheism, the metaphysical position that, for some propositions p, the conjunction p & $\sim p$ is actually *true*. Within classical logics-as-formal-systems, accepting a contradiction as true has the consequence that *every* proposition is true. To avoid this consequence, Priest advances a paraconsistent logic-as-formal-system; in a paraconsistent system, it is not the case that p & $\sim p$ entails q, for any randomly chosen proposition q (Priest 2006b).

Priest advocates dialetheism not only as a logic-as-metaphysical-system but also as a framework for reading Heidegger.[5] He argues that

---

[5] See Priest (2002) and Priest (2016).

Heidegger's investigation of Being may be advanced by placing it within dialetheism. Doing so would allow a Heideggerian to maintain both that Being is not an entity (thereby respecting the ontological difference) and that Being *is* an entity (thereby ensuring that we can make assertions about it).[6]

Finally, Priest's work is valuable in that he reflects explicitly on how formal systems can be revised and lays out criteria that should govern the selection of a logic-as-formal-system. The nature and basis of such revisions will turn out to be a crucial issue for our understanding of Heidegger's project.

In "Revising Logic" (Priest 2014b), Priest distinguishes several notions of logic, expounding dimensions of the concept different from those captured in the Heideggerian distinctions I have just explored. These notions are (in his nomenclature) (1) *logica utens*, or how people actually reason, (2) *logica docens*, or logic as it is formalized and taught, and (3) *logica ens*, or the set of all truths regarding what follows from what. Priest's concept of *logica docens* is close to what I have labeled "logic-as-a-formal-system," and so I will focus on his account of how it can be revised.

Priest characterizes *logica docens* as an attempt to give "a theory of the validity of ordinary arguments: what follows (deductively) from what" (Priest 2014b, 216). Coming up with an adequate formal system is like coming up with a theory in any domain: Researchers aim to match theory to data in such a way as to best satisfy theoretical virtues like "simplicity, non-(ad hocness), unifying power, fruitfulness." In the case of logic, the "data" are "those particular inferences that strike us as correct or incorrect" (Priest 2014b, 217).

Stated thus baldly, this position smacks of psychologism, that is, the view that the aim of logics-as-formal-systems is to formally characterize the inferences we are psychologically inclined to make. This is in opposition to the idea that logical systems aim to capture rules of truth – the inferences that are *actually valid*, not the inferences we happen to *think* are valid. Priest, however, is no friend of psychologism. He makes clear that the inferences to which we should try to match our theory are the inferences that, *upon reflection*, we regard as correct. And in determining what inferences are correct we appeal to the norms of our inferential

---

[6] Priest claims that Heidegger *should* have been a dialetheist. Filippo Casati (2019) goes further, building a strong exegetical case that, in his later work, and especially in *Contributions to Philosophy (of the Event)*, Heidegger *does in fact* embrace dialetheism.

practice, including perhaps the very formal system that we are trying to fit to the data (Priest 2014b, 219). This appeal may seem to involve a vicious circularity, but it does not: The correction of our actual inferences by reference to a formal rule is like the way theory informs data in the empirical sciences.

On this picture, as we gather more data or examine our data more closely, we may change our theory. For example, Priest argues that logicians like Frege and Russell attended more closely to mathematical inferences than their predecessors had and developed formal, "mathematical" logical systems, which they adopted in preference to Aristotelian syllogistic and its descendants. Modern logic-as-a-formal-system supersedes syllogistic; it is not just an addition to or correction of it. Even though it involves rejecting the previous logic-as-formal-system (and so is "illogical" in that sense), this revision is still rational in a broader sense, in that it is justified according to the canons of rational theory choice.

Priest's case for rejecting the principle that contradictions are necessarily false exemplifies this general account of the revision of logic. Priest offers many arguments for dialetheism and paraconsistent logical systems.[7] A representative one begins with the Russell paradox, generated by defining the set R of all sets that are not members of themselves. If R is a member of itself, then it is (by definition of R) not a member of itself. On the other hand, if R is not a member of itself, then (by the definition of R), it is a member of itself. Letting p be the proposition that R is a member of itself, we can conjoin these conditionals to get the biconditional p *if and only if* $\sim p$. This biconditional implies the conjunction p *&* $\sim p$. Hence, it is true both that R is a member of itself and that R is not a member of itself.[8]

Responses to this paradox are legion. But apart from the scant handful of dialetheists, they all start from the position that the contradiction must be avoided. So they all look for flaws in the argument (the definitions or the reasoning from those definitions) that leads to it. Priest surveys these attempts and argues that none is rationally acceptable: He thinks each one rests on one or another arbitrary assumption. It is more reasonable to adopt a paraconsistent logic-as-formal-system that tolerates true contradictions; this will better model our inferential practices. This revision allows us to adopt a dialetheic logic-as-metaphysical-system that asserts as true the conclusion that R both is and is not a member of itself. Priest's case implicitly relies on the

---

[7] These are systematically presented in Priest (2006b).
[8] This is an instance of the argument schema in Priest (2006b, 10–12).

kinds of considerations governing theory choice that he formulates explicitly
in "Revising Logic": for example, the arbitrariness of other resolutions of the
paradox counts against them, while the fact that dialetheism's solution to
one paradox suggests similar solutions to others counts in its favor.

It is worth noting that this account of a rational change of one's logic-
as-formal-system does not make an appeal to *logica ens*, the third of the
three concepts of logic that Priest identifies. Given the definition of *logica
ens* as the set of all truths about what really follows from what, this is sur-
prising: One would think that in constructing a formal system a logician
should aim to capture the inferences that actually *are* correct, rather than
merely the inferences that people *judge* to be correct. To make sense of this
situation, we can appeal again to the analogy Priest draws between logical theorizing and theorizing in the empirical sciences (Priest 2014b, 216).
Logica ens occupies the place of (for example) the actual movements of
physical bodies like the earth and sun; in constructing theories of dynam-
ics, we aim ultimately to provide formal models of the movements of these
bodies, but that to which we match these theories is not the celestial bodies
themselves, but the data we have about their movement. In similar fashion, one could say that the inferences that (upon reflection) we recognize
as correct (*logica utens*) are the data about *logica ens* that we attempt to
match when we construct a *logica docens*. Thus, for Priest, even though we
do not actively consult *logica ens*, it remains the ultimate goal in constructing a logic-as-formal-system. And this goal is a set of timeless truths – all
the truths about what actually follows from what. By positing this domain
of logical truths, Priest is, I suspect, trying to assure us that, undergird-
ing the assessment of theoretical pluses and minuses that is the business
of logic-as-discipline-of-formalization, there lies an ultimate ground or
authority to which that theorizing is answerable.

8.5   Priest versus Heidegger

Priest's account of how one might come to reject one formal system and
embrace another is *rationalist*. Despite the fact that the formal system
he embraces is one that violates what most philosophers would consider
a core tenet of rationality, he defends it by offering arguments that are
meant to be intelligible to traditional logicians. A reader of Heidegger
might therefore hope that Priest's work could provide a model for understanding Heidegger's own questioning of the principles of classical logics-
as-formal-systems: Perhaps his philosophizing about Being should be seen
as rationally defensible according to broader canons of rationality.

I will ultimately offer a kind of explanation and defense of Heidegger's contra-logical philosophizing. But that explanation will be radically different from the kind of rational appeals that Priest offers on behalf of his paraconsistent logic-as-formal-system.

As a first step toward understanding the differences between Priest and Heidegger, let's consider how they come to challenge traditional logics-as-formal-systems. Priest's motivation for advocating paraconsistent logics originates within logic-as-a-discipline-of-formalization: Classical formal systems allow for paradoxes, and Priest advances dialetheism (and the paraconsistent logic that makes it viable) as the most reasonable way of resolving them. By contrast, Heidegger's challenge to the principle of non-contradiction is motivated by his substantive claims in the arena of logic-as-metaphysical-inquiry. Heidegger does not go hunting up paradoxes, but rather has a paradox thrust upon him, in the form of theses (1)–(3) above and related claims about truth, Dasein, and the nature of philosophy.

This difference in the origins of their projects has consequences for the kind of inquiry they pursue and for the canons of rationality to which they may appeal. Priest treats logical theorizing as a kind of scientific investigation of a realm of entities (viz., those inferences that, upon reflection, we recognize as correct). Because he thinks of his investigation as a science, he draws on the sciences for the canons of rationality that govern it; his goal is to find the optimal fit of theory to evidence, where optimality of fit is to be assessed by appeal to the theoretical virtues appropriate to any science.

Heidegger's investigation lies at a different level. As we have seen, it is essential to his conception of his project that it does not investigate *entities* – or if it does, it is only as a propaedeutic for the investigation of Being. His investigation is therefore not *scientific*; its aim instead is to uncover the heretofore hidden *essence* of scientific investigation, which essence lies in the character of Dasein. Since he is trying to explain the source of the theoretical virtues characteristic of science, it would be inappropriate for him to evaluate his own theorizing in light of those very virtues.[9] Similarly, whereas Priest can presuppose concepts like meaning, truth, and validity (or at least he can postpone consideration of them while he advocates paraconsistent systems), Heidegger's project is precisely to explicate such notions.

---

[9] This is part of what Heidegger means when he says that his thinking is "more rigorous" than the "exact" thinking defined by classical logics-as-formal-systems ("Postscript to 'What Is Metaphysics?'"; GA9, 308/235).

Finally, Heidegger's philosophy has no place for *logica ens*, the set of timeless truths regarding what *really* follows from what. For Heidegger, to embrace the idea of a *logica ens* is to suppose that it is possible for Dasein to get outside its own modes of thought, so as to be able to contemplate what is really the case, apart from any thing that Dasein takes to be the case. Such a "sideways-on" perspective on our own thought is a fiction.[10]

Priest's willingness to embrace contradictions makes him look like an ally of Heidegger's rejection of the sovereignty of classical logical systems. Indeed, the dialetheic logical-metaphysics that Priest advocates initially looks to be a promising solution to the conundrum Heidegger faces as a consequence of his theses (1)–(3). But the fundamental differences in the scope and bases of their respective inquiries entail that Priest's *way* of revising logical principles cannot be Heidegger's. To find a model for how *Heidegger* might wish to revise logic, we will have to look elsewhere.

8.6   Wittgenstein on Logic

Wittgenstein might seem to offer little aid and comfort to Heidegger's way of doing philosophy. Heidegger frames his whole project as a meta-physical investigation of Being. Almost any page of Heidegger's writings is full of neologisms and jargon, as he attempts to plumb the depths of Being. By contrast, Wittgenstein says that "the essence of things ... already lies open to view, and ... becomes *surveyable* through a process of ordering" (*Philosophical Investigations* §92).[11] He offers this description of his philosophical method: "What *we* do is to bring words back from their metaphysical to their everyday use" (PI §116). Wittgenstein does not envision rejecting the principle of noncontradiction; Heidegger at least contemplates doing so. But on closer examination we will find that Wittgenstein's description of the relation between language and logic and human activity aligns him with Heidegger's Dasein-first approach to metaphysics. Like Heidegger, Wittgenstein is not advocating one logic-as-formal-system among others, but is trying to understand the status of formal systems vis-à-vis the rest of language. This leads him to explore the notion of attunement. This notion will provide a key for describing the connection between anxiety and Heidegger's challenge to the sover-eignty of logic.

---

[10] McDowell (1994, 34–36) coins the expression "sideways-on" and argues that it is an illusion to sup-pose that we could achieve a sideways-on understanding of our own thought.

[11] Wittgenstein (2009); subsequent references are to PI and section number.

Like Heidegger, Wittgenstein is suspicious of the notion of a *logica ens*. If there were such a thing, it would define what configurations of reality were possible and so would set parameters on what we could experience. It would be the "logic" that Wittgenstein describes as a structure of crystalline purity:

> Thinking is surrounded by a nimbus.—Its essence, logic, presents an order: namely, the a priori order of the world; that is, the order of *possibilities*, which the world and thinking must have in common. But this order, it seems, must be *utterly simple*. It is *prior* to all experience, must run through all experience; no empirical cloudiness or uncertainty may attach to it.—It must rather be of the purest crystal. But this crystal does not appear as an abstraction, but as something concrete, indeed, as the most concrete, as it were the *hardest* thing there is .... (PI §97)

This way of thinking about logic – as a crystalline structure dictating the a priori order of the world and of thought – has a powerful appeal. But Wittgenstein thinks that it is a myth. To see why, we may begin by considering what this structure is supposed to do. At a minimum, it is to provide "strict and clear rules for the logical construction of a proposition" (PI §102) and to determine the logical relations among propositions – to specify what follows from what, what inferences are correct and what incorrect. But a system of logical rules cannot deliver determinations of correctness and incorrectness *by itself*; its rules have to be understood and applied *by us*. This will require us to determine whether something falls under a rule, whether one instance is relevantly similar to another instance, whether a particular individual falls under a given concept, and so on. For a formal system of rules to yield usable conclusions, thinkers must be able to agree on such judgments.

Wittgenstein argues that recognizing this fact will lead us to reconceive the character of logic:

> It is not only agreement in definitions, but also (odd as it may sound) agreement in judgments that is required for communication by means of language. This seems to abolish logic, but does not do so.—It is one thing to describe methods of measurement, and another to obtain and state results of measurement. But what we call "measuring" is partly determined by a certain constancy in results of measurement. (PI §242)

Wittgenstein distinguishes agreement in definitions from agreement in judgments and says that both kinds of agreement are required for communication by means of language. Why might this claim sound odd, and why does it seem to abolish logic? If you have a conception of logic as an a priori system that determines the possibilities of thought and of reality, then you should think that all that we need to secure communication is agreement in definitions. Let's assume that communication between two people is a matter of their exchanging linguistic expressions to which they assign the same meanings. On the conception of logic at issue, such communication is achieved when speakers assign the same meanings to the component words of their expressions; logic in this sense may be thought of as a syntax that enables them to derive the meaning of whole expressions from the meanings of their parts. Whether the communicators go on to assign the same truth-values to the same statements – that is, whether they agree in their judgments – is irrelevant to whether they have a shared understanding.

When Wittgenstein says that agreement in judgments is *required* for communication, he is therefore rejecting this conception of logic – and this is why his remark "seems to abolish logic." Agreement in judgment is often a contingent matter. Different speakers might assign different truth-values to a given proposition for all kinds of reasons: different experiences, different background beliefs, different degrees of skill in reasoning, even different values (theoretical and moral). If *what our expressions mean* turns out to depend on *whether we agree*, then it looks as though logic – as what establishes the meanings of and logical relations among our propositions – is being made to depend on contingencies; and that is to "abolish logic."

Why is agreement in judgments *required* for communication in language? Wittgenstein presents his argument through an analogy with measuring. In this analogy, "describ[ing] methods of measurement" is likened to establishing the definitions and logical rules that together yield specifications of the meanings of sentences; "obtaining and stating results of measurement" would then be like using language to communicate. In the case of measuring, we expect different measurers to get the same results (to achieve "a certain constancy in [their] results"). Indeed, Wittgenstein says that these agreements in results "partly determine" what measuring is.[12] Think about how we react when measurers get different results. When the difference is within a tolerable margin of error we just think this is to be expected, and move on. But if the difference is significant, we look for an explanation: Perhaps the measurers were careless, or their instruments

---

[12] I am deliberately moving from Wittgenstein's point that "*what we call 'measuring'* is partly determined by a certain constancy in results of measurement" (my emphasis) to the claim that what measuring *is* is partly so determined. For Wittgenstein, investigating what we call *x* is a chief way of investigating what *x* is.

were mis-calibrated. But if significant differences could not be explained in such a way, or if they were persistent or extreme, then we would not judge that these agents were *measuring* (even if they were going through the motions of measuring, following "procedures," as they call them). It would be hard to understand *what* they were doing. Even if we *could* come to understand their pseudo-measuring activity, it would have a role in their lives very different from the role measuring has in ours.[13]

Similarly, agreement in judgments is the expected consequence of our establishment of a shared language; that is, we will agree about when a statement in the language is true, and when false. What happens when we disagree? We look for an explanation: Perhaps there are differences in our background beliefs, or in our experiences; or perhaps the discrepancy arises from differences in the care we take in reasoning, or the meanings we assign to our expressions. Finding such explanations can secure agreement in judgments at a deeper level, even when our initial judgments diverge. But if we cannot agree in our judgments at some level – if you insist on saying it is night when I say it is day, and there is no accounting for the difference – then we are not communicating. The idea that logic has fixed the meaning of our utterances, even though we disagree so thoroughly, gets no grip here. Or, to reformulate the conclusion: If we are communicating, then we will largely agree in our judgments.

There is another dimension of the dependence of communication on agreement in judgments. For, at another level, agreement in judgments is not just the necessary consequence of communication, it also makes communication possible. This dimension emerges from Wittgenstein's reflections on rule-following. Language use is a normatively structured activity, and our sharing norms depends on our agreeing at a level that goes deeper than simply accepting a body of rules. We can bring out this aspect of agreement by considering one of Wittgenstein's most famous thought experiments, which I will call "the parable of the wayward pupil."

The pupil has been taught to write series of integers according to the instruction "+n," and has been tested on series carried as high as 1000. Now we order him to continue the series "+2," and he writes 998, 1000, 1004, 1008, 1012.

> We say to him, "Look what you're doing!"—He doesn't understand. We say, "You should have added *two*: look how you began the series!"—He answers, "Yes, isn't it right? I thought that was how I *had* to do it."—Or

---

[13] For examples of what it takes to make sense of pseudo-measuring activity, see Cavell (1979, 115–118) and Cerbone (2000).

> suppose he pointed to the series and said, "But I did go on in the same way."—It would now be no use to say, "But can't you see …?"—and go over the old explanations and examples for him again. (PI §185)

Because the pupil finds it natural to continue the series in a wayward fashion, our communication with him is (at least temporarily and in this regard) blocked. There is no more fundamental level of principles the pupil *must* accept and to which we could appeal to get him to the correct continuation. (This does not mean that there is no way to teach him to continue the series correctly, but just that such teaching will take a form different from drawing out the consequences of his prior commitments.) To communicate with someone else, we have to agree on a wide range of things. At a fundamental level, we have to agree that vocables or inscriptions that are in some respects different (because spoken in different vocal registers or in different accents, or because written in different hands or fonts) are in the relevant sense *the same*. We have to agree that going on from 1000 to 1002 to 1004 is going on *in the same way* as going from 100 to 102 to 104. The idea of the wayward pupil surprises us into recognizing the multifarious dimensions of agreement in judgment that are presupposed in something as clearly defined as continuing the series "+ 2."

In his reflections on Wittgenstein, Stanley Cavell gives an indication of the range of these agreements:

> We learn and teach words in certain contexts, and then we are expected, and expect others, to be able to project them into further contexts. Nothing insures that this projection will take place (in particular, not the grasping of universals nor the grasping of books of rules), just as nothing insures that we will make, and understand, the same projections. That on the whole we do is a matter of our sharing routes of interest and feeling, modes of response, senses of humor and of significance and of fulfillment, of what is outrageous, of what is similar to what else, what a rebuke, what forgiveness, of when an utterance is an assertion, when an appeal, when an explanation—all the whirl of organism Wittgenstein calls "forms of life." Human speech and activity, sanity and community, rest upon nothing more, but nothing less, than this. (Cavell 1976, 52)

This sharing of sensibilities, this whirl of organism, is what, in *The Claim of Reason*, Cavell describes as "mutual attunement in judgments" (Cavell 1979, 115).

> The idea of agreement here is not that of coming to or arriving at an agreement on a given occasion, but of being in agreement throughout, being in harmony, like pitches or tones, or clocks, or weighing scales, or columns of figures. That a group of human beings *stimmen* in their language *überein*

says, so to speak, that they are mutually voiced with respect to it, mutually *attuned* top to bottom. (Cavell 1979, 32)

What is the conception of logic that this leaves us with? For Wittgenstein, our ordinary language has a "grammar" – a rich and nuanced web of conceptual relations among its possible propositions. This grammar is reflected in our judgments regarding the implications of its propositions and how they are connected to evidence and action. A logic-as-formal-system is an abstraction from the grammar of our language. A formal system is clear and certain ("crystalline" if you will): free from ambiguity, readily teachable, capable of delivering definitive verdicts as to which inferences are correct and which incorrect. Such a system aspires to command assent the way 1000 + 2 = 1002 commands assent.[14] It has these features, *because we have built them into it*; we would not accept a logic-as-formal-system that lacked them. A logic-as-formal-system is a priori, not because it commands us from the platonic heights of *logica ens*, but because it presents in perspicuous form the commitments already implicit in our concepts. Accordingly, our grammar is the source and touchstone of any analysis in terms of a logic-as-formal-system. Cavell asks: "How does the logician know that (1) 'Nobody is in the auditorium' must be transcribed differently from (2) 'Peabody is in the auditorium'?" The answer Cavell finds in Wittgenstein is that the logician draws on his "knowledge of what we ordinarily mean in using an expression, or the knowledge of the particular circumstances in which an expression is actually used" (Cavell 1976, 62).

Since a logic-as-formal-system expresses necessary relations among propositions, it can look as though Wittgenstein's conception of the relation between logics-as-formal-systems and language leaves the notion of necessity insufficiently grounded, as though what is necessary depended on what we believe to be necessary. Cavell expresses this worry as follows: "[Wittgenstein's] philosophy provides, one might say, an anthropological, or even anthropomorphic, view of necessity; and that can be disappointing; as if it is not really *necessity* which he has given an anthropological view of. As though if the a priori has a history it cannot really be the a priori in question" (Cavell 1979, 118–119).

The fact is that the a priori does have a history. Logics-as-formal-systems that were accepted by our ancestors have been replaced by different and incompatible formal systems. This is not just a matter of replacing unwieldy

---

[14] Cavell (1979, 118) identifies these features as belonging to anything that we would count as logic, by which he means a logic-as-formal-system.

or less powerful formal systems with ones that do more, better. For example, Aristotelian syllogistic regarded inferences as valid that we now regard as committing the "existential fallacy."[15] This is not truth replacing error, but instead a realignment of our concepts (in this case, the content of universal categorical propositions) that is akin to a Kuhnian paradigm shift. But the fact that the concept of necessity has a history should not make us think that the grammar from which it is derived is arbitrary or merely conventional, or simply a reflection of psychological propensities to connect one concept with another. Our concepts reflect our form of life, the kind of creature we are. They evolve as our form of life evolves, with the kind of inner "logic" that we see in the emergence of one genre of music from another, or in the transition from one political order to another. These changes may not be predictable, but they are neither random nor matters of unfettered decision nor expressions of mere psychological tendencies – though it is true that if people made different decisions or had different psychologies, our concepts would be different.[16]

We may summarize this area of Wittgenstein's thought by saying that our being able to communicate depends on our being mutually attuned – on our agreeing in our judgments of sameness and difference, similarity and dissimilarity, and so on, so that we can agree in the application of our words. A logic-as-formal-system is derived from the grammar embedded in our language, so it too depends on our attunements. And these attunements are malleable in some dimensions: They spring from the special biological endowment of *Homo sapiens*, and they are shaped by education and culture, by our individual experiences and psychologies. This last observation, on the malleability of our attunements, will provide a key for interpreting Heidegger.

8.7   Anxiety as Attunement

We are now in a position to offer an interpretation of Heidegger's attitude toward "logic" in "What Is Metaphysics?" (1929). As I argued above, Heidegger's investigation of Being in *Being and Time* (1927) yields the inconsistency expressed in theses (1)–(3). But it is not until "What

---

[15] Priest (2014b, 213) makes a similar argument.

[16] Compare Wittgenstein's remark: "If anyone believes that certain concepts are absolutely the correct ones … then let him imagine certain very general facts of nature to be different from what we are used to, and the formation of concepts different from the usual ones will become intelligible to him" (Part II of the *Investigations*, entitled "Philosophy of Psychology: A Fragment" in the 4th ed., §366).

Is Metaphysics?" that Heidegger explicitly broaches the possibility of overthrowing "logic." What moves Heidegger against logic in "What Is Metaphysics?" appears at first to be something utterly different from the status of Being, namely, the status of what Heidegger calls "the Nothing." But as it turns out, the Nothing and Being are intimately connected. "What Is Metaphysics?" starts with Heidegger's observation that science requires a special attitude in which Dasein submits itself to entities, letting them have "the first and last word" (GA9, 104/83). Metaphysics seeks to understand the relationship of scientific Dasein to entities, to understand and explain how entities are revealed for scientific investigation. Heidegger claims that this revelation takes place through a fundamental experience of Dasein: This is anxiety, an "attunement" in which Dasein encounters the Nothing – "In the clear night of the Nothing of anxiety the original open-ness of entities as such arises: that they are entities – and not Nothing" (GA9, 114/90). This encounter is supposed to explain the possibility of science, but it raises a paradox structurally parallel to the paradox of Being. For the Nothing is not an entity; accordingly it does not make sense to say that the Nothing *is* this or *does* that. Yet Heidegger also appears to make many assertions about the Nothing, for example that the Nothing *is that in the face of which Dasein has anxiety.* The Nothing is, and it is not.

Indeed, for Heidegger, the Nothing and Being are linked by more than the parallel conundrums that attend attempts to philosophize about them. Experiencing the Nothing brings Dasein face to face with Being: Being "manifests itself only in the transcendence of a Dasein that is held out into the Nothing" (GA9, 120/95). Indeed, Heidegger endorses Hegel's dictum "Pure Being and pure Nothing are therefore the same" (GA9, 120/94). Accordingly we may take the problem of talking about the Nothing to be the same as the problem of talking about Being.

As I remarked above, Heidegger's response to this paradox is fundamentally different from Priest's superficially similar response. Priest weighs the theoretical costs and benefits of retaining versus rejecting the principle of noncontradiction. By contrast, Heidegger describes, in evocative but elusive detail, Dasein's *experience of the Nothing.* His argument is *not* that we should reject the principle of noncontradiction in order to solve metaphysical problems regarding Being and the Nothing. That may be true (in Heidegger's opinion), but the case for allowing (self-contradictory) talk about the Nothing is based not on theoretical considerations, but rather on what experience reveals to us. Indeed, Heidegger even claims that the legitimacy of his metaphysical investigation "can be demonstrated only on the basis of a fundamental experience of the Nothing" (GA9, 109/87).

How can an experience of any kind make it legitimate to talk about the Nothing, when doing so violates the principle of noncontradiction? Can an "experience" prove that the Nothing both is and is not an entity? Or prove that the Nothing can be a topic of assertions?

For Heidegger, the principle of noncontradiction belongs to a family of logics-as-formal-systems that he regards as "the *traditional* interpretation of thinking"; this is the "logic" whose sovereignty he seeks to overcome (GA9, 117/92; cf. GA9 107/85, 120/95). In the "Postscript to 'What Is Metaphysics?'" Heidegger comments on this traditional logic as follows:

> Why does the lecture place this term in quotation marks? So as to indicate that "logic" is only *one* interpretation of the essence of thinking, indeed the one that, as its very name shows, rests upon the experience of Being attained in Greek thought. (GA9, 308/235)

If the Greeks' experience of Being can give us the logic-as-formal-system that has devolved into what Heidegger decries as mere "logistics" (GA9, 308/235), then perhaps Dasein's experience of the Nothing can give us access to a possibility of thought that can tolerate the peculiar descriptions of Being and the Nothing that Heidegger finds himself forced into.

As I read Heidegger, the experience of anxiety is supposed to provide that new way of thinking. It is a shift in Dasein's attunements so that what before was paradoxical becomes comprehensible, what before made no sense becomes sensical. Like the Wittgensteinian attunements that allow us to agree in our applications of rules and projections of words into new contexts, these attunements lie at a level different from the rules of logical systems. They are not stances I can be argued into. But a special experience can impel me to adopt them.

The idea that anxiety is akin to the Wittgensteinian notion of attunement is suggested by Heidegger's terminology. Anxiety, like related states such as profound boredom and joy at someone else's existence, is what he calls a *Gestimmtsein*, or a way of being in tune; Heidegger also refers to such states as *Stimmungen*, or moods. These are etymologically connected to *Stimme*, or voice, and the verb *stimmen*, which can mean *to give voice to something* or *to tune a musical instrument*. Cavell stresses exactly these etymological features when he chooses the term "attunement" for the concept he finds in Wittgenstein. This etymological commonality does not prove that anxiety is an attunement in precisely Cavell's sense. But it does indicate that both concepts pertain to being in tune with something. Wittgenstein emphasizes being in harmony with other speakers. Heidegger emphasizes being in tune with the world, with entities as a whole.

The power of an experience to shift the boundaries of intelligibility may be illustrated with two examples. One is the experience of coming to see a new aspect. So long as I see a duck-rabbit drawing only as a duck, the suggestion that it is a picture of a rabbit makes no sense to me: I cannot see how the words "It's a rabbit" could describe this image. The possibility that the drawing can be so described becomes intelligible when – through a switch in my visual experience – I see it as a rabbit. Perhaps anxiety is an analogous switch in my perception. Normally, my experience is of *this* determinate thing and *that* determinate thing; in anxiety, entities do not change, but now I experience a new aspect: indeterminateness. This experience is what Heidegger describes as anxiety making the Nothing manifest (GA9, 111/88). Because language imputes some level of determinateness to whatever we talk about, we end up saying things like "The Nothing is ... and is not ...." Our traditional logics-as-formal-systems reject this talk as nonsensical, but perhaps Heidegger is suggesting that the novel perception produced by anxiety gives meaning to our attempts to describe the Nothing.

A second example of how an experience can alter one's attunements so that what seemed incoherent becomes meaningful, and even true, is religious conversion, according to some accounts of it. The claim that God is three persons in one or that Jesus's death atones for our sins is unintelligible to someone without Christianity's commitments. But a religious conversion (which might be described as the experience of being touched by grace) can so alter the convert's understanding – their sense of what makes sense – that these theological doctrines become intelligible to them. The convert does not learn anything new, but everything appears transformed. Perhaps the "clear night of the Nothing" similarly transforms someone who undergoes it so that the Nothing and Being become intelligible.

8.8 The Locus of Anxiety

The understanding acquired by the convert and the perception delivered by seeing a new aspect remain inaccessible to those untouched by grace and those to whom the aspect has not dawned. If the new attunements that come with anxiety work in a similar fashion, then those who have experienced anxiety will be able to philosophize about Being in ways that will be unintelligible to those who have not. The revision of the logics-as-formal-systems that Heidegger calls for will be available only to those thinkers who have undergone this fundamental experience.

This conclusion would mean that Heidegger is offering an esoteric philosophy, one whose insights are available only to the initiated. This would make his metaphysics a specialized discipline, which could be pursued only by those whose experience of anxiety has attuned them for it. The critics who think there is nothing to Heidegger's invocation of the Nothing could be dismissed as unqualified because they are not appropriately attuned. However, this conception of Heidegger's philosophy is incompatible with the role he claims for metaphysics. In "What Is Metaphysics?" he says that encountering the Nothing is an essential occurrence in human existence:

> [S]cientific Dasein is possible only if in advance it holds itself out into the Nothing. … Only because the Nothing is manifest can science make entities themselves objects of investigation. (GA9, 121/95)

Furthermore, not just science but *any* attitude toward entities depends on Dasein's relationship to the Nothing: "Human Dasein can comport itself toward entities only if it holds itself out into the Nothing" (GA9, 120/96). And, as we have seen, it is in anxiety that Dasein encounters the Nothing: "With the fundamental attunement of anxiety we have arrived at that occurrence in Dasein in which the Nothing is manifest" (GA9, 112/89). These statements entail that anxiety – the mood that makes the Nothing manifest – is a necessary precondition for doing science and indeed for any comportment toward entities.

Each of us comports ourselves toward entities: We use tools, interact with other people, engage in more or less theoretical reflections about entities. But have we all experienced anxiety? Have we all been held out into the Nothing? Or is anxiety, as the condition for the ability to comport oneself toward entities, a feature of *Dasein* but not of each human being? How are we to understand the experience of anxiety if it really is the condition for human life as we know it?

There are at least three routes Heidegger could take in answering this question. One way to understand the way anxiety makes possible our encounters with entities is to hold that undergoing anxiety is an experience only for a few intrepid individuals. They serve as pioneers, achieving an understanding that reveals entities; they then open that understanding to the rest of us. This interpretation is suggested by Heidegger's description of the "anxiety of those who are daring" (GA9, 118/93). Alternatively, we could think of anxiety as a cultural and historical phenomenon. Just as the Greeks achieved an experience of Being that they expressed in *logos*, so a new era can achieve an experience of the Nothing that expresses itself in a new contra-"logical" metaphysics. On this view, it is *Dasein* who is anxious, and Dasein's anxiety is different from the anxiety of individual human beings. Finally, we can maintain that anxiety is ubiquitous: Every human being has anxiety and so has encountered the Nothing, and this is what enables each of us to relate to entities.

I believe that the most illuminating of these three interpretations is the one that seems most implausible, namely, the interpretation according to which every human being has experienced anxiety. It seems obviously false: While no doubt all adults have been anxious, worried, fearful at some points in their lives, has *everyone* tumbled into the abyss of indeterminateness that is the experience of anxiety Heidegger describes? Many people will deny having undergone that form of anxiety. Are they wrong about what they have experienced?

Heidegger would say that they are. Human beings have an inveterate tendency to deny, repress, and cover up essential features of our existence. An experience can shape us, even when we repress the memory of it, or even when we prevent it from coming to consciousness in the first place. So it is with our experience of the Nothing. If anxiety runs through each of us, then each of us satisfies this necessary condition for encountering entities. And each of us is, in principle, capable of understanding Heidegger's metaphysics. But this does not entail that we actually are attuned to understand it, for it could be that we need to uncover anxiety – to experience it in a self-conscious, reflective manner – in order to get what Heidegger is saying about the Nothing.

We cannot decide to understand: "We are so finite that we cannot even bring ourselves originally before the Nothing through our own decision and will" (GA9, 118/93). But perhaps we can decide not to *refuse* to understand. I have argued that, if Heidegger seeks a revision of the formal rules of logic, the revision would have to come from so altering our attunements that we made new judgments of what makes sense, of what is possible. I suggest that we remain open to the possibility that Heidegger's philosophical investigation of Being is tenable, despite the contradiction it embodies. If we are to find the sense in this investigation, we will have to excavate the anxiety that we generally and for the most part repress and cover up.[17]

[17] I thank Sebastian Pendleton-Witherspoon for invaluable feedback on earlier drafts. And I am profoundly grateful to Filippo Casati for many fruitful conversations. His insights into Heidegger and Priest, Cavell and Wittgenstein, opened up routes for thinking about the topic of this chapter that I would not have found without him.

CHAPTER 9

Heidegger and the Authority of Logic

Kris McDaniel

Was Heidegger hostile to logic?[1] Not any more than he was hostile to chemistry, or to history, or to the systematic study of phonemes. Rather, he was hostile to a particular view about the *authority* of logic, one in which putative logical propositions *demand* assent and serve to constrain our thinking about nonlogical subject areas such as metaphysics. On my view, Heidegger is less interested in revising or rejecting principles such as the law of noncontradiction than he is in defending his right to revise or reject these principles if his metaphysical investigations demand that he do so.[2]

In this chapter, I argue that, given his metaphysics, his rejection of the authority of logic is defensible. This observation in turn supports Heidegger's claim that logic should be based on metaphysics rather than the other way around (GA26, 36, 127–128).[3] Logic, in Heidegger's view, is not a "secure" (*gesicherte*) discipline that can act as a border police of our metaphysical territory (GA26, 132). Moreover, Heidegger rejects the tendency "to isolate logic and base logic on itself alone" (GA26, 70).

In this chapter, I explore the implications of the metaphysical views of the Heidegger of roughly the era of *Being and Time* for the question of the authority of logic. Since the question of the authority of logic is itself vexing, and since the question of what Heidegger's views are during this time is highly contested, I expect resistance to what follows. In order to make the debates I anticipate profitable, I first discuss some related

---

[1] In what follows, I focus solely on the Heidegger of *Being and Time* and related roughly contemporary texts, rather than the "post-turn" Heidegger. For the claim that this Heidegger is hostile to logic, see Fey (1974); Friedman (2001, 156); Philipse (1998, 9–15); Shirley (2010, 1–8); and White (1985, 22–25).
[2] This interpretation of Heidegger's attitude toward logic is not particularly novel; see, for example, Fay (1974, 85–87, 93). What will hopefully be novel is my account of why Heidegger's metaphysical system would license this attitude. Käufer (2001) suggests that what Heidegger is hostile to is traditional (pre-Fregean) logic rather than rigorous thinking per se.
[3] See also Mohanty (1988, 125–127) and Shirley (2010, 32).

questions about logic and then state putative answers to them that have the following features. First, they jointly provide an account of why and in what way logic is (allegedly) authoritative. Second, Heidegger was familiar with these putative answers, and he took himself to have good grounds for rejecting them.

Here are the questions about logic to which putative answers are forthcoming. Some of these questions are about the epistemic status of logic: Are logical judgments rationally revisable? Is logic a priori? Do logical claims have a kind of methodological priority over other claims? These questions will be the focus of Section 9.1.

Other questions are about the metaphysical status of logic: Does logic have a distinctive ontology of logical objects? Do logical objects have distinctive metaphysically fundamental properties, such as intentional properties or the properties of being true or false? Is logic a topic-neutral science? And is there a science of objects as such – that is, a formal ontology – that is properly construed as a part of logic? These questions will be the focus of Section 9.2.

Heidegger's views enter the discussion in Section 9.3. There are two relevant aspects of Heidegger's metaphysics that I discuss. First, Heidegger claimed that the ultimate ground for all intentionality is to be found in Dasein's mode of being, which in turn implies that the ultimate grounds for truth and falsity are to be found in the same source. Second, I interpret Heidegger as endorsing *ontological pluralism*.[4] Ontological pluralism is the view that there are modes of being. There are various kinds of beings, such as people, lumps of matter, trees, and hammers, but there are also various kinds of being corresponding to these different kinds of beings. It's not merely that a person isn't a lump of matter; it's not even the case that a person *is* in the way that a lump of matter *is*. Given ontological pluralism, even if there are distinctively logical objects, there is a further question about how these distinctively logical objects *are* – that is, there is a further question about the mode of being of logical objects. Moreover, I argue that Heidegger's views on the source of truth and falsity along with Heidegger's particular version of ontological pluralism imply that many of the putative answers to the questions discussed in Sections 9.1 and 9.2 are false, which in turn undercuts the alleged explanation for the authority of logic.

---

[4] See McDaniel (2013, 2016, and 2017, chap. 1) for defenses of this interpretation of Heidegger; McDaniel (2017) also discusses many other versions of ontological pluralism besides Heidegger's. See also Carman (2013) and McManus (2013a and 2020) for critical assessments of this reading of Heidegger.

As we'll see, questions concerning the authority of a formal theory to dictate or constrain a metaphysics are not new. Nor are they dead questions. There are several places in the contemporary literature in which certain principles stated in a formalized language are taken to be inviolable constraints on theorizing. Here are three examples: David Lewis's (1986 and 1991) use of classical mereology to rule out a metaphysics of structural universals and states of affairs; Timothy Williamson's (2013) adoption of a quantified S5 modal logic as modal metaphysics enough; and Kit Fine's (1994, 1995, and 2012) articulation of a logic of grounding, which in turn rules out structuralist metaphysical systems. My view is that none of these theories comes even close to being authoritative in the sense that I articulate.[5] One might think that nonetheless logic has a special status that these other formal theories lack – but if logic itself lacks this status, certainly classical mereology, S5 modal logic, and the logic of grounding do as well.

9.1   Epistemic Questions about Logic

Here are three interrelated epistemic questions about logic: Are logical judgments rationally revisable? Is logic a priori? Do logical claims have a kind of methodological priority over other claims?

Let's begin with the first question, which we'll refine so that it is not easily answered affirmatively. To revise a judgment is to increase or decrease how strongly you hold that judgment. And it obvious that it is often rational to do this. Students who are learning logic often start from a reasonably low degree of confidence in some of their logical judgments, and through practice come to have rationally higher degrees of confidence in those same judgments. But this fact isn't really relevant for us here, which is why the first pass at the question needs refining. What about experts – highly trained logicians with years under their belts? Consider such an expert and a given logical judgment about which she is highly confident. Perhaps it is the principle of noncontradiction. But then she reads some philosophy – perhaps Graham Priest (2006b) on dialetheism – and as a result she becomes somewhat less confident, albeit still fairly confident. That she is now less confident is not irrational.

Note that, contra Quine (1970, 100; 1951, 40), the question of whether a logical judgment is rationally revisable doesn't seem to be especially closely

---

[5] Heidegger would presumably agree. Note that, on the reading of Heidegger's metaphysics defended in McDaniel (2013), Lewis's mereology is inconsistent with Heidegger's views on the nature of material objects. On nonstandard views about grounding, see Bliss (2013, 2014) and Barnes (2018).

tied to the question of whether logical judgments are empirical – at least not with some clarity on what it is for a judgment to be a priori.[6] (More on this soon.) For it seems that both the student and the expert logician rationally change their degrees of confidence in their logical judgments not via the acquisition of new empirical information, but rather by simply doing further thinking. Reading Graham Priest is the occasion for the change in judgment, but in principle, the expert logician could have worked through these thoughts on her own.

Also note that, if logical judgments are rationally revisable, they don't have a kind of absolute methodological priority over all other types of judgments.[7] One type of judgment has methodological priority over another type if and only if it is never the case that one can rationally decrease one's confidence in judgments of the first type in light of one's confidence in judgments of the second type. Suppose, for example, that I am fairly confident in a law of logic (perhaps it is the principle of noncontradiction) but also fairly confident in some metaphysical thesis (perhaps it is the thesis that for every predicate, there is a corresponding abstract property). Suppose I learn that these two theses are inconsistent with one another. Suppose I read my Graham Priest or other relevant texts and, as a result, my confidence in the logical principle drops – and in fact drops below my confidence level in my metaphysical thesis. Why shouldn't then my confidence in my metaphysical thesis provide me with rational grounds for further dropping my level of confidence in the law of logic?

We've seen some evidence that the question of whether logical judgments can be rationally revised itself requires revision if we want to consider a question that is not easily answered affirmatively, and also that this question is in some way connected up with the other two questions. Here is the central question we will discuss: Can a person be situated with

---

[6] In what follows, I will have very little to say about the nature of rationality or theories thereof. For a nice discussion of Quine on the revisability of logic, see Bryant (2017).

[7] The distinction between thinking and experiencing might be challenged by a phenomenologist, since thinking itself might be an experiential activity in which something is revealed to the thinker. For example, Brentano (1995, xxv) writes, "My psychological standpoint is empirical; experience alone is my teacher. Yet I share with other thinkers the conviction that this is entirely compatible with a certain ideal point of view [*Anschauung*]." (A better translation here would have substituted "intuition" for "point of view.") And, as will be discussed briefly later, Husserl's (2005b) account of the a priori in Investigation III is one in which resting on the intuition of essences is the defining characteristic of a justified a priori judgment. And, as Dan Dahlstrom has suggested to me, if Heidegger is right that all thinking is an affect-laden process, this might provide further reason to be suspicious of a hard distinction between thinking and experiencing. (There might still be a hard distinction between empirical and a priori judgment, however, if something like the Husserlian view of the a priori is correct.) I thank Dan Dahlstrom for helpful discussion here.

respect to a judgment about some logical principle so that the judgment is no longer rationally revisable, is a priori (in some suitable sense), and as such this judgment should trump those judgments inconsistent with it? And if this is possible (i.e., if a person can be so situated in their judgment about a logical principle), what are the conditions under which this is actual?

Heidegger was familiar with the following answers to these questions.[8] There is a distinctive domain of characteristically logical entities: propositions in themselves, abstract concepts or meanings, and the web of logical relations that connect them.[9] These logical entities in turn have *essences*, and they are essentially such that they obey the laws of logic. (This is what makes true logical claims *laws*.) In principle, these essences can be *fully presented in a completely adequate manner* to creatures such as ourselves.[10] When an essence is fully presented to a person, that person can articulate and understand that essence and via that understanding have knowledge of that essence. This knowledge is propositional: It is a known judgment. This judgment is a priori in the truest sense of that term, because the best account of what it is for a judgment to be a priori is this: A judgment is a priori if and only if it is knowable by way of knowledge of the essences of things.[11] And when an essence is presented to a person, and that person has articulated and understood that essence, the judgment so derived is not rationally revisable – because the essence is, as it were, in full view, and one cannot rationally revise a judgment when the truth-maker for the judgment has presented itself in a fully adequate manner and it is fully apparent that the truth-maker is a truth-maker for that judgment. Because this judgment is not rationally revisable, it has a kind of methodological priority over judgments that can be rationally revised. And so, at least in principle and often in fact, a person can have secure knowledge in a body of logical truths that can constrain theorizing about other topics. Finally, because the source of the best kind of knowledge of logical truths

[8] That's because these answers are defended by Husserl (2005a and 2005b). See Dahlstrom (2001, 15–16) for a discussion of the influence of the *Logical Investigations* on Heidegger's development.

[9] Mohanty (1988, 108–109) plausibly attributes this sort of metaphysics to the very early Heidegger; see Heidegger (GA1, 292–293, 301).

[10] By way of contrast, a physical object such as a car is never fully presented in a completely adequate manner, since we always see it only by having a part of it, for example its front side, but never the whole all at once. As Daniel Dahlstrom has suggestively expressed to me, a physical object always has a hidden side, but when an essence is fully presented in a completely adequate manner, there is no hidden side of it remaining to be seen.

[11] See Husserl's (2005a) third *Logical Investigation* for an argument that this is how the a priori should be conceived.

is our insight into the essence of logical objects, logic is a self-standing and independent science that needs or requests no assistance from any other disciple in order to justify its laws.[12]

Perhaps there are other theories about why logic is authoritative, and I invite the reader to consider whether the kinds of considerations discussed in Section 9.3 are applicable to these theories. I discuss only this theory of the authoritativeness of logic in what follows. Note that this is a view in which logic is a *stable* discipline, since its principles are known via insight into the essences of an unchanging body of abstract objects. And on this view, logic is *isolatable* from other disciplines – it need take no lessons from psychology or speculative metaphysics – and so logic can be "based on logic alone."

However, this particular answer is up to its eyeballs in metaphysics. So let me say a bit more about this metaphysics next.

9.2 Metaphysical Questions about Logic

The first metaphysical question about logic – does logic have a distinctive ontology? – received the beginning of an affirmative answer in the previous section: The ontology of logic is an ontology of abstract meanings/concepts/propositions that have essences that can be discerned by us. But what is the mode of being that they enjoy? And what is the metaphysical status of the distinctively representational properties, preeminent among them truth, that they exemplify?

Is the mode of being of logical objects the same mode of being as the mode of being of everything else? For an ontological pluralist like Heidegger, this claim is a nonstarter, but note also that few if any of his philosophical influences accepted it either. Brentano (1966, 56–93) denied that there are logical entities such as propositions full stop, and so the question of their mode of being does not arise for him. Bolzano (Bolzano 2014, vol. 1, §§48–49, pp. 59, 173) and Husserl (2005a, 149–150) denied

---

[12] Compare with GA26, 71. As James Kinkaid has suggested to me, similar remarks would hold for *regional ontologies* as well, since those also are a body of a priori truths known via insight into the essences of the particular kind of entity – that is, the region of entity – in question. One difference that makes no difference here is that formal ontology is understood by Husserl as providing a system of analytic laws, while regional ontological truths are synthetic (2005b, 72). But this difference is definitional rather than epistemological because Husserl understands the analytic/synthetic distinction largely in terms of the topic-neutral/topic-specific distinction (2005b, Third Investigation). That a regional ontology is synthetic makes it no less authoritative. I am inclined to ascribe to Heidegger the view that the regional ontology of Dasein is authoritative in my sense, while formal ontology is not. See McDaniel (2014) for a discussion of a phenomenological approach to ontology.

that they have the mode of being of reality, which you and I enjoy and whose mark is temporality, and affirmed instead, respectively, either that they simply are or that they have ideal being rather than real being. Lotze (1884, 438–440) distinguished between the mode of being that substances have from the mode of being enjoyed by events – they have occurrence – and distinguished both of these from the mode of being of true propositions, which he labeled "validity." It is unclear to me what ontological status Lotze attributed to false propositions, and I think it was unclear to Heidegger as well.[13] In Heidegger's discussion of Lotze's theory of validity, Heidegger repeatedly says that it is the mode of being of true propositions but in that context doesn't mention false propositions at all (GA21, 70), and in Heidegger's discussion of falsity, there is no further mention of Lotze (GA21, 168–175). Moreover, Heidegger (GA21, 74) explicitly wonders whether, for Lotze, truth just is validity.[14]

Where Lotze was unclear, Meinong (1960, 90–91) was explicit. According to Meinong, a true objective has a distinctive kind of being – it subsists – while a false objective has no being at all, but nonetheless there are false objectives.[15] A similar view is defended by Reinach (1982, 335–442), for whom states of affairs are what we assert and deny, and they are the bearers of logical and explanatory relations; states of affairs have subsistence rather than existence as their mode of being, but they do not have subsistence essentially, and what corresponds to a true assertion is a subsisting state of affairs.

Now for the question of the metaphysical status of truth and other representational properties. Do logical objects have distinctive metaphysically fundamental properties, such as intentional properties or the properties of being true or false? As noted above, for Meinong and Reinach (and perhaps for Lotze) truth just is subsistence (or validity?), and so there is no need for a distinctive property of being true. Truths are subsisting facts; falsehoods are facts that lack any sort of being. (We could call them "alternative facts.") Given this theory, a proposition – what Meinong calls an

---

[13] Other commentators also seem unclear on this. Mohanty (1988, 111) characterizes validity as the mode of being of "propositions and truths" – but isn't this redundant if truths are among the propositions? Dahlstrom (2001, 41–46, 108, 388) tells us that it is truths that are valid and that validity is truth's form of actuality. Käufer (2005b, 149) says both that validity is the mode of being of the logical, but also that truth is defined in terms of validity; these are jointly consistent only if false propositions lack the mode of being of the logical.

[14] See also GA24, 282–283.

[15] Note that there are true objectives about the nonexistence of objects – for example, the object that the perpetual motion machine does not exist is true, and this objective subsists, despite the nonexistence of the object that it is about.

"objective" and Reinach a "state of affairs" – is what it is about in virtue of being identical with what it is about.

For Bolzano and Husserl, however, truth is not reducible to a mode of being, as true and false propositions have the same mode of being.[16] Thus, for them, the question of the nature of propositional truth (and falsity) is less straightforward: How for them does a proposition manage to represent? Bolzano (2014, 92–93) briefly indicates support for a relatively deflationary form of a correspondence theory of truth: A proposition is true when it states what belongs to its object.[17] Husserl has a much richer account. In his sixth *Logical Investigation*, he provides an account of how we acquire the concept of propositional truth. First, we can "see" the propositional content of a judgment because a proposition is itself a universal that is exemplified by the judgment itself, and so we can "see" the proposition in the judgment in a way analogous to how we can "see" the type *fear* in a specific instance of fear – or see the redness that the red rose exemplifies. We can also "see" states of affairs via a faculty that Husserl calls *categorial intuition*, and in some cases we can "see" that a state of affairs and the judgment made true by that state of affairs "coincide."[18] This is an account not of the nature of truth but rather of the etiology of (one of) our concepts of truth – by way of tracing this concept back to the original intuitions from which it is "derived." But this etiology of the concept also suggests an account of what that concept is about, namely, that truth itself consists in the correspondence of a proposition with a state of affairs.[19]

Propositions don't merely have truth-values, but in general, they represent that something is the case. Perhaps a proposition represents a state of affairs if and only if that state of affairs is what would make it true. This proposal doesn't settle which direction of the bi-conditional explains the other, or whether they are both equally primary. Let's provisionally assume that the left-hand side explains the right-hand side, that is, the explanation for why a given state of affairs would make a proposition true is that the proposition represents that state of affairs. We make this provisional assumption in order to ask the next thorny question, namely: Is what a

---

[16] See Bolzano (2014, 1.84). See also Russell (1992, section 427), who criticizes Lotze's claim that validity is the being of truth. Russell's criticism is that both false and true propositions have being (and neither exists), and so truth neither is a mode of being nor corresponds to one.

[17] Interestingly, Lapointe (2011, 81–83) notes that, elsewhere, Bolzano denies that truths are grounded in what they are about.

[18] Heidegger (GA20, 64) sympathetically discusses Husserl's notion of categorial intuition.

[19] See also Okrent (1988, 110–115, 122) and Dahlstrom (2001, 63–94).

proposition represents grounded in something external to the proposition, or is it somehow grounded only in something internal to the proposition, such as its constituents and how they are arranged, or is it an ungrounded, primitive fact about the proposition? We are going to return to this question in the next section.

But first, one final aspect of the metaphysics of logic needs to be discussed, namely, the metaphysics of formal ontology. Husserl conceived of pure logic as dividing into two interdependent parts: formal apophantic logic, which is the logic of propositions and meanings and the subject of our discussion so far, and formal ontology, which is the systematic study of objects in general.[20] Both formal apophantic logic and formal ontology are "topic-neutral" sciences, but in different ways: Formal apophantic logic describes laws that govern all propositions regardless of what they are about, while formal ontology describes laws that govern all objects regardless of what kind of thing those objects are. And just as the laws of formal apophantic logic (henceforth, simply "logic" unless the context demands a clearer disambiguation) are best known – that is, known in a way that gives them authority – by way of intuitions of the essences of the logical, so too the principles of formal ontology are best known – that is, known in a way that gives them authority – by insight into the essence of objecthood as such, that is, of what it is to be *something*.

This is serious metaphysics. Perhaps this is the kind of metaphysics that is necessary to prevent both logic and ontology from collapsing into a disreputable psychologism that reduces their laws to merely locally valid empirical psychological generalizations.[21] But what is most relevant is that it is a metaphysics that imbues formal logic and formal ontology with the authority to constrain debates about particular topics (such as, for example, the study of culture) or particular objects (such as, for example, human beings) from above. Without this metaphysics, it is hard to see why logic and formal ontology would have this special status.

Heidegger rejected the claims that logic and formal ontology are authoritative. Unsurprisingly, he also rejected the metaphysics that underwrites these claims. And although he is not as explicit about this as one would like, there are plausible arguments built around premises that Heidegger explicitly accepts against this metaphysics. Let's discuss them next.

---

[20] See Husserl (2005a, 17–21; 2005b, 3). Husserl characterizes formal ontology as the science of something in general and its derived forms (Husserl 1973, 11).

[21] Bolzano (2014, 64–65) and Husserl (2005a) were motivated to endorse this ontology partly out of a desire to avoid this kind of reductive psychologism.

9.3   Heidegger and the Metaphysics of Logic

The logical and inferential relations that propositions bear to each other are a function of what those propositions represent. If what a proposition represents is an internal feature of that proposition, rather than determined by something external to the proposition, then the logical and inferential relations that propositions bear to each other are internal to the propositions considered collectively. And if that is the case, then, in principle, insight into the nature of propositions would suffice to "see" how those propositions are logically and inferentially related – and this in turn would ground authoritative knowledge of the laws of logic.

However, this picture falls apart if what propositions represent is not determined by something internal to the propositions themselves. According to Heidegger, both the truth-values of propositions and even their representational properties – their intentionality – are derived features. I focus on representational features more generally rather than truth specifically.[22]

Heidegger's remarks on these matters can be found in many places, but here is what I take to be a fair summary of Heidegger's argument. First, propositions represent only in virtue of being types of possible judgments that would have the same representational content. But possible judgments have content only in virtue of a deeper fact, namely, that Daseins – the kind of being that we are – are essentially such as to be open to the world.[23] What this means is rather involved, to say the least, but part of what it is to be essentially open to the world is for one's actions to have a primitive kind of intentionality – they involve a kind of understanding of something *as* something. Heidegger explicitly says that this understanding of something as something is pre-predicative and does not involve conceptual synthesis.[24] By this, he does not mean that possessing this understanding is temporally prior to the forming of judgments, but rather that it is prior in the order of explanation: That we are essentially such as to take things as being some way is what explains why judgments can be true or false, why they can represent what they represent.

---

[22] Dahlstrom (2001) is devoted to presenting and defending Heidegger's views on truth. One of the most prominent of these views is his rejection of what Dahlstrom calls "the logical prejudice," which is the uncritical assumption that the primary bearers of truth are propositions, judgments, or assertions. See also Okrent (1988, 97–107) and Carman (2003, 256–258).

[23] See Heidegger (SZ 218–224; GA26, 150–160, 168–169; GA21, 150–151) for the relevant texts. For discussion of this idea, see Wrathall (1999, 79–82). See also Dahlstrom (2001, 399–400); Shirley (2010, 5–6); and Käufer (2005b, 151).

[24] See Philipse (1998, 55–56). Okrent (1988, 53–54, 127) claims that the basic bearer of intentionality for Heidegger is "practical" and prior to perception.

So on Heidegger's view, propositions are not inherently intentional entities, and so the logical relations between them that are grounded in their representational content are not inherent facts about them either. It is certainly worth wondering what Heidegger should say about the Meinongian/Reinachian (and possibly Lotzean) view that propositions represent by virtue of being identical with what they represent. (It is hard to think of a view in which the representational features of a proposition are more internal than this!) Relatedly, one might think that even if the representational features of propositions are derivative, nonetheless there are inherent "syntactical" or structural properties of propositions, and in virtue of those alone some logical relations obtain. Heidegger could respond by claiming that what makes an internal structural relation be a genuinely logical relation is that it be in some way interpreted as being a logical relation – and, in turn, requires that these structural relations stand in relations to Dasein that make them meaningful.[25] So even if these structural relations are themselves internal relations, that these internal relations are logical relations is not internal to the propositions themselves.

Now for a premise that I think Heidegger doesn't explicitly assert, but I'll make explicit: If propositions have their representational content derivatively, then it is not part of the essences of propositions that they stand in logical and inferential relations to one another. This premise is necessary for the argument to go through, because without it, one could grant that the representational properties of propositions are derivative while still endorsing that they belong to the essences of the propositions that have them. Note that this now-made-explicit premise doesn't imply that any putative law of logic is in fact false. We do not, for example, have the materials to constitute any sort of threat to the law of noncontradiction. What we do have is a threat to the claim that the law of noncontradiction is binding on our theorizing. For if the laws of logic are not discernible by an inspection into the essences of logical entities, but that they are discernible is a necessary condition of the laws of logic to be authoritative, then it follows that the laws of logic are not authoritative.

---

[25] Here is a very simplified model to illustrate this idea. Pretend that there are continuum-many propositions. Then each proposition can be assigned a unique real number such that the relation of greater than or equal to corresponds to the relation of entailment: A proposition entails another proposition just in case the second is greater than or equal to the first. Now consider a view that dispenses with propositions as a distinct set of entities, but holds that these numbers can be interpreted as propositions, and that the relation of greater than or equal to can be interpreted as the relation of entailment. On this view, even if the relation of greater than or equal to is internal to the numbers as such, that this relation can be interpreted as the relation of entailment is not.

So does Heidegger reject principles of standard logic such as the law of noncontradiction? I think not really, although there are interesting arguments that he should.[26] But he is open to rejecting it, because he does not view it as authoritative.[27]

This discussion so far has presupposed that Heidegger believes that there are such abstract objects as propositions to begin with. If there are no propositions, then they have no essences to inspect, and so we have a more direct argument against the case for the authority of logic developed in Sections 9.1 and 9.2. Heidegger's take on whether there are such things is not crystal clear, to put it mildly, which is in sharp contrast to his earliest views on this issue.[28] Heidegger does often mention a mode of being enjoyed by abstracta, but this could be because he wants to discuss any mode that one of his interlocutors might believe in, rather than only those that he himself recognizes.[29] And there are places in which he is outright dismissive, such as where Heidegger (GA 24, 306) calls the postulation of a third realm of propositions an "invention that is no less doubtful than medieval speculation about angels." My impression, which is certainly not decisively supported by the textual evidence, is that Heidegger is indifferent to whether there are propositions – but he is confident that *if* there are propositions, they do not have their representational properties inherently, and so consequently we cannot read off the laws of logic by discerning their essence.[30]

Heidegger's challenge to the authority of logic also threatens Husserl's account of the etiology of our logical concepts, which, recall, is supposed to come from our intuitions of the essences of logical objects.[31] I am not aware of a systematic exploration of the origins of our logical concepts in Heidegger's works, but there is one notable and infamous suggestion about one of them, namely, that the origin of the concept of negation comes from our experience of nothingness.[32] Although this topic is very

---

[26] See Casati (2019) for a discussion of whether Heidegger should accept true contradictions in order to solve "the paradox of being." See also McDaniel (2016) for an ontologically pluralist resolution to the paradox of being.

[27] See Heidegger (GA26, 6), in which Heidegger questions whether the law of noncontradiction can be replaced.

[28] I thank Daniel Dahlstrom for reminding me of Heidegger's earlier acceptance of propositions.

[29] See, for example, Heidegger (SZ 215–218), where he also asks about the mode of being of the relation between the real and the ideal.

[30] Heidegger (GA21, 23–24) questions whether there are propositions, and later (GA21, 92–93) seriously considers the view that propositions are fictional entities. See also Carman (2003, 90–91).

[31] As Philipse (1998, 57) notes, Heidegger agrees with Husserl that all our concepts in some way derive from encounters with entities.

[32] See GA9, 107–108. See also Fay (1974, 85–86) and Philipse (1998, 12–13) for critical commentary. Note that Philipse takes Heidegger in this passage to deny the law of noncontradiction. However,

interesting, I won't pursue it here – I want to focus on the question of authority rather than the question of etiology. However, when it comes to the origins of our ontological concepts, the question of etiology will be discussed as well.

So let's turn to a discussion of formal ontology, the ontological counterpart to formal aphophantic logic. Husserl's view seems to have been that these two disciplines are, as it were, two sides of the same coin.[33] This claim has some plausibility. A thesis in formal ontology will be equivalent to a universally quantified statement that consists wholly of logical and formal ontological vocabulary. Roughly, what qualifies a term as a bit of basic formal ontological vocabulary is that it cannot be analyzed into simpler terms but it can still be applied to each kind of object, that is, it is a "topic-neutral" expression; the formal ontological vocabulary consists of the basic formal ontological vocabulary plus any other expression definable wholly in terms of it. Husserl thought the formal ontological vocabulary would include expressions such as "object," "part," "whole," "essence," "depends on," "property," "relation," and "state of affairs," among others. Every logical law will have a corresponding formal ontological law. Consider, for example, the law of noncontradiction that states that no proposition is both true and false. A corresponding formal ontological principle is that no object both has and lacks a given property.[34] It is hard to see how principles like the former would be authoritative if principles like the latter were not.

In general, a consequence of the claim that formal logic and formal ontology are two sides of the same coin is that formal ontology is authoritative if and only if formal logic is authoritative. If this bi-conditional is true, and the Heideggerian argument for the conclusion that formal aphophantic logic is not authoritative is sound, then formal ontology is also not authoritative.

---

as I am sure will be of no surprise at this point, I think what is going on is this: Heidegger is asserting that the law of noncontradiction is not authoritative, and so he is in within his rights to seriously consider metaphysical views that falsify it. See also Shirley (2010, 86–90, 141–144) and White (1985, chap. 1). James Kinkaid has directed my attention to a somewhat different account of the origin of our concept of negation that is suggested by Heidegger (SZ 284–287); he has also suggested to me that Heidegger (SZ 356–364) tentatively offers an etiology of our concept of a conditional. See also Kinkaid (2020) for an excellent discussion of phenomenological approaches to logic.

[33] Husserl (2005a, 150, as well as 2005b, Third Investigation). See also Dahlstrom (2010, 397–398), who argues that formal logic and formal ontology are not identical but are in an important sense equivalent.

[34] Compare again with Dahlstrom (2010, 397–398).

That's all well and good, but I'd like to approach things from the opposite direction – by first assessing whether there is an independent case for the conclusion that formal ontology is not authoritative. This is what we'll discuss next.

Recall that what would make formal ontology an authoritative science is the possibility of directly seeing that the laws it prescribes are true. And in order to directly see that the laws of formal ontology are true, being an object (in the most capacious sense), being a property, being an essence, and so forth, must have essences that can be directly intuited and are such that formal ontological laws are true according to them. On my reading of Heidegger, neither of these conditions is satisfied.

Let's start by examining objecthood, since formal ontology is meant to be a science of objects in general. Since everything is an object, "object" itself is not a bit of basic formal ontological vocabulary, but instead is definable simply in terms of being something: x is an object if and only if there is some y such that $x = y$. This conception of an object was recognized by Heidegger, albeit he used a different technical term to mark it in the following passage: "On the whole the word 'thing' here designates whatever is not simply nothing. In this sense the work of art is also a thing, so far as it is some sort of being" (GA5, 5). Since what is not simply nothing is something, "thing" as used here has the meaning of "object" as used above.

So does *being something* have an essence that we can directly intuit? And does this essence (along with the essences of other formal ontological features) license formal ontological laws? To say the least, asking what the essence of *being something* is and inquiring into the meaning of being are very similar tasks. I've now come to think that they are the same task, or at the very least, that doing the latter requires doing the former plus doing something more, such as inquiring into how *being* is understood and understandable by creatures like us.[35] In earlier work, I took the question that Heidegger posed to us to be answered by providing an account of what modes of being there are and how they are related to each other and to being itself. I also interpreted Heidegger to be claiming that the various modes of being he recognizes are more metaphysically fundamental than being itself, such that the latter is in some way to be understood in terms of the former.[36] I now think that, for Heidegger, this relation of metaphysical

---

[35] Compare with Okrent (1988, chap. 6).
[36] McDaniel (2017, chap. 1).

fundamentality should be understood in terms of essential dependence, and the reason why being itself is to be understood in terms of modes of being rather than the converse is that a real definition can be given of the former in terms of the latter.[37]

However, the real definition of *being* – that is, the meaning of being – isn't transparent to us, but rather must be clarified by first better understanding the various modes of being, beginning with the mode of being most familiar to us – namely, our own mode of being – and by destroying any preconceptions about these modes or being itself that we have inherited from our traditions. Prior to this clarification and destruction, Heidegger (SZ 8) thinks we have a merely "average, everyday" understanding of being (SZ 8).[38] See, for example, this passage:

> There is an understanding of the expression "being," even if it borders on a mere understanding of the word. The question is asked on the basis of this indeterminate pre-understanding of the expression "being." What is meant by "being"? (GA20, 194)

That the essence of being is not transparent to us is not enough to eliminate formal ontology as an authoritative discipline since it is conceivable that, if its essence became clear, we would be able read off formal ontological truths from that essence – provided that the other allegedly formal ontological features also have essences that can be made transparent and that would collectively ground formal ontological laws. (More on why Heidegger closes this latter possibility off in a moment.) If being were, for example, the only mode of being, or if being were more metaphysically fundamental than any of its modes, then there might be discernible laws governing beings as such, because all beings would have the same simple, unitary, and maximally capacious mode of being. And so even if it is currently not clear to us that being is this way, what matters for the authority of formal ontology is that the essence of being could become this clear.

However, by Heidegger's lights, the prospects for authoritative formal ontology are worse than that. Although being is obscure to us, our understanding of being is clear enough for us to see that being is unified merely by analogy rather than having a simple and unitary nature all of its own. This is noted here:

---

[37] See "The Essence of Being" in *Shadows of Being* (ms). I also argue there that we can still inquire into the essence of being and its modes, even if being and its modes are not themselves beings.

[38] Heidegger (GA26, 185) subtly stresses the difficulty of the project of getting clearer about being by noting that although our first concepts are of being, our last concept is of being.

> The ontological difference between the constitution of Dasein's being and that of nature proves to be so disparate that it seems at first as though the two ways of being are incomparable and cannot be determined by way of a uniform concept of being in general. Existence and extantness are more disparate than say, the determinations of God's being and man's being in traditional ontology … Given this radical distinction of ways of being in general, can there still be found any single unifying concept that would justify calling these different ways of being ways of being? (GA24, 250)

And so beings are not importantly alike simply by being beings. And although everything is an object, being something, by which being an object is defined, is not itself metaphysically fundamental, and the tenuous web of analogies by which it is constructed is not sufficiently sturdy to support authoritative formal ontological laws. This is why we mustn't assume that there are metaphysically important features that everything must have regardless of its mode of being.[39]

To return to a well-worn analogy, there are many ways in which something can be healthy. A physical organism can be healthy, as can the food that it eats and the waste products that it discharges. But these ways of being healthy are importantly different from one another, and this is why it would be absurd to assume that there is a true universally quantified conditional of the form "if x is healthy, then…" that could be a law of the science of healthy things qua healthy. In general, if a feature F is unified merely by analogy, the prospects for a science of F things qua being F is rather dim. As for health, so too for being itself.[40]

I ask those readers of *Being and Time* who claim that Heidegger there defends a univocal conception of being: Why then does Heidegger not pursue a project of formal ontology? I hope it is clear on my reading of Heidegger why this project would not seem a promising one to pursue.[41] To be clear, Heidegger certainly does pursue ontology – there's *Sein* in the title of the main book after all! – but he doesn't pursue it by way of an alleged insight into the essence of being that reveals formal laws. Instead, our most reasonable hope for discovering features that apply to all objects – though not features that apply to all objects *as such* – is via an examination

---

[39] Compare with SZ 16–17.
[40] See also Philipse (1998, 112), who suggests that, for Heidegger, those logical propositions that apply to all domains do so "only analogously."
[41] See also Philipse (1998, 110–115), who mentions two reasons that Heidegger does not pursue formal ontology, one of which is that he believes that *being* is not topic neutral; the other reason is that Heidegger believes that the "philosophical attitude" is not a "theoretical attitude." For a discussion of other versions of ontological pluralism that also threaten the prospects of formal ontology, see McDaniel (2017, chap. 4).

of a specific kind of object and its mode of being, namely, Dasein, and
then attempting to determine the ways in which the other modes of being
are related to the mode of being of Dasein.[42] This approach to ontology is
nonformal: Rather than beginning top-down with principles that apply to
all objects as such that thereby constrain investigations of the ontology of
specific types of being, this approach begins bottom-up, so to speak – or,
if you like, in terms of what is *fundamental*, not necessarily metaphysically,
but in the order of what is most apt for us to begin our inquiry. And this
way of pursuing ontological investigation offers no promise that there even
are interesting ontological principles true of all objects to be discovered.

Note that Heidegger also denies that other putative formal ontological
features have a unitary essence. For example, being a property is merely
analogous – we can attribute properties to things such as ourselves, and we
can attribute properties to things such as tables or protons, but what it is
for Dasein to have a property is importantly different from what it is for a
table or a proton to have a property. There is no univocal notion of *having*
to be had.[43] Since what it is to be a property is to be among the kinds of
thing that can be had, being a property lacks a unitary nature as well.

What about *essence*? According to Heidegger (GA24, 156–171), Dasein
doesn't have an essence in the way that other items in Heidegger's metaphysics do. At best, although in a sense it makes sense to consider both the
whatness of a thing – its essence – and the whether of a thing – its mode of
being, if it exists at all – this division is not univocal across categories. But
Heidegger goes so far as to tell us that for the kind of thing that we are, it
is better to distinguish not the *what* from the whether, but, rather, the *who*
from the whether:[44]

> If the Dasein exhibits an ontological constitution completely different from
> that of the extant-at-hand, and if to exist, in our terminological usage,
> means something other than mere *existere* and *existentia* (*einai*), then it also
> becomes a question whether anything like *Sachheit*, thingness, whatness,
> reality, *essentia*, *ousia*, can belong to the ontological constitution of Dasein.
> *Sachheit*, thingness, whatness, reality, *realitas*, or *quidditas*, is that which
> answers the question *Quid est res*, what is the thing? Even a rough consid-
> eration shows that the being that we ourselves are, the Dasein, cannot at all
> be *interrogated* as such by the question *What is this?* We gain access to this

---

[42] This examination is the so-called existential analytic of Dasein.
[43] See SZ 42, 44. For a defense of this interpretation of Heidegger, see Okrent (1988, 20–21, 26, 180).
Note that pluralism about both objects and properties fits nicely with but does not mandate pluralism about essence, which will be discussed next.
[44] See GA24, 169–171 and GA20, 326. See also Shirley (2010, 38).

being only if we ask: *Who* is it? The Dasein is not constituted by whatness—but if we may coin the expression—by *whoness* ... the basic concept of essential, whatness, first becomes really problematic in the face of the being we call Dasein. The inadequate founding of the thesis [that with respect to every being we can distinguish that it exists from the essential features it must have in order to exist[45]] as a universally ontological one becomes evident. If it is to have an ontological significance at all, then it is in need of a *restriction* and a *modification*.... Formulated more generally, the thesis that *essentia* and *existentia* belong to each being merely points to the general problem of articulation of each being into a being *that* it is and the *how* of its being ... under the heading "*being*," we now have *not only essentia* and *existentia* but *also whoness* and *existence* in our sense [i.e., the kind of Being exemplified by Dasein]. The articulation of Being varies each time with the way of Being of a being. (GA24, 170–171)

Note that in this passage Heidegger claims that the articulation of being varies along each mode of being. Because the modes of being are so different from one another, we should not expect structural features, such as division of essence and existence, to apply across the board to objects that enjoy different modes of being – contrary to what the proponents of formal ontology tell us we should expect.[46] Moreover, not only should we not expect this particular division of essence and being to apply across the board, phenomenological investigation itself reveals a counter-example to this thesis: The phenomenological investigation into our own mode of being shows that our essence is exhausted by our mode of being, which is not the case for other objects.[47]

"Object," which is understood in terms of being something, as well as "property" and "essence," are three critically important bits of putative formal ontological vocabulary.[48] But in each case, there is no corresponding univocal essence, and given that, it is unlikely that there is a fundamental metaphysical theory that makes use of them. There might well be true universally quantified statements in which they appear – in fact, it is

---

[45] This is the thesis Heidegger is examining in this portion of *Basic Problems of Phenomenology* (GA24, 108–171).

[46] See also GA20, 325 as well as GA34, 2–5, in which Heidegger evinces skepticism that the same notion of essence can apply to tables and truth.

[47] See SZ 41–43. See McDaniel (2017, chap. 9) for a metaphysical interpretation of Heidegger's claim.

[48] What about mereological properties, which are so important to the formal ontology developed in Husserl's (2005b) Third Investigation? Here there is not much text, but James Kinkaid has called my attention to an intriguing footnote in which Heidegger suggests that there might be "categorial variation" in the division of parts to wholes (SZ 244 n. 1). Other putative formal ontological features should be assessed on a case-by-case basis. I am inclined to think, for example, that Heidegger is a pluralist about possibility; such an interpretation is suggested by Shirley (2010, 46) as well.

trivial that there are. But no collection of these true universally quantified statements collectively constitutes the laws of an authoritative science of formal ontology that is capable of setting constraints on what our metaphysics can look like. Such putative principles might be true, but they do not in themselves demand assent, and are rationally revisable in light of phenomenological investigations into particular domains of objects.

Recall the following bi-conditional: Formal logic is authoritative if and only if formal ontology is authoritative. We have examined independent challenges to both sides of the bi-conditional – and if both sides are false, it seems then that the bi-conditional is true. It is mildly amusing that both Heidegger and Husserl would have had very different reasons for their endorsement of it.[49]

---

[49] I thank Ross Cameron, Daniel Dahlstrom, and James Kinkaid for helpful comments on an earlier draft of this paper.

CHAPTER 10

On the Limits and Possibilities of Human Thinking

Filippo Casati

Among the many core activities of our lives, thinking is certainly one of the most important. We think about numbers while doing mathematics, about art while visiting a museum, about cells while studying biology, and about planets while reading an astronomy book. Despite thinking's ubiquity in human life, Heidegger believes that it is not clear what this activity actually is. According to Heidegger, "an understanding of [our] thinking" can be achieved only by engaging with "its intrinsic possibilit[ies]" (GA26, 26) and, for this reason, he devoted a significant part of his philosophy to exploring such possibilities. What is *possible* for our thinking? Is it possible to think about *anything*? Or is there something that our thinking *cannot* grasp? And what about all the logical laws that govern our thoughts? *Can* those laws be violated? Is there thinking that *is not* subject to logical regimentation?

In the present chapter, I begin by addressing these questions in light of what Heidegger considers one of the basic problems of philosophy, including his own, namely, the alleged incompatibility between the notion of Being, our thinking, and logic. I then turn to how Heideggerians have dealt with this incompatibility via what I call *irrationalist* and *rationalist* interpretations. According to the former, Heidegger believes that there is something beyond the limits of our thinking and our logic. In other words, there is something that our thinking and thereby our logic *cannot* do, that is, grasp Being. According to the latter interpretation, Heidegger either does or should believe that there is nothing beyond the limits of our thinking and our logic. There is nothing that our thinking and, with it, our logic *cannot* do, including grasping Being. However, both of these interpretations, I argue, face *exegetical* and *philosophical* problems. I conclude by defending an alternative way of addressing the incompatibility between our thinking, logic, and the notion of Being. In this connection I note Heidegger's suggestion, in some of his late works, that the *real* problem lies in the philosophical illusion that we can actually assess the limits of our thinking and, thereby, our logic. Heidegger's philosophy aims, I submit, at freeing us from such a philosophical illusion by delivering an experience that reminds us that we can never look at our thinking, as it were, from "on high," that is, from a standpoint that would enable us to grasp its limits or determine that it has no limits whatsoever.

10.1   The Basic Problem

During the summer semester of 1928, Heidegger delivers his last course at the University of Marburg. This course, published exactly fifty years later as *The Metaphysical Foundations of Logic*, has become one of the most representative presentations of Heidegger's early view of the relation of philosophy and logic. From the beginning of this course, he argues that, if "Being [is] the theme of philosophy," philosophy is "a risky venture" (*ein Wagnis*), indeed, "an inverted world" from a logical point of view (GA26, 13). By means of this metaphorical jargon, Heidegger introduces "the basic problem" at the juncture of philosophy and logic (GA26, 18).

In order to understand why philosophy might represent "a risky venture" or "an inverted world" in the eyes of a logician, let's begin by discussing how Heidegger accounts for what he takes to be its theme. In keeping with the Aristotelian legacy, Heidegger believes that philosophy is neither about a specific entity (e.g., a stone, a tree, an animal, or a human being) nor about a specific cluster of entities (e.g., all material bodies, plants, animals, or humans). Philosophy, on the contrary, attempts to understand the Being of all these entities, that is, what makes any entity the entity it is. Heidegger writes:

> [Philosophy] is the investigation not of this or that being [i.e., entity], this thing, this stone, this tree or this animal, this human being, nor the investigation of all material bodies, all plants, animals, humans—that would in each case be the investigation of a specific region of that which is, of being [i.e., an entity]. ... Rather, what should be investigated is the τὸ ὂν ᾗ ὄν—beings [i.e., entities] with regard to [B]eing, i.e., solely with regard to what makes a being [i.e., an entity] the being [i.e., the entity] it is. (GA26, 12)

Heidegger is firmly convinced that even though Being makes stones, trees, animals, or human beings what they are, Being is not a stone, a tree, an animal, or a human being. Being is not itself an entity. As Heidegger writes: "Being lies beyond every entity and every possible character that an entity might possess. *Being is the transcendens pure and simple*" (SZ 38). In other words, "Being is not a being [i.e. an entity]" (GA40, 67). And, if so, since philosophy is about Being, philosophy is about no entity whatsoever.

At this point, the tension between philosophy and logic should already be clear, but Heidegger's discussion of the latter makes it even more obvious. Soon after introducing what he takes to be the theme of philosophy, Heidegger claims that, according to a "traditional conception" (GA26, 1), logic is the study of our thinking and the rules governing it. Moreover, he claims that thinking is always thinking about something, that is, the entity that is thought. "Logic, the science of λόγος, is the science of thinking" (GA26, 1) and "thinking is a thinking of something. All real thinking has its theme, and thus relates itself to a definite object, that is, to a definite being [i.e., a definite entity]" (GA26, 2). If so, Heidegger takes logic to be the study of our thinking about specific subject matters where these subject matters are the entities about which we think. For instance, Heidegger claims that "[there is] the logic of thinking in physics, the logic of mathematical thinking, of philological, historical thinking" (GA26, 2). Since thinking is always about an entity, thinking in physics is about "physical thing[s]," mathematical thinking is about "geometrical objects," philological and historical thinking is about "historical event[s]" and "linguistic phenomen[a]" (GA26, 2). Thus, the logic of thinking in physics governs our thinking about physical entities, the logic of mathematical thinking governs our thinking about geometrical entities, the logic of philological and historical thinking governs our thinking about historical entities and linguistic entities.

What about the logic of philosophical thinking, then? To begin with, Heidegger argues that, since the theme of philosophy is Being, the logic of philosophy should be the logic of our thinking about Being. If so, our thinking about Being ultimately amounts, Heidegger concludes, to thinking about nothing because Being is no thing; it is not an entity. At this point, Heidegger distinguishes between two equally ruinous ways of interpreting such a conclusion. On the one hand, he believes that we might understand our thinking about nothing as not thinking at all, and he argues that this interpretation fails to articulate the logic of philosophical thinking. For logic is the study of our thinking and this first understanding jettisons that very activity. On the other hand, Heidegger believes that we might understand our thinking about nothing as thinking about nothingness, and he specifies that, like thinking about Being, thinking about nothingness is thinking about what is not an entity. Even in this second case, Heidegger argues that such an understanding fails to articulate a logic for philosophical thinking. For our thinking about what is not an entity is still thinking about something; it is still thinking about an entity and, as such, it is thinking about neither nothingness nor Being. He writes:

Is its theme [i.e., philosophy's theme] then a [matter of] thinking about nothing? "Thinking about nothing" is ambiguous. First of all, it can mean "not to think." But logic as the science of thinking obviously never deals with not thinking. Secondly, it can mean "to think nothingness," which nonetheless means to think "something." In thinking of nothingness, or in the endeavor to think "it," I am thoughtfully related to nothingness, and this is what the thinking is about. (GA26, 3)

In light of these remarks, the very theme of philosophy appears to be a "risky venture" for logic because the latter does not really seem to be equipped to deal with the former. In other words, the notion of Being seems to represent "an inverted world" in the eyes of a logician because the world inhabited by her is uniquely constituted by what Being is *not*, that is, entities. Therefore, philosophy and logic seem to follow two irreconcilable paths: While the path of philosophy points toward Being *only*, the path of logic points toward entities *only*. And, for this reason, any attempt to have a philosophical logic, that is, a logic that governs our thinking about Being, appears to be destined to fail. This is the "basic problem" highlighted by Heidegger at the beginning of his last course at Marburg.[1]

10.2   Between Irrationalism and Rationalism

From Heidegger's last course at Marburg to the very end of his intellectual trajectory, the alleged incompatibility between philosophy and logic remains a central issue for him. And for Heideggerians, despite an impressive amount of intellectual energy devoted to its discussion, the status of this incompatibility remains the topic of endless debates. Within the field of these interpretations, I believe it is possible to identify two main ways in which scholars have understood Heidegger's attempt to relieve this alleged tension between philosophy and logic. On the one hand, some scholars believe that, since the very theme of philosophy seems to resist logic, Heidegger decides to jettison the latter by endorsing the idea that Being lies beyond the limits of our thinking and our logic. If so, there is something that our thinking and our logic *cannot* do, that is, grasp Being. And, for this reason, they also believe that Being needs to be addressed by means of something *other than* logically grounded thought. This is what I call the *irrationalist interpretation*. On the other hand, there are scholars

---

[1] What I here designate Heidegger's "basic problem" has been addressed and discussed by many contemporary scholars. See, for instance, Casati (2018), Dahlstrom (1994; 2001), McManus (Chapter 7, this volume), Moore (2012; 2015a), Priest (2001), and Witherspoon (2002).

who believe that Heidegger, far from jettisoning logic, retains it while endorsing the idea that nothing, not even Being, lies beyond the limits of our thinking and our logic. If so, there is nothing that our thinking and our logic *cannot* do, including grasping Being. This is what I call the *rationalist interpretation.*

The irrationalist interpretation has a very honorable history and it finds one of its early supporters in Hans-Georg Gadamer. "Heidegger's philosophy," he claims, "juxtaposes itself against logic" (Gadamer 1994, 47). Many other interpreters echo Gadamer's interpretation, arguing that "Heidegger seeks what no logic can accomplish" (Pöggeler 1987, 221–222) because "the question of Being cannot be raised as long as we remain within the bounds of logic" (Philipse 1998, 15). As is evident from these quotations, the very core of the irrationalist interpretation is represented by the idea that Being escapes logical reasoning; for Being is not an entity and logic regiments thinking that is, in turn, concerned with entities *only*. If so, the notion of Being determines the limits of both our thinking and our logic because, according to Heidegger himself, Being is exactly what lies beyond both.

At this point, it is important to notice that, according to the irrationalist interpretation, the failure of thinking about Being and the impossibility of having a philosophical logic do not necessarily entail the failure of Heidegger's whole philosophical enterprise. Most, if not all, of the interpreters who support the irrationalist interpretation argue that Heidegger's philosophy should not be read as an exercise in logical reasoning; on the contrary, it is a way of *experiencing* what cannot be grasped by our thinking and our logic. If so, Heidegger's work is a tool by means of which we can reach what our thinking and our logic fail to properly grasp. Far from delivering rational arguments, his writings offer "an original experience of the truth of Being" (Blattner 1999, 300), "the experience [of] the wonder of all wonders" (Caputo 1990, 26), and "the original experience of *Entschlossenheit* (the released openness to Being)" (Davis 2007, 50).

In order to have a better understanding of how Heidegger's writings can deliver an experience of Being, it might be fruitful to follow Ed Witherspoon in resorting to the distinction between saying and showing that is often employed by interpreters of Wittgenstein's *Tractatus*. As we have already seen in Section 10.1, Heidegger engages in the philosophical attempt to think about Being and, in one of his last lectures at Marburg, he argues that such an attempt leads us to face an inevitable failure because thinking is always thinking about entities and Being is not itself an entity. Witherspoon thus argues that Heidegger takes such an inevitable failure in thinking about Being as *showing* something about Being itself.

As Witherspoon writes, "they [i.e. thinking and logic] show something through their breaking down" (Witherspoon 2002, 104). In failing, our thinking and our logic offer an *experience* of Being; in misfiring, they disclose some ineffable truths about something, namely Being, which lies beyond the limits of our thinking and our logic.

Concerning the rationalist interpretation, I believe it is possible to identify at least two ways in which it has been defended. On the one hand, some advocates of the rationalist interpretation deny that Heidegger faces any incompatibility between the theme of philosophy and what he calls a "traditional account of logic." In so doing, they defend an interpretation of Heidegger's philosophy that contradicts the one I presented in Section 10.1. On the other hand, some other advocates of the rationalist interpretation acknowledge the fact that Heidegger faces the aforementioned incompatibility and, for this reason, they argue that such an incompatibility should force him to revise some of his philosophical assumptions. In so doing, they defend an interpretation of Heidegger's philosophy that is consistent with the one I presented in Section 10.1.

Let's begin by considering the first way of defending the rationalist interpretation as it has been articulated by one of its most passionate advocates, Stephen Käufer. Käufer denies that Heidegger faces any incompatibility between Being, our thinking, and our logic by rejecting the idea that thinking is always thinking about an entity. He claims that, since Heidegger does *not* endorse this view, Heidegger does not face any issue in thinking about Being either. If so, Käufer concludes that "there is no need to read Heidegger as an irrationalist" (Käufer 2005a, 482). In my view, Käufer's interpretation is fraught *exegetically*. It disregards and fails to make sense of numerous texts in which Heidegger claims that Being is "mysterious" (GA16, 12, 29, 56) and "enigmatic" (SZ 4, 136, 392; see also GA29/30, 517–518; GA45, 208).[2] If there is no problem in thinking about Being, what makes it so mysterious? If we face no troubles in thinking about Being, why does Heidegger believe that it is so enigmatic? With no clear answer to these questions, this first way of accounting for the rationalist interpretation, epitomized by Käufer's interpretation, does not appear promising and, for this reason, I will not discuss it further.

There is, however, a second, more auspicious way of defending the rationalist interpretation and Denis McManus's work can be read as voicing

---

[2] Neglect of these passages perhaps also explains why Käufer ignores a great number of Heideggerians who have argued in favor of the idea that Heidegger's notion of Being resists our thinking and our logic.

some of its core ideas. To begin with, McManus is exegetically sensitive to passages where Heidegger affirms that Being does indeed resist our thinking and our logic. Furthermore, he claims that this incompatibility between Being, our thinking, and our logic must be taken as a "reductio ad absurdum" (McManus 2013a, 667). In other words, McManus argues that, since Heidegger's philosophical assumptions force him to conclude that Being resists our thinking and our logic, Heidegger should (and perhaps does) revise some of his assumptions in such a way that Being does not resist our thinking and our logic anymore. Even though McManus does not, in my view, do enough to clarify which assumption is supposed to be revised, it is clear that such a revision is meant to help Heidegger's philosophy accommodate the idea that nothing, not even Being, lies beyond the limits of our thinking and our logic.

The irrationalist and the rationalist interpretation are thus radically different. While the irrationalist interpretation sees our thinking and our logic as having limits beyond which lies Being, the rationalist interpretation sees our thinking and our logic as having no limits whatsoever. While the irrationalist interpretation entails that there is something that our thinking and our logic *cannot* grasp, the rationalist interpretation entails that there is nothing that our thinking and our logic *cannot* grasp. Now, given the aim of the present chapter, it is also important to notice that, regardless of these very significant differences, these two interpretations share a very important feature as well. For different reasons and with different outcomes, both of them fall into the very same philosophical temptation, that of dealing with the limits of our thinking and our logic. Both of them are concerned with what is *possible* and *impossible* for our thinking and our logic.

10.3   Neither Irrationalism nor Rationalism

Prima facie, both the irrationalist and the rationalist interpretations seem to be *exegetically* grounded, and countless interpreters, on both sides of the barricades, have been hunting for passages in which Heidegger endorses one or the other of these two interpretive stances. For instance, the advocates of the irrationalist interpretation could find much favorable textual evidence in *Pathmarks*. In this collection of essays, Heidegger echoes some of the thoughts presented in his last course at Marburg by discussing all the unavoidable difficulties we face while thinking about Being. However, contrary to what he did in *The Metaphysical Foundation of Logic*, Heidegger begins to question the very possibility of grasping Being with our thinking and our logic. Heidegger not only notices that the notion of Being seems to resist our thinking and our logic, but also begins to question the "supreme importance [of logic]" by asking whether "we [are] allowed to temper [its] rules" (GA9, 85). Many years later, Heidegger reiterates the same set of questions. Are we sure, he wonders, that our dealing with Being has to be subject to our thinking and some logical laws? Heidegger seems to believe that we need to call into question this very assumption by arguing that "it becomes necessary to ask the question, which is barely posed whether this thinking [i.e., the thinking about Being] already stands within the law of its truth when it merely follows thinking whose forms and rules are conceived with 'logic'" (GA9, 235). In line ostensibly with the irrationalist interpretation, these passages appear to confirm Heidegger's "suspicion regarding logic" (GA9, 235) and, in so doing, they also suggest that Being transcends the limits of our logical thoughts.

However, advocates of the rationalist interpretation have solid exegetical ground to rely on as well. For instance, considerable favorable textual evidence for this interpretation that can be found in a series of lectures that Heidegger delivers during his Rectorate at the University of Freiburg, subsequently published under the title *Being and Truth*. In these lectures devoted to illuminating the essence of language, Heidegger notes the essential role that being silent plays in language and the paradoxical necessity of talking about being silent. He insists that doing so cannot mean relegating this silence as a "dark and mystical thing" to "emotional premonitions" and "irrationality"; in a line that strongly supports the rationalist interpretation of his philosophy, he immediately adds: "So long as we are engaged in philosophy, this must not be" (GA36/37, 107). Thirty years later, Heidegger reproposes the same idea by arguing that, as with any rigorous philosophical position, his own work should not be interpreted as promoting either mysticism or irrationality. In a manner consistent with the rationalist interpretation, he writes: "My thinking is essentially divorced from every 'mysticism' and mere sinking into the darkness of obscurity for its own sake" (GA55, 32).

In light of what I have discussed until now, not only is it difficult to deny that a lot of work has been done in order to articulate philosophical defenses of both the irrationalist and the rationalist interpretations, but it is difficult to deny that these two ways of reading Heidegger are exegetically grounded as well. Their philosophical and exegetical sophistication and complexity are certainly undeniable. Having said that, I still believe that both of them rely on a *philosophical* problem that might be better addressed by beginning to discuss a less pressing *exegetical* issue. Such an issue arises from the fact that, in some of his later works, Heidegger expresses evident dissatisfaction with both the irrationalist and the rationalist labels. His philosophy, Heidegger claims, is beyond this distinction because neither the rationalist nor the irrationalist interpretation seems to be appropriate in describing what he wants to achieve by means of his seemingly futile attempts to think about Being. Thus, Heidegger sees his philosophy as separated from both the rationalist desire to jettison what resists our thinking and the irrationalist aspiration to welcome what cannot be grasped by our thoughts. "My philosophy," he writes, "is divorced both from reckoning of mere logic and from the hollow dizziness of a mystical profundity" (GA55, 132). In keeping with this observation, Heidegger invites us to engage with his philosophy "more thoughtfully," and he specifies that "'more thoughtfully' means here: outside the distinction of 'rational' and 'irrational'" (GA71, 260).

Of course, these quotations are not meant to be taken as a fatal criticism of either the irrationalist or the rationalist interpretation. Given the complexity of all these issues, it is reasonable to assume that, during so many years of philosophical work, Heidegger could have oscillated between a rationalist and an irrationalist stance. Having said that, I believe that these quotations are still important because they should encourage us to wonder about the reasons for Heidegger's ultimate dissatisfaction with both the irrationalist and the rationalist interpretations. Why was Heidegger unhappy with these two exegetical options? What can we learn from his dissatisfaction? Should we take their rejection as Heidegger's way of suggesting that there is a third way to deal with these philosophical issues? These are the philosophical questions that will be addressed in the next section.

10.4 On Stillborn Children

As has already been anticipated in Section 10.3, the exegetical issue faced by the irrationalist and rationalist interpretations might be taken as the symptom of a more pressing philosophical issue. For both interpretations seem to be committed to the same mistake, that is, thinking about something that cannot be thought. In order to see how this is the case, let's begin by considering the irrationalist interpretation. As already discussed in Section 10.1, the irrationalist interpretation argues that Heidegger develops a special philosophical practice. Since Being cannot be captured by our thinking and our logic, Heidegger abandons any argumentation about Being and, in so doing, he tries to deliver what certain interpreters (e.g., Blattner, Caputo, and Davis) call "an original experience of Being itself." In other words, the irrationalist interpretation presents Heidegger's philosophy as an attempt at *showing* what cannot be grasped otherwise. Now, the substantial philosophical problem faced by this reading becomes immediately evident as soon as we notice that, in order to formulate the irrationalist interpretation, we already find ourselves thinking about Being. In order to understand what Heidegger's philosophy is supposed to do, don't we need to understand that Heidegger's philosophical practice is meant to show Being? And, if so, aren't we already thinking about Being when we claim that, according to the irrationalist interpretation, Being is what is shown by Heidegger's philosophical practice? It seems to me that we must answer all these questions in an affirmative way because, if Being cannot be grasped by our thinking and our logic, we should not be able to think about the irrationalist interpretation and mount logical arguments in its favor. That is to say, the very attempt to think about the irrationalist interpretation and argue in its favor seems to require us to engage in two activities: *thinking* about *Being* and *arguing* that *Being* is shown by Heidegger's philosophical practice. Unfortunately, according to the irrationalist interpretation, we should not be able to engage in either of these activities.

In order to present this problem in the clearest way possible, let's consider how Witherspoon accounts for the irrationalist interpretation and how he explains Heidegger's attempt at *showing* Being. As noted earlier, Witherspoon believes that, according to Heidegger, any attempt to think about Being leads to a necessary failure. However, such a failure is somehow revealing: With their breakdown, our thinking and our logic show something about Being, that is, its ability to resist both our thinking and our logic. As Witherspoon writes: "[T]hey [i.e., our thinking and our logic] show something through their breaking down" (Witherspoon 2002, 104). At this point, it should be evident that, in spelling out his own account of the irrationalist interpretation, Witherspoon is thinking about Being. And it should be even more evident that, while reading Witherspoon's account of the irrationalist interpretation, we ourselves follow him in arguing that something is shown about Being by witnessing the breakdown of our thinking and our logic. Once again, the pressing philosophical problem faced by this reading is that, according to the irrationalist interpretation, Witherspoon should not be able to think and argue about Being – and neither should we.[3]

---

[3] It is important to notice that Witherspoon is well aware of this problem and he addresses it in the last section of his 2002 paper. Also, the criticism I mount here against the irrationalist interpretation echoes criticisms directed at the traditionalist interpretation of Wittgenstein's *Tractatus*. For the *locus classicus* of these criticisms, see chaps. 1 and 6 of Diamond (1991); see, too, Conant (2002).

It is important to notice that Heidegger seems to be aware of this line of thought and it is possible to find some traces of it in his *Bremen Lectures*. To begin with, he compares our thinking with light. Thinking, he notes, *enlightens* both the world and our own thinking. Leaving metaphors aside, we can also say that, through our thinking, we decode and understand the complexity of both our world and ourselves. On the one hand, we can think about the world; for instance, we can think about tables, cups, and numbers. On the other hand, we can think about our own thoughts; for instance, we can think about our own thoughts while dealing with tables, cups, and numbers. For this reason, Heidegger writes that "thinking moves and stands in a light that, to all appearances, it itself ignites" (GA79, 137). At this point, Heidegger notices that the comparison between thinking and light invites us to ponder shadows, too. As there might be something that remains in the shadow because it is not possible to enlighten it, there might be something that remains unthought because it is not possible to think about it. Following scholars who endorse the irrationalist interpretation, we could also argue that, as there might be something that escapes and resists light, there might be something that escapes and resists our thinking as well. If so, as the shadow (de)limits light, what is not thinkable (de)limits our thinking.

At this point, however, Heidegger adds that characterizing the shadow as what (de)limits light is as problematic as it is common. Contrary to what the irrationalist interpretation claims, Heidegger explicitly argues that, however the shadow might be characterized and whatever is concealed by it, such a shadow cannot be understood as the boundary of light. He writes: "Wherever the shadow is seen it is only understood as the limit of brightness. But the shadow is something more and other than a limit" (GA79, 137). The shadow has to be something different from a limit because the very gesture of identifying the limit of what is enlightened, the very idea that there is something on the other side of that limit, necessarily presupposes our ability to see whatever is *not* enlightened. And, of course, this is not possible because what lies in the dark cannot be seen *at all*. In the same way, Being has to be different from something (de)limiting our thought because the very gesture of identifying the limit of our thought, the very idea that there is something on the other side of that limit, necessarily presupposes our ability to think about what is *not* thinkable, that is, Being itself. And, as we have already argued above, this is not possible because what is unthinkable cannot be thought *at all*. If so, any attempt to draw the limit of our thinking is destined to fail because the very attempt to advocate for the existence of something irrational (i.e., the existence of something that resists our thinking) presupposes a rational position (i.e., the idea that everything is *somehow* thinkable). The underlying reasoning here is patent: In order to advocate for the existence of something unthinkable, it seems necessary to think about it. If so, the very idea that there is something irrational (i.e., the idea that there is something that resists our thinking) is nothing more than a "stillborn child" of the rationalist position (i.e., the idea that nothing is unthinkable). As Heidegger puts it: "This shadowing arises neither from a realm of shades and ghosts, nor is it dispatched with the cheap remark that next to the rational there would also be the irrational; for the irrational always remains *a stillborn child* of rationalism" (GA79, 138, my emphasis).

If the irrationalist interpretation appears to be a "stillborn child," the rationalist interpretation does not seem to fare much better. In order to see why this is the case, let's recall that, according to the rationalist interpretation, Heidegger should (and perhaps does) revise some of his ideas *because* his notion of Being resists our thinking and our logic. At this point, the problem should be evident as soon as we realize that, in order to articulate and defend such a philosophical position, the advocates of the rationalist interpretation must be able to think about something (i.e., Being) that resists our thinking and our logic. Only in this way would they be able to argue that Heidegger should (and perhaps does) revise some of his ideas *in light of* the fact that Being resists our thinking and our logic. And, if so, the advocates of the rationalist interpretation find themselves wrestling with the same problem faced by the advocates of the irrationalist interpretation. They seem to be committed to thinking about something that cannot be thought, that is, something that lies beyond the limits of our thinking and our logic.[4]

Even though it is certainly difficult to find sufficient clear textual evidence for Heidegger's commitment to this line of thought, it is still reasonable to believe that he would not have disagreed with it. For the criticism that I have directed at the rationalist interpretation relies on the same kind of argument that Heidegger seems to employ against the irrationalist one. In both cases, the issue arises from the fact that, for different reasons and with different aims, the irrationalist and the rationalist interpretations deal with the limits and the possibilities of our thought. If the former argues that something (i.e., Being) lies beyond the limits of our thinking, the

---

[4] Since Section 10.2 discusses the rationalist interpretation by appealing to McManus (2013a), it deserves noting that not all his works are subject to the criticism presented in Section 10.4; see, for example, his chapter in this volume (Chapter 7).

latter argues that nothing, not even Being, lies beyond the limits of our thinking. If the former claims that there is something that is not possible for our thinking (i.e., grasping Being), the latter claims that there is nothing that is not possible for our thinking, even grasping Being. Both interpretations attempt to understand what is possible or impossible for our thought by examining its limits. Unfortunately, as the arguments presented in this section show, such an attempt commits the advocates of the irrationalist interpretation and the rationalist interpretation alike to think something that cannot be thought and, hence, the very attempt to do so, under either interpretation, seems patently futile.

In light of what we have discussed in this section, it should be clear that *any* attempt to deal with the limits of our thinking and our logic is destined to face the very same problem. Both the attempt to maintain that there is something beyond the limits of our thinking (the irrationalist interpretation) and the attempt to deny that there is something beyond the limits of our thinking (the rationalist interpretation) are destined to fail. For this reason, Heidegger seems to encourage us to reject the former without this rejection entailing the acceptance of the latter, and vice versa. If so, the issue is neither the viability of one of these two exegetical positions nor the necessity of finding a third way to philosophize about the limits of our thinking and our logic. On the contrary, according to Heidegger, the issue is dispelling the philosophical illusion to which the irrationalist and the rationalist interpretations alike fall prey, that is, the philosophical illusion that pushes us to believe that we can articulate sensible philosophical positions about the limits of our thinking and our logic.

Heidegger challenges the very idea that our thinking and our logic can deal with their own limits. In other words, engaging with such limits is not among the very many possibilities of our thinking and our logic, because both the attempt to draw these limits and the attempt to deny their existence are somehow committed to the same, unavoidable mistake. What is left is accordingly our everyday thinking about entities and the logic we employ in order to regulate such thinking. What remain for us are all our meaningful attempts to *illuminate* specific regions of the world with the light of our thinking, a thinking that is, in turn, governed by logical principles. Entities remain at our disposal, ready to be managed, understood, thought, and even questioned; our ordinary encounter with them lingers, as do our thoughts about them and the rules governing all these different thoughts.

Since we can, and indeed do, think about material, geometrical, historical, and linguistic entities, we can and, indeed, do have a logic that is apt for governing our thinking about all these entities as well. And what about the Being of these entities? What about our attempts to think about it? Well, if our thinking about entities and our logic of thinking about those entities can be investigated by our philosophical enterprises, the limits of our thinking and what, by lying beyond them, determines those limits cannot be. While our thinking about entities and our logic of thinking about those entities can be dissected with our philosophical lancet, the limits of our thinking, our logic, and, thereby, Being itself cannot be. We would need to be able to "look" at Being as we "look" at entities in order to take Being as something about which we can actually think. However, since Being is not an entity, this is *not* possible. And, if so, we can neither defend nor deny the existence of the limits of our thinking, because this would require us to think about what lies on the other side of those limits, that is, Being itself.

Our thinking is *not* something that we can, so to speak, "look down upon from above" in order to grasp its boundaries or to realize that it has no boundaries whatsoever. The very attempt to find an available point of view from which we can either glance over the limits of our thinking or ascertain their nonexistence is the very temptation from which Heidegger wants to free us. According to Heidegger, only when we are liberated from this philosophical desire can we finally realize that our thinking is something that does not "lie over against us" because we are constantly immersed in it. Thinking is the *Heimat* in which all our mundane activities take place. Thinking is something we always *inhabit*. It is something in which we are "caught up" and which, for this reason, we can never "overtake." Heidegger writes:

> The relationship of thinking [and] Being therefore does not lie over against us. We ourselves are held within it. We can neither overtake it, nor even merely check up with it because we ourselves are caught up in this relationship. (GA79, 164)

10.5   Of Signposts and (Formal) Indications

Before concluding, it is important to address a concern that is difficult to ignore. As I argued in Section 10.4, Heidegger believes that the irrationalist and the rationalist interpretations fail because both of them are committed to the same mistake, that is, thinking about what cannot be thought. But, if so, doesn't Heidegger's position face the same issue? The answer to this question seems to be affirmative because, in order to argue that the irrationalist and rationalist interpretations are mistaken and in order to show that their mistake lies in the attempt to deal with the limits of our thinking, Heidegger deals with these limits as well. For instance, when Heidegger argues that we cannot think and, therewith, articulate *any* philosophical position about the limits of our thought, Heidegger himself seems to think and thereby articulate a philosophical position about the limits of our thought. If so, Heidegger seems to fall prey to the same issue he finds in the irrationalist and rationalist interpretations.

Heidegger is aware of this problem and, in the last part of his *Bremen Lectures*, he tries to address it in the following way. He argues that his work should *not* be taken as a sample of thoughts by means of which he theorizes about our thinking and deals with its limits; the aim of his lectures is *not* to articulate a philosophical position according to which we can or cannot deal with such limits. For whoever reads Heidegger's lectures in this way would condemn his own work to the same mistake Heidegger identifies in the irrationalist and rationalist interpretations. In order to avoid such a misreading of his own work, Heidegger repeatedly claims that what he delivers in his lectures are *not* statements that compose the body of a philosophical treatise, but "signposts" (*Wegweiser*; GA79, 104, 133, 142, 158, 163, 166–167).

Even though it is certainly difficult to understand what these signposts are, the fact that Heidegger describes them in a way akin to "indications" might encourage us to clarify his ideas by presenting these signposts as having a formally *indicative* nature. As I have already argued elsewhere (Casati 2019), Heidegger believes that formal indications have two essential features. First of all, formal indications force us to abandon any *theoretical* way of engaging with their subject matter. As Dahlstrom puts it, "[a formal indication] *points to a phenomenon* in such a way that it enjoins against any preemptive or external characterization of it" (Dahlstrom 1994, 782, my emphasis). Crowell echoes Dahlstrom by claiming that "[a formal indication] inhibits the tendency toward *'blind, dogmatic fixation' upon verbal formulas*" (Crowell 2001, 141, my emphasis). Secondly, formal indications have an *existential* impact on us. Thus Dahlstrom claims that "[formal indications] *transform* the individual who philosophizes" (Dahlstrom 1994, 783, my emphasis) and Crowell asserts that "[they] are indicators ... of tasks that yield the fullness of evidence in the phenomenological sense, the *'authentic'* possession of an object" (Crowell 2001, 141, my emphasis).

In light of what I have discussed up to this point, it seems quite plausible to argue that Heidegger's remarks on the limits of our thinking have both these features. To begin with, it should be clear that, in keeping with the first feature possessed by formal indications, these remarks cannot have a *theoretical* nature. According to the interpretation presented in this chapter, Heidegger believes that the problem faced by both the irrationalist and rationalist interpretations arises from the attempt to think about, that is, to theorize, the limits of our thought (where "to theorize something" is to disengage, step back, and look at it). Since Heidegger takes thinking about the limits of our thought in this way to be problematic, his remarks about such limits cannot be *theoretical* in nature.

Heidegger's "signposts" are meant neither to *argue* in favor of the existence of the limits of our thought nor to *argue* against it. They are meant neither to *show* the limits of our thinking and our logic (à la Witherspoon) nor to *reduce to absurdity* the very idea that these limits exist (à la McManus). Far from delivering any kind of *intellectual* result, Heidegger's signposts do nothing more than "point to a phenomenon," that is, the *experience* of our own thinking as something that does not "lie over against us." Beyond any "blind and dogmatic fixation," Heidegger's signposts help us to uncover the foolishness of any attempt to explore the limits of our own thinking. Heidegger's signposts remind us that our own thinking is something in which we are constantly and necessarily immersed. If so, Heidegger's lectures are not so much a *theoretical* exercise concerned with the limits of our thinking as they are an exercise "compelling us to *experience*" (GA79, 142, my emphasis) our own thinking as an inescapable *Heimat* in which the entirety of our activities take place. He writes:

> As soon as we get involved with the basic principles of thinking and ponder them, we see ourselves compelled to *experience* our thinking for the first time in its essential provenance so as to be properly there where, as thinking beings, for a long time we already are. The path into this *experience* is pointed out to us by the *signposts* that we have mentioned several times. (GA79, 142, my emphasis)

What about the second feature of Heidegger's formal indication? Well, Heidegger is very clear in suggesting that, as with formal indications, his signposts (*Wegweiser*) are meant to achieve an *existential* change by "transforming the individual who philosophizes." Literally translated, they show (*weisen*) us the way (*Weg*). On the one hand, through Heidegger's signposts, we experience our own thinking as the *Heimat* in which anything we do takes place. On the other hand, such an experience is supposed to free us from the illusion that we can, so to speak, "look at our own thinking from above" in order to survey its limits. In so doing, this experience releases us from the temptation to find a point of view from which we can assess the boundaries of our thought. Whoever understands Heidegger's philosophy will, thus, realize that what prima facie looks like an unavoidable "wretchedness of the human condition" (i.e., our uncompromising inability to *argue* either in favor of or against the existence of the limits of our thought) is instead that specific feature that determines human beings *as human beings*. This is how *we* inhabit *our* world and how *we* are related to *our* thinking. This is how *we* are. It is *our* "essence."

Given the interpretation defended in this chapter, such an uncompromising inability is the condition under which *we* are what *we* are. Human beings *are* those entities for whom there is no point of view that is outside their own thinking. And, if so, it would be highly misleading, if not patently wrong, to think that we lack this point of view and, indeed, misleading because no human being can have such a point of view in the first place. For this reason, Heidegger thinks that we should not complain about our inability to *argue* either in favor of or against the existence of the limits of our thought. If we properly understand Heidegger's philosophy and we appreciate what we experience through his indications and signposts, we should erupt in joy (as he puts it) because there is nothing that humans either miss or lack. In accord with the second feature of formal indications, Heidegger presents this *existential* change in the following way:

> We may note, in addition, that the awkwardness and helplessness that our contemplation must go through do not merely stem from the limitations of our capacities, but instead are essential. This gives no right to whine about the wretchedness of the human, but is instead a cause for jubilation over the fullness of the enigma that remains the lot of thinking. (GA79, 165,)

PART IV

Logical Principles and the Question of Being

CHAPTER II

The Resonant Principle of Reason

Katherine Withy

The principle of sufficient reason is a logical principle first fully formulated by Gottfried Wilhelm Leibniz. It holds that "there can be found no fact that is true or existent, or any true proposition, without there being a sufficient reason for its being so and not otherwise, although we cannot know these reasons in most cases" (Leibniz 1989, 646). Leibniz holds this to be one of two "great principles" governing reason; the other is the principle of (non-) contradiction (Leibniz 1989, 646). The principle of (non-)contradiction was formulated much earlier, by Aristotle, and it seeks to guarantee that our thinking is consistent. But it is not clear what virtue of thinking the principle of sufficient reason guarantees or why it had to wait for Leibniz for its full formulation. Heidegger addresses these two issues in his 1955–56 lecture course "The Principle of Reason" (*Der Satz vom Grund*) at the University of Freiburg and in his 1956 address of the same title.[1] He speaks of the principle of reason rather than the principle of sufficient reason because he thinks that the latter is a historically specific version of the former. The former, the principle of reason, is a fundamental logical and ontological principle of a distinctively Heideggerian sort. Heidegger thinks that it resonates for thinking in different ways at different times. In modernity, it resonates as the principle of sufficient reason, which expresses the ontological commitments definitive of modernity, which Heidegger also associates with the technological worldview and the dominance of the natural sciences. It is because the principle of sufficient reason belongs to modernity in this way that it was not formulated earlier – including by the ancient Greeks, for whom the principle of reason, insofar as it resonates at all, resonates differently.

---

[1] Both the lecture course and the address are included in *Der Satz vom Grund*, translated into English as *The Principle of Reason*. Since the pagination given in the running head of the English translation matches that of the 1957 edition rather than the *Gesamtausgabe* edition, I include page references to both the *Gesamtausgabe* edition (GA10) and the English edition (PR) throughout. I quote from the English translation but replace its "beings" with "entities" for *das Seiende*. I transliterate all Greek. See also "On the Essence of Ground" (GA9, 123–176) and Caputo (1975).

Heidegger's goal in his lectures on the principle of reason is to bring us to experience some of the different ways that the principle can resonate. Rather than tell a straightforward history of its resonance or identify the core principle and then list its variations, Heidegger leads his audience through a series of meditations on the principle of reason and the principle of sufficient reason, which he claims is necessary preparation for coming to hear the claim that the principle of reason as such makes on us, as well as for coming to understand why it has appeared as it has in the history of philosophy (GA10, 77/PR, 52). To undertake that intellectual journey, the reader can turn to Heidegger's text. In this chapter, my goal is to reconstruct Heidegger's interpretation of the principle of reason as a principle that resonates variously in the history of philosophy.[2]

11.1   Leibniz's Strict Formulation of the Principle of Reason

Within Leibniz's writings, Heidegger distinguishes three versions of the principle of reason:

1. The principle of causality, which says that nothing is without a cause (*nihil est sine ratione seu nullus effectus sine causa*) (GA10, 32–33/PR, 21).
2. "The short formulation" (GA10, 33/PR, 21), which says that nothing is without a reason (*nihil est sine ratione*).
3. The strict formulation, which says that for every truth the reason can be rendered (*quod omnis veritas reddi ratio potest*) (GA10, 34/PR, 22).

Heidegger rejects the principle of causality as equivalent to the principle of reason, on the grounds that not all reasons are causes (GA10, 33/PR, 21). The short formulation is the version of the principle that resonates differently throughout the history of philosophy; it is the core of the principle. The strict formulation is the version of the principle that is distinctive of modernity.

The strict formulation of the principle applies, on its face, to statements (GA10, 35/PR, 22). Statements are bearers of truth, and they are so because statements are judgments. Judgments make claims by bringing together a subject and a predicate. In order for a judgment to be true, the connection between the subject and the predicate must be justified, and to be justified it must be grounded in some account (*ratio*). There must be a

---

[2] For an assessment of whether Heidegger's account is adequate as an interpretation of Leibniz, see Dahlstrom (2011).

reason (*ratio*) that can be given to support the connection of the subject and the predicate: "If it is not given, judgment remains without justification. It lacks evident correctness. Judgment itself is not truth. Judgment is only true when the reason for the connection is specified, when the *ratio*, that is, an account, is given" (GA10, 174/PR, 119). (Heidegger does not consider the possibility that truth and justification do not always travel together; I make no claim as to Leibniz's own account.) So, a true statement is one for which we can give and ask for justifying reasons. For every true statement, a reason can be rendered. Applied to judgments, then, it is not the case that "we cannot know the[] reasons in most cases" (Leibniz 1989, 646). Instead, "*it is always necessary that there be a foundation for the connecting parts of a judgment* [, ... that is,] a reason that one can always render" (Leibniz, cited in GA10, 174/PR, 119)).

But the principle, as formulated, also applies – and, in fact, applies first of all – to thinking. Modern philosophers, according to (Heidegger, take thinking to be judging. What a judgment in a statement requires is thus also required of thought. A thought for which the reason can be rendered is "true" (or perhaps – better – counts as knowledge) in that it successfully represents an object to the thinking subject: "When the reason [*Grund*] for the connection of representations has been directed back – and expressly rendered – to the I, what is represented first comes to a stand [*Stehen*] such that it is securely established as an object [*Gegenstand*], that means, as an Object [*Objekt*] for a representing subject" (GA10, 175/PR, 119; cf. GA10, 34/PR, 22). The presence of objects thus depends on the successful judgment and the reason or account that grounds it. (Heidegger does not specify what sorts of things can ground judgment in modern philosophy, but Schopenhauer offers four, corresponding to four types of truth: Judgments can be grounded in another judgment (logical/formal truth), in an empirical representation (material/empirical truth), in space and time as the forms of intuitive empirical cognition (transcendental truth), or in the formal conditions of thought (metalogical truth) (Schopenhauer 2012, 100–103)).

Heard strictly and modernly, the principle of reason is both a logical and an ontological principle. It is a logical principle insofar as it is a rule governing successful thinking – provided that thinking is conceived in a distinctively modern way. Indeed, conceived in the modern way, thinking by its very nature stands under the direct authority of the principle of reason. The principle of reason is thus "the supreme fundamental principle of cognition" (GA10, 42/PR, 27). Its grandeur also derives from its status as an ontological principle. Since "entities are entities as objects for a consciousness" (GA10, 113/PR, 77), the rules governing successful thinking are also the rules for being an entity at all: "The principle now says that every thing counts as existing when and only when it has been securely established as a calculable object for cognition" (GA10, 175–176/PR, 120).

We can now see why the strict version of the principle of reason was not formulated until the modern period: It makes a claim on thinking only when thinking is understood as a subject representing an object. If the human being's relationship to entities is understood or experienced differently, the principle of reason will not place the claim on thinking that it does for Leibniz and other modern philosophers.

11.2 The Short Formulation as an Ontological Principle

The "short formulation" of the principle of reason – that nothing is without (a) reason – is not specifically tied to modernity. Heidegger thinks that it offers insights – provided that we listen to it in a certain way. We tend to hear the principle of reason as a claim about entities: *for every entity, there is a reason*. There are different ways to hear this ontic claim. It might range over everything that is, or only over true propositions about things that are. In the former case, it might guarantee a reason for the fact *that* each entity is, or also – or instead – for the fact that it is *this* way rather than some other way. Finally, the reason that is guaranteed might be a cause (as in the principle of causality), or a justification, or some other sort of ground. Sorting out what type of ontic claim the principle of reason makes is what most reflection on the principle consists in. But Heidegger wants to hear the principle of reason not as an ontic claim but as an ontological claim. To tune our ear to its purported ontological dimension, Heidegger plays with where the emphasis falls as we hear the principle. Rather than hearing it as saying that *nothing* is *without* reason, try hearing it as saying that nothing *is* without *reason*: "The pitch has shifted from the 'nothing' to the 'is' and from the 'without' to the 'reason'" (GA10, 76/PR, 50). The emphasis on "*is*" is what makes the principle of reason resound as a claim about what it takes to be. The claim is: To have being is to have reason, or ground – "The principle of reason now speaks as a word of being. The word is an answer to the question: what, after all, does 'being' mean? Answer: 'being' means 'ground/reason'" (GA10, 183–184/PR, 125).

Heard ontologically, the principle of reason speaks as an answer to the question of being. That question comes from us, the entity that understands being, whom Heidegger calls Dasein. Cases of Dasein are those entities who track the difference between what is and what is not, and what is *this* and what is *that*. We are open to both the existing and the essencing – together, the being – of entities. This openness to being leads us to ask (in our essence, if not in our lives): What is it to be? What is it that makes the difference between being at all and not being? And, what is it that unifies being at all with being *this* rather than that – and, for that matter, with being true, and being actual? It is because we are entities who essentially move around within the scope of the question of being that we can hear what the principle of reason says, and that what it says can make a claim on us. The principle of reason rings out in answer to our question about being: Nothing *is* without *reason*; having reason is being. Being means reason.

Or rather, being means *ground*. Heidegger's *Grund* can mean either *reason* or *ground*, as can the Latin *ratio*. Identifying being with ground makes explicit the relationship that being has with what is: It is that by virtue of which, or on the basis of which (*woraufhin*), entities are (SZ 6). An entity *is* by virtue of, or on the basis of, its *is-ing* or *be-ing*. Being is thus whatever it is that grounds entities as things that are. Situating being as the ground of entities does not tell us what it "is," but it does indicate, formally, what role being plays vis-à-vis entities. This formal indication of being is a foundational principle of Heidegger's ontology. He hears in the principle of reason the same claim.

From this ontological version of the principle of reason, the ontic version can be derived: "[b]ecause entities are brought into being by being *qua* ground/reason, every entity inevitably is allotted a ground/reason. For otherwise it would not be" (GA10, 184/PR, 125). That is, because all entities are by virtue of being, every entity has a ground or reason – namely, its being. This ground will account for the fact that the entity is rather than not, as well as for the way in which the entity is, or for what it is, as opposed to some other way or what. Thus each entity will have its ground in being as both that-being (existing) and what-being (essencing). This derivation puts a definite ontological spin on the ontic version of the principle of reason, which otherwise could have been making any of a number of different sorts of claims – about causation or justification, existence or essence, propositions or entities. Now, it makes a claim about all entities that points toward their ontological status: Everything that *is* has a ground in being, in the sense that it has both that-being and what-being.

At this point, Heidegger might be accused of changing the subject. In what sense can it be true that the principle of reason says that being is the ground of entities, and so that each entity has a ground in being? Presumably, this is not remotely what Leibniz heard in the principle that he formulated. It is not among Schopenhauer's four meanings of the principle of sufficient reason.[3] And it is not what contemporary discussions of the principle of sufficient reason or of grounding are concerned with. From this perspective, Heidegger has indeed changed the subject. At the same time, Heidegger is talking about the one thing that he has always been talking about and listening out for in the history of philosophy: the question of being. He derives some insights about this enduring topic from his interpretation of the principle of reason, which I explore in Sections 11.3 and 11.4, before returning to Heidegger's historical interpretation of the principle of reason in Section 11.5.

11.3   Being as the Abyssal Ground of Entities

From the principle of reason's claim that being is the ground of entities, or that all entities have a ground in being, Heidegger concludes that "[o]nly entities have—and indeed necessarily—a ground/reason" (GA10, 184/PR, 125). The force of this "only" is to deny any ground to being, which thus falls outside the scope of the principle of reason (GA10, 76/PR, 51). Heidegger puts this by saying that the principle of reason speaks of being not only as ground but also as "a-byss" (GA10, 87/PR, 59). The Greek *abussos* means *bottomless* or *groundless* (LSJ[4], s.v. "ἄβυσσος"). Lacking a ground or bottom makes being abyssal. And, since being is essentially abyssal, it is (in contemporary parlance) not apt to be grounded.

Obviously, it does not follow from the fact that *all* entities have a ground in being that *only* entities have any sort of ground. Heidegger supports his claim by asserting that that which grounds cannot have a further ground (GA10, 169/PR, 113). On its face, this is a rather poor argument. There is no reason that *being* a ground should preclude *having* a ground. But Heidegger's actual point is narrower: Being the ground *of entities*

---

[3] Schopenhauer distinguishes four, interconnected ways of hearing of the (single) principle of sufficient reason. Which of these resonates with us depends on the sort of reason or ground we are seeking. The four are (1) the law of causality (*all events have causes*), which governs the material sciences; (2) the principle of reason of knowing (*a judgment counts as knowledge only if it is justified*), which governs logic and the classificatory sciences; (3) the principle of sufficient reason of being, which governs mathematics; and (4) the law of motivation (*there is always a motivation behind an agent's action*), which governs morality and the anthropological sciences (Schopenhauer 2012, passim). Schopenhauer's law of causality is Heidegger's principle of causality and Schopenhauer's principle of reason of knowing corresponds to Heidegger's Leibnizian strict formulation. There is nothing like the law of motivation in Heidegger's analysis. Schopenhauer's principle of sufficient reason of being has to do with space and time, unlike Heidegger's ontology, which has to do with the intelligibility of entities as that and what they are.

[4] LSJ stands for Liddell-Scott-Jones (1940).

precludes having a ground *in the way that entities do*. I draw this narrower interpretation from Heidegger's worry that "[e]very founding and even every appearance of foundability has inevitably degraded being to some sort of an entity" (GA10, 166/PR, 111). To think being as having a ground is to think it as an entity – if, that is, we think it as having a ground of the same sort that entities have. To avoid this mistake, we must deny being an ontological ground.

But it does not yet follow that only entities have grounds, for being might be grounded in some way other than the way in which entities are grounded. That is, it is possible to attribute a ground to being without mistakenly treating it as an entity, if we afford it a distinctive type of ground. Heidegger does not respond to this worry, but I can do so on his behalf by suggesting that being, as an ontological ground, is supposed to be a regress-stopper. The third-man regress is known for threatening Plato's account of forms, which are posited to explain why sensible particulars have the properties that they do. If the forms have such properties themselves, then something further will be needed to explain why the forms have the properties that they do, and so on. The regress begins, and it posits an infinite chain of (both explanatory and causal) grounding relations. We might be worried that this sort of regress threatens if we allow being to have a ground of any sort.[5] Entities are grounded in being (ground$_1$), which is grounded in something else (ground$_2$), which is in turn grounded in something else (ground$_3$), and so on. We can perhaps avoid the regress by appealing again to the formal indication of being as whatever it is that grounds entities as things that are. If *being* names whatever grounds entities, then it will refer not only to ground$_1$ but to any posited ground$_2$ and ground$_3$, all the way to ground$_n$. The entire series would then count as the being in which entities are grounded – and it itself would not have a ground. Being would remain abyssal.[6]

This is not a particularly satisfying response to the worry, however, because it rests on a stipulative interpretation of Heidegger's formal indication of being as that on the basis of which entities are and are what they are. Our dissatisfaction brings to our attention that we do not actually know what being "is." We know that it "is" not an entity (and so it cannot

---

[5] Heidegger, for his part, does not seem to be worried about a regress. He is aware of this sort of regress (GA10, 17/PR, 12), but as far as I know he never discusses it as a problem for being. For a discussion of the third-man regress in relation to being, and specifically as a way of motivating the ontological difference, see my "The Trouble with the Ontological Difference" (Withy forthcoming b).

[6] Alternatively, one could argue that being is self-grounding, in the way that some hold that God is self-grounding. Whether this interpretation preserves being's ungroundedness is a difficult issue.

be said *to be*, hence my scare quotes around "is"). We know that it "is" the ground of entities, and that it has no further ground. One of the reasons that we might have wanted to posit a ground for being is precisely in order to better grasp what it "is." A ground for being would be intimately related to it yet distinct from it and so would allow us to set being off from something that it is not. Such contrasting is one way of making sense of what being "is." Lacking a ground means lacking this contrast case, and it leaves being oddly indeterminate. It is *abussos* in that it is not only *groundless* but also *boundless* and thereby *unfathomed* and perhaps *unfathomable* (LSJ, s.v. "ἄβυσσος"). The only contrast case that we do have is with entities: Being is not an entity, but each entity has its ground in being. And yet even this gives us little guidance as to what being "is," for *entity* and *being* are defined in terms of one another. Being is the ground of entities; entities are that which have a ground in being. There is nothing other than this grounding relationship that could help us to grasp being as distinguished from entities and so give us a sense of what it "is."

So, although the principle of reason speaks of being and appears to answer the question of being by saying that being is a ground, its speaking is still shot through with silence. But this silence is telling. The silence is due to being's self-withdrawing, and it is being's self-withdrawing that gives being – and with it, the principle of reason – a history.

11.4   The Self-Withdrawing of Being

Heidegger thinks that being, as the ground of entities, shows up differently in different eras. For the ancient Greeks, for instance, the entity appears as "*phusis tis*, the sort of thing that is an emerging-on-its-own" (GA10, 117/ PR, 79) and being appears as emerging (*phusis*). In the medieval period, entities are "the *ens creatum* of the medieval scholastics, entities created by God" (GA10, 117/PR, 79) and to be is to create or be created. In the modern period, as we have seen, entities are objects and being is objectness (GA10, 117/PR, 79). In each era, being is given in a different way. Heidegger calls this differential granting the *destiny* (*Geschick*) of being. In this sense, being is historical. Being is historical because it is self-withdrawing or self-concealing (GA10, 95/PR, 65). Such self-withdrawing is an essential feature of being: "being proffers itself to us, but in such a way that at the same time it, in its essence, already withdraws" (GA10, 95/PR, 65). There are three main interpretations of this withdrawal in the literature, and I want to offer a fourth – one that draws directly on what the principle of reason, on Heidegger's ontological interpretation, says about being.

One interpretive current takes the self-withdrawing of being to be the fact that, in each era, one take on what it is to be is offered while alternatives are hidden (e.g., Wrathall 2011, 33; Bartky 2010, 266). Being is proffered to us *in one way* and *other ways in which it could be proffered* are withdrawn. (For example, in the modern period, to be is to be an object, and the possibility of being as emerging (*phusis*) is withheld. The moderns thus could not experience entities as emerging into appearing but only as objects set off from a subject.) I agree that this withholding does obtain, and Heidegger does criticize some eras for concealing alternatives more thoroughly than others (e.g., GA10, 118/PR, 80). But I do not think that this is the self-withdrawing of being. When Heidegger speaks of the self-withdrawing of being, he does not say that *one* style of being shows up while *others* are withheld, but instead that when *entities* appear in their being, *being* is both given and withheld. It is given in the sense that "being must of itself and already beforehand shine, so that particular entities can appear" (GA10, 93/PR, 63). It is withheld in the sense that being "never lies over against us as do particular entities that are present here and there. Being is in no way as immediately familiar and overt to us as are particular entities" (GA10, 93/PR, 63).[7]

A second interpretive current makes sense of passages such as this by holding that it is precisely because being is the ground of entities that it is concealed. As the ground, it is always presupposed and is thereby background to the foreground of entities. When entities show up to us, the condition of possibility of their doing so is thus not apparent to us (see, e.g., Polt 2006, 144). This interpretation trades on the intuition that a ground, background, or condition of possibility is not available to us when we are focused on that which is made possible, foregrounded, or grounded. The interpretation presumably has its roots in Gestalt psychology's account of the perceptual foreground and background, yet I do not know of anyone who has tried to work out precisely how and why this analogy with Gestalt-psychological perception, or even the intuition that grounds are always hidden, holds in the case of being.

---

[7] Wrathall tries to take account of passages such as this by arguing that an understanding of being – say, being as objectness – is invisible to us when we are relating to entities in terms of it (e.g., as objects). He concludes from this invisibility that alternative understandings of being must be withheld (Wrathall 2011, 33). The missing premise must be something like: *in order for an understanding of being to be invisible, it must be the only one available.* More argument would be needed to establish that this is true – particularly if different eras conceal alternative understandings of being to greater or lesser degrees.

A third, but related, interpretive current tries to capture the idea that being is an invisible background with a different sort of image: Being is pervasive, atmospheric, like light or air (see, e.g., Dreyfus 2005a, 409; Sheehan 2015, 116). Heidegger sometimes speaks this way himself, using an analogy with light:

> Being itself is unquestioned and taken for granted, for it is only in the light of being that entities can be asked about, and the question concerning what entities are can be answered. However, the light itself remains unnoticed, just as one takes the day for granted and in its "light" concerns oneself with the matters of the day. (GA55, 98)

The thought seems to be that being is ubiquitous and familiar and so taken for granted. It is less familiar to us than entities precisely because it is maximally familiar. But, while Heidegger does sometimes say things along these lines, I do not believe that this is, strictly, the self-withdrawing of being. It may be true that being is ubiquitous and taken for granted, but usually when things are so it is relatively easy to draw our attention to them. Heidegger (at least in his later period) does not seem to think that this is true of being. Why not? Why must being remain in the background? I am tempted to say: because it is a ground or condition of possibility. But that brings us straight back to the second interpretation.

I would like to suggest a fourth interpretation that will explain what the third interpretation is trying to get at while acknowledging the second's focus on being as a ground.[8] It is important not just that being is the ground of entities but also – as the principle of reason hints – that it is an abyssal ground. Being is abyssal in the sense that it is ungrounded but also in the sense that it is boundless and so unfathomable. It is so because, as I said, it lacks the determinacy that would be afforded it by a contrast case. Entities appears to us determinately – as grounded in being (and so distinct from it), as *that* they are (rather than not), and as *what* they are (rather than not). Entities show up meaningfully insofar as they show up as set off from what they are not. Being does not show up with this sort of meaningful determinacy. As we saw, it cannot be set off from a ground, and it is set off from entities only formally.[9] Indeed, Heidegger considers the distinction between being and entities to be one that we cannot grasp.

---

[8] For more on this interpretation, see Withy 2022.

[9] Being also cannot be set off from *lēthē*, which is the nothingness that is other than being, because *lēthē* cannot be grasped by us. When we try to approach *lēthē* in the mood of angst, we encounter it only as "wholly repelling" (GA9, 114).

"Though the two elements of the difference, that which is present [i.e., entities] and presencing [i.e., being] disclose themselves, they do not do so as different" (GA5, 365) – and they cannot, since we have no access to a field of commonality within which their difference could be manifest. As a result, "this distinction as a whole is in its essence a *completely obscure distinction*" (GA29/30, 518). Heidegger identifies this obscurity with the self-withdrawing of being: "the oblivion of being is oblivion to the difference between being and the entity" (GA5, 365). Being is self-withdrawing because our only ways of making sense are ways of making determinate, and this making determinate works for entities but not for being. As Heidegger puts it in his lectures on the principle of reason, being

> never lies over against us as do particular entities that are present here and there. Being is in no way as immediately familiar and overt to us as are particular entities. … From this we come to see that, compared to entities which are immediately accessible, being manifests the character of holding itself back, of concealing itself in a certain manner. (GA10, 93/PR, 63)

The familiarity of entities comes from their ontic determinacy. But being cannot be set off from any contrast case and so cannot be rendered determinate in this way. This is why we would describe being as a kind of pervasive atmosphere – not because it is familiar or presupposed, but because it is boundless and so unfathomable. In the principle of reason's claim that being is the abyssal ground of entities, this self-withdrawing of being is announced, obliquely.

I have suggested that the self-withdrawing of being is being's lack of ontic determinacy. It must be because of this ontic indeterminacy that being has a history. Yet the history of being is a history of its various determinate appearings – now as *phusis*, now as being created, now as objectness. For my interpretation of the self-withdrawing of being to be plausible, I must resolve the apparent tension between this historical determinateness and being's ontic indeterminacy. Notice, first, that being's indeterminacy with regard to *what* it is in contrast to entities is not impacted by its historical determinateness. Rather than taking a stand on what being is in contrast to entities, the various destinings of being take a stand on being's ground. This is the second point. In the modern period, to be is to be an object posited by a subject. *Being* is thus *being posited by a subject* and so has an efficient cause: the subject. In the medieval period, to be is to be created by God. *Being* is thus *being created by God* and so has God as its efficient cause. (The ground of God's being as creator remains a problem.) For the Greeks, in contrast, to be is to emerge into presence. As we will see in Section 11.5, while such emerging is always correlated with, and sometimes enabled by, the *logos* of the human being, emerging into presence is not caused by or grounded in the human being. For the Greeks, *phusis* appears as an abyssal ground. The Greeks thus preserve the indeterminacy of being with respect to ground. But the medievals and the moderns do not. By positing an efficient cause for being, they posit a ground for it. In doing so, they neglect or forget the indeterminacy, and so the self-withdrawing, of being. Forgetting the self-withdrawing of being by positing one or another ground for being thus allows the various post-Greek destinings of being their various historical characters. In sum, being can appear variously throughout its history because its indeterminacy can be recognized or forgotten, and, if forgotten, it can be covered over in various ways.

As being shows up differently in different eras, so too does any principle that speaks of being, including the principle of reason. How the principle of reason resonates will thus depend on the era's take on being, and it will change over time. In this sense, the principle (*Satz*) of reason is something like a musical movement (*Satz*), which changes and develops over time and drives the listener along with it (GA10, 132/PR, 89). To hear the principle of reason properly, then, we must listen to it as Mozart recommended, "'listening to everything at once'" (GA10, 99/PR, 67), getting its entire history and development in view. For Heidegger, that means trying to hear how the principle of reason spoke to the ancient Greeks and how this resonated through the Roman era and into modernity.

11.5   The Principle of Reason as Heard by the Ancient Greeks

According to Heidegger, the principle of reason resonated with the ancient Greeks insofar as being and ground were closely associated for them. This close association is present, but obscured, in the Greek concept of *logos*. The concept of *logos* is the right place to look for a Greek version of the principle of reason, since *logos* is the antecedent of the Latin *ratio* (reason/ ground). It has a wide semantic scope, covering:

I.   Computation, reckoning
II. Relation, correspondence, proportion
III. Explanation
IV. Debate
V.   Continuous statement, narrative, oration
VI. Verbal expression or utterance
VII. A particular utterance, saying

VIII.   Thing spoken of, subject matter

IX.   Expression, utterance, speech (LSJ, s.v. "λόγος")[10]

So while *logos* is usually associated primarily with both speaking and thinking, it is so specifically in the context of a reckoning with things, and especially a reckoning that aims to explain or account for them. The third sense of *logos*, explanation, is further elaborated:

1. Plea, pretext, ground
2. Statement of a theory, argument
3. Law, rule of conduct
4. Thesis, hypothesis, provisional ground
5. Reason, ground
6. Formula
7. Reason, law (LSJ, s.v. "λόγος")

So, a *logos* is an account, whether in thinking, speaking, or theorizing, that reckons with entities by giving them explanatory or justificatory grounds. Those grounds are themselves *logoi*. Identifying those grounds is precisely the sort of *logos* that philosophical thinking aims at, according to both Heidegger (GA10, 163/PR, 109) and Aristotle. Thus Aristotle frames the philosophical project of the early philosophers of nature, the *phusiologoi*, as aiming to give a *logos* that identifies grounds, the principle (*archē*) and/ or causes (*aitiai*) of things – specifically, of *phusis* (Aristotle 1984, *Phys.* 184a10–184a16).

As we have seen, Heidegger takes *phusis* to be the Greek conception of being. If the concept of *logos* is to speak of both ground and being, then it must speak of *phusis* – not in the sense that a *logos* can be given of *phusis*, but in the sense that *logos* and *phusis* must overlap semantically.

Phusis is usually translated as *nature*. It can refer narrowly to natural things, broadly to all things, and ontologically to the nature either of natural things only or of all things as such. In the Greek experience, natural things are what they are by bursting forth into presence, as plants do from the soil. (The verb associated with *phusis*, *phuein*, means *to bring forth* or *to grow* in the sense of springing up (LSJ, s.v. "φύω").) Compare Aristotle's claim that a natural entity is one that "has within itself a principle of motion and of stationariness (in respect of place, of growth and decrease, or by way of alteration)" (Aristotle 1984, *Phys.* 192b12–192b16). Such bursting forth

---

[10] The final item in the entry is "the word or wisdom of God," which is obviously a later meaning.

into presence is the nature of all things.[11] It is that by virtue of which they are: being (GA10, 102/PR, 69). So, for the ancient Greeks, to be is to burst forth into appearing. (It is also to withdraw from appearing: Heraclitus says that *phusis kruptesthai philei*, *phusis* loves to hide (22B123; or Kirk, Raven and Schofield 1983, fragment 208). Heidegger takes this to be an expression of the self-withdrawing of being (GA10, 95/PR, 64)).

How does *phusis* as arising into appearing resonate in the concept of *logos*? It does so in the *logos* as uttering or speaking, because speaking is a way in which entities arise into presence (GA10, 161/PR, 107). Heidegger gives a long argument for this in his lectures on the principle of reason and a shorter one in *Being and Time*. The shorter argument asserts that *logos* means "the same as *dēloun* [manifest]: to make manifest what one is 'talking about' in one's discourse. … The *logos* lets something be seen (*phainesthai* [to allow to appear])" (SZ 32, insertions mine). When we speak, we allow what is spoken of to manifest itself. This is a version of entities bursting forth into presence, *phusis*. The longer argument connecting *logos* with *phusis* appeals to the verb associated with *logos*, *legein* (or *legō*), which means gathering or reckoning (GA10, 160/PR, 107; LSJ, s.v. "λέγω"). All forms of *logos* are forms of gathering, in the sense that they lay things out in relation to one another so as to reckon with them in terms of one another (GA10, 160/PR, 107; Withy forthcoming a). A statement, for example, gathers a subject and predicate together so as to make sense of the former in terms of the latter. A speech or story gathers events together into a narrative or explanation that makes sense of something on the basis of its broader context. In bringing one thing together with another in this way, the *logos* allows one thing to manifest itself *as* what it is in terms of or on the basis of another. In doing so, the *logos* allows the entity to show up as what it is. It makes manifest, or brings into appearing. We thus hear being as *phusis*, arising into appearing, speaking in the concept of *logos*. As gathering and so manifesting, the concept of *logos* overlaps semantically with *phusis*.

So, according to Heidegger, the Greek concept of *logos* speaks of both ground (as *archē* and/or *aitia*) and being (as *phusis*): "[l]ogos is at once presencing and ground. Being and ground belong together in *logos*" (GA10, 161/PR, 107). But the connection between the two is concealed, in the sense that it is not explicit that or how they belong together – namely, that being is the ground of entities (GA10, 164/PR, 110). Thus the principle of reason speaks to the ancient Greeks but in a silent, concealed way.

---

[11] Interestingly, Heidegger does not think that the Greeks extended their experience of the being of natural things to the being of all things, but rather that they first experienced *phusis* as "pure emerging" and, on that basis, experienced natural entities accordingly (GA55, 87).

Even if we can follow Heidegger's argument step by step, it does not have the feel of an insight. Still, it is not wholly implausible. Consider that the short formulation of the principle of reason expressed in ancient Greek terms would hold that nothing *is* without an *archē* or *aitia*, where that *archē* is being as *phusis*. That is: Nothing is without bursting forth into presence. Notice now that Aristotle, for example, closely associates *phusis* with the *archē* – not only in the sense that philosophy aims to identify the *archē* of *phusis*, but in the sense that *phusis* is itself a sort of *archē* (Aristotle 1984, *Phys.* 192b23). Positing *phusis* as a sort of principle or ground connects it deeply, albeit obscurely, to the *logos*. Indeed, Aristotle takes the *logos* to be an accurate guide to the structure of reality – as do Heraclitus (cf. GA10, 168/PR, 112) and Parmenides.[12] This could be the case only if the *logos* has an ontological dimension. But, as far as I know, none of the Greeks inter-rogated either the ontological dimension of the *logos* or the logical dimen-sion of *phusis*. This lends some plausibility to Heidegger's claim that the relationship between being (*phusis*) and ground (*logos*), articulated in the principle of reason, spoke to the Greeks in a concealed way.

Because the relationship between being and ground was concealed from the Greeks, ground came to be understood ontically rather than onto-logically. The deep connection between being and ground was replaced with the commonplace idea that every entity has some (ontic) ground or reason (GA10, 162/PR, 108). This withdrawal of the ontological "allows something else to come to the fore, namely ground/reason in the shape of *archai*, *aitiai*, or *rationes*, of *causae*, of Principles, *Ursachen* [causes] and Rational grounds" (GA10, 165/PR, 110). This is decisive for what happens next, in the Roman period, and it sets the stage for how the principle of reason resonates in modernity.

11.6 The Romans Ruined Everything

We have seen, in ancient Greece, a close connection between being as *phusis* and the *archē* given as a ground in the *logos*. Since *archē* means not only *foundation* or *first principle* but also *origin* and *source of action*, stating the *archē* of something is giving a *logos* that tells us where that thing comes from and what governs any change that it undergoes (LSJ, s.v. "αρχή").

---

[12] This assumption is clearly behind Aristotle's approach in, for example, the *Categories* (Aristotle 1984). Heraclitus is explicit that we learn about the nature of reality by listening to the *logos* (22B1 and 22B50; or Kirk, Raven, and Schofield 1983, fragments 194 and 196). Parmenides explicitly derives ontological conclusions from what can be said and thought (Kirk, Raven, and Schofield 1983, "VIII. Parmenides of Elea," *passim*).

Identifying the *archē* of something thus gives us a firm basis for working with it – something that we can depend on and use to predict and antici-pate what will happen in "the blooming, buzzing confusion" (James 1981, 462) of bursting forth into presence. This idea of the *archē* as a dependable basis is, according to Heidegger, carried over into the Roman appropriation of *logos* as *ratio*. The Latin *ratio* means *a reckoning, account, calculation*, or *computation* (Lewis and Short, 1879, s.v. "ratio"). Heidegger claims that it is based on the verb *reor* (GA10, 148/PR, 100), which means *to reckon* or *to calculate* (Lewis and Short, 1879, s.v. "reor").[13] According to Heidegger, "[t]o reckon or count on something means to expect it and thereby to figure it as something upon which to build" (GA10, 149/PR, 100). The expecta-tion – and, eventually, demand – for a dependable basis is determinative for how grounds and reasons come to figure in the modern epoch of being.

We can hear that demand in Leibniz's formulation of the principle of *sufficient* reason. The reason rendered by the subject as the ground of its judgment must be enough – for what? To "securely establish an object [*Gegenstand*] in its stance [*Stand*]," which is to say, to bring the object to its "*perfectio*, … the completeness [*Voll-ständigkeit*] of the determinations for the standing [*Stehen*] of an object [*Gegenstand*]" (GA10, 50/PR, 33). Only then can the object be counted on and count as securely posited by the judging subject. The secure positing that brings the object to a stand is one that can be reproduced by any judging subject at any time, who can thus represent, and so reckon with, the same object (GA10, 175/PR, 120). Such representing is a knowing that is objective, neutral, and certain.

Certain, neutral, objective knowledge is what modern science aims at. Heidegger thus sees modern science as the explicit and developed form of the cognition posited by modern philosophers (GA10, 44/PR, 28), now directed specifically at knowing nature (GA10, 88/PR, 56). The various types of sci-entific knowledge of nature are in turn organized in the modern university (GA10, 37–38/PR, 24), which drives the distinctively modern effort to be able to reckon with everything, to calculate everything, to understand everything on a secure, certain, and single basis. It seeks complete rationalization of real-ity: total calculability, certainty, and coherence. This is "the modern manner of thinking in which we daily reside without expressly perceiving or noticing the demand of reason to be rendered in all cognition" (GA10, 50–51/PR, 33).

At this point in his story, Heidegger draws on the account of technology that he provided in "The Question Concerning Technology" (1949, GA7).

---

[13] Lewis and Short (1879) also list as meanings *to believe, think, suppose, imagine, judge, deem*.

There, he argued that the modern technological worldview experiences entities as mere resources to be exploited. It thereby occludes both other ways of experiencing entities (e.g., as emerging into appearing) and our own essential activity as understanders of being who make sense of entities. Indeed, we ourselves are experienced as mere "human resources," with productive energies to be tapped by economic and other systems.

These are the systems that, in *The Principle of Reason*, Heidegger characterizes as driven by the demand for total calculability and sufficient reason. He is especially concerned with the atom bomb, which was developed in the 1940s and is the purest possible manifestation of both the worldview that thinks in terms of harnessable energy and the modern drive for total control. In line with the fears of the times, Heidegger's rhetoric quickly becomes apocalyptic, yet his concern is not with the ontic devastation of the bomb but with the ontological devastation wrought by the worldview that birthed it. Being "overpowered" by the principle of sufficient reason (GA10, 130/PR, 123) "threatens everything of humans' being-at-home and robs them of the roots of their subsistence" (GA10, 47/ PR, 30). Heidegger does not elaborate on this threat and I will not further explore it, except to point out that his worries about "the withdrawal of roots" (GA10, 48/PR, 31) are clearly connected to the anti-Semitism and anti-urbanism that led him to his affiliation with the Nazis.

So, what began with the Greek quest for the dependability of an *archē* has become the demand for total certainty (GA10, 181–182/PR, 124). This demand speaks so loudly that we can no longer hear the possibility of which Angelus Silesius speaks when he describes the rose as being "without why. It blooms because it blooms" (GA10, 53/PR, 35).[14] The rose is an entity that escapes the principle of sufficient reason (insofar as it is not subject to the demand, placed on cognizers, to render sufficient reason) but it does not escape all grounding. It is grounded in its being or appearing, as "a pure arising on its own, a pure shining" (GA10, 85/PR, 57). That we can make little sense of this shows how "mighty" the principle of sufficient reason is (GA10, 47/PR, 30). But it also means that there is a sense in which the principle of reason, in fact, remains silent and asleep (GA10, 86/ PR, 56). For the principle of reason speaks of being as the abyssal ground of entities and we still do not hear that message clearly, if at all.

We can now see why the principle of sufficient reason had such a long "incubation period" (GA10, 5/PR, 4): because its full articulation belongs

---

[14] For more on Heidegger's appeals to Silesius, and so to Meister Eckhart, see Caputo 1986.

wholly to the modern era, in which not only is our relationship to entities conceived as that of a subject representing an object, but the demand for total control and calculation rings in our ears and blocks out any other resonance of the principle of reason.

11.7   About the Story We Just Heard

Heidegger's histories of philosophy are less actual histories than just-so stories. They can be illuminating, but they are not necessarily historically accurate. Consider the claim that the principle of sufficient reason is a distinctively modern idea. Connecting the principle to modern technology and the epistemology of modern philosophy puts both these and the principle of sufficient reason in a new light. But, as Heidegger acknowledges (GA10, 80/PR, 53), versions of the principle of sufficient reason can be found, more or less explicitly, throughout the history of philosophy. Anaximander (12A26; Kirk, Raven, and Schofield 1983, fragment 124) and Parmenides (28B8; Kirk, Raven, and Schofield 1983, fragment 296) make use of it. Leibniz himself cites Archimedes as anticipating it (Leibniz and Clarke 2000, 7).[15] It can also be found in the medieval philosophers Ibn Sina (aka Avicenna; Richardson 2014, 744), Ibn Rushd (aka Averroes; Kukkonen 2000), and Peter Abelard (Melamed and Lin 2020). There are surely others.

Of course, reasoning by appeal to something like the principle of sufficient reason is not the same as stating it as a logical principle. It is still deeply puzzling why the principle was not explicitly articulated earlier – but it remains puzzling, at least to me, even after charitably reconstructing Heidegger's interpretation of its incubation period. Heidegger's explanation, in short, is that a transformation took place in the way that the Latin language gave uptake to a Greek term, and that that transformation later determined "the spirit of the seventeenth century" (GA10, 39/PR, 25; cf. GA54, 63 and 100). But while linguistic shifts can be powerful, Heidegger does not establish that this particular shift is decisive. His discussion of the verb *reor* is too underdeveloped. Further, in light of what I said in the previous paragraph, there is a much simpler way to resolve the puzzle: Odds are that someone prior to Leibniz *did* formulate the principle, just not in a way that we have been in the habit of acknowledging when we construct histories of philosophy.

---

[15] I owe this reference to Melamed and Lin (2020).

Heidegger's goal, however, is not to tell an accurate history of philosophy so much as to bring us into a certain experience of questioning. Hearing the principle (*Satz*) of reason ontologically will bring us to a leap (*Satz*) into being: "the leap from the principle of reason into the principle of being" (GA10, 79/PR, 53). So leaping, we consider being as the abyssal ground of entities – and so, as an unfathomable, indeterminate, open question for us. We thus come to the question of being.

We come also, and thereby, to our own essence, as the entity for whom being is at issue. We are sense-makers who make sense of entities on the basis of their that-being and what-being – and yet we cannot make sense of that ground. Since the principle of reason speaks of this, learning to hear it is an exercise in self-knowing. We learn from the principle both that there is finitude in our access to being (i.e., that being is abyssal) and that, on the basis of the access to being that we do have, we are always, everywhere, able to make (at least some) sense of entities (i.e., that all entities have a ground in being). By virtue of the latter, Heidegger's principle of reason guarantees a minimal, ontic pan-intelligibility: For every entity, some sense can be made of what and that it is. And just as the commitment to there being an explanation or a cause for everything drives the human quest for knowledge, so too the guaranteed intelligibility of entities drives us as sense-makers, everywhere making what sense we can of all that we encounter.

So, we are "constantly addressed by, summoned to attend to, grounds and reason" (GA10, 3/PR, 3) in that we are constantly called to make sense of entities on the basis of their being. We can now understand in what respect the principle of reason is a logical principle. It does not have normative authority over our thinking (as does, for instance, the principle of non-contradiction). It does not license us to make inferences (as does, for instance, *modus ponens*). The principle says of us that we allow entities to reveal themselves as that and what they are by gathering (*legein*) them together with their being. It tells us that being logical in this original sense is our "modus vivendi" (GA10, 16/PR, 11) and it thereby "lays claim to us in our essence" (GA10, 101/PR, 68).[16]

---

[16] I thank Dave Cerbone and Dan Dahlstrom for helpful comments on a draft of this paper. I thank Filippo Casati for conversations about the material.

CHAPTER 12

Heidegger's Contradictions

Daniel O. Dahlstrom

*Alles Wort und somit alle Logik steht
unter der Macht des Seyns.* (GA65, 79)

Heidegger uses "contradiction" in different ways but flags it primarily as a basic rule of formal logic, enjoining avoidance of contradiction at all costs. However, his characterization of the principle of noncontradiction (hereafter PNC) is messy if not contradictory. At times he characterizes the PNC unmistakably as a rule for what is asserted insofar as the latter is on hand (*vorhanden*) in some sense. From this vantage point, far from being ontologically innocuous, compliance with the PNC is of a piece with a commitment to thinking that restricts what there is to what is on hand. Yet if so, Heidegger himself is guilty of doing just that since he invokes the PNC throughout his corpus, applying it not only to the thought of many others but also to his own discussions of what, he claims, is decidedly not on hand.

Is Heidegger caught in such a contradiction? In this chapter I hope to show how he responds on different levels to the dilemma indicated. He countenances narrow and broad ontological interpretations of the PNC and, on the latter interpretation, his adherence to the principle is not contradictory without much further ado, if at all. Yet this broad interpretation of the PNC is no more neutral than the narrow interpretation of it that ties it to what is merely "on hand." Instead it is grounded, he contends, in our way of being-here together as well as in the hidden clearing that, by virtue of appropriating the being of beings and being-here to one another, yields the sort of decisive disjunction of possibilities that the PNC can only presuppose.[1]

---

[1] I want to thank James Kinkaid for his helpful comments on an earlier draft of this chapter.

12.1   Senses of "Contradiction"

Widersprechen, like the Latinate *contradict*, literally signifies "speak against" and Heidegger, for the most part, follows a common practice of using the term in the strict sense as a principle of logic. Thus, when something is said or written that states the opposite ("the contra") of something else said or written, the statements contradict one another. Heidegger's observations that "the Antigone chorus' final words do not contradict what it says earlier" or that rationalism and irrationalism play out "under the most contradictory titles" are just two examples of his use of the term in this strictly logical sense (GA40, 173, 188). Indeed, he faults his own use of "fundamental" in the expression "fundamental ontology" for "contradicting" the provisional character of the existential analysis, a contradiction that leads him to drop the rubric "fundamental ontology" altogether (GA14, 40).

Heidegger applies "contradictory" in this strict sense quite conventionally to "judgments" (GA10, 180; GA24, 42), "propositions" (GA20, 431; GA24, 48), and "assertions" (GA14, 7f; GA46, 158). This logical use of "contradiction" complies with what he variously calls the "principle of contradiction" (*Satz vom Widerspruch*), the "ground rule of noncontradictoriness" (*Grundregel der Widerspruchslosigkeit*), and a "law of thinking" (*Denkgesetz*). These normative expressions ("rule," "law") mandate the avoidance of contradictions because the conjunction of the two contradictory propositions cannot obtain. And it cannot obtain because what is designated by one proposition and what is designated by its opposite cannot jointly exist. Thus, given p, it is impossible for $\sim p$ to be or to be consistently thought or asserted. Ruled out for the same reason is any combination of an assertion's grammatical subject with a grammatical predicate that expresses something incompatible with what is signified by that subject, as in Heidegger's example "the triangle laughs" (GA8, 159).

As the foregoing gloss makes clear, the various injunctions noted correspond to the PNC as a principle equally fundamental for logic and ontology, for thinking and being, namely, the principle that what is contradictory is unthinkable and impossible while something is thinkable or possible if and only if it is noncontradictory. Note, too, that while the PNC, understood in this way, is arguably not wedded to a particular sort or manner of being, it does suppose some notion of possibility and impossibility.

Heidegger also applies the logical sense of contradiction to representations or thoughts (GA15, 383). The logical use of "contradiction" may, indeed, derive, as Heidegger insists, from a certain interpretation of λόγος, but if so, it is a λόγος that may be spoken, written, or merely thought. The contradictory

items, moreover, may be not only "assertions" but also collections of assertions or bodies of thoughts, for example "contradictory theories" or "contradictory conceptions of being" (GA14, 7; GA54, 45; GA56/57, 22). Still
wielding the term in this specific sense, Heidegger also makes the metonymical move from contradictory assertions, thoughts, or theories to the person
responsible for them: "The poet contradicts himself ... a simultaneous affirming and denying of the same" (GA10, 55f; GA39, 57). Similarly, the observation "Heraclitus contradicts himself" indicates that the ancient thinker makes
claims that appear prima facie to contradict one another (GA55, 110).

While Heidegger uses "contradiction" in the strictly logical sense just
glossed, he also follows a common practice of using *widersprechen* in a
broad sense to flag cases of some thing, event, or phenomenon opposing,
conflicting with, ruling out, or canceling its counterpart. Thus, life and
death, day and night "contradict" one another (GA55, 26). Interpreting
earlier thinking as definitive instead of grasping it more radically on the
basis of new possibilities "would contradict" genuine research (GA22,
32; see, too, GA14, 63; GA15, 324). Heidegger also appeals to this broad,
extra-linguistic use of the term when he observes that "Heraclitus' remarkable sentences assert something contradictory in itself" (GA55, 111).

Nor does Heidegger shy away from using the term in a third sense that
is a hybrid of the strict and broad senses. Thus he notes how "the naked
facts contradict ... arbitrary theses" (GA27, 127; GA29/30, 402) and how
an interpretation of Kant "contradicts" a fact (GA25, 338). Onomatopoeia
seems to "contradict" the claim that words are not copies of what they
signify (GA52, 33f).

12.2 Appearances of Contradiction: Vagueness and Ambiguity

Adhering to the PNC and locating genuine contradictions in the strictly
logical sense reviewed above require univocal terminology. Heidegger frequently addresses alleged instances of contradictions with the aim of demonstrating that what may appear contradictory proves on further reflection
to be nothing of the sort. In some cases, for example, he exposes some
vagueness, thereby removing the appearance of contradiction. Thus, he
exonerates Nietzsche, on grounds of vagueness, from various charges of
contradiction (even as he critically exposes interpretations of Nietzsche's
work for being contradictory; GA46, 158, 168, 343). In early Freiburg lectures he acknowledges the apparent – but only apparent! – contradiction
of attempting to gain access to a concept of philosophy that is indefinable
(GA59, 175). So, too, his claim that the question of being has not been

posed appears, he concedes, preposterous at first, indeed, "contradicting" his own earlier gloss on Aristotle's framing of the question (GA31, 36f). Yet, whatever their kinship, the two questions are quite distinct and the apparent contradiction can be traced to the vagueness of the phrase "the question of being." Heidegger similarly contests that a contradiction – rather than simply a difference in meaning – obtains between his talk of being itself and being as appropriation (GA14, 52), or between thinking as experiencing and as a preparation for experiencing (GA14, 63).

Along similar lines, Heidegger insists in different lectures that the appearance of methodological inconsistency on his part is in fact traceable to an *ambiguity* at the heart of philosophy. He introduces this ambiguity at the outset of his 1929/30 lectures by noting that philosophy (here equated with metaphysics) is neither a science nor a worldview, but a questioning of things in their entirety and at the profoundest level that accordingly includes putting ourselves in question. Philosophy's basic concepts are sui generis (*ureigene*) since they require holistically grasping (*begreifen*) things and ourselves but only by virtue of having been gripped (*ergriffen*) by a basic attunement (GA29/30, 9–13, 86f, 200, and passim). Hence, the task arises of awakening such a basic attunement but also, as a necessary preliminary step, assuring ourselves that it grips us here and now, in our own contemporary situation. "What attunement," Heidegger asks, "is to be awakened for *us today?*" (GA29/30, 104).

In this connection Heidegger turns briefly to early twentieth-century philosophies of culture that, taking cues from Nietzsche, pit life and spirit against one another. He criticizes them, not so much for their portrayal of human existence as something culturally on hand, but for managing only a portrayal without awakening a basic attunement and conveying what being-here actually means, confronted with the need to make decisions (GA29/30, 113).

Still, Heidegger concedes that awakening a basic attunement requires proceeding from some expression or other in which we are merely portrayed. The task of philosophy, that of awakening a basic attunement, accordingly appears to be a matter of portraying something on hand, even though – he alleges – it is something completely different. Nor can we shake the impression that everything we say merely portrays our situation and that we are identifying an attunement as something on hand that underlies our situation and expresses itself in it. The inability to shake this impression is part and parcel of the *ambiguity* (*Zweideutigkeit*) of philosophy. Nor is it removed by asserting a theoretical difference between portraying and awakening a basic attunement: "The more authentically we begin, the more we leave the ambiguity in play and the harder the task is for each individual to decide for themselves whether they actually understand or not" (GA29/30, 114).

Nonetheless, portraying the attunement that expresses itself in our contemporary situation is not the same as awakening it, even if that awakening necessarily piggybacks on that portrayal. This construal of philosophy (portraying something as though it were on hand on the way to awakening it as a way of being-here) is not a contradiction but an ambiguity, albeit an inescapable ambiguity in Heidegger's eyes. Philosophy is inherently subject to ambiguities, since it must draw on ordinary language to say what is not ordinary and since it is taken to be universally accessible to human beings in everyday life and yet is nothing less than an assault on the latter.[2] This acknowledgment of philosophy's ambiguity, like that of Heidegger's practice of exposing the vagueness that gives rise to the appearance of contradiction, further demonstrates adherence to the PNC in the strict sense.

12.3   Ontological and Post-ontological Interpretations of the Principle of Noncontradiction

While Heidegger uses *widersprechen* in the three ways mentioned in Section 12.1, he only thematizes the strict use explicitly. As noted, this sense of "contradiction" takes the form of injunctions, for example, rules of logic and laws of thinking, because the PNC places a constraint on what there is and thereby on what we can think and meaningfully say: "What is contradictory cannot *be*" (GA40, 83, 196; GA8, 159). It is possible, of course, to make contradictory claims, that is, to mouth contradictions, but it is equally possible to avoid doing so; hence the designations "rule" and "law." But while these injunctions presuppose the avoidability of certain conjunctions of propositions or predicates, the normative force of what they enjoin follows from the impossibility of the state of affairs or whatever it is that is designated by those conjunctions. In this sense, the necessity underlying the PNC, the "rule" to avoid contradiction, can be – and traditionally has been – understood as no less ontological than logical.[3]

---

[2] See GA29/30, 18, 21, 30–32 and GA40, 11–14, 20f, and 33–34.

[3] Two points of qualification here: (1) Heidegger takes this reading of the PNC as jointly logical and ontology from an array of philosophers: Aristotle (GA22, 173, 317; GA23, 8; GA33, 66; GA40, 196), Leibniz (GA22, 47; GA26, 61, 65ff), Wolff (GA23, 195f), Baumgarten (GA36/37, 56), and Kant (GA24, 52; GA26, 6). (2) Heidegger appears (see below) to retain the PNC even in the wake of eschewing ontology generally; hence, a post-ontological PNC.

12.3.1 *The Narrow, Ontological Interpretation of the Principle of Noncontradiction and the Dilemma It Presents*

As flagged above, there is a traditional interpretation of logic that is of a piece with a certain interpretation of being. On this interpretation, logic (comprising the PNC as well as principles of implication, equivalence, and so on) is exclusively concerned with assertions about what is on hand, that is, beings. This view of logic goes hand in hand with an interpretation of being that equates it with being on hand and is thus exhausted by what is on hand (e.g., things, properties, states of affairs, events, and so on that are the objects of assertions).[4]

At times Heidegger appears to endorse this interpretation. For example, after noting that an attunement, like what sleeps, is in a sense both here and at the same time not here, he acknowledges that to assert as much is an "outright contradiction." Yet the PNC, he quickly adds, is a principle of the old metaphysics; "a completely determinate construal of being" underlies it and, as such, "it must not only be put in question but shaken up [rattled, unsettled: *erschüttern*] from the ground up" (GA29/30, 91). Later in the same lectures he criticizes metaphysics' exclusive orientation to logic and its focus on the assertion, the linguistic expression of taking one thing *as* another, with the assumption that both are "*on hand* in the widest sense" (thereby leaving the logician herself – being-here and not on hand – in logical limbo; GA29/30, 424). The reason why sentences in the form of assertions dominate logic is nothing less than our everyday way of relating (comporting ourselves) to entities as something simply on hand, our "tendency to take everything we encounter as something on hand."[5] On this understanding, logic and the PNC, as its basic principle, are the basis for the old metaphysics, a metaphysics that takes things exclusively as being on hand (a metaphysics of presence).

Heidegger iterates these points in several lectures during the 1930s. In the Winter Semester 1933/34 he tells his students: "Logic is the doctrine of thinking, thinking that is conceived as the grasp of entities (what is on hand)" (GA36/37, 103). In the Summer Semester 1934 he iterates that logic is concerned with assertions "taken as something on hand" and that the PNC, as

---

[4] This parallel or even apposition of "logic" and "ontology" (or "metaphysics"), often highlighted by Heidegger (GA65, 79, 247, 280, 469; GA66, 189–190) is exemplified by their paired formality: just as *formal* logic, in a decontextualizing analysis, abstracts forms of inference from language, so *formal* ontology abstracts formal properties of what is said to be, for example, the state of affairs (*Sachverhalt*). Heidegger opposes *Wahrverhalt* to the latter; see Dahlstrom (1994b).

[5] GA29/30, 432, 438f, 479; this tendency, Heidegger notes, is a legacy of Greek thinking; see GA29/30, 462, 464; GA36/37, 102f; GA40, 201.

the basic rule for assertions so construed, forms part of the inner structure of logical inference (GA38, 3f). In his 1935 lectures he goes even further, claiming that logic not only connects two things on hand but construes the connection itself as something on hand (GA40, 199). Not surprisingly, during this period he further contends that the logic that has come down to us (*die herkömmliche Logik*) is grounded in a completely specific answer to the question of what beings are and, as a result, thinking that follows its laws exclusively is unable to understand, let alone unfold the question (GA36/37, 280; GA40, 27). To the extent that the *logos* in the sense of the assertion dominates how being is understood (merging formal logic and formal ontology), being is experienced and conceived as being on hand (GA40, 204). There is accordingly no *question* of being; any such question is pointless (GA65, 442).

Heidegger takes himself here to be battling against the ontological inertia of everyday use of assertions. The assertion that '*a* is *b*' allegedly draws, as noted, on the pre-predicative process of taking *a* as *b*, a process that typically relates one thing or aspect on hand to another. This process can conflate the relation, putting it on the same level (*nivellieren*), without regard for context or content, with the terms (*relata*) of the relation, taken as something merely on hand. Echoing his remarks about the inherent ambiguity of philosophy, he notes how the very articulation that is essential to philosophizing makes it susceptible to a substantive misunderstanding to which a commonplace understanding inevitably falls prey, namely, that of discussing everything it comes across, in philosophy no less, "*as something on hand*," taking it, in effect, "on the same level as the things it works on [*betreibt*] on a daily basis" (GA29/30, 422ff).

Thanks to its everydayness, this practice is particularly seductive, Heidegger submits, inclining us to generalize it and accounting for the decisive importance of the form of the assertion for (formal) logic:

> The basic feature of everyday being-here is that undifferentiated comportment toward entities as just on hand. The corresponding form of speech in which such comportment expresses itself initially and for the most part ... is this indifferent normal form of the assertion: a is b. Because the λόγος in this form first imposes itself and, indeed, precisely as something also on hand in the everyday, human way of talking with one another and, furthermore, as the form of speech that is predominantly, most on hand, this λόγος determines the theory of the λόγος, logic. (GA29/30, 438; see, too, 22, 414, 423–426, 450–451)

On this account of the genesis of traditional logic as a logic of assertions, its source lies in the everyday, pre-ontological practice of relating to what is on hand, a practice that subsequently underwrites the ontological equation of being with being on hand.[6] The PNC figures into this process by articulating, for traditional logic and the metaphysics bound up with the latter, a necessary constraint on what is on hand, namely, the impossibility of something being and not being on hand (present and absent) in the same respect.

The foregoing array of texts demonstrates Heidegger's view, not only of the narrow, ontological interpretation of the PNC but also of how, with its focus on the "on hand" (*vorhanden*, "present-at-hand"), it has held sway over Western metaphysics (GA65, 469). But it also presents an obvious dilemma since, as noted above (Section 12.2), he holds thinkers (himself included) to the PNC, a practice that appears to align with the narrow ontological interpretation of it. When he undertakes to show that what appears to be a contradiction is merely the result of vagueness or ambiguity, is he not subscribing to that narrow interpretation?

But there are other possibilities. He may be employing an ontologically innocuous interpretation of the PNC, that is, a conception putatively untied to any ontology. Or he may have his sights on a more robust understanding of the PNC, one that aligns with a different sense of "being," even while underscoring and accounting for the narrow sense. On the more robust understanding, making assertions is not wedded, any more than the "as" structure on which it rests is, to taking its components or the relation between them as on hand. So, too, while assertions alone can be contradictory in the strict sense, PNC would not be a law of thinking merely of things on hand.

To be sure, to the extent that Heidegger refrains from explicitly suggesting an alternative interpretation of PNC, his invocation of contradiction often comes across as a dialectical ruse, a concession, on the one hand, to readers and listeners who, he is right to presume, may take the PNC to be of a piece with the ontologically narrow sense but a ladder, on the other hand, that will need to be kicked away, at least in some cases and, indeed, most notably when it comes to thinking, not of beings, but of being.

12.3.2 *Attunements and the Case for a More Expansive Reading of the Principle of Noncontradiction*

Heidegger's discussion of attunements in the 1929/30 lectures appeals to the narrow ontological interpretation of the PNC even as a basic flaw in the analysis points to an interpretation that departs from that traditional

---

[6] Somewhat surprisingly, Heidegger makes no mention of being handy (*Zuhandensein*) in this connection, perhaps because this mode of being is foreign to a logical analysis that presumes the equivalence of being and being on hand (present-at-hand).

interpretation. In those lectures, as already noted, Heidegger declares that speaking of an attunement, as something both here and not here, is an "outright contradiction."[7] He contrasts an attunement's presumably unavoidable contradictoriness with the impossibility of something on hand – his example is a rock – having and not having the same property. A rock is either on hand or not on hand, but an attunement is supposedly at once here and not-here, present and away – and being both at once is essential to the kind of being – being-here – proper to a human being (GA29/30, 95). For the same reason, Heidegger stresses, awakening an attunement cannot mean observing, knowing, or – as noted above – portraying it as though it were something on hand (GA29/30, 91–97). On this reading, there is no contradiction in affirming that in a basic attunement we are both here and not here, since the contradiction only applies to what is on hand. In other words, the contradiction disappears with the removal once again of an ambiguity, that is, the moment it becomes clear that attunements are not on hand or not, like the properties of a rock. Summing up the import of this contrast, Heidegger observes: "But a human being's being-here and being-away is something totally different from being-on-hand and not being-on-hand" (GA29/30, 96).

Yet if it is totally different and the law of contradiction applies exclusively to what is assertably on hand or not, it would seem to follow that the law of contradiction does not apply to being-here. In this case, Heidegger's characterization of basic attunements as contradictory ("an outright contradiction") is itself contradictory, that is, contradicting the restriction of the PNC to what is on hand. Or, if not blatantly contradictory, the characterization is at best the sleight of hand suggested above, designed to distinguish what is on hand and thus subject to the PNC from what is not.

But are our basic attunements contradictory? In order for them to be contradictory in the strict sense of the term, the language used to depict them cannot be vague or ambiguous. The contradiction would be the claim that in a basic attunement we are both here and not here *in the same respect* (and not, as Heidegger contends, simply *at the same time*).[8] Yet there is little reason to think that such is the case, particularly when we consider Heidegger's own paradigm in this respect: profound boredom.

---

[7] This discussion arises because philosophizing cannot be introduced by talking about it but only by engaging in questions that emerge from a basic mood. Hence, the "first and genuine basic task" is, he submits, to awaken such a mood.

[8] It is tempting here to defend Heidegger's claim that moods are contradictory by having recourse to "contradiction" in the broader sense noted in Section 12.1. Yet this defense runs afoul of the fact that Heidegger flags basic moods' contradictoriness in order to eliminate recourse to the narrow ontological interpretation of contradiction.

In a state of profound boredom, everything, including ourselves, fades into irrelevance, counting as much and as little as everything else: "Beings as a whole do not vanish but instead show themselves precisely as such in their indifferentness" (GA29/30, 208). Herein lies the component of boredom that Heidegger dubs "being left empty" (*leergelassen*) by it, as everything and every possibility withdraw. Yet they withdraw precisely from someone, the "Dasein in us" that is held out toward entities as a whole in this vapid condition, and they do so, moreover, by presenting no possibilities for doing anything; they simply lie fallow, unexploited. Herein lies the second component of profound boredom, that of being held out toward those fallow possibilities and thus suspended or kept in limbo (*hingehalten*) with respect to them.

On a certain level of vagueness (one that trades on an ambiguity), it is fair to say that we are both here and not here in a state of profound boredom. Because of the complete withdrawal of any significance on the part of entities as a whole, we are *not here* in any normal ways of being here, engaging in the possibilities that they present us. At the same time, however, there is a sense in which we are *here* in the second structural component, held out to that indifferent totality of beings and held up or held in limbo by it. Talk of "us" here is a bit of a misnomer, since who we are itself becomes insignificant at this point, leading Heidegger to stress the anonymity, "the undifferentiated no one" who is held in limbo (GA29/30, 207). We do not relate to entities as a whole in any ordinary sense of the term both because they withdraw from us as a whole and because who we respectively are in any engagement with them is absent. We are both here and not here in profound boredom.

Yet it seems clear, given Heidegger's painstaking differentiation of the two complementary components of profound boredom, that, while we are not here in one respect, we are here in quite another. We are not here as-we-normally-are because everything has withdrawn from us and we are here as-we-normally-are-not because profound boredom holds us in limbo. Any semblance of contradiction is removed if we attend to the different respects, that is to say, if we eliminate ambiguous characterizations of being here in a state of profound boredom. Thus, the analysis of boredom confirms that basic attunements are only apparently contradictory but not – as Heidegger would presumably have us conclude – by virtue of not being on hand and thus not subject to the PNC. Instead only the vagueness or ambiguity of the relevant descriptions gives them the veneer of contradiction, a veneer that can be stripped away to show that they remain in accord with the PNC. If this critique of Heidegger's reading of the contradictoriness of basic attunements holds, that reading fails to underwrite the notion that the

PNC is necessarily confined to assertions about beings and what is on hand. And that would arguably be a bonus for Heidegger, since it would mean that he is not contradicting himself when he says, with due vagueness, that we are both here and not here in a basic attunement.

12.3.3 An Existential Interpretation of the Principle of Noncontradiction and the Question of Language

Heidegger regularly qualifies his reservations about the narrow ontological interpretation of the PNC and its implications for metaphysics. However, those reservations indicate neither a rejection of the *logos* that traditionally forms the centerpiece of logic (GA36/37, 278) nor any intention of denying logic's merits (GA40, 129). He stresses, as noted above, that his aim is not to establish another logic but to "shake up" logic in a way that is grounded on a transformation of our being-here itself (GA38, 8, 11).[9] While annoyingly allusive, this repeated talk of the need to shake up traditional logical thinking "from the ground up" can hardly be read as signaling its suspension or dissolution (GA29/30, 91; GA38, 8, 11). In his 1934 lectures on logic he briefly notes, to be sure, current debates about the nature and merits of logic as a university discipline and about the legitimacy of the question of its status as a science. But he refuses to take any position on these questions. His aim instead is to "inquire what actually goes on here" in logic, conceived as the rules of thinking, and what ultimately grounds it (its *Grund, Ursprung*; GA38, 11).

Perhaps the most explicit example of this inquiry, as it pertains to the PNC, is found in Heidegger's commentary on Baumgarten's metaphysics. Heidegger draws attention to the fact that this metaphysics starts with a consideration, not of the being of beings, but of their being possible, followed by an account of what is rational, that is, grounded. This starting point gives rise to the question of what underlies possibility: "What is, for the *entire* metaphysics, the *absolute first principle, principium absolute primum*? Answer: the *principium contradictionis*, the fundamental principle of contradiction" (GA36/37, 56). Despite the initial strangeness of this claim, it hits upon, Heidegger adds, "a major piece" of the foundation of Western metaphysics, echoing comments cited earlier about Western metaphysics' logical origins.

After briefly mentioning the kinship of contradictoriness and nothingness (a point to which we return below), Heidegger asks for the ground

---

[9] He also speaks of metaphysics having "a different logic" from "sound" common sense (*gesunder Menschenverstand*) even as he flags a basic attunement's "pre-logical" openness to beings (GA29/30, 293, 498–512).

(*Grund*) of the PNC's dominance over metaphysics and the reason for its indisputability. The ground or reason is somewhat unexpected, he submits, given previous ways of construing and treating the axiom – not least his own! The account of the ground – not to be found anywhere else in Heidegger's corpus to my knowledge – amounts to a ringing defense of the PNC, properly construed:

> The demonstration of the unprovability and indisputability of the law of being that the principle of contradiction expresses leads back to a *completely unexpected ground* – unexpected for the entire previous construal, interpretation, and manner of treatment of the axiom. This ground in which what obtains is grounded is *human beings' being-here [Dasein]* and not human beings in general but *historical* human beings being-here in their being-with-one-another, belonging *to* one another and obligated *to* one another, where there is a specific spirit to their ways of being-with-one-another, that of a people and the language it speaks. (GA36/37, 57)

Language, as Heidegger emphasizes here and elsewhere, is not *essentially* a tool, an object of linguistics, or a means of expression. The essence of language is far more the centerpiece of how a people is historically here (*Dasein des Volkes*), holding sway over and sustaining the world it forms (GA38, 169; see, too, GA29/30: 346, 414, 442f, 468).

At the same time, however, language would not be possible if speakers as such were unable to relate/comport themselves to beings *as such* – which they in turn could not do if they did not understand being in general. "That means, however," Heidegger adds, "understanding what pertains, among other things, to the essence of being." He immediately clarifies this at first obscure remark by stating that he is referring to the sameness of what is understood at all. Were this sameness not preserved, agreement with one another about one and the same thing would not be possible. Nor would anyone be able to relate to entities as self-same – and, to that extent, no one could be the human being he or she is. In short, there is no getting around the need to sustain the sameness of the same (*Unumgänglichkeit der Wahrung der Selbigkeit des Selbigen*) – and this means safeguarding the being of beings (*Bewahrung des Seins des Seienden*); and not being able to get around it is, furthermore, a condition of existing as human beings (GA36/37, 58). Contradiction violates that sameness. The PNC accordingly expresses in a negative form nothing other than the sustainment of that sameness. So understood, it is "no empty proposition of logic," but a fundamental component of being here at all, something "all its own and quite primitively" (*ureigene*; GA36/37, 59).

Yet this talk of need, safeguarding, and possibility – all analogues of the normative character of the PNC – also indicates that the sameness is not simply a given. What is given, Heidegger stresses, is the necessity of a decision to acknowledge it, a decision that is possible in turn only by "passing over into the realm of not-being, the nil, the contrary, and the erroneous" (GA36/37, 59). Only where this realm is conceived as necessary, he adds, is there "greatness, something to be affirmed, the sublime and true" (GA36/37, 59).

The pompous ring of such pronouncements aside, Heidegger is in effect identifying the ground of the PNC in possibilities that present being-here with a decision. There would be no need to safeguard being or sustain the sameness of what is the same (two metonymical expressions for the PNC as "the first law of being"), were there not the possibility of not-being and the necessity of recognizing that possibility, both of which are integral to a decision to be-here.

> Standing behind the obtaining and acknowledgment [*Bestand und Anerkennung*] of the first law of being is the decision whether a human being wants to exist as a human being or not; that is to say, whether she elevates the λόγος to being the dominating *power* of being-here or not; whether she stands for her essential possibility or not! (GA36/37, 59)

Because Heidegger's equation of the PNC in this way with "the first law of being" coincides with its grounding in a decision pertaining to Dasein and the possibilities afforded it, it is not out of place here to tap into the terminology of SZ and designate it an *existential interpretation* of the PNC. Regardless of how it is named, it departs markedly from his usual practice of panning, as noted above (Section 12.3.1), what he takes to be the traditional, narrow ontological interpretation of the PNC. Precisely because he repeatedly ties the PNC to a metaphysics that prioritizes being on hand, the text just cited from the Baumgarten commentary might seem to be an outlier. But there are reasons to think otherwise.

In the first place, in these 1933/34 lectures he explicitly distinguishes this account from previous construals of the PNC and subsequently notes the "distance" between the PNC's "origin" and its subsequent treatment in late Scholasticism. So, too, after describing how, in the systems of Wolff and Baumgarten, it serves as a self-evident point of departure, an axiom beyond question and a ground rule for the derivation of all ontic determinations, he notes the lack of any inquiry "by means of which the basic principle is supposed to be conceived *as such* and grounded in its *essential content*" (GA36/37, 59f). Thus, he clearly entertains a way of understanding the PNC and its ground that escapes the purview of traditional metaphysics or ontology, whether Scholastic or Wolffian, and, with the latter, a certain interpretation of logic and its principles. In lectures on logic, it may be recalled, he states that his aim is not to establish another logic but instead to carry on a decade's work at shaking up that logic (GA38, 8, 11).

That shake-up, moreover, takes the form of locating the question of logic within the broader framework of the question of language as the potentially transformative experience of bespeaking how we find ourselves appropriated by beyng, that is, by a set of disjunctive possibilities that cannot both stand (hence, the PNC) and call for a decision (GA38, 13; see, too, GA29/30, 414). Herein lies a second reason to think that the existential interpretation of the PNC (grounding it in Dasein) is no outlier, namely, its appeal to the interconnectedness of language and comportment to beings. If we listen to the way we talk, we hear the self-sameness of being-here, being handy, and being on hand, disclosed in the respectively attuned understanding of being-here; that is to say, in the different ways that we comport ourselves, for example to others, hammers, and the chemical composition of water. On pain of contradiction, we cannot speak of being-here as though it were the same as being handy or on hand. In this way, the PNC is of a piece with understanding and speaking of what it means for different entities to be and, indeed, to be what they are and not something else. Just as "there is language only for an entity that by its very essence transcends" (GA29/30, 447), that is, moves beyond beings to their respective being, so, too, the PNC transcends beings and applies to the respective being of beings. Not surprisingly, Heidegger even characterizes the PNC at one point as "transcendental," albeit "pointing back to something more originary that does not have the character of a proposition [*Satz*] but belongs far more to the happening of transcendence as such (timeliness)" (GA9, 173).

Of course, this existential (transcendental and timely) understanding of language underlying the PNC is not the understanding of language supposed by traditional logic. Toward the conclusion of his 1934 lectures on logic, Heidegger dubs this inquiry into the essence of language "logic" because language (λόγος) has been the subject of "logic" from its inception and yet "the previous logic precipitously flattens, externalizes, and misconstrues the essence of language" (GA38, 169). So, too, in his *Introduction to Metaphysics*, Heidegger stresses that, in the guise of the assertion, the *logos* itself has become something on hand in order to acquire and guarantee truth as a matter of correctness (GA40, 196). Yet precisely because traditional logic, through its analysis of language, lays claim to the validity of the supreme rules of any determination of being, "its claim must be grasped in a more originary fashion and ruthlessly renewed on the basis of the originary concepts of the essence of language" (GA38, 169). There is no rule of thinking more supreme than the PNC and, as noted above,

Heidegger grounds it in the existential, that is, the discursively transcendental, manner of being proper to being-here.

12.4   Sameness and Nothingness: An Unavoidable Contradiction?

While Heidegger's account of the contradictoriness of profound boredom is flawed, it illustrates that he has no difficulty subjecting talk of different ways of being, not simply being on hand, to the PNC. It is no less a contradiction to assert that a tool is handy and not handy in the same respect as it is to say that I am here and not here in the same respect (e.g., alive and dead). So, too, assertions do not transform what is asserted into something on hand, even when, in accordance with the PNC, they maintain the sameness of something not on hand, that is, a hammer and its handiness, a human being and its being-here. Despite occasional indictments of the PNC's traditional amalgamation to a metaphysics of presence, Heidegger not only lends it this broader reach, but also signals its existential origins. The PNC holds thanks to our transcending character of being-here with one another as interlocutors, capable of talking about the same thing. We are always already discursively relating to things as beings and that means, too, moving beyond (transcending) them not simply to their being but to that self-sameness of their respective being that adherence to the PNC assures.

Yet even if this ontologically – or, more advisedly, this post-ontologically – more copious and arguably more defensible construal of the PNC is granted, it still fails to address the elephant in the room, the overriding concern of Heidegger's deliberations, namely, his attempt to characterize being itself and, indeed, to do so not only by making assertions about it that do not reduce it to an entity, but also by having it encompass what is no more and is yet to come. He paints the elephant in many colors: the nothingness inherent in being; the hiddenness presupposed by truth as unhiddenness; the refusal that is being's supreme gift (GA65, 240–242); the U-turn (*Kehre*) that being takes insofar as it turns toward and away from us at once (GA65, 311, 351); the conflict between the sheer opacity (*reinste Verschlossenheit*) of the earth and the supreme transparency (*höchste Verklärung*) of the world (GA65, 29, 410). To be sure, thinking with Heidegger along any of these disparate yet affiliated lines, we could not be farther from a block universe of things on hand. Each of these tropes attempts to identify being – or, better, 'beyng' (see below) – as something that is happening. Nonetheless, each trope can be read as contradictory (e.g., reading the following genitives as appositives akin to "the city *of* Boston": the nothingness of being, the hiddenness of the unhiddenness, the gift of the refusal, the opacity of the transparent). Given the reading of the

PNC glossed in the previous section, namely, that it is existentially grounded and not restricted to things on hand, the following question has unmistakable recursive (reflexive) bite: Are these tropes, these ways of speaking of being, not patent contradictions? Do they not confirm, albeit indirectly, the conclusion that making assertions about being devolves into logical – even if post-ontological – paradox?

Within the scope of this chapter, it is not possible to pursue these questions across the multiple tropes mentioned, not least because Heidegger's own pronouncements on the subject are less than straightforward. To be sure, despite the strident defense of the PNC that he offers in the Baumgarten lectures, he frequently calls the scope of the PNC into question, and at some junctures even embraces contradiction.[10] Being "does not bother itself" (*kümmert sich nicht*), he notes, with the measly contradictions of our thinking and it is always short-sighted to think of noncontradictoriness as "the measure for the essence of beings" (GA65, 74f; GA66, 156; GA67, 206–207; GA71, 41). The PNC holds for being (or beingness) as "constant presence," not to be confused with the abyss of "beyng" and its nothingness (GA66, 394–396).[11] Although he restricts the PNC in this way to consideration of beings and being (contrary to his practice elsewhere, as noted earlier), it does not keep him from offering that "contra-diction" is precisely *contra* a truth that is "*not sufficiently inceptual*" and, in this sense, contradiction is the "establishment [*Ergründung*] of an inceptual, basic positioning in the truth of beyng" (GA69, 13–15, 157). Basic principles (*Grund-sätze*) like PNC, when we think them through sufficiently, require a "leap" from every ground into the abyss (*Abgrund*). In this same spirit, criticizing the demand for univocity and for steering clear of contradiction, Heidegger rhetorically asks: "Must not the thinking that develops logic stand above logic? Does 'outside logic' mean 'illogical'"? (GA71, 295; GA10, 19–20).

These comments on contradiction seem to provide ample support for reading the tropes mentioned earlier as outright contradictions. Prima facie they provide fuel to the fire, as it were, of a dialetheist interpretation of Heidegger's thinking. Still, there is more to the story, not least given his discussion of "beyng" in the *Contributions* where he takes pains not only to abide by the PNC, but to do so in the course of grounding it.

In that discussion, "beyng" stands for the hidden clearing in which we relate to things, to each other, and to ourselves. More precisely, he

---

[10] While defense of the PNC is part of a lecture, criticisms of its scope occur largely in unpublished writings.

[11] GA71, 296: "One hunts for contradictions and acts as though he were in possession of eternal truth."

understands that clearing as an "appropriation" (*Ereignis*) – after 1936 the "guiding word of his thinking" (GA9, 316n) – that stands for the fact that to be-here is for us to appropriate and to be appropriated by the being of beings. He uses the archaic term "*Seyn*" to flag something that is but is other (and more original) than the being of beings (*Sein des Seienden*), namely, the mutual appropriation that constitutes and underlies beings' presence to us. So construed, one might claim that beyng (qua appropriation) both is and is not the case; insofar as it grounds the being (that is, the presence) of beings, it pre-eminently *is*, while not being similarly present itself (after all, it remains hidden).[12] But then the claim that appears contradictory ("beyng both is and is not the case") trades on an equivocation (equivocating between "is the case" designating it as ground and "is the case" designating it as being present, that is, the presence of an entity/a being). In short, on this reading, Heidegger is not indulging in contradiction.

Yet he appears to incur contradiction on another level in the course of elaborating how there is a history to beyng, so conceived, namely, inasmuch as it confronts us with an "either/or": either experiencing and heeding it as that hidden clearing or not. Leaving beyng in hiddenness is, as he puts it, "fundamentally different" from experiencing it as hidden (GA65, 255). Beyng's historical character means that it is something unfinished, that is, that its "either/or" is yet to be decided.[13] Particularly with regard to "the transition from modernity to something other than it," Heidegger reviews a number of decisions entailed by this "either/or," such as "whether human beings venture beyng and thus going under *or* content themselves with beings" (GA65, 91–92, 101). But the essence of the decision comes down to a decision whether beyng completely withdraws from view or its withdrawal is the primary truth, marking another inception of history. Notably, that inception coincides with countenancing that beyng "needs the *not* to obtain and, with it, the opposite [*das Gegen*], everything

---

[12] In this vein Heidegger repeatedly notes that "beyng is," indeed, "only beyng is," while "beings are not" (GA65, 472f; GA66, 89–92, 112, 202; GA69, 142, 144; GA71, 31, 172f); and in these contexts he identifies *beyng* with *appropriation* (GA65, 470; GA66, 100, 343; GA69, 106, 134; GA71, 121). So, too, far from being contradictory, talk of beyng as nothing (e.g., GA66, 59; GA69, 168; GA71, 124) trades on its difference from beings and their being as well as on the no more and not yet (that is also neither a being nor being).

[13] The emphasis on a decision and possibilities presented by beyng is consistent with the general view espoused in SZ: "*Höher als die Wirklichkeit steht die* Möglichkeit" (SZ 38). Just as the thrown projection that constitutes Dasein as the clearing (depicted in SZ) is a dynamic – δύναμις-like – field of possibilities, both determinate and indeterminate, marking the movement (κίνησις) where we are coming from and where we are going, so, too, the hidden clearing (the grounding appropriation depicted in the 1930s works) is to be understood in terms of mutually exclusive, history-defining possibilities.

that is not the case"; so, too, he suggests that the "nothing" – "equal in rank" (*gleichrangig*) and inherent (*zugehörig*) to beyng – provides human beings with an inkling of it (GA65, 91, 101–102, 245).

This talk of the necessity of the "not" and the "opposite" raises once again the specter of contradiction but, if so, it cannot be in terms of the traditional ontological interpretation of the PNC. Indeed, Heidegger goes out of his way to underscore the absence of the conditions for contradiction in that sense. "Being" in this connection, he stresses, does not mean "being-on-hand," and "not-being" (the other disjunct, that which corresponds to the "not" and the "opposite") is not something "completely disappearing" (*völliges Verschwinden*). Instead, each disjunct encompasses its viable opposite, in what may well be "the road not taken." He accordingly describes the disjunct "not-being" as "being and yet not" and likewise the other disjunct "being" as "permeated by the not and yet nonetheless being."[14]

Negation in this connection is clearly not equivalent to the truth functional operator by the same name and so, too, the PNC, insofar as it applies to beings on hand (the ontological interpretation), cannot be in play in this account (GA65, 410). Yet we have seen that Heidegger understands the PNC in a more expansive (post-ontological) sense. So the question remains: Does talk of "being and yet not" and the like to characterize each disjunctive possibility (entailed by beyng) violate the PNC in that more expansive sense?

While the general issue remains fraught, it is worth noting that Heidegger, in the passage highlighted, is describing possibilities and, while there is a sense in which possibilities both are and are not, we can say so without incurring contradiction. A seed's potential, for example, is a possibility that both is in one respect and is not in another respect. In a similar way, each of the disjuncts historically presented by beyng (indeed, equivalent to it) can be said to be and yet not to be, but not in the same respect. So once again no contradiction is at hand, at least not without further ado. The negation at play in each case, moreover, is twofold, contrasting the possibility with its alternative and with what is (fully) realized. In this sense (shades of Spinoza), the negation determines a respectively requisite possibility, reinforcing the dynamic meaning of the abyssal and nongeneric character of beyng noted earlier. Indeed, "the *most hidden* essence of the *not*" is, Heidegger observes, "the not yet and no longer" (*Noch-nicht und Nicht-mehr*; GA65, 410).

---

[14] GA65, 101: "… *Nichtsein meint hier nicht: völliges Verschwinden, sondern Nichtsein als eine Art des Seins: Seiend und doch nicht; und ebenso Sein: nichthaft und doch gerade Seiend.*"

Heidegger observes that logic and metaphysics generally fail to articulate the ground of the yes and no (the affirmability *and* deniability) that they presuppose (GA65, 247). Their opposition lies, he submits, in the prevailing of beyng (*Wesung des Seyns*) and its ground is the hidden appropriation (*Er-eignung*) that assigns us to beyng (and presumably the decision it entails). He adds that this amounts to "the 'not' and the 'no' being even more original in beyng," a remark consistent with the preceding gloss and with his view that the truth of beyng, understood as unhiddenness, presupposes hiddenness (GA65, 247, 255, 332). By noting how beyng essentially contains mutually disjunctive possibilities that confront us with an original either/or, Heidegger is in effect explaining what is presupposed by the law of the excluded middle and its counterpart, the PNC. He is doing what he claims logic and metaphysics fail to do. As the hidden clearing, beyng – along with the possibilities that it entails – can be said to be and not to be (to be present and absent) but not, to be sure, in the same respect. That is to say, it *is* as the clearing but it remains hidden from us, as we attend to beings and their being, and thus we cannot attribute to it the being, that is, the presence, of a being/an entity. At the same time, both of the possibilities entailed by it obtain by countenancing their negation, but they cannot both stand, and therein lies the grounding of the PNC.

This reading is speculative, to be sure. Heidegger is often more adept at gesturing and insinuating than asserting (a practice that he often defends as necessary). Nonetheless, this reading has textual support and if something akin to it is sustainable, his understanding of beyng as the hidden clearing (appropriation) does not violate the PNC and, furthermore, grounds it in a noncontradictory manner by identifying the fundamental, disjunctive possibilities that it entails/supposes.

To be sure, if the line of interpretation offered here holds, rescuing Heidegger's analysis from a dialetheist challenge on certain levels, the issue of his contradictions is hardly resolved. The issue persists not least because once again his practice of avoiding contradiction in his analysis of beyng (along with his defense of contradiction in the Baumgarten lecture) runs counter to his dismissal of the PNC and embrace of contradiction in several passages cited above. Seeing no way to reconcile those passages with Heidegger's noncontradictory analysis of beyng and its possibilities, I can only conclude that in this respect at least Heidegger contradicts himself – even if, sharing Emerson's disdain for hobgoblins, he wouldn't have it any other way.

References

Selected Works by Heidegger

GA Heidegger, Martin. *Gesamtausgabe.* 102 vols. Edited by Friedrich-Wilhelm von Hermann, Peter Trawny et al. Frankfurt: Klostermann, 1975– (as of 2022, only volumes 72, 92, and 93 have not been published).

SZ Heidegger, Martin. *Sein und Zeit.* Tübingen: Niemeyer, 1957.

SZ *Sein und Zeit.* Translated as *Being and Time.* Translated by John Macquarrie and Edward Robinson. New York: Harper & Row, 1962.

GA1 *Frühe Schriften.*

GA2 *Sein und Zeit.* For translation, see SZ above.

GA3 *Kant und das Problem der Metaphysik.* Translated as *Kant and the Problem of Metaphysics.* Translated by Richard Taft. Bloomington: Indiana University Press, 1997.

GA5 *Holzwege.* Translated as *Off the Beaten Track.* Translated and edited by Julian Young and Kenneth Haynes. Cambridge, UK: Cambridge University Press, 2002.

GA7 *Vorträge und Aufsätze.*

GA8 *Was heisst Denken?* Translated as What Is Called "Thinking"? Translated by Fred D. Wieck and J. Glenn Gray. New York: Harper & Row, 1976.

GA9 *Wegmarken.* Translated as *Pathmarks.* Edited by William McNeil. Cambridge, UK: Cambridge University Press, 1998.

GA10 *Der Satz vom Grund.* Translated as *The Principle of Reason.* Translated by Reginald Lilly. Bloomington: Indiana University Press, 1991.

GA11 *Identität und Differenz.* Edited by Friedrich-Wilhelm von Herrmann. Frankfurt: Klostermann, 2006.

GA12 *Unterwegs zur Sprache.* Translated as *On the Way to Language.* Translated by Peter D. Hertz. San Francisco: HarperCollins, 1982.

GA13 *Aus der Erfahrung des Denkens.*

GA14 *Zur Sache des Denkens.* Translated as *On Time and Being.* Translated by Joan Stambaugh. New York: Harper Torchbooks, 1972.

GA15 *Seminare.* Translated as *Seminars.* Translated by Andrew J. Mitchell and François Raffoul. Bloomington: Indiana University Press, 2003.

GA16 *Reden und andere Zeugnisse eines Lebensweges.*

GA17 *Einführung in die phänomenologische Forschung.* Translated as *Introduction to Phenomenological Research.* Translated by Daniel O. Dahlstrom. Bloomington: Indiana University Press, 2005.

GA18 *Grundbegriffe der aristotelischen Philosophie.* Translated as *Basic Concepts of Aristotelian Philosophy.* Translated by Robert D. Metcalf and Mark B. Tanzer. Bloomington: Indiana University Press, 2009.

GA19 *Platon: Sophistes.* Translated as *Plato's Sophist.* Translated by Richard Rojcewicz and André Schuwer. Bloomington: Indiana University Press, 1997.

GA20 *Prolegomena zur Geschichte des Zeitbegriffs.* Translated as *History of the Concept of Time.* Translated by Theodore Kisiel. Bloomington: Indiana University Press, 1992.

GA21 *Logik: Die Frage nach der Wahrheit.* Translated as *Logic: The Question of Truth.* Translated by Thomas Sheehan. Bloomington: Indiana University Press, 2016.

GA22 *Grundbegriffe der antiken Philosophie.* Translated as *Basic Concepts of Ancient Philosophy.* Translated by Richard Rojcewicz. Bloomington: Indiana University Press, 2008.

GA23 *Geschichte der Philosophie von Thomas v. Aquin bis Kant.*

GA24 *Die Grundprobleme der Phänomenologie.* Translated as *Basic Problems of Phenomenology.* Translated by Albert Hofstadter. Bloomington: Indiana University Press, 1982.

GA25 *Phänomenologische Interpretation von Kants Kritik der reinen Vernunft.* Translated as *Phenomenological Interpretation of Kant's Critique of Pure Reason.* Translated by Parvis Emad and Kenneth Maly. Bloomington: Indiana University Press, 1997.

GA26 *Metaphysische Anfangsgründe der Logik im Ausgang von Leibniz.* Translated as *The Metaphysical Foundations of Logic.* Translated by Michael Heim. Bloomington: Indiana University Press, 1984.

GA27 *Einleitung in die Philosophie.*

GA28 *Der Deutsche Idealismus (Fichte, Hegel, Schelling) und die philosophische Problemlage der Gegenwart.*

GA29/30 *Die Grundbegriffe der Metaphysik: Welt, Endlichkeit, Einsamkeit.* Translated as *The Fundamental Concepts of Metaphysics: World, Finitude, Solitude.* Translated by William McNeill and N. Walker. Bloomington: Indiana University Press, 1995.

GA31 *Vom Wesen der menschlichen Freiheit. Einleitung in die Philosophie.* Translated as *The Essence of Human Freedom.* Translated by Ted Sadler. London: Continuum, 2002.

GA32 *Hegels Phänomenologie des Geistes.* Translated as *Hegel's Phenomenology of Spirit.* Translated by Parvis Emad and Kenneth Maly. Bloomington: Indiana University Press, 1988.

GA33 *Aristoteles: Metaphysik IX.* Translated as *Aristotle's* Metaphysics *Theta 1–3: On the Essence and Actuality of Force.* Translated by Walter Brogan and Peter Warnek. Bloomington: Indiana University Press, 1995.

GA34 *Vom Wesen der Wahrheit. Zu Platons Höhlengleichnis und Theätet.* Translated as *The Essence of Truth: On Plato's Cave Allegory and Theaetetus.* Translated by Ted Sadler. New York: Continuum, 2002.

GA36/37 *Sein und Wahrheit*. Translated as *Being and Truth*. Translated by Gregory Fried and Richard Polt. Bloomington: Indiana University Press, 2010.

GA38 *Logik als die Frage nach dem Wesen der Sprache*. Translated as *Logic as the Question Concerning the Essence of Language*. Translated by Wanda Torres Gregory and Yvonne Unna. Albany: State University of New York Press, 2009.

GA39 *Hölderlins Hymnen "Germanien" und "Der Rhein."* Translated as *Hölderlin's Hymns "Germania" and "The Rhine."* Translated by William McNeill and Julia Ireland. Bloomington: Indiana University Press, 2014.

GA40 *Einführung in die Metaphysik*. Translated as *Introduction to Metaphysics*. Translated by Gregory Fried and Richard Polt. New Haven: Yale University Press, 2014.

GA41 *Die Frage nach dem Ding*. Translated as *The Question Concerning the Thing*. Translated by Benjamin Crowe and James Reid. London: Rowman & Littlefield, 2018.

GA45 *Grundfragen der Philosophie. Ausgewählte "Probleme" der "Logik."* Translated as *The Basic Questions of Philosophy: Selected "Problems" of "Logic."* Translated by Richard Rojcewicz and André Schuwer. Bloomington: Indiana University Press, 1994.

GA46 *Zur Auslegung von Nietzsches II. Unzeitgemässe Betrachtung*. Translated as *Interpretation of Nietzsche's Second Untimely Meditation*. Translated by Ullrich Haase and Mark Sinclair. Bloomington: Indiana University Press, 2016.

GA52 *Hölderlins Hymne "Andenken."* Translated as Hölderlin's Hymn "Remembrance." Translated by William McNeill and Julia Ireland. Bloomington: Indiana University Press, 2018.

GA54 *Parmenides*. Translated as *Parmenides*. Translated by Richard Rojcewicz and André Schuwer. Bloomington: Indiana University Press, 1992.

GA55 *Heraklit Der Anfang des abendländischen Denkens (Heraklit) 2. Logik. Heraklits Lehre vom Logos*. Translated as *Heraclitus: The Inception of Occidental Thinking and Logic: Heraclitus' Doctrine of the Logos*. Translated by Julia Goesser Assaiante and Montgomery Ewegen. London: Bloomsbury, 2018.

GA56/57 *Zur Bestimmung der Philosophie*. Translated as *Towards the Definition of Philosophy*. Translated by Ted Sadler. London: Continuum, 2002.

GA58 *Grundprobleme der Phänomenologie*. Translated as *The Basic Problems of Phenomenology*. Translated by Scott M. Campbell. London: Bloomsbury, 2013.

GA59 *Phänomenologie der Anschauung und des Ausdrucks. Theorie der philosophischen Begriffsbildung*. Translated as *Phenomenology of Intuition and Expression*. Translated by Tracy Colony. London: Continuum, 2010.

GA60 *Phänomenologie des religiösen Lebens*. Translated as *Phenomenology of Religious Life*. Translated by Matthias Fritsch and Jennifer Anna Gosetti-Ferencei. Bloomington: Indiana University Press, 2004.

GA61 *Phänomenologische Interpretationen zu Aristoteles: Einführung in die phänomenologische Forschung*. Translated as *Phenomenological Interpretations of Aristotle*. Translated by Richard Rojcewicz. Bloomington: Indiana University Press, 2001.

GA62 *Phänomenologische Interpretationen ausgewählter Abhandlungen des Aristoteles zur Ontologie und Logik*.

GA63 *Ontologie: Hermeneutik der Faktizität.* Translated as *Ontology: The Hermeneutics of Facticity.* Translated by John van Buren. Bloomington: Indiana University Press, 1999.

GA65 *Beiträge zur Philosophie (Vom Ereignis).* Translated as *Contributions to Philosophy (of the Event).* Translated by Richard Rojcewicz and Daniela Vallega-Neu. Bloomington: Indiana University Press, 2012.

GA66 *Besinnung.* Translated as *Mindfulness.* Translated by Parvis Emad and Thomas Kalary. London: Athlone, 2016.

GA67 *Metaphysik und Nihilismus.*

GA68 *Hegel.* Translated as *Hegel.* Translated by Joseph Arel and Niels Feuerhahn. Bloomington: Indiana University Press, 2015.

GA69 *Geschichte des Seyns.* Translated as The History of Beyng. Translated by William McNeill and Jeffrey Powell. Bloomington: Indiana University Press, 2015.

GA71 *Das Ereignis* Translated as *The Event.* Translated by Richard Rojcewicz. Bloomington: Indiana University Press, 2013.

GA73 *Zum Ereignis-Denken.*

GA76 *Leitgedanken zur Entstehung der Metaphysik, der neuzeitlichen Wissenschaft und der modernen Technik.*

GA79 *Bremer und Freiburger Vorträge.* Translated as *Bremen and Freiburg Lectures: Insight Into That Which Is and Basic Principle of Thinking.* Translated by Andrew J. Mitchell. Bloomington: Indiana University Press, 2012.

GA86 *Seminare: Hegel – Schelling.*

GA87 *Seminare: Nietzsche: Seminare 1937 und 1944.*

GA94 *Überlegungen II–VI (Schwarze Hefte 1931–1938).* Translated as *Ponderings II–VI.* Translated by Richard Rojcewicz. Bloomington: Indiana University Press, 2014.

GA95 *Überlegungen VII–XI (Schwarze Hefte 1938–1939).* Translated as *Ponderings VII–XI.* Translated by Richard Rojcewicz. Bloomington: Indiana University Press, 2017.

GA100 *Vigiliae I, II/Notturno, (1952/53 bis 1957).*

Heidegger, Martin. 1963. "Letter to William J. Richardson, April 1962." Translated by William J. Richardson. In William J. Richardson, *Through Phenomenology to Thought.* The Hague: Martinus Nijhoff. Pages viii–xxiii.

Heidegger, Martin. 1966. *Discourse on Thinking.* Translated by John Anderson and Hans Freund. New York: Harper & Row.

Heidegger, Martin. 1976. "The Theological Discussion of 'The Problem of a Non-Objectifying Thinking and Speaking in Today's Theology' – Some Pointers to Its Major Aspects." In *The Piety of Thinking.* Translated by J. G. Hart and J. C. Maraldo. Bloomington: Indiana University Press. Pages 22–31

Heidegger, Martin. 2002. *Supplements: From the Earliest Essays to* Being and Time *and Beyond.* Edited by John van Buren. Albany: State University of New York Press.

Heidegger, Martin. 2008. *Basic Writings.* Edited by David Krell. London: Harper Perennial.

Heidegger, Martin. 2010. "Wilhelm Dilthey's Research and the Current Struggle for a Historical Worldview." In *Becoming Heidegger: On the Trail of His Early Occasional Writings, 1910–1927.* Edited by Theodore Kisiel and Thomas Sheehan. 2nd ed. Seattle: Noesis Press. Pages 238–274.

Heidegger, Martin. 2013. *Nature, History, State: 1933–1934.* Translated and edited by Gregory Fried and Richard Polt. London: Bloomsbury.

Works by Other Authors

Arendt, Hannah. 1978. *The Life of the Mind.* New York: Harcourt.

Aristotle. 1984. *The Complete Works of Aristotle: Revised Oxford Translation.* 2 vols. Edited by Jonathan Barnes. Princeton: Princeton University Press.

Augustine. 1998. *The City of God against the Pagans.* Translated and edited by R. W.Dyson. Cambridge, UK: Cambridge University Press.

Bahoh, James. 2020. *Heidegger's Ontology of Events.* Edinburgh: Edinburgh University Press.

Barnes, Elizabeth. 2018. "Symmetric Dependence." In *Reality and Its Structure.* Edited by Ricki Leigh Bliss and Graham Priest. Oxford: Oxford University Press. Pages 50–70.

Bartky, Sandra L. 2010. "Heidegger's Philosophy of Art." In *Heidegger the Man and the Thinker.* Edited by Thomas Sheehan. New Brunswick, NJ: Transaction Publishers. Pages 257–275.

Blattner, William. 1995. "Decontextualization, Standardization and Deweyan Science." *Man and World,* 28(4): 321–339.

Blattner, William. 1999. *Heidegger's Temporal Idealism.* Cambridge, UK: Cambridge University Press.

Blattner, William. 2007. "Ontology, the A Priori and the Primacy of Practice." In *Transcendental Heidegger.* Edited by Steven Crowell and Jeff Malpas. Stanford: Stanford University Press.

Bliss, Ricki. 2013. "Viciousness and the Structure of Reality." *Philosophical Studies,* 166 (2): 399–418.

Bliss, Ricki. 2014. "Viciousness and Circles of Ground." *Metaphilosophy,* 45 (2): 245–256.

Bliss, Ricki, and Graham Priest. 2017. "Metaphysical Dependence, East and West." In *Buddhist Philosophy: A Comparative Approach.* Edited by S. M. Emmanuel. Oxford: John Wiley & Sons. Pages 63–87.

Bliss, Ricki, and Kelly Trogdon. 2016. "Metaphysical Grounding." In *The Stanford Encyclopedia of Philosophy.* Edited by Edward N. Zalta. https://plato.stanford .edu/entries/grounding/

Bolzano, Bernard. 2014. *Theory of Science.* 4 vols. Translated by Paul Rusnock and Rolf George. Oxford: Oxford University Press.

Brandom, Robert. 1992. "Heidegger's Categories in *Being and Time.*" In *Heidegger: A Critical Reader.* Edited by Hubert L. Dreyfus and Harrison Hall. London: Blackwell. Pages 45–64.

Brandom, Robert. 1994. *Making It Explicit: Reasoning, Representation, and Discursive Commitment.* Cambridge, MA: Harvard University Press.

Braver, Lee. 2014. *Heidegger: Thinking of Being.* Cambridge, UK: Polity.

Brentano, Franz. 1960. *Von der mannigfachen Bedeutung des Seienden nach Aristotles.* Hildesheim: Olms.

Brentano, Franz. 1966. *The True and the Evident.* New York: Routledge.

Brentano, Franz. 1995. *Psychology from an Empirical Standpoint*. 2nd ed. New York: Routledge.

Bronzo, Silver. 2015. "Words, Sentences, and Speech Acts: An Interpretation and Defense of the Context Principle." Doctoral dissertation, University of Chicago.

Bryant, Amanda. 2017. "Resolving Quine's Conflict: A Neo-Quinean View of the Rational Revisability of Logic." *Australasian Journal of Logic*, 14 (1): 30–45.

Camp, Elisabeth. 2004. "The Generality Constraint and Categorial Restrictions." *Philosophical Quarterly*, 54 (214): 209–231.

Caputo, John. 1975. "The Principle of Sufficient Reason: A Study of Heideggerian Self-Criticism." *Southern Journal of Philosophy*, 13 (4): 419–426.

Caputo, John. 1986. The Mystical Element in Heidegger's Thought. New York: Fordham University Press.

Caputo, John. 1990. *The Mystical Element in Heidegger's Thought*. New York: Fordham University Press.

Carman, Taylor. 2003. *Heidegger's Analytic*. Cambridge, UK: Cambridge University Press.

Carman, Taylor. 2008. *Merleau-Ponty*. New York: Routledge.

Carman, Taylor. 2013. "The Question of Being." In *The Cambridge Companion to Heidegger's Being and Time*. Edited by Mark Warthall. Cambridge, UK: Cambridge University Press. Pages 84–100.

Carnap, Rudolf. 1959. "Overcoming of Metaphysics through Logical Analysis of Language." In *Logical Positivism*. Edited by A. J. Ayer. Glencoe, IL: Free Press. Translation of "Überwindung der Metaphysik durch logische Analyse der Sprache." *Erkenntnis*, 2 (1932): 219–224.

Carta, Emanuela. 2021. "Husserl on Eidetic Norms." *Husserl Studies*, 37(2): 127–146.

Casati, Filippo. 2018. "Heidegger's *Grund*: (Para-)Foundationalism." In *Reality and its Structure*. Edited by Ricki Leigh Bliss and Graham Priest. Oxford: Oxford University Press. Pages 291–313.

Casati, Filippo. 2019. "Heidegger and the Contradiction of Being: A Dialetheic Interpretation of the Late Heidegger." *British Journal for the History of Philosophy*, 27 (5): 1002–1024.

Casati, Filippo. 2020. "The Recent Engagement between Analytic Philosophy and Heideggerian Thought: Logic and Language." *Philosophy Compass*, 15 (2): 1–14.

Casati, Filippo, and Graham Priest. 2018. "Heidegger and Dogen on the Ineffable." In *The Significance of Indeterminacy: Perspectives from Asian and Continental Philosophy*. Edited by Robert H. Scott and Gregory S. Moss. New York: Routledge. Pages 279–309.

Casati, Filippo, and Michael Wheeler. 2016. "The Recent Engagement between Analytic Philosophy and Heideggerian Thought: Metaphysics and Mind." *Philosophy Compass*, 11 (9): 486–498.

Cavell, Stanley. 1976. "The Availability of Wittgenstein's Later Philosophy." In *Must We Mean What We Say?* New York: Cambridge University Press. Pages 44–72.

Cavell, Stanley. 1979. *The Claim of Reason: Wittgenstein, Skepticism, Morality, and Tragedy*. New York: Oxford University Press.

Cerbone, David. 2000. "How to Do Things with Wood." In *The New Wittgenstein*. Edited by Alice Crary and Rupert Read. London: Routledge. Pages 293–314.

Conant, James. 2000. "Elucidation and Nonsense in Frege and Wittgenstein." In *The New Wittgenstein*. Edited by Alice Crary and Rupert Read. London: Routledge. Pages 179–218.

Conant, James. 2002. "The Method of the *Tractatus*." In *From Frege to Wittgenstein. Perspectives on Early Analytic Philosophy*. Edited by Eric Reck. Oxford: Oxford University Press. Pages 374–463.

Crowell, Steven. 2001. *Husserl, Heidegger, and the Space of Meaning: Paths toward Transcendental Phenomenology*. Evanston: Northwestern University Press.

Crowell, Steven. 2013. *Normativity and Phenomenology in Husserl and Heidegger*. Cambridge, UK: Cambridge University Press.

Crowell, Steven. 2017. "Competence over Being as Existing: The Indispensability of Haugeland's Heidegger." In *Giving a Damn: Essays in Dialogue with John Haugeland*. Edited by Zed Adams and Jacob Browning. Cambridge, MA: MIT Press. Pages 73–103.

Cussins, Adrian. 2003. "Content, Conceptual Content, and Nonconceptual Content." In *Essays on Nonconceptual Content*. Edited by York H. Gunther. Cambridge, MA: MIT Press. Pages 133–165.

Dahlstrom, Daniel. 1994a. "Heidegger's Method: Philosophical Concepts and Formal Indications." *Review of Metaphysics*, 47 (4): 775–795.

Dahlstrom, Daniel. 1994b. "Heidegger's Critique of Husserl." In *The Early Heidegger: New Texts, New Perspectives*. Edited by Ted Kisiel and John van Buren. Albany: State University of New York Press. Pages 231–244.

Dahlstrom, Daniel. 2001. *Heidegger's Concept of Truth*. Cambridge, UK: Cambridge University Press.

Dahlstrom, Daniel. 2005. "Heidegger's Transcendentalism." *Research in Phenomenology*, 35: 29–54.

Dahlstrom, Daniel. 2010. "Hermeneutic Ontology." In *Theory and Applications of Ontology: Philosophical Perspectives*. Edited by Roberto Poli and Johanna Seibt. Dordrecht: Springer. Pages 395–415.

Dahlstrom, Daniel. 2011. "Being and Being Grounded." In *The Ultimate Why Question: Why Is There Anything at All Rather Than Nothing Whatsoever?* Edited by John F Wippel. Washington, DC: Catholic University of America Press. Pages 125–145.

Dastur, François. 1987. "Logic and Ontology: Heidegger's 'Destruction' of Logic." *Research in Phenomenology*, 17: 55–74.

Dastur, François. 2003. "Heidegger et les 'Recherches logiques.'" In *Husserl: La représentation vide, suivi de "Les Recherches logiques, une œuvre de percée."* Edited by Jocelyn Benoist and Jean-François Courtine. Paris: Presses Universitaires de France. Pages 265–281.

Dastur, François. 2007. *Heidegger: La Question du Logos*. Paris: Vrin.

Davidson, Donald. 1984. "What Metaphors Mean." In *Inquiries into Truth and Interpretation*. Oxford: Oxford University Press. Pages 245–264.

Davis, Brett. 2007. *Heidegger and the Will: On the Way to Gelassenheit*. Evanston: Northwestern University Press.

Deleuze, Gilles, and Félix Guattari. 1986. *Nomadology: The War Machine*. New York: Semiotext(e).

Denker, Alfred, Hans-Helmuth Gander, and Holger Zaborowski (eds.). 2004. *Heidegger-Jahrbuch* I: *Heidegger und die Anfänge seines Denkens*. Freiburg/ Munich: Alber.

Derrida, Jacques. 1992. "'Il faut bien manger' ou le calcul du sujet." In *Points de Suspension: Entretiens*. Edited by Elisabeth Weber. Paris: Galilée. Pages 269–303.

Diamond, Cora. 1991. *The Realistic Spirit: Wittgenstein, Philosophy, and the Mind*. Cambridge, MA: MIT Press.

Donnelly, Maureen. 2011. "Using Mereological Principles to Support Metaphysics." *Philosophical Quarterly*, 61 (243): 225–246.

Dreyfus, Hubert. 1991. *Being-in-the-World*. Cambridge, MA: MIT Press.

Dreyfus, Hubert. 2005a. "Heidegger's Ontology of Art." In *A Companion to Heidegger*. Edited by Hubert Dreyfus and Mark Wrathall. Malden, MA: Blackwell. Pages 407–420.

Dreyfus, Hubert. 2005b. "Overcoming the Myth of the Mental." *Proceedings and Addresses of the American Philosophical Association*, 79: 47–65.

Dummett, Michael. 1994. *The Origins of Analytic Philiosophy*. Cambridge, MA: Harvard University Press.

Duns Scotus 1997. *Opera Philosophica*. Volume III: *Quaestiones super Libros Metaphysicorum Aristotelis, Libri I–V*. Edited by R. Andrews, G. Etzkorn, T. Noone et al. St. Bonaventure, NY: Franciscan Institute.

Dutilh Novaes, C. 2015. "A Dialogical, Multi-Agent Account of the Normativity of Logic." *Dialectica*, 69 (4): 587–609.

Edwards, Douglas. 2018. *The Metaphysics of Truth*. Oxford: Oxford University Press.

Fay, Thomas. 1974. "Heidegger on Logic: a Genetic Study of His Thought on Logic." *Journal of the History of Philosophy*, 12 (1): 77–94.

Feyerabend, Paul. 1991. *Three Dialogues on Knowledge*. Oxford: Blackwell.

Fine, Kit. 1994. "Essence and Modality." *Philosophical Perspectives*, 8: 1–16.

Fine, Kit. 1995. "Ontological Dependence." *Proceedings of the Aristotelian Society*, 95: 269–290.

Fine, Kit. 2012. "Guide to Ground." *Metaphysical Grounding: Understanding the Structure of Reality*. Edited by Fabrice Correia and Benjamin Schnieder. Cambridge, UK: Cambridge University Press. Pages 37–81.

Frege, Gottlob. 1979. *The Posthumous Writings*. Oxford: Blackwell.

Frege, Gottlob. 1980. *Foundations of Arithmetic*. Translated by J. L. Austin. Evanston: Northwestern University Press.

Frege, Gottlob. 1997. "On Concept and Object." Translated by Peter Geach. In *The Frege Reader*. Edited by Michael Beaney. Oxford: Blackwell. Pages 181–194.

Friedman, Michael. 2001. *A Parting a Way: Carmap, Cassirer, Heidegger*. Chicago: Open Court.

Gadamer, Hans-Georg. 1994. *Heidegger's Ways*. Albany: State University of New York Press.

Gadamer, Hans-Georg. 2006. *Truth and Method*. London: Continuum.

Glock, Hans-Johann. 2015. "Nonsense Made Intelligible." *Erkenntnis*, 80 (1): 111–136.

Goldfarb, Warren. 1997. "Metaphysics and Nonsense: On Cora Diamond's *The Realistic Spirit*." *Journal of Philosophical Research*, 22: 57–73.

Goldfarb, Warren. 2011. "*Das Überwinden*: Anti-Metaphysical Readings of the *Tractatus*." In *Beyond the Tractatus Wars*. Edited by Rupert Read and Matthew A. Lavery. New York: Routledge. Pages 6–22.

Golob, Sacha. 2013. "Heidegger on Assertion, Method, and Metaphysics." *European Journal of Philosophy*, 23 (4): 878–908.

Golob, Sacha. 2014. *Heidegger on Concepts, Freedom and Normativity*. Cambridge, UK: Cambridge University Press.

Grimm, Jacob, and Grimm, Wilhelm. 2021. *Deutsches Wörterbuch von Jacob Grimm und Wilhelm Grimm*. Digitalized version by Trier Center for Digital Humanities, Version 01/21. www.woerterbuchnetz.de/DWB

Gurwitsch, Aron. 1929. *Phänomenologie der Thematik und des reinen Ich. Studien über Beziehungen zwischen Gestalttheorie und Phänomenologie. In Psychologische Forschung*. Volume 12. Pages 279–381. Translated as "Phenomenology of Thematics and of the Pure Ego: Studies of the Relation between Gestalt Theory and Phenomenology." In *Studies in Phenomenology and Psychology*. Translated by Richard M. Zaner. Evanston: Northwestern University Press, 1966. Pages 175–287.

Gurwitsch, Aron. 1931. *Die mitmenschlichen Begegnungen in der Milieuwelt*. Edited by Alexandre Métraux. New York: De Gruyter.

Habermas, Jürgen. 1990. "Discourse Ethics: Notes on a Program of Philosophical Justification." In *Moral Consciousness and Communicative Action*. Translated by Christian Lenhardt and Shierry Weber Nicholson. Cambridge, MA: MIT Press. Pages 43–116.

Hacker, P. M. S. 2000. "Was He Trying to Whistle It?" In *The New Wittgenstein*. Edited by Alice Crary and Rupert Read. London: Routledge. Pages 352–389.

Harman, Gilbert. 1984. "Logic and Reasoning." *Synthese*, 60 (1): 107–127.

Hartmann, Klaus. 1974. "The Logic of Deficient and Eminent Modes in Heidegger." *Journal of the British Society for Phenomenology*, 5 (2): 118–134.

Hartmann, Klaus. 1981. "No Logic of Modes in Heidegger?" *Journal of the British Society for Phenomenology*, 12 (1): 74–75.

Hatab, Lawrence. 2016. "The Point of Language in Heidegger's Thinking: A Call for the Revival of Formal Indication." *Gatherings: The Heidegger Circle Annual*, 6: 1–22.

Haugeland, John. 1998. "Truth and Rule-Following." In *Having Thought: Essays in the Metaphysics of Mind*. Cambridge, MA: Harvard University Press. Pages 305–363.

Haugeland, John. 2013. *Dasein Disclosed*. Edited by Joseph Rouse. Cambridge, MA: Harvard University Press.

Holton, Richard. 2010. "The Exception Proves the Rule." *Journal of Political Philosophy*, 18 (4), 369–388.

Husserl, Edmund. 1913. *Ideen zu einer reinen Phänomenologie und phänom-enologischen Philosophie*. In *Jahrbuch für Philosophie und phänomenologische Forschung*, Halle: Max Niemeyer.

Husserl, Edmund. 1970. *Logical Investigations*. 2 Vols. Translated by J. N. Findlay. London: Routledge & Kegan Paul.

Husserl, Edmund. 1973. *Experience and Judgment*. Translated by James S. Churchill and Karl Ameriks. Evanston: Northwestern University Press.

Husserl, Edmund. 2005a. *Logical Investigations*, vol. I. Translated by J. N. Findlay. London: Routledge.

Husserl, Edmund. 2005b. *Logical Investigations*, vol. II. Translated by J. N. Findlay. London: Routledge.

Husserl, Edmund. 2014 (translation of Husserl 1913). *Ideas for a Pure Phenomenology and Phenomenological Philosophy. First Book: General Introduction to Pure Phenomenology*. Translated by Daniel O. Dahlstrom. Indianapolis: Hackett.

James, William. 1981. *The Principles of Psychology*. Cambridge, MA: Harvard University Press.

Kant, Immanuel. 1902–2009. *Kants Gesammelte Schriften*. Berlin: de Gruyter.

Käufer, Stephan. 2001. "On Heidegger on Logic." *Continental Philosophy Review*, 34 (4): 455–476.

Käufer, Stephan. 2005a. "The Nothing and the Ontological Difference in Heidegger's 'What is Metaphysics?'" *Inquiry*, 48 (6): 482–506.

Käufer, Stephan. 2005b. "Logic." In *A Companion to Heidegger*. Edited by Hubert L. Dreyfus and Mark Wrathall. Oxford: Blackwell. Pages 141–156.

Kinkaid, James. 2020. "What Would a Phenomenology of Logic Look Like?" *Mind*, 129 (516): 1009–1031.

Kirk, G. S., J. E. Raven, and M. Schofield. 1983. *The Presocratic Philosophers: A Critical History with a Selection of Texts*. 2nd ed. Cambridge, UK: Cambridge University Press.

Kisiel, Theodore. 2006. "Die formale Anzeige als Schlüssel zu Heideggers Logik der philosophischen Begriffsbildung." In *Heidegger und die Logik*. Edited by Alfred Denker and Holger Zaborowski. Amsterdam: Rodopi. Pages 49–65.

Kistner, Ulrike. 2011. "The Exception and the Rule: Fictive, Real, Critical." *Telos*, 157: 43–59.

Koslicki, Kathrin. 2015. "The Coarse-Grainedness of Grounding." *Oxford Studies in Metaphysics*, 9: 306–344.

Kukkonen, Taneli. 2000. "Plenitude, Possibility, and the Limits of Reason: A Medieval Arabic Debate on the Metaphysics of Nature." *Journal of the History of Ideas*, 61 (4): 539–560.

Lachenman, Daniel. 1981. "Philosophic Truth and the Existentiell: The Lack of Logic in *Sein und Zeit*." *Journal of the British Society for Phenomenology*, 12 (1): 55–73.

Lafont, Cristina. 2002. "Replies." *Inquiry*, 45 (2): 229–248.

Lapointe, Sandra. 2011. *Bolzano's Theoretical Philosophy: An Introduction*. New York: Palgrave Macmillan.

Leibniz, G. W. 1989. *Philosophical Papers and Letters*. 2nd ed. Edited and translated by Leroy E. Loemker. Dordrecht: Kluwer Academic.

Leibniz, G. W., and Samuel Clarke. 2000. *Correspondence*. Edited by Roger Ariew. Indianapolis: Hackett.

Lewis, Charlton, and Charles Short. 1879. *A Latin Dictionary*. Oxford: Clarendon Press.

Lewis, David. 1986. "Against Structural Universals." *Australasian Journal of Philosophy*, 64 (1): 25–46.

Lewis, David. 1991. *Parts of Classes*. Oxford: Blackwell.

Liddell, Henry, and Robert Scott. 1940. *A Greek–English Lexicon*. Revised by Sir Henry Stuart Jones. Oxford: Clarendon Press.

Lotze, Hermann. 1884. *Lotze's System of Philosophy. Part I: Logic*. Translated by Bernard Bosanquet. Oxford: Clarendon Press.

Martin, Lillien J. 1914–15. "Ueber die Abhängigkeit visueller Vorstellungsbilder vom Denken." *Zeitschrift für Psychologie*, vol. 70, 3/4: 212–275.

Martin, Wayne. 2006. *Theories of Judgment: Psychology, Logic, Phenomenology*. Cambridge, UK: Cambridge University Press.

McDaniel, Kris. 2009. "Ways of Being." In *Metametaphysics: New Essays on the Foundations of Ontology*. Edited by David Chalmers, David Manley, and Ryan Wasserman. Oxford: Clarendon Press. Pages 290–320.

McDaniel, Kris. 2013. "Heidegger's Metaphysics of Material Beings." *Philosophy and Phenomenological Research*, 86 (1): 332–357.

McDaniel, Kris. 2014. "Metaphysics, History, Phenomenology." *Res Philosophica*, 91 (3): 339–365.

McDaniel, Kris. 2016. "Heidegger and the 'There Is' of Being." *Philosophy and Phenomenological Research*, 93 (2): 306–320.

McDaniel, Kris. 2017. *The Fragmentation of Being*. Oxford: Oxford University Press.

McDowell, John. 1994. *Mind and World*. Cambridge, MA: Harvard University Press.

McManus, Denis. 2006. *The Enchantment of Words: Wittgenstein's* Tractatus Logico-Philosophicus. Oxford: Oxford University Press.

McManus, Denis. 2012. *Heidegger and the Measure of Truth*. Oxford: Oxford University Press.

McManus, Denis. 2013a. "Ontological Pluralism and the Being and Time Project." *Journal of the History of Philosophy*, 51 (4): 651–673.

McManus, Denis. 2013b. "The Provocation to Look and See: Appropriation, Recollection and Formal Indication." In *Wittgenstein and Heidegger*. Edited by David Egan, Stephen Reynolds, and Aaron Wendland. New York: Routledge.

McManus, Denis. 2014. "Austerity, Psychology, and the Intelligibility of Nonsense." *Philosophical Topics*, 42 (2): 161–199.

McManus, Denis. 2015a. "On Being as a Whole and Being-a-Whole." In *Division III of* Being and Time: *Heidegger's Unanswered Question of Being*. Edited by Lee Braver. Cambridge, MA: MIT Press. Pages 175–197.

McManus, Denis. 2015b. "Wittgenstein, Moore and the Lure of Transcendental Idealism." *Philosophical Topics*, 43 (1/2): 125–148.

McManus, Denis. 2017. "Beholdenness to Entities and the Concept of 'Dasein': Phenomenology, Ontology and Idealism in the Early Heidegger." *European Journal of Philosophy*, 25 (2): 512–534.

McManus, Denis. 2020. "Review of *The Fragmentation of Being* by Kris McDaniel." *European Journal of Philosophy*, 28 (3): 833–837.

Meinong, Alexius. 1960. "On the Theory of Objects." In *Realism and the Background of Phenomenology*. Edited by Roderick Chisholm. Glencoe, IL: Free Press. Pages 76–112.

Melamed, Yitzhak, and Martin Lin. 2020. "Principle of Sufficient Reason." In *The Stanford Encyclopedia of Philosophy*. Edited by Edward N. Zalta. https://plato.stanford.edu/archives/spr2020/entries/sufficient-reason

Mohanty, Jitendra N. 1988. "Heidegger on Logic." *Journal of the History of Philosophy*, 26 (1): 107–135.

Moore, Adrian W. 2003. "Ineffability and Nonsense." *Proceedings of the Aristotelian Society*, 77: 169–193.

Moore, Adrian W. 2012. *The Evolution of Modern Metaphysics: Making Sense of Things*. Cambridge, UK: Cambridge University Press.

Moore, Adrian W. 2015a. "Being, Univocity and Logical Syntax." *Proceedings of the Aristotelian Society*, 115 (1): 4–25.

Moore, Adrian W. 2015b. "Replies." *Philosophical Topics*, 43: 329–383.

Nelson, Eric. 2006. "Die formale Anzeige der Faktizität als Frage der Logik." In *Heidegger und die Logik*. Edited by Alfred Denker and Holger Zaborowski. Amsterdam: Rodopi. Pages 31–49.

Nietzsche, Friedrich. 2002. *Beyond Good and Evil*. Cambridge, UK: Cambridge University Press.

Nietzsche, Friedrich. 2005. *The Anti-Christ, Ecce Homo, Twilight of the Idols, and Other Writings*. Cambridge, UK: Cambridge University Press.

Noë, Alva. 2005. "Against Intellectualism." *Analysis*, 65: 278–290.

Okrent, Marl. 1988. *Heidegger's Pragmatism*. Ithaca, NY: Cornell University Press.

Owen, G. E. L. 1986. *Logic, Science and Dialectic*. Ithaca, NY: Cornell University Press.

Parapuf, Andreea. 2005. "Die defizienten Modi in *Sein und Zeit* und ihre Rolle für die Fundamentalontologie Heideggers." *Studia Universitatis Babes-Bolyai – Philosophia*, 2: 29–57.

Philipse, Herman. 1998. *Heidegger's Philosophy of Being: A Critical Interpretation*. Princeton: Princeton University Press.

Pöggeler, Otto. 1987. *Martin Heidegger's Path of Thinking*. Atlantic Highlands, NJ: Humanities Press.

Poli, Robert. 1993. "Husserl's Conception of Formal Ontology." *History and Philosophy of Logic*, 14 (1): 1–14.

Polt, Richard. 2006. *The Emergency of Being: On Heidegger's Contributions to Philosophy*. Ithaca, NY: Cornell University Press.

Polt, Richard. 2019. *Time and Trauma: Thinking through Heidegger in the Thirties*. London: Rowman & Littlefield International.

Priest, Graham. 1979. "The Logic of Paradox." *Journal of Philosophical Logic*, 8: 219–241.

Priest, Graham. 1998. "What Is So Bad about Contradictions?" *Journal of Philosophy*, 95: 410–426.

Priest, Graham. 2001. *Beyond the Limits of Thought*. 2nd ed. Oxford: Oxford University Press.

Priest, Graham. 2006a. *Doubt Truth to Be a Liar*. Oxford: Oxford University Press.

Priest, Graham. 2006b. *In Contradiction*. 2nd ed. Oxford: Oxford University Press.

Priest, Graham. 2014a. *One*. Oxford: Oxford University Press.

Priest, Graham. 2014b. "Revising Logic." In *The Metaphysics of Logic*. Edited by P. Rush. Cambridge, UK: Cambridge University Press. Pages 211–223.

Priest, Graham. 2015. "Stop Making Sense." *Philosophical Topics*, 43: 285–299.

Priest, Graham. 2016. "The Answer to the Question of Being." *Beyond the Analytic-Continental Divide: Pluralist Philosophy in the Twenty-First Century*. Edited by Jeffrey A. Bell, Andrew Cutrofello, and Paul M. Livingston. London: Routledge. Pages 249–261.

Priest, Graham, Francesco Berto, and Zach Weber. 2018. "Dialetheism." In *The Stanford Encyclopedia of Philosophy*. Edited by Edward N. Zalta. https://plato.stanford.edu/entries/dialetheism

Quine, W. V. O. 1951. "Two Dogmas of Empiricism." *Philosophical Review*, 60 (1): 20–43.

Quine, W. V. O. 1969. *Ontological Relativity and Other Essays*. New York: Columbia University Press.

Quine, W. V. O. 1970. *Philosophy of Logic*. Englewood Cliffs, NJ: Prentice-Hall.

Radloff, Bernhard. 2007. *Heidegger and the Question of National Socialism: Disclosure and Gestalt*. Toronto: University of Toronto Press.

Reinach, Adolf. 1982. "On the Theory of Negative Judgment." In *Parts and Moments: Studies in Logic and Formal Ontology*. Edited by Barry Smith. Munich: Philosophia Verlag. Pages 309–376.

Richardson, Kara. 2014. "Avicenna and the Principle of Sufficient Reason." *Review of Metaphysics*, 67 (4): 743–768.

Rickert, Heinrich. 1913. *Die Grenzen der naturwissenschaftlichen Begriffsbildung*. 2nd ed. Tübingen: Mohr.

Rosen, Gideon. 2010. "Metaphysical Dependence: Grounding and Reduction." In *Modality: Metaphysics, Logic, and Epistemology*. Edited by Bob Hale and Aviv Hoffmann. Oxford: Oxford University Press. Pages 109–137.

Roubach, Michael. 2008. *Being and Number in Heidegger's Thought*. New York: Continuum.

Rubin, Edgar. 1921. *Visuell Wahrgenommene Figuren. Studien in Psychologischer Analyse*. Copenhagen: Gyldendalske Boghandel.

Russell, Bertrand. 1937. *A Critical Exposition of the Philosophy of Leibniz*. London: Allen and Unwin.

Russell, Bertrand. 1992. *Principles of Mathematics*. 3rd ed. London: Routledge.

Russell, Gillian. 2020. "Logic Isn't Normative." *Inquiry* 63 (3–4): 371–378.

Scanlon, T. M. 1998. *What We Owe to Each Other*. Cambridge, MA: Harvard University Press.

Schaffer, Jonathan. 2009. "On What Grounds What." In *Metametaphysics: New Essays on the Foundations of Ontology*. Edited by David Chalmers, David Manley, and Ryan Wasserman. Oxford: Clarendon Press. Pages 347–384.

Schear, Joseph. 2007. "Judgment and Ontology in Heidegger's Phenomenology." In *The New Yearbook for Phenomenology and Phenomenological Philosophy*, 7. Edited by Steven Crowell and Burt Hopkins. New York: Routledge. Pages 127–158.

Schopenhauer, Arthur. 2012. "On the Fourfold Root of the Principle of Sufficient Reason." In *Arthur Schopenhauer: On the Fourfold Root of the Principle of Sufficient Reason and Other Writings*. Translated and edited by David E. Cartwright, Edward E. Erdmann, and Christopher Janaway. Cambridge, UK: Cambridge University Press.

Searle, John. 2000. "The Limits of Phenomenology." In *Heidegger, Coping, and Cognitive Science: Essays in Honor of Hubert L. Dreyfus*. Edited by Mark Wrathall and Jeff Malpas. Cambridge, MA: MIT Press. Pages 71–93.

Searle, John. 2010. *Making the Social World*. Oxford: Oxford University Press.

Sheehan, Thomas. 2015. *Making Sense of Heidegger: A Paradigm Shift*. London: Rowman & Littlefield.

Shirley, Gref. 2010. *Heidegger and Logic: The Place of Lógos in* Being and Time. New York: Continuum.

Simons, Peter. 2012. "To Be and/or Not to Be: the Objects of Meinong and Husserl." In *Categories of Being: Essays on Metaphysics and Logic*. Edited by Leila Haaparanta and Heikki J. Koskinen. Oxford: Oxford University Press. Pages 241–257.

Spiegelberg, H. 1965. *The Phenomenological Movement*, vol. 1. 2nd ed. The Hague: Martinus Nijhoff.

Steinberger, Florian. 2017. "The Normative Status of Logic" In *The Stanford Encyclopedia of Philosophy*. Edited by Edward N. Zalta. https://plato.stanford.edu/archives/spr2017/entries/logic-normative

Tolley, Clinton. 2006. "Kant and the Nature of Logical Laws." *Philosophical Topics*, 34 (1/2): 371–407.

Turner, Jason. 2010. "Ontological Pluralism." *Journal of Philosophy*, 107: 5–34.

van Inwagen, Peter. 2009. "Being, Existence, and Ontological Commitment." In *Metametaphysics: New Essays on the Foundations of Ontology*. Edited by David Chalmers, David Manley, and Ryan Wasserman. Oxford: Clarendon Press. Pages 472–507.

van Inwagen, Peter. 2014. "Modes of Being and Quantification." *Disputatio*, 6 (38): 1–24.

White, David. 1985. *Logic and Ontology in Heidegger*. Athens: Ohio University Press.

Williamson, Timothy. 2013. *Modal Logic as Metaphysics*. Oxford: Oxford University Press.

Wilson, Jessica. 2014. "No Work for a Theory of Grounding." *Inquiry*, 57 (5–6): 535–579.

Witherspoon, Edward. 2000. "Conceptions of Nonsense in Carnap and Wittgenstein." In *The New Wittgenstein*. Edited by Alice Crary and Rupert Read. London: Routledge. Pages 315–351.

Witherspoon, Edward. 2002. "Logic and the Inexpressible in Frege and Heidegger." *Journal of the History of Philosophy*, 40 (1): 89–113.

Witherspoon, Edward. 2003. "Much Ado about the Nothing: Carnap and Heidegger on Logic and Metaphysics." In *A House Divided: Comparing Continental and Analytic Philosophers*. Edited by C. G. Prado. Amherst, NY: Humanity Books. Pages 291–322.

Withy, Katherine. 2022. *Heidegger on Being Self-Concealing*. Oxford: Oxford University Press.

Withy, Katherine. Forthcoming a. "Heidegger on Human Being: The Living Thing Having *Logos*." In *Human: A History*. Edited by Karolina Hübner. Oxford: Oxford University Press.

Withy, Katherine. Forthcoming b. "The Trouble with the Ontological Difference." In *The Cambridge Critical Guide to Being and Time*. Edited by Aaron Wendland. Cambridge, UK: Cambridge University Press.

Wittgenstein, Ludwig. 1961. *Tractatus Logico-Philosophicus*. Translated by D. F. Pears and B. F. McGuinness. London: Routledge & Kegan Paul.

Wittgenstein, Ludwig. 1969. *The Blue and Brown Books*. Oxford: Blackwell.

Wittgenstein, Ludwig. 2009. *Philosophical Investigations*. Edited by P. M. S. Hacker and Joachim Schulte. Translated by G. E. M. Anscombe, P. M. S. Hacker, and Joachim Schulte. Chichester: Wiley-Blackwell.

Wrathall, Mark. 1999. "Heidegger and Truth as Correspondence." *International Journal of Philosophical Studies*, (1): 69–88.

Wrathall, Mark. 2011. *Heidegger and Unconcealment*. Cambridge, UK: Cambridge University Press.

Index

Printed in the USA
CPSIA information can be obtained
at www.ICGtesting.com
CBHW072222120424
6858CB00004B/153

9 781108 798792